SCHOOL OF
ORIENTAL AND AFRICAN STUDIES
UNIVERSITY OF LONDON

London Oriental Series
Volume 40

LONDON ORIENTAL SERIES · VOLUME 40

THE TRADITIONAL LITERATURE OF CAMBODIA

A Preliminary Guide

BY
JUDITH M. JACOB
Formerly Senior Lecturer in Cambodian
School of Oriental and African Studies
University of London

OXFORD UNIVERSITY PRESS
1996

Oxford University Press, Walton Street, Oxford OX2 6DP
Oxford New York
Athens Auckland Bangkok Bombay
Calcutta Cape Town Dar es Salaam Delhi
Florence Hong Kong Istanbul Karachi
Kuala Lumpur Madras Madrid Melbourne
Mexico City Nairobi Paris Singapore
Taipei Tokyo Toronto
and associated companies in
Berlin Ibadan

Oxford is a trade mark of Oxford University Press

Published in the United States
by Oxford University Press Inc., New York

British Libary Cataloguing in Publication Data
Data available

Library of Congress Cataloging in Publication Data
Jacob, Judith M.
The traditional literature of Cambodia : a preliminary guide / by Judith M. Jacob.
(London oriental series; v. 40)
Includes bibliographical references.
1. Khmer literature—History and criticism. I. Title. II. Series.
PL4328.J33 1996 895'.932—dc20 95–20959
ISBN 0–19–713612–5

1 3 5 7 9 10 8 6 4 2

Typeset by Graphicraft Typesetters Ltd., Hong Kong

Printed in Great Britain
on acid-free paper by
Bookcraft Ltd.
Midsomer Norton, Bath

London Oriental Series

*No. 1 PHONETICS IN ANCIENT INDIA
W. SIDNEY ALLEN

*No. 2 THE DIACRITICAL POINT AND THE ACCENTS IN SYRIAC
J. B. SEGAL

†No. 3 THE MANICHAEAN HYMN CYCLES IN PARTHIAN
MARY BOYCE

*No. 4 THE BACKGROUND OF THE REBELLION OF AN LUSHAN
EDWIN G. PULLEYBLANK

*No. 5 SOCIAL POLICY AND SOCIAL CHANGE IN WESTERN INDIA 1817–1830
KENNETH BALLHATCHET

*No. 6 THE HEVAJRA TANTRA
D. L. SNELLGROVE Two volumes

*No. 7 THE GĀNDHĀRĪ DHARMAPADA
Edited with an Introduction and Commentary by JOHN BROUGH

*No. 8 THE HISTORY OF THE CAUCASIAN ALBANIANS BY MOVSÉS DASXURANÇI
Translated by C. J. F. DOWSETT

†No. 9 KURDISH DIALECT STUDIES, Vol. I
D. N. MACKENZIE

†No. 10 KURDISH DIALECT STUDIES, Vol. II
D. N. MACKENZIE

*No. 11 NINETEENTH-CENTURY MALAYA
The Origins of British Political Control
C. D. COWAN

*No. 12 THE HEBREW PASSOVER FROM THE EARLIEST TIMES TO A.D. 70
J. B. SEGAL

†No. 13 THE MORPHOLOGY OF THE TIGRE NOUN
F. R. PALMER

*No. 14 JAINA YOGA
A Survey of the Medieval Srāvakācāras
R. WILLIAMS

*These volumes are out of print.
†These volumes are distributed by SOAS

†No. 15 TIDDIM CHIN
A Descriptive Analysis of Two Texts
EUGÉNIE J. A. HENDERSON

*No. 16 NESHRI'S HISTORY OF THE OTTOMANS
The Sources and Development of the Text
V. L. MÉNAGE

†No. 17 EASTERN ARABIAN DIALECT STUDIES
T. H. JOHNSTONE

*No. 18 THE NINE WAYS OF BON
Excerpts from gZi-brjid
Edited and translated by DAVID L. SNELLGROVE

*No. 19 TIBETAN TEXTS CONCERNING KHOTAN
R. E. EMMERICK

†No. 20 SAKA GRAMMATICAL STUDIES
R. E. EMMERICK

*No. 21 THE BOOK OF ZAMBASTA
A Khotanese Poem on Buddhism
Edited and translated by R. E. EMMERICK

†No. 22 THE 'SŪTRA OF THE CAUSES AND EFFECTS OF ACTIONS' IN SOGDIAN
Edited by D. N. MACKENZIE

*No. 23 THE KHOTANESE ŚŪRANGAMASAMĀDHISUTRA
R. E. EMMERICK

†No. 24 A DICTIONARY OF THE MON INSCRIPTIONS FROM THE SIXTH TO THE SIXTEENTH CENTURIES
Incorporating materials collected by the late C. O. BLAGDEN
H. L. SHORTO

†No. 25 THE FINANCIAL SYSTEM OF EGYPT A.H. 564–741/ A.D. 1169–1341
HASSANEIN M. RABIE

*No. 26 THE TREASURY OF GOOD SAYINGS: A TIBETAN HISTORY OF BON
SAMTEN G. KARMAY

†No. 27 POPULATION PRESSURE IN RURAL ANATOLIA 1450–1600
M. A. COOK

*No. 28 THE MODAL SYSTEM OF ARAB AND PERSIAN MUSIC A.D. 1250–1300
O. WRIGHT

*These volumes are out of print.
†These volumes are distributed by SOAS

*These volumes are out of print.
†These volumes are distributed by SOAS

CONTENTS

FOREWORD

In offering this book to the public I am acutely aware that it is very much a preliminary reference work for Khmer traditional literature. There are many deficiencies of which I am conscious: not least the fact that I have prepared the work in England. I have made the odd trip to Paris but was never in Cambodia in the 1960s and 1970s. Then, where there are conflicting statements, for example as to the authorship of a work, I have not denied anything; I have simply entered the claim of the writer; often I do not know whence his 'facts' came. However, I feel that I am helping future researchers to start where I leave off instead of at the beginning of the task.

I thank the Publications Committee of the School of Oriental and African Studies for meeting the cost of publication.

J. J.

ABBREVIATIONS OF TITLES OF JOURNALS

A	*Anthropos*
AA	*Arts Asiatiques*
ASEMI	*Asie du Sud-est et Monde Insulinde*
BEFEO	*Bulletin de l'École Française d'Extrême-Orient*
BSEI	*Bulletin de la Société des Études Indochinoises*
CA	*Cambodge d'Aujourd'hui*
CN/NC	*Cambodge Nouveau/New Cambodia*
EA	*Extrême-Asie*
EC	*Études Cambodgiennes*
FA	*France-Asie*
IB	Institut Bouddhique
IIEH	*Bulletins et Travaux de l'Institut International pour l'Étude de l'Homme*
JA	*Journal Asiatique*
JSS	*Journal of the Siam Society*
KS	*Kambujasuriyā*
MKS	*Mon-Khmer Studies*
NC	*New Cambodia/Cambodge Nouveau*
RC	*Réalités Cambodgiennes*
RI	*Revue Indochinoise*

1

INTRODUCTION

THE KHMERS AND THEIR COUNTRY

Cambodians or Khmers are a race of people occupying the Mekong river basin in what was known as Indochina but is now 'Mainland South-East Asia'. They are bordered by Thailand to the north-west, by Laos to the north-east, and by Vietnam to the east and south. The racial and linguistic family to which the Cambodians belong is known as the Mon–Khmer family. The Mons, now separated from the Khmers, form minority groups in Thailand and Burma but from the seventh century onwards they ruled several kingdoms in what was to become Lower Burma and were finally defeated by the Burmese in the sixteenth century. Both the the Mons and the Khmers have literatures. The best-known 'relatives' of the Khmers are the Surin of Thailand. Other Mon–Khmer minorities live in Burma, Thailand, Vietnam, Malaysia, and Cambodia.

THEIR HISTORY

Indians came from the second century AD to trade and later to settle on the west coast of Indochina. They gradually brought to the Khmers the Hindu and Buddhist religions, ideas of kingship, the art of writing, Sanskrit literature, a knowledge of law, and the skill to build and decorate monuments. From the Chinese Annals we learn that there was an Indianized state called Funan in the south of Cambodia. The Indian connection is reflected in the legend which tells how an Indian, the Brahmin Kaundinya, came to Cambodia and married Soma, the daughter of the king of the Nagas (or Underworld people). Then, in the second half of the sixth century the kingdom of Tchenla, later divided into Water and Land Tchenla, rose to power in Cambodia. Another legend relates that the hermit Kambu Svayambhuva (whose name explains the use of the Indian name Kambuja for the Khmer country) married the heavenly nymph Mera, a gift of the god Çiva. Finally, at the end of the ninth century AD there was the beginning of the Angkor kingdom in the north of Cambodia, near the Great Lake. This kingdom flourished until the fourteenth century and produced monuments and sculptures which have taken a proud place among the treasures of the world.

The first historical documents in Cambodia are the inscriptions in Sanskrit and Khmer. The earliest dated inscriptions are AD 611 (Khmer) and AD 613 (Sanskrit) but there were earlier dated Sanskrit inscriptions in Champa to the south. The script is known as the *Devanāgarī* and is from South India. The Sanskrit inscriptions are poetical; they extol the virtues of the gods and tell about the king's learning and great deeds. The inscriptions in Khmer are prosaic and inform the population in halting prose, via those who could read, about the organization of the religious foundations which were established in the kingdom. Gradually the picture emerges of rich men and officials close to the king offering land and goods to build the foundations. There was an elaborate system of serfs who grew vegetables, rice, and fruit, some at least working half their time for the foundation and half for a private employer. Many ceremonies took place at the monastery during the year. The statues of the gods were bathed, anointed, dressed, and carried round the community. Students and visiting professors stayed at some monasteries.

The existence of monuments in Korat (now Thailand), in Laos, and in Vietnam as well as in Cambodia indicates the extent of the kingdom at its apogee. We know from the inscriptions of the pre-Angkor period, seventh to ninth centuries, and of the Angkor period, ninth to fourteenth centuries, that Indian epics were read and studied. We know the names—Sanskrit names but they could belong to Khmers—of six poets who wrote, in Sanskrit, during the Angkor period. Some inscriptions were in Khmer, some in Sanskrit, some in both languages, and a few in Pali, the language of Buddhism. The inscriptions in Khmer could be regarded as the beginning of Khmer literature. During the Angkor period the Khmer language developed, using many Sanskrit loan-words. This book does not include the inscriptions, either those of the Angkor period or those of the Middle period (16th–19th centuries). They have in any case been, and are still being, well documented and studied by such people as Étienne Aymonier, Léon Feer, Georges Cœdès, Saveros Pou, Claude Jacques, Philip Jenner, and Khin Sok.

The Angkor period came to an end around AD 1430 after attacks by the Siamese. The Cambodian king and court moved away from Angkor. Many books and many of the writers, who were monks or royalty, were taken to Siam. Cambodia began to suffer the predatory attacks not only of the Siamese but also of the Vietnamese and for five centuries its fortunes were very low. Lovek, Srī Santhor, Lvea Em, Oudong, and Phnom Penh were the places which became the capital for a time. During the nineteenth century the Vietnamese persuaded the king of Cambodia to form an alliance with a Vietnamese princess. The French intervened and saved the country from submission to Vietnam by making it a Protectorate of France, along with Vietnam and Laos, in 1863. From the end of the nineteenth century until the present day Phnom Penh has been the capital.

In 1953, after ninety years of colonial rule, Norodom Sihanouk gained Cambodia's independence from France. He abdicated and became head of state. In 1970 he was overthrown in a *coup d'état* and Lon Nol, a protégé of the USA, was instated. The American war against North Vietnam spilled over into Cambodia. The Communist party of Cambodia, now known as the Khmer Rouge, were gaining territory, forcing young people to join their ranks and moving closer to Phnom Penh. By 1974 Phnom Penh was housing three million people of whom two million had fled either from the Khmer Rouge or from the American bombing. Rockets were being fired into the capital. Rice was in short supply. On 17 April 1975 the Khmer Rouge took the capital and imposed their harsh regime, causing the deaths of at least a million people. At the end of 1978 the Vietnamese marched in, drove the Khmer Rouge towards the west, and established a pro-Vietnamese government. The Khmer Rouge continued to attack until May 1993, when, under the auspices of the United Nations, elections were held. Norodom Sihanouk was crowned king again; his son, Ranariddh, and the President of the recent government, Hun Sen, are joint Presidents. The Khmer Rouge have reverted to sporadic warfare.

RELIGION

From the thirteenth century onwards Hinayana Buddhism was the official religion, although Brahmans remained at court and carried out private royal rituals—the tonsure of princes and princesses, engagements, weddings, and funerals—until the abdication of Norodom Sihanouk. It must be remembered too that the cosmogony of Hinduism was the background of Buddhist tales. Buddhism wielded a profound influence over the literature. The *Cpāp'* is a genre which preaches Buddhist morality, showing how the wise man, who observes the precepts, will conduct himself in society. In the lyrics and folktales the poets or the characters exclaim against the *karma* which has separated them from their loved one or placed them in a frightful situation. The *Rāmakerti* presents *Rām* as the Buddha but is permeated, like the verse-novels, with references to the Hindu gods and the Hemavant. In addition to the beliefs which came from India, animism has a strong hold over Cambodians. An odd-shaped tree or rock is inhabited by a local spirit who may or may not be kindly. He must be propitiated by offerings of rice and other foods and has power over illness, fertility, life, and death in his locality. There are also other spirits, those of the dead, who are to be found in any locality and who may be hostile. These beliefs are represented in the literature. Folktales or verse-novels tell of the wife who asks the spirit to help her get rid of her husband or of the queen who wants a child.

WRITING MATERIALS AND MANUSCRIPTS

Apart from writing on stone, the Khmers, like their neighbours the Siamese, wrote on palm-leaf, *sliḳ riṭ*. The *Latania* palm-leaves were first treated to make them supple. Then they were cut up, laid on top of each other, and flattened for a week in a wooden press. The pages were approximately 2 inches deep and 14 or 26 inches wide. An iron stylus was used to engrave the writing. Then a black dye was applied, which did not affect the shiny surface but filled the channels. Both sides of the manuscript were engraved and one side numbered. The pages were kept together by means of two cotton strings which went through two holes; the strings were tied loosely so that the pages could be turned and placed at the back as they were read. Other manuscripts, *krāṃṅ*, consist of paper made from the bark of the mulberry, *Snāy Salvadora*, chopped up with rice-straw and boiled with water and chalk, then left to dry as a thin layer in the sun. The resulting yellowish paper was usually painted black. The writing was done with sticks of chalk or carbon. For more lasting writing a copper or bamboo pen was used, filled with Chinese ink or gamboge. The long piece of paper was folded concertina-wise.

There are two scripts for Cambodian. The *mūl* is regarded as being more beautiful and was kept for texts. The Pali texts, that is the Buddhist literature for the Buddhism which originated in South India, were written in *mūl* script. In recent times it has been used for shop names and for headings in books and newspapers. The *crīeṅ* was the script used for every day. Although there must have been written materials in the Angkor period other than the inscriptions on stone, they and subsequent manuscripts have either been eaten by insects or have crumbled in the heat or have been lost. Manuscripts were kept either at the palace or in the monasteries or later at the Institut Bouddhique. The oldest manuscripts, from the eighteenth century, were preserved at a monastery in Battambang. Manuscripts were copied and recopied, at the palace or in the monasteries, with all the updating of language and the mistakes which that involves. It is very common for there to be no author's name on the manuscript in its present form. The name of the author may have been on the cover and have become torn and lost. The name of the copyist is sometimes on the manuscript, with or without the indication that he is the copyist and not the author!

PRINTING

Printing was possible in Vietnam from 1862 at the Autorité coloniale en Indo-Chine but in Cambodia the first time Khmer characters were printed was in 1908, when *Paṇṭāṃ Tā Mās*, 'The recommendations of Grandfather *Mās*', was published. There was opposition by monks to publishing Cambodian texts. Religious texts needed the authorization of both Orders of monks, the Mahanikay and the Thommayut, as well as of the Council of Ministers. It was in the 1920s that Chuon-Nath and Huot-Tath, with the help of Louis Finot, the Director of the École Française d'Extrême-Orient, achieved the authority to publish all kinds of texts.

THE LANGUAGE

The Khmer language is basically monosyllabic but many words may be lengthened to an iambic disyllable (⏑–) by the addition of prefixed or infixed consonants. Depending on the phonetic nature of these consonants, the juncture with the consonants of the base word may be marked by aspiration or by the presence of a very restricted set of vowels. Thus the word /kaət/ 'to be born, to arise, to rise (of the moon)' is related to the prefixed form /bɔŋ-kaət/ 'to give rise to, produce' and to the infixed /k-hn-aət/ 'period of the rising moon' and /k-ɔmn-aət/ 'birth'. The language resembles other South-East Asian languages and Chinese in having no inflexions to indicate number, person, agreement, tense, or aspect. Instead it is rich in particles by which these facts may be indicated *when necessary*. It is a language which does not need to repeat the subject or object or indicator of time, once they have been established, until they are changed. The language was heavily influenced by Sanskrit during the Angkor period, borrowing words, chiefly nouns, for many new ideas connected with government, religion, law, literature, and writing. Pali, the language of Buddhism, also had its turn, particularly from the thirteenth century onwards. By the time that we have literary works in manuscript form, both Sanskrit and Pali loan-words were equally in use. The Inscriptions Modernes d'Angkor, which date from the sixteenth to the nineteenth centuries, show a new stage of development in Khmer prose. Now it is free and flowing and is marked by the poetical features of assonance and alliteration. Fervent Buddhist faith was expressed in these inscriptions, which were written during the bleak centuries when Cambodia was attacked from both sides. Thai borrowings were of a different nature. They were the names of artefacts of current use, such as *mīoeṅ* 'city' and *hmuot* 'company, unit'. Finally, from the middle of the nineteenth century, French words came into the language.

POETIC STYLE

The Khmer interest in the use of language for the creation of poetry has always been an absorbing one. Sanskrit and Pali borrowings or the 'high' vocabulary are widely used, often with a Khmer word, for example *bralap' sandhyā* 'dusk, dusk'. Native Khmer vocabulary offers a wealth of alliterative, chiming, and rhyming words: *caṅ cāp'* 'to capture', *yon yān* 'hanging heavily', *caom-raom* 'to surround' are examples of each of these. The alliteration may involve more than one syllable, for example *srabon-sraban'* 'wilted'. They are used to the full in poetry. Four alliterative syllables may occur in succession, for example *me min mūl metrī* 'you are not my lover'. More often, however, two pairs of alliterating syllables occur in succession, for instance *khdār khdar chloey chlaṅ* 'with reverberating responses'. In the second half of the nineteenth century, when imitation of the Siamese was very much in vogue, all kinds of experiments with repetition were made: *ora: kdau ūrā kduol* 'my heart inflamed with anger' or *kher ṭūc mdiṅ khiṅ ṭūc mdec* 'angry in what way'.

I have never heard or read in an evaluation of a Khmer poet any reference to inspiration. Praise has always been given for their *prājñā* 'cleverness'. However, undoubtedly, there is feeling and appreciation of the beauty of natural objects. Poets are particularly aware of the light: the golden light of the sun, the twinkling of jewels, the shining, gold skin of the heroine. Gold is a term of love, 'treasure'. Some terms seem strange to Westerners. They speak of the lungs, liver, and even bile in connection with the emotions; the loved one is as dear as the lungs or even *is* the lungs. Heroes as well as heroines weep tears not only in the verse-novels but in the lyrics too. Cambodians are acutely conscious of the feeling of anger; it is like a fire which is lit in the breast. Contempt is an emotion which has many means of expression. Heroes and their enemies boost their own courage by deriding the opponent.

THE LITERATURE

Because of Cambodia's troubles following the fall of Angkor no literature survives which can be precisely dated to the fifteenth century or even the sixteenth. The earliest written extant literature consists of the *Rāmakerti I* (Reamker or Cambodian Rāmāyaṇa), the *Cpāp'* 'Codes of Conduct', and the *Lpoek Aṅgar Vat*, 'The founding of Angkor Vat'. It seemed that the precise date of the last-named was known: AD 1620 (see Pou 1975*a*). However, in the first fifteen hundred stanzas of *Rāmakerti I* and in the *Cpāp'* there are grammatical and lexical features which seem older than anything in the *Lpoek Aṅgar Vat* and Khing Hoc Dy now casts doubt on the dating (1993: 123). Pou gives the date for *Rāmakerti I* as sixteenth to seventeenth centuries and the same dating might apply to the *Cpāp'*. Cambodian literature was 'borrowed' by the Siamese when they rose to the ascendant after the fall of Angkor. After many centuries during which changes were made to the texts, the Cambodians gradually retrieved much of their literature in the nineteenth century. The authors are very often unknown and it is usual for the work to be known by its title. In the lists of works available from the Buddhist Institute, for example, published at the end of every book, is a list of titles without any authors' names.

Earlier than any of the extant texts, however, are four groups of oral literature, for which names of authors are not relevant: folktales, songs, riddles, and proverbs. Some of the folktales probably go back to the days before the arrival of the Indians. They are concerned with the next meal and the nature of tigers, monkeys, and crocodiles. Songs illustrate the melancholy, sentimental side to the Cambodian character. Riddles, together with some folktales, show Cambodians at leisure, demonstrating a wry kind of humour. Proverbs demonstrate the wisdom and philosophy of the Khmers. All have to a greater or less extent been written down now.

There is a religious element in most of the literature. The *Rāmakerti* was Hindu originally but the Cambodian versions, both literary and popular, represent the hero, *Rām*, as the Buddha. The *Cpāp'* were Buddhist moral poems in essence though they give most interesting details of the life of the ordinary people and have many a humorous touch. The next genre which we come to chronologically is the *Sātrā Lpaeṅ*. These are 'verse-novels' in which the novelists told at great length the stories of some of the Bodhisatvas (persons who would later be born as the Buddha). Usually the author would choose to write about a Bodhisatva who lived as a prince but there are some verse-novels whose hero is a humble animal such as a frog. The literature which comes next historically is the lyric, *kaṃṅāby*. Many lyrics must have been lost but the manuscript of the work of the eighteenth- to nineteenth-century court poets was owned by, and has been published by, Princess Malika. Like songs, they readily express the feelings of the poets, usually about their loved ones, from whom they are often separated.

The Chronicles, *Baṅsāvatār*, one may presume, were written during each reign—sometimes changing the reports of the previous reign to suit the current king's image! The first full account, from earliest, legendary times, is that of Nong, prepared in AD 1818. This was brought up to date during the reign of Norodom in 1903 and again in 1941. The oldest fragment of Chronicle is from AD 1796. There were many private Chronicles, narrating the activities of members of families; these were kept by the family.

Religious literature may be divided into that which is to be studied or heard in the monastery and that which is meant for pleasure. The three sections of the Pali Canon, known as the Tripitaka and consisting of the Vinaya (Discipline), the Sutta (formulae), and the Abhidhamma (High Law), were translated into Khmer from Pali. This was completed, in 110 books, in 1969, published by the Buddhist Institute. As a result of the work on the Tripitaka, a number of translations of less familiar jatakas were published in the journal *Kambujasuriyā*. The best-known parts of the Canon, however, known for a long time from the *samrāy* (text and loose translation or version), are the familiar jatakas (*jātak*) or birth stories of the Buddha. The 'ten' *jātak*, telling of the last ten lives of the Buddha before he entered Nirvana, and the extra-canonical texts, the 'fifty *jātak*', which are known only to Burma, Laos, Thailand, and Cambodia, are very popular. They were written in Pali, probably by a Laotian monk, in the fifteenth century. Religious themes and texts have also been translated into verse.

Another religious work which has been a source for the literature is the *Trai Bhūm* (The Three Worlds), which has given authoritative details about the sixteen paradises, the world of men, and the layers of hells. The Siamese text of this work, written during the reign of the last king of Sukhoday, was the source of the Khmer version. There is also a large collection of treatises or *kpuon*, on subjects such as astrology, law, medicine, which were written in verse because that is easier to remember but which are not included in this study of literature. Most of the literature is poetry—to make the reading more pleasant, as the poet Ban-Teng said.

PUBLICATIONS

Adolf Bastian travelled through Siam and Indochina, sat with villagers in the evenings when stories were told, and gave summaries of the tales he heard (1868). In 1871 Garnier published his version of a Chronicle. Feer in 1877 saw how much like Siamese literature Cambodian literature was. In the 1880s many people—Aymonier, Cabaton, Guesdon, Leclère, Moura, Pavie, Taupin—published books or articles of, about, or including Cambodian literature. All were interested in the stories, folktales or verse-novels, and proverbs of which they gave versions and sometimes texts as well.

The attitude of the French to Cambodian literature was dismissive. In any case their main interest was to find out—what Cambodians had forgotten—the history of the remarkable monuments at Angkor, by deciphering the inscriptions and examining the buildings. The first general books on Cambodia or Indochina, by Moura and G. Maspero, for example, were unanimous in their low opinion of the literature. Songs and folktales were regarded by Chéon, Cœdès, Guesdon, and Maspero as spontaneous and genuine. All other writings were erudite but mediocre. Aymonier described the literature (1904: 43–5) as monotonous, repetitive, unoriginal, and completely subordinate to Indian literature. He published his *Textes Khmers* (mostly favourite stories) with a 'traduction sommaire' in 1878. Pavie translated folktales and verse-novels in 1898. Plon-Nourrit published many texts, chiefly *Cpāp'* and verse-novels, in Paris at the beginning of the century. In 1911–12 *Kambujavarokās* published the *Cpāp'* in Phnom Penh.

So far all publications had been by the French or as a result of their interest but in 1926 the journal *Kambujasuriyā* was launched by the Buddhist Institute, which gave a forum for reports by Khmers on religious and secular social events, for articles by Khmers on Buddhist teaching, for the study of proverbs, and for the publication of In's *Gatilok* and of folktales. Long works which were later published by the Buddhist Institute were serialized and in 1939 one of the earliest Western-style novels, Kim-Hak's 'The waters of the Tonle Sap' was published in sections. The Commission des Mœurs et Coutumes invited readers, particularly in more remote parts of the country, to send folktales for publication. The Buddhist Institute published nine volumes of folktales from 1959 to 1974. In 1958–62 twenty-five of the fifty *jātak* were translated from Pali and published. During the 1960s some literary history and criticism by Khmers began to appear. Dik-Kéam, Léang-Hap An, and Ly-Théam Teng wrote lives of the poets (Srī Dhammarājā, Nong, Ang Duong, Mok, and Seth) and studies of text (Reamker, *Haṅs Yant*). An anthology of parts of the Chronicles was published by Eng-Soth. Saram Phan and others wrote in French (and even English) in an effort to make their songs and stories more widely known. And as Khmer literature was now taught at the Université Royale des Beaux Arts of Phnom Penh, there appeared a course of Khmer literature on the radio, two or three books on literature in Khmer, and many editions of works for teaching.

Meanwhile the French were very active. Martini was a lone voice from 1938 until 1977 in the study of the Reamker (*Rāmakerti*). Then, after publishing the *Inscriptions Modernes d'Angkor* (*BEFEO* 1970–5, first as Lewitz later as Pou), Pou began her monumental work on the text of the *Rāmakerti*, using manuscripts available in Paris. Pou's comments on the literature of the Middle Period, particularly on the Inscriptions, on the *Cpāp'* and on the *Rāmakerti* will be found in the editions of these works, in various articles and in the *Études sur le Rāmakerti*. She divided the literature of the Middle Period, sixteenth to nineteenth centuries, into the Haute and Basse Époques, the former from the beginning to the eighteenth century, the latter from the eighteenth to the middle of the nineteenth.

In the 1950s Bitard wrote about the satire in Khmer folktales while Solange Bernard (later Solange Thierry or Bernard-Thierry) translated songs and folktales, wrote articles on the literature, and in 1985 produced *Le Cambodge des contes*. In the 1970s Chandler and Milne translated folktales into English and Huffman produced some of the texts. Pou and Jenner edited and translated the old *Cpāp'*.

The Centre de Documentation et de Recherche sur la Civilisation Khmère (CEDORECK), with its journal, *Seksa Khmaer*, has continued to publish and reprint in Paris during the years since the Khmer Rouge take-over. And in Paris, where in the 1960s Sarkar researched on the Indian contacts with Cambodian literature, a new generation of Khmer researchers has come into being. Khin Sok and Mak Phœun have produced editions and translations of the Chronicles with comparisons between manuscripts. Khing Hoc Dy has written on the literature, chiefly of the nineteenth century, and has produced the first two volumes on Khmer literature in a Western language.

CAMBODIAN TRADITIONAL LITERATURE AS DEALT WITH IN THIS BOOK

By and large the literature which was written on palm-leaf or paper manuscripts has formed the basis of this study, though I have included books in some genres, such as the *Cpāp'*, which have continued into the modern period when no manuscripts were involved. The definition of the term 'literature', as meaning works written for pleasure, would exclude not only the *Cpāp'*, which are didactic in character, but also the Chronicles, which contain many repetitive passages of information, and the proverbs. So the definition is taken the other way round. Works of a technical nature intended entirely for instruction or information are excluded. Thus treatises on medicine and astrology and the direct translations from Pali of religious texts are not treated in this book.

BIBLIOGRAPHIC REFERENCES to Works of a General Nature about the Literature

For details see Bibliography; references to works on specific genres and versification are given at the end of the introduction to each genre in Ch. 2 and at the end of Ch. 3.

Aymonier 1904, Bausani 1970, Bernard 1949, 1952, Bernard-Thierry 1953, 1955*a*, *b*, *c*, Bitard 1951, 1955*c*, Cabaton 1901, Cœdès 1931, 1942, Dik-Kéam 1962*b* (Khmer), Feer 1877, Gorgoniev 1966 (Russian), Guesdon 1906, Jacob 1979, 1989, Keng-Vannsak 1961, 1967, 1968, Khim Sam-or 1961 (Khmer), Khing Hoc Dy *passim* and especially 1990 and 1993, Khuon Sokhamphu 1963 (Khmer), Khuon Sokhamphu and Heng-Yann 1956 (Khmer), Kourov 1958 (Russian), Lay-Kry 1965 (Khmer), Léang-Hap An 1967, 1968–71 (Khmer), Lewitz 1972, Long-Séam 1980 (Russian), Ly-Théam Teng 1959*b*, 1960, 1967, 1969 (Khmer), Ma Lay Khem 1970*a*, *b*, Martini n.d., 1948, Maspero 1928–30, Népote and Khing Hoc Dy 1981, 1987, Nhok-Thaem 1959 (Khmer), Pavie 1898, Piat 1974, 1975, Pou 1977*b*, 1982*a*, 1983*a*, Ray-Buc 1956 (Khmer), *Saem Sūr* 1965 (Khmer), Sarkar K. K. 1961, 1968, Sidtha Pinitpouvadal 1966, Taupin 1886, Terral-Martini 1959, Thierry 1953, 1959, 1968, 1969, 1971, 1982*a*, Trinh Hoanh 1967, Vandy Kaonn 1973, 1981, n.d.

2

THE GENRES

The following terms are used by Cambodians with reference to the literary documents:

gambīr 'treatise (especially religious)'.

kpuon 'technical treatise'. These are documents on medicine, law, magic, divination, astrology, etc. and as such do not concern us in this book, despite the fact that they are, for the purpose of memorizing, usually versified. The Chronicles, which do form part of the present work because of the legends which are told in them, are, however, included among *kpuon* (Au Chhieng (1953: x).

samrāy Pali Buddhist texts loosely translated into Khmer with some comment, often preceded by the relevant few lines of Pali. The translation is usually much longer than the original.

sātrā 'manuscript'. It may be either a *sātrā sḷik ṛit*, 'palm-leaf manuscript', or a *krāṃṅ*, 'a folded paper manuscript' (see p. 7).

tamrā 'manual, treatise'.

When we come closer to the contents of the documents the following terms are used:

baṅsāvatār 'chronicles'. These may be the annals of a king, of a monastery, or of a family.

bāky paṇṭau, *paññhā* 'riddles, puzzles'.

cpāp' 'codes'. This is a class of didactic Buddhist verse, among the earliest extant poetry.

daṃnuk caṃrīeṅ 'songs'. Many are very old. Some are read as poems as well as being sung.

jātak 'a birth story of the Buddha', i.e. one of his previous lives.

kaṃṇāby 'poem, lyric'. The term suggests a shorter poem than is found among the *lpaeṅ*, q.v., and one which is not a narrative. It is, however, a general term for 'poetry': *kaṃṇāby nirās* or *nirās*, 'travel or separation poem', is a long account of a journey, to France for example, with indications of regret at leaving the loved one; *kaṃṇāby saṅvās*, 'love poem'.

kābyasāstr 'versification'.

lpaeṅ 'works for pleasure'. The majority of compositions are long versified narrations of the *jātak*, 'birth stories of the Buddha'.

lpoek 'poetic composition of moderate length'. The term has changed its meaning as time has passed. Khing Hoc Dy (1983) says that some *lpoek* have been close to *lpaeṅ*, some have been more religious in character, and some, in the twentieth century, have been the equivalent of fables.

nirās See under *kaṃṇāby*.

rīoeṅ breṅ 'folktales, legends'. These are the folktales of oral tradition, some of which were written down at least by the end of the nineteenth century but perhaps before that.

rīoeṅ lkhaon 'versified plays (for dance drama)'. These were adaptations of the *lpaeṅ* in which a chorus told the story and the characters danced. There were no plays in the Western style, in which the characters themselves spoke conversational prose, until the mid-twentieth century.

subhāsit or *bhāsit* 'proverbs, sayings'. Many of these are quite long, being citations from the poems known as the *Cpāp'*, q.v.

The decision to divide Khmer literature arbitrarily into ten genres in order to decribe it will not, I hope, give offence. I am using terms which are in circulation in Cambodia. There is no well-known term for 'epic' but it is practical to separate off the works connected with the Rama story, in particular the Reamker (Rāmakert(i)), and the *Lpoek Aṅgar Vat* from the ordinary *lpaeṅ*. The ten genres are then in an approximate historical order:

Genre or G.1	*Rīoeṅ Breṅ* 'folktales, legends'.
Genre or G.2	*Daṃnuk caṃrīeṅ* 'songs'.
Genre or G.3	*Subhāsit* or *Bhāsit* 'proverbs'.
Genre or G.4	*Bāky Panṭau*, *Paññā* 'riddles, puzzles'.
Genre or G.5	*Cpāp'* 'codes of conduct'.
Genre or G.6	*Rāmakert(i)* (Reamker) and *Lpoek Aṅgar Vat*.
Genre or G.7	*Lpaeṅ, Sātrā Lpaeṅ* 'narrative poetry'.
Genre or G.8	*Kaṃṇāby* or *Bāky Kāby* 'poems, lyrics'.
Genre or G.9	*Baṅsāvatār* 'chronicles'.
Genre or G.10	*Samrāy* 'popular Buddhist literature'.

G.1. *Rīoeṅ Breṅ*: FOLKTALES, LEGENDS

The folktales have a delightful spontaneity, vigour, and realism.[1] They have seemed to some to be, together with songs, the real literature of Cambodia. They reveal the Khmer character, especially their humour and philosophy of life. Many of the 'Khmer' folktales are found in other parts of South-East Asia; others have their origin in the Indian collection of folktales, the Pañcatantra. Their style is simple with plenty of colloquial speech. Everything is told in chronological order. This takes away from the possibility of surprise for the audience as well as for a character. However, the Khmer audiences knew the tales in advance in any case and there was a build-up of anticipation.

Some stories show no trace of any political structure and may predate Indian influence. They tell whether there will be a 'catch' for the evening meal. The saying *Ŝī brịk khān lṅāc* 'Eat in the morning, miss at night' really applies. There are the *Anak Tā* or local spirits, who may help people, if they are prayed to and given offerings. They live in odd-shaped trees, rocks, caves, etc.

The background of the folktales is the ordinary life of the peasant. We go with father and son to stay for a few months and grow rice on the borders of the Tonle. We go on a day's expedition to the jungle to cut wood for building or to collect creepers for making fences. Stock characters are the husband and wife, usually peasants, the rich man, and, in tales which were formed after the coming of Indian influence or which were modified to conform to such a time, the king, his *caturastambh* (four pillars or ministers), the judge, the soothsayer, and the monks. The husband is often less clever than his wife. She tends to be either wily and faithless or, on the other hand, a woman with *grap' lakkh(ṇ)*, 'all the signs' (i.e. good, beautiful, and destined to have good fortune).

There are many collections of tales about one or two characters. *Ā Khvāk' Ā Khvin**, the Blind Man and the Cripple, is the story of two slaves who decide to escape and who in the end are cured of their infirmities and become king and second king. A story of this kind, about the escape of a blind and a crippled slave, is known in other parts of South-East Asia, including Indonesia. *Ā Ḷev**, A Lev, was a boy who told each of his parents that the other was dead so as to have the pleasure of eating funeral foods! He, like Thmenh Chey*, rises from

[1] Folktales which are told in full in Ch. 6 are marked with an asterisk.

poverty to wealth by tricks and lies, always with money as the main goal. In *Cau Kāṃpit Pandoḥ** (Mr Whittling Knife) we follow the adventures of a young man who is given three maxims, as he leaves the religious life: not to fall asleep on guard, when others do; to keep busy; and not to talk in bed. (These have become proverbial sayings in Cambodia.) The story of the *Daṃbaek 4 nāk'**, Four Bald Men, is found in other parts of South-East Asia too. Ridiculed because of their baldness, they set off to acquire some hair and later in their old age they set off to acquire a wife.

The tale of the rabbit *Subhā Dansāy** in prose narrates many separate adventures. He is surely Brer Rabbit in a different setting, escaping from death over and over again. The rabbit is also Judge Rabbit in many tales, though this is not mentioned in the collection of stories. Judge Rabbit takes on legal cases and makes the right man win, by unusual means. So when the man who put his trap at the bottom of the tree has been tricked by the other (who went early in the morning and transferred the catch to his snare at the top of the tree), he goes to Judge Parrot and learns that whoever returns first with a meal for the judge and himself wins the case. He appeals to Judge Rabbit, who goes with him to the house of Judge Parrot. 'Why so late? The case is decided already.' 'I was waiting to watch a fish fly up to eat a tamarind leaf.' 'Never have I seen such a thing.' 'And never have I seen a four-footed animal trapped at the top of a tree.'

Probably the most well-known of the collections of tales about one character is Thmenh Chey* or Thnenh Chey, *Dhmeñ Jăy*, *Dhneñ Jăy*. He is a likely lad, who begins life as an ordinary boy with no particular prospects. Soon, however, he is tricking people and winning contests of wit until even the king is convinced of his cleverness. In the end he saves Cambodia from the Chinese by answering their riddles.

A complete *sātrā*, *Kịn Kantrai**, forms volume 3 of the *Prajuṃ Rīoeṅ Breṅ Khmaer*, published by the Commission des Mœurs et Coutumes. It is composed of tales in which judges find themselves quite unable to make a decision and have to refer the matter to the king. Two men, one chasing a runaway slave and the other a runaway cow, meet on a bridge; both refuse to give way. The king awards to the man chasing the slave because he crossed by the bridge, whereas the cow swam across the river! There are many stories with four or three men. Four men went to dig up some buried gold. When they had divided it in four there remained one piece. Who should have it? The king decides that the man with the heaviest digging stick should have it.

Frequently stories are concerned with stupid behaviour. There is the couple who try to empty the sea for the sake of the treasures which are at the bottom of it. There is the wife who puts her head deep into the cooking pot to lick up the last drops and sticks there. A monk tells his pupil to buy the cheapest food. The pupil buys a block of salt. On the way home it is heavy and the monk puts it down the bank of the river, to be collected next day—it dissolves in the water.

There is black comedy. We laugh when a man gazes at his dead companion, lying with his mouth gaping open under a fallen tree, and says, assuming he is still alive and thinking that he has pulled down the tree, 'So strong!—and smiling too!' There is the moment in *Māyā Srī** when she puts her hand into the jar to push down the head of her lover and finds that he is dead in the boiling water.

Betting is a pastime which plays a prominent part in the folktales. Two men decide to make a wager for a pretty wife. They stake their power to prove that a cart is not a cart. 'What is this?' 'A hub.' 'What is this?' 'The seat.' At court, however, they are defeated when the wife is similarly treated. 'What is this?' 'An arm', etc. A Lev bets the rich men all their wealth that the pretty girl will offer him betel. She is secretly his wife and has been told to do so beforehand. Thmenh Chey bets that he can give an order to His Majesty with impunity. In fact he says to the king, 'Look behind you first and then I'll give my order'. But the king has already obeyed the order and looked behind him.

Verbal play and sophistry are dearly loved by the Cambodians. A worm saves himself from being eaten by a crow by posing four riddles which the crow cannot answer. A would-be son-in-law, spending three days in a tub of water as a test, is taken to court because he stretches out his hand to a distant fire, pretending to warm it. Judge Rabbit gives the judge a tasteless meal with the seasoning ingredients placed at the side. 'You say the heat of the fire on top of a mountain reaches the young man. Well, why shouldn't the seasoning reach the food?' Thmenh Chey is a past master at sophistry. For example, when he is told not to shout, he whispers from a distance to his master that his house is on fire. The riddles which the Chinese ask him to solve are absurd questions such as how many seeds there are in three melons. The man who could cure snake-bite had no thanks from the tiger whom he cured and who did not believe he had been bitten. Judge Rabbit said to him, 'Go to sleep again and when you wake up, if you are not dead, you may eat the man'. Judge Rabbit and the man went far away.

Magic is an ingredient in many folktales. A Lev trains 500 robbers, with their heads shaved, to recite 'magic Pali' words, while leaping into a well which they have dug—this will enable them to steal as he has done. Later he draws lines on a slate as though he is able to prophesy and tells the robbers' wives that they will come home soon. Judge Rabbit pretends to read a 'letter' from Indra which is only insect bites on a leaf. A king and his court, returning through the jungle after studying the magic art, are hungry. They turn themselves into a tiger. The king is the head, the queen the body, the four ministers are the legs, and the astrologer the tail.

All kinds of deception are practised in the stories. The Blind Man shows how big he is by throwing out, for the *yaks* (ogre) to see them, a wickerwork tray, a turtle, and a rope, pretending that these are his liver, his fleas, and the hair on his feet. Similarly A Lev says his name is 'Grandson-in-law'. Then, when he rows off and grandma calls out 'Grandson-in-law is going off with my granddaughter' no one worries about her cries. An illiterate increases his standing by prophesying where a lost plough could be found. His servant had hidden it in an agreed place.

The folktales are interlarded with instances of mistreatment of relatives. Children are taken to the forest and abandoned when there is not enough to eat. Wives trick their husbands and try to kill them in order to marry the lover. A grandmother is killed by her grandson for allowing the meat to shrink in cooking. Prospective sons-in-law are almost driven away by the difficulty of the tasks which are set for them. In some stories the son-in-law has to build a silver bridge or a five-roomed house in one night. The gods help him. One would-be son-in-law has to do more mundane things. He must plough a field 'until a certain rock weeps', hunt like a dog for turtles, and carry a sack of 'rice'. His father-in-law is in the sack and he knows it. When crossing a bridge he makes sounds like an elephant about to cross the bridge to frighten the father. All these tasks he performs well because, having listened under the roof of the house at night, he knows about them in advance.

The clergy are figures of fun. The pupil cooks a fish for the monk but eats the flesh and leaves him the bones. 'The flies ate the flesh.' 'Swat the flies.' He does so, not omitting the one on the teacher's nose! Later the monk says he has been carrying out a rite to make himself invisible. The pupil pretends he cannot see him and the monk goes visiting, his clothing not covering him properly. A Lev tricks a monk by arranging an assignation for him with a 'beautiful girl', actually a Chinaman whom he has tricked in the same way.

The tales about humans have many repetitive features: 500 thieves, 500 dogs, seven daughters, three maxims. The last-named are given to the young man, for example, as he leaves the monastery and starts out in life. They consist of three of the following: he must not talk to his wife in bed; he must not eat when others do, even if hungry; he must keep busy; he must keep an eye on his mother-in-law. As the story unfolds we find that the three maxims are applicable. *Cau Kāṃpit Pandoḥ*, Mr Whittling Knife, for example, on the boat at night, stays awake and is busy attacking the *yaks* (ogre), saving the crew, and acquiring three boons. Then in several stories the term /baːt/ is used to trick people, because it may mean 'one piece' or 'a beggingbowlful'. Thmenh Chey collects taxes and it turns out that he expects a beggingbowlful of silver from everybody, not one piece. Similarly, A Lev exacts the greater amount from the monk and the Chinese man, who thought they would pay one piece of silver for the favour he did them. Books of Lies are found now and again. *Ā Kuhak Ŝī* is put in a sack ready to be drowned. He sends his uncle home to fetch his Book of Lies to be drowned with him—though in fact he escapes drowning by changing places with a leper whom he persuades that he has been cured of leprosy by being in the sack. Thmenh Chey, to prove to the king that he can lie, asks him to send to his home for his non-existent Book of Lies. Both *Cau Kāṃpit Pandoḥ* and the boy whose life is influenced in turn by the gods, Good Luck and Bad Luck, guard the palace at night in place of the rich man whom they serve. They refrain from eating and therefore do not fall asleep and impress the king with their dutifulness and the power of their weapons.

Many stories concern animals. They have characteristics which man would like them to have. The tiger is a foolish creature who copies the fish-eagle and tries to catch fish by jumping from a tree into shallow water. He is taken in and runs away when he hears the rabbit boasting about how many tigers he has eaten. The crocodile is friendly but also foolish. One is a monk's pet. It carries him on its back until it meets an enemy crocodile. Then it transfers him to its mouth, beats the enemy and is dismayed to find its master dead. Another, in *Nāṅ Raṃsāy Sak*'*, is the pet of *Mīkā* and is sent by her to kill *Rājakul*. Monkeys are naughty and often come to a bad end. There is a tale which explains the variety of serpents. Once there was only one kind called *Bas' Keṅ Kaṅ** until the birth of all kinds of serpents from the union of *Keṅ Kaṅ* with a faithless wife. The serpent had returned her chopper which had fallen into its hole on condition that she would take him as her lover.

Some of the Buddhist stories have become folktales. *Khyaṅ Săṅkh* is an example. This has come down to us as a full-length verse-novel (IB 1961) but has also been a popular folk drama (described in Thiounn and Cuisinier 1956: 91–5) and folktale. Others which are known both as long *jātak* verse-novels and as popular stories are *Săṅkh Silp Jăy* (IB 1962), *Sradap Cek* (IB 1962 by Ngin), and *Varavaṅs Sūravaṅs* (*KS* 1970 Ly-Théam Teng ed.). *Laksaṇavaṅs* is written as a long verse-novel but is not a *jātak*, though it resembles one; it is a popular story. Only a résumé in Feer 1877 is available in print.

BIBLIOGRAPHIC REFERENCES

For details see Bibliography.

Texts

Many texts are not mentioned below. They are in the Bibliography but they are extremely unlikely to be obtainable.

The earliest texts of folktales were published by É. Aymonier (1878) in Saigon from a manuscript and were accompanied by translations or versions. In Paris, Plon-Nourrit published several works including some folktales in 1900–3. Then from 1932 to 1969 the journal *Kambujasuriyā* in Cambodia published the best-known favourite stories. Corbet published selections, undated but certainly before 1946, from the folktales and other tales.

Finally, the Commission des Mœurs et Coutumes published between 1959 and 1974 nine volumes of the *Prajuṃ Rīoeṅ Breṅ Khmaer*, Collection of Khmer Folktales. They used the stories already printed in *Kambujasuriyā* but towards the end went on to add tales which people sent in at their request. The result is that in the first two volumes all the tales are good ones and most of the best and most well-known are to be found there. The titles are set out in the Bibliography under Commission des Mœurs et Coutumes. The stories are told in a slightly old-fashioned style in volumes 1 and 2. Volume 3 is the *Sātrā Kịṅ Kantrai* (legal tales), which include the story about the poor man who sets his house to windward of the rich man, to smell his food; that of two men who claim possession of an umbrella; and the tale of the monkey who steals the king's diadem. Volume 4 continues with popular tales, including the origin of the *kūn lok* bird, of the mosquito and of the thunder, and the story of the Indrī bird and Çiva. It also includes the poetic (G.7) texts, *Mā Yoeṅ* and *Lpoek Cacak*. In volume 5 there are tales from the Chronicles, about the foundaton of Angkor and the city of Phnom Penh. The legend of Phnom Pros Phnom Srey, built by the efforts of two teams, one men, one women, is there and the story of the Phnom Neang Kangrei (*Rathasenajātak* G.7) is recorded. In volume 6 there are many tales which explain the names of places and do not have much of a story. This volume has the legend of the hills,*Varavaṅs* and *Sūravaṅs* (G.7), however. The stories in volume 7 tell of the origins of animals or plants.

They include that of the Mouse which becomes king and the story of the Areca and Betel. Volume 8 gives the origin of various Nak Ta (*Anak Tā*); it includes, in *Pravatti Anak Tā Ghlaṃṅ Mīoeṅ* and *Anak Tā Kraham Ka*, two famous historical events which have become legendary. (Volume 9 came out in 1974 and I have not seen it.)

Other texts are available in Cedoreck (1981 *Dhanañjăy*), Dik-Kéam (1962*a*), Huffman (1972) with vocabulary, In (1936), and Midan (1927, 1933) with introduction and translation.

Versions

From an early date (Aymonier 1878) there was a keen interest in the Khmer folktales among the French. Leclère (1895), Pavie (1903), Monod (1922), Martini and Bernard (1946), Khing Hoc Dy (1985), and Thierry (1988) all published books of translated tales. Nevermann (1956) and Velder (1971) followed suit but based their German versions on translations into French. There are English versions in Dik-Kéam (1962), Chandler, and Milne. Apart from these collections there are many separate stories in translation. See the following in the Bibliography:

Anakota 1977, Aung *c.*1969, Aymonier 1878, Bharati 1949, Bitard 1956*b*, 1959, *Cambodge d'aujourd'hui* and *Cambodia Today* 1958–9, Carrison 1987, Chandler 1971, 1976, 1978, Dik-Kéam 1962*a*, Fabricius 1969, 1970, Foshko and Deopik 1981 (Russian), Garnett *et al. c.*1965, Gerny-Marchal 1913, 1919, Gorgoniev 1973 (Russian), Institut Bouddhique (reprints of Pavie) 1969–71, Khing Hoc Dy 1985*a*, 1990: 96–113, Laporte 1970–1, Leclère 1895, Leuba 1913, 1959, Malherbes 1958, Mao (Chuuk Meng) 1961, Marounova 1972 (Russian), Martini 1948, 1949*b*, 1955, Martini and Bernard 1946, 1949, 1955, Marx 1908, Men-Riem 1962, Midan 1927, 1933, Milne 1972, Monod 1922–43 (repr. 1985), Nevermann 1956 (German), New Cambodia 1970–1, Nicolas 1947, Notton 1939, Nouth-Oun 1953*a*, *b*, *c*, Pavie 1898–1921 (repr. 1988), Poulichet 1913, *Réalités Cambodgiennes* 1960, 1969, 1971, Rebert 19—, Soth-Polin 1966, Thierry 1955, 1971–2, 1981*a*, *b*, 1982, 1988, Tvear 1969–71, Velder 1971 (German).

Studies

Despite the interest of Cambodian folklore, study of it began only after the Second World War. See Bernard (1949 and 1952), Bernard-Thierry (1953, 1955, 1959), Bitard (1951 and 1955), Chau Seng and Kong-Huot (1967), Jacob 1982, Khing Hoc Dy 1977, 1990: 96–113, Porée 1955, Thierry 1953, 1959, 1968, 1971, 1976 (Thesis), 1977, 1978, 1982, 1985, Vandy-Kaonn 1973, 1981, n.d.

G.2. *Daṃnuk caṃrīeṅ*: SONGS

As Tricon said (Tricon and C. Regismanset 1923: 35–42), the real Khmer poetry is to be found in their songs. It is in this medium of expression that the Cambodians have most readily put into words their innermost thoughts and moods. They have a natural feeling for music and rhythm and a remarkable facility with words. Cambodians abroad find that their traditional songs and instrumental music are the most poignant reminders of home and that, under some cirumstances, they cannot bear to hear them. At times of leisure Cambodians in their own country would sit somewhere cool with a guitar or one-stringed violin to play and sing, all alone, a traditional or a spontaneously composed song.

Traditional popular melodies number approximately 300 (op. cit. 36). Most airs, if not all, may be used alone as instrumental music or may accompany certain songs. There are set songs which are used, or have in the past been used, at ceremonies such as weddings, funerals, the New Year, the Water Festival, or occasions when offerings are made to spirits.

Many other traditional songs, also sung to old melodies, are associated with the less formal and more individual situations in everyday life. These include the kind of song which every country would have in its repertoire: love songs—Khmer love songs are usually sad—lullabies, and songs sung when the return of a loved one is awaited or a separation is necessary. A tendency to wistfulness characterizes Khmer songs but there are some humorous ones too. In one song the husband urges the wife to make herself and the house look nice, ready for a guest; the tax inspector is coming and they must make a pleasant impression on him. More than one song pokes fun at the Buddhist clergy, usually by suggesting that a monk is looking out for a girl-friend or a wife.

There are two categories of song which are characteristic not only of Cambodian life but of that of South-East Asia generally: work songs and alternating songs, which are known as *Āÿai*. Special songs are sung during activities such as transplanting, harvesting, or threshing rice or carrying out any hard manual work in the heat or during a storm. Alternating songs are particularly enjoyed at festivals or at times when a rest is taken after some seasonal work. A group of boys and a group of girls, or one boy and one girl, sing alternate stanzas. Most of the songs have now been written down, that is to say one version has been recorded by a poet, but formerly the singers improvised freely. The content of the song is flirtatious in intent but this is expressed very indirectly and with the utmost discretion. The surface meaning of a stanza may concern a flower or animal but is of course intended to refer to the singers themselves. Songs such as these may be accompanied by music and dancing; they give the young people the opportunity to relax a little from the usual strictures of their upbringing. Alternating songs composed entirely impromptu by one man and one woman singer are a very popular form of entertainment. The singing may be accompanied by miming and dancing and may take place with some improvised scenery.

The boat song, *Pad Uṃ Dūk* (lit. Song for rowing boats), is a rather special category. Dik-Kéam, in a very well-worth-while study (1964) gives the texts of eleven such songs. King Norodom, he tells us, is said to have composed his own *Pad Uṃ Dūk* when on a long river journey, hoping that the singing would help the oarsmen in their task. Dik-Kéam gives the text of Norodom's long poem, followed by ten other, shorter boat songs, mostly based on Norodom's. The poems describe the places passed on the journey and refer to the flora and fauna which may be seen. Dik-Kéam tells us incidentally that the boat songs are sung also when a sailing boat or raft is the means of conveyance. It is said that boat songs originated with the famous folktale character Thmenh Chey (*Dhanañjăy*). He was being taken by the king's men in a boat to a place where he would be thrown into the river to drown as a punishment. He suggested to the men that he should sing as they rowed. He sang, 'Thmenh Chey's overboard!' and they responded with the syllables '*Hai oe, hai oe!*', a refrain often sung in modern times by oarsmen. After a number of repetitions of song and refrain he jumped overboard. When the man at the stern called out, 'Thmenh Chey's overboard!', the rest took no notice. They just sang their refrain and Thmenh Chey escaped. The refrain in many *Pad Uṃ Dūk* is a repetition of part of the last verse and is sung by the oarsmen, as in the case just mentioned, while the passengers sing the song. The songs may also be sung as alternating songs, with girls in one boat and boys in another, singing the stanzas and refrains in turn. A further use of the boat songs, in modern times at least, has been as an accompaniment for the popular Lam Thon dance.

Traditional Khmer songs of all the above kinds were written down on *krāṃṅ* (see section on 'Writing Materials and Manuscripts' in Chapter 1) as *kpuon khnāt* (books of rules) which have been used as sources for printed articles and books (e.g. Gironcourt 1941, Pou 1973). The Institut Bouddhique did have (see *Kambujasuriyā* 1941 (13) 13: 23) approximately 300 recordings of songs, chiefly Khmer but including some from Laos, Thailand, China, and Japan.

Detailed Western study of Khmer songs began, to the best of my knowledge, in 1890 with an article by Chéon consisting of a page of comment and translations into French of eight 'poems'. The first serious work on Cambodian songs came in 1913 with Roeské's 'Métrique Khmère, Bat et Kalabat'. Roeské found that the songs he examined all had four verses to a stanza, each verse having four syllables, and that the rhyme schemes involved an end rhyme between the last verse of one stanza and both the second and third verses of the next. This scheme is illustrated as the seventh metre, *Pad Bāky Puon*, in the chapter on Versification below. Roeské noted an internal rhyme between the end syllable of the first verse of the stanza and the first syllable of the second verse. However, with regard to the number of verses in a stanza, texts of songs published later, for example by Huffman and Pou, include some with six or eight verses (apart, that is, from those set out with a refrain at the end of each verse). Roeské published nine songs, with text, in both orthography and transcription, and translation into French.

With the publications in which Tricon was involved we have the musical notation for the first time as well as text and translation. The 1921 publication deals with twenty-five songs. Only Roeské had so far given the Khmer orthography for the songs he published. Transcriptions, without diacritics, are unfortunately very unsatisfactory for Cambodian; even with the translation and a knowledge of the language it is not always easy to interpret the transcription! However, Gironcourt, like Roeské before him, gave, in his 1941 publication, the orthography, plus transcription, translation, and notation of thirty-six songs. The text of twenty-two of these was supplied by the Princesses Malika and Pengpas Yukanthor. The remainder include some songs of the countryside and of the hill tribes.

In the post-war period there have been some translations of songs into French without texts or notation (Bernard, Bernard-Thierry, Saram Phan, and Yon) and at last some studies by Cambodians in Khmer containing texts and comment (Dik-Kéam, Ly-Théam Teng, and Pech-Sal). Finally, we have had in the 1970s the translation into French of the treatise on marriage with the text in Khmer orthography and translation of twenty-one marriage songs (Pou 1973), and Huffman's Cambodian Literary Reader (Khmer text) which contains the texts with vocabulary of four songs.

BIBLIOGRAPHIC REFERENCES

For details see Bibliography.

Bou-Po 1961 (Khmer text in orthography of four songs incorporated into a story). Chéon 1890 (1 page of comment; translation into French of 8 songs).

Chhim-Soum 1951 (*Āÿai*; text of song). Coedès 1931 (brief comment). Commission des Mœurs et Coutumes 1951. Dhingra 1958, 1959 (oriental collection; slight Khmer element). Dik-Kéam 1964 (introduction to *Pad Uṃ Dūk* 'Boat songs' and text of 11 songs; Khmer text throughout). Gironcourt 1941 (text in both orthography and transcription, French translation and musical notation of 21 traditional and 39 country or tribal songs). Huffman 1977 (text in Khmer orthography, with vocabulary translated into English, of 4 songs of which 2 are *Āÿai*). Institut Bouddhique 1951 *Caṃrīeṅ jāti niyam*, Part I. Institut Bouddhique 1970 (25 songs in French translation). Keng-Vannsak 197— (songs for guitar). Khing Hoc Dy 1990 (versions and study). Laspeyres 1958 (songs for guitar). Lesur 1946 (5 songs). Lewitz 1973 (text and version of 21 marriage songs). Louvey 1965 (*Āÿai*). Ly-Théam Teng 1960 (comment in Khmer, pp. 38–43). 1964*a* and *c* (note in Khmer on music; text in Khmer of 3 songs). 1969*a* (Khmer text of 10 songs). Maspero 1929 (comment including list of a few well-known songs). Moura 1883 (text in transcription and translation of 4 short songs). Pech-Sal 1970 (comment in Khmer on music and singing; Khmer text of 21 Cambodian songs and 5 Khmer Loe (hill tribes) songs). Roeské 1913 (comment; text in orthography and French translation of 9 songs). Saram Phan *et al.* 1965 (not seen; assume it contains translation into French of some *Āÿai* songs). Srey-Ou and Nhoung-Sœung 1951 and 1977 (*Āÿai*). Thiounn, Samdach Chauféa 1933 (not seen; Khmer text of songs with refrains?). Tricon 1915 (text in orthography, translation into French, and notation of 8 songs). Tricon and Bellan 1921 (text in transcription, translation into French, and notation of 57 songs). Tricon and Regismanset 1923 (text in transcription, translation into French, and notation of 6 songs). Yon 1965 (not seen; Vandy Kaonn says it contains discussion of *Āÿai*).

G.3. *Subhāsit or Bhāsit*: PROVERBS

The *subhāsit* 'good sayings, proverbs, maxims' and *bhāsit* 'sayings' which are found in the published collections seem unbelievably numerous but Cambodians have traditionally taken an interest both in the provision of advice on moral questions and in correct and, if possible, cleverly composed discourse. Collections of proverbs include the short, meaningful, pithy ones such as *tak' tak' beñ paṃbaṅ* 'Drip by drip the node of bamboo is filled', *kuṃ ciñcim khlā sgam* 'Don't keep a thin tiger as a pet' or *chmā min nau, kaṇṭur ḷoeṅ rājy* 'When the cat's away the mouse becomes king' but many well-known sayings are longer, being quotations of two or more verses from didactic poems. Some of these are excerpts from the *Cpāp'* (Genre 5) of which perhaps only a small part would need to be quoted in a situation to which the proverbs applied. For instance

dịk ḷoeṅ trī sī sramoc
dịk hoc sramoc *sī trī*

When the waters rise the fish eat the ants.
When the waters sink the ants eat the fish.

(Rhymes are indicated with underlining).

Others refer to situations in folktales, for example *ṭek yap' kuṃ niyāy nịṅ srī* 'Don't talk to your wife in bed at night'. This warning occurs in more than one folktale but foolish husbands disregard it and the robber, hidden under the house (built on stilts), hears where some treasure is hidden.

Either because they are, like the example cited above, quotations from poetry or in some cases perhaps because they are so composed from choice, proverbs are often rhymed, as *praheḥ* pāt' *prayatn gaṅ'* 'If you're careless you'll lose things. If you take care they'll still be there.'

Something of a fashion seems to have sprung up in the post-World War II period for taking a proverb and composing a poem explaining the meaning of it. Sometimes the poem, long, complex, and full of 'high' vocabulary, seems more difficult to understand than the proverb! See Chhim-Soum 1965 and 1966*a* and Méas-Yutt 1966 for examples of this. Some poets took Pali moral sayings, several lines long, and wrote poems illustrating their meaning. These are not considered to be Khmer proverbs, for the purposes of the present study.

No hard and fast line can be drawn between *bhāsit* 'sayings', *subhāsit*, 'good sayings, maxims', and *cpāp'* 'codes of conduct' because all involve good advice. Bou-Po (1951) wrote an article concerning twelve 'expressions proverbiales', giving a little moral encouragement as he discussed each one. According to Bou-Po's note at the head of his article the twelve expressions were ones which were passed on from generation to generation yet I have not found any of the twelve in the 284-page book of proverbs of Nuon-Bouth and Choum-Muong (1961)!

BIBLIOGRAPHIC REFERENCES
For details see Bibliography.

Texts
Chap-Pin 1945–6, Chhim-Soum 1965 and 1966*a*, *Damnīem* n.d., Guesdon n.d., Khing Hoc Dy 1990: 73–6, Nhok-Thaem 1943–4, Nuon-Bouth and Choum-Muong 1961, Pannetier 1915, Ray-Buc 1949, San-Kong 1944, Tieng-Day Chhoun 1957.

Versions

Dhingra 1958: 127, Dik-Kéam 1967*c*, Khing Hoc Dy 1990: 73–6, Pannetier 1904, 1915, 1949, and 1955, Parmentier 1969, Yukanthor 1947.

Studies

Bou-Po 1951, Chap-Pin 1945–6 and 1958*a*, Chhim-Soum 1965 and 1966*a*, Kem-To 1955, Khing Hoc Dy 1990: 73–6, Lebedev 1959 (Russian text), Méas-Yutt 1966, Nhoung-Sœung 1966, Pou 1979*b*, *Tau Ĥīṅ* 1955, 1965.

G.4. *Bāky Paṇṭau, Pañhā*: RIDDLES, PUZZLES

The Khmers have as a national characteristic a lively interest in the use of words. Their facility in rhyming, punning, or using rapidly formed Spoonerisms have often been the subject of admiring comment. They delight in pastimes which are based on a play of words and in getting the better of someone by verbal wit. Riddles provide an excellent means of indulging their skill.

There was a traditional procedure attached to the posing of riddles in the old days. It was an amusement which would take place in the evenings, probably among men sitting outside in some central area of the village. The answer to most riddles was the name of an animal, plant, or object of daily use. If the person had difficulty in answering he could ask what kind of thing it was. If he then, after being given enough time, failed to answer correctly, he was subjected by the other man to a humiliating experience. Examples of this are: being sent to a place where he would be kicked and beaten; having to listen to insults being said about his parents; being told to go and fetch some worms and touch them with his tongue. He could avoid this by giving a gift to the one who had asked the riddle. The defeated contestant had to answer a second riddle correctly before being allowed to ask one himself.

It is said that King Ang Duong enjoyed riddles and composed some himself. Many others were composed by poets and learned men whose names are not known. The rhythm of most riddles suggests a particular poetic metre and some are long enough for it to be clear which metre is used. Usually there is at least one internal rhyme even if a riddle is short; for instance

*ṭoem p̈un aṅr*ae *phl*ae *p̈un aṅrut*

Its trunk is as big as a pestle and its fruit is as big as a lobster pot.
Answer: Fish tail palm.

Some riddles are constructed round the fact that a particular word occurs in the compound name of, for example, four plants. The answer will then consist of all four plant names. In 1968 riddles were regarded as sufficiently instructive to be included in the school curriculum!

Our evidence for riddles goes far back in time since there are many examples of them in well-known folktales and legends. The famous folktale character Thmenh Chey (*Dhanañjăy*), saves Cambodia by his cleverness (and a little luck) when the king of China poses three riddles and threatens to take the country if they are not correctly answered. A similar incident forms part of a local legend told in *Sāvatār Vatt Atthāras*, 'The history of Vatt Attharas'. See Bibliography under *Kambujasuriyā*. III Texts of folktales and legends 1950: 9 and 10. In several folktales a pun occurs, in connection with money or silver, between the words *pād* 'monetary unit' and *pātr* 'bowlful' (both pronounced /baːt/), the question being which was intended at the time when the agreement to pay was made. In the folktale *Rīoeṅ k-aek niṅ ṭaṅkūv* 'Story of the crow and the worm', told in *Prajuṃ Rīoeṅ Breṅ Khmaer* 1, No. 23, the worm saves himself from being eaten by the crow by 'allowing' that the crow shall eat him provided that he can answer a *prasnā* 'enigma, puzzle'. The crow is required to name the sweetest, the sourest, the most malodorous, and the most fragrant things. According to the correct answer, these are virtues and vices, not substances with physical properties, and the crow fails his test. The enjoyment of this kind of philosophic question and answer may suggest Buddhist influence and such well-known works as the *Milindapañhā* in which questions of doctrine are posed and answered. However, a delight in contests of verbal dexterity may surely pre-date Buddhist influence?

BIBLIOGRAPHIC REFERENCES

Publication on the subject of riddles is slight but see the following references in the Bibliography:

Chap-Pin 1944. *Kambujasuriyā* 1V Riddles 1942 and 1968. Khing Hoc Dy 1977*c*, 1990: 113–16.

G.5. *Cpāp'*: CODES OF CONDUCT

The *Cpāp'* is a genre of didactic, Buddhist poetry. The older and better-known *Cpāp'* (*Kerti Kāl*, *Kūn Cau*, *Rājaneti*, *Kram*, and *Trīneti*) have been shown by Pou, by means of linguistic criteria, and Jenner, who used rhyming coefficients, to be at least as old as the seventeenth century. They precede the poem which is No. 38 of the Inscriptions Modernes d'Angkor and is dated 1623 saka (AD 1702). They may therefore be presumed to be older than most of the extant literature and possibly as old as the first books of the Reamker (Khmer *Rāmāyaṇa*). The writing of *Cpāp'* continued until the 1950s but it is the old *Cpāp'* which have been well loved and much quoted so that many short passages have become proverbial. Most of the *Cpāp'* were written by monks and were used to teach reading, writing, and moral principles in the monastery schools. No names of authors are known for the earliest *Cpāp'*. In the nineteenth century the authors, Mai, Nong, Ngoy, and King Ang Duong are known. The *Cpāp'* are addressed to ordinary people, to children or young people of both sexes, or to royalty. They teach how the good Buddhist should behave in society. Their charm is in the illustrations from the peasant life (or the royal life) of the day.

The style of writing of the *Cpāp'* is very simple and easy to memorize, though many words and turns of phrase are used which are unfamiliar now. Two metres only, the *Kākagati* and the *Brahmagīti*, are used for the early and most of the later *Cpāp'*. Each stanza makes a complete statement. Often the message given in a stanza is illustrated in the next stanza or several stanzas by references to natural phenomena or to the expected behaviour of people. In the *Cpāp' Kūn Cau* the faithful, whose nature is sweet, are likened to the jackfruit (st. 16), which is hard outside but delicious inside; and obstinate, stupid people are worse than iron, which is hard but can be worked, or the wild elephant, which can be tamed (sts. 54–6). Similes such as this which are quite long and have probably only one point of reference to the compared object are very common. Metaphors are used too.

The *Cpāp' Kram* is the shortest and simplest of the poems. It urges the pupils to a disciplined attitude. 'O all you novices, your mothers have put you under the authority of the teacher. Strive to learn, like the masters. Don't be irresponsible, like when you were at home' (st. 6). At st. 33, it continues, 'The teacher may be compared with your mother and father. He can give you the code of conduct and instruct you in the Dharma, following the Path of all the Buddhas.' The *Kerti Kāl* reminds the owner of a house of his responsibilities. 'You must make your house spick and span. No dust! Clean the ground by scratching and sweeping it to perfection so that it creates pleasure. Keep your needles safe and put your money away carefully in your purse. When you give orders to slaves, watch their faces so that you will know for certain whether they are bad or good . . . Put in a post to moor your boats. Make sure you have punt-poles, ropes and anchors. Watch out for an unfavourable wind lest it beat (on the boats) and break them in pieces' (sts. 18–25).

A very well-known passage in the *Kūn Cau* (sts. 9–11) describes the Dharma, whose light lasts for ever. It excels that of fire, because that is extinguished, and that of the sun, because the sun goes down. Buddhists must not be like the egret which goes from place to place and will not settle (st. 53).

Two of the *Cpāp'*, the *Kūn Cau* (sts. 41–2) and the *Cpāp' Prus* (sts. 52–90) tell of the ill-effects of the three follies (women, alcohol, and betting). The author of the *Cpāp' Prus* tells a tale of woe, when the Chinese money-lenders want their payment. 'Sometimes they tie your feet together and hang you upside down. Your eyes will stare fixedly, while your face is strained and grimacing. They will claim their money—immediately! And what a fine fellow you'll look! Won't you be ashamed in front of the market women, who will stop and listen? Your face will be like a dead man's. Your mouth will gape open like a baby's. And you will groan loudly, '*Aḥ, Ūy, Oey!* Please, Uncle, let me go! I'll find money for you. I'll get it for you tomorrow.' The *Cpāp' Prus* urges the householder to prepare carefully for the night (sts. 17–19, 22–3). 'After dusk, check all your various goods. Put your knife at your side and water at your feet. Put the box (of offerings) level with your shoulders for the gods who look after us. And make sure the fire outside on the hearth shall not go out. Don't let it be extinguished—while you say you forgot. Every day you must see to it without fail and not go and ask for it from the neighbours. Sometimes in the dark of night it happens that you have forgotten and your children need to go to the lavatory. There is no fire on the hearth to light a torch—it is totally extinguished. You rush off, dripping with perspiration, to find some fire. You are unhappy and uncomfortable because you were lazy and did not think it might be needed night or day and you are miserable having to go far for it.'

The idea that a house has an air of content because the wife is a good manager is expressed more than once. The *Rājaneti* puts it like this (st. 11), 'The kite flies because of the wind, the officer is glorious because his men keep him secure, possessions are kept safe because the woman knows how to save. It is a contented house because the wife is good.'

The political situation where the people are oppressed is the subject of part of the *Trīneti* (sts. 7–8). 'The people are like fish. The officials and generals are the water. If it becomes very warm, more so than usual, the people become afraid and do not know where to turn for help. Now the officials may be compared to tigers or venomous spotted snakes. All the people turn to them for help and they suddenly turn into ferocious *yaks* (ogres), with no pity.'

BIBLIOGRAPHIC REFERENCES

For details see Bibliography.

Texts

The old *Cpāp'* were among the texts published in 1900 and 1901 by Plon-Nourrit and in 1911 by Kambujavarokās and they were among the first texts published in *Kambujasuriyā*. (1932 onwards). They were published by the Bibliothèque Royale, Imprimerie Royale, and Imprimerie Nouvelle at about the same time. The Institut Bouddhique published the old texts and Ngoy's works in the 1940s and 1950s.

See Bibliography for the following:

Bibliothèque Royale, Cedoreck 1980, Imprimerie Royale, Imprimerie Nouvelle, Institut Bouddhique, Kambujavarokās, *Kambujasuriyā* I, *Cpāp'* 1932 onwards, Khing Hoc Dy and Jacqueline Khing (see under 'Studies'), Pou (see under 'Studies').

Versions

In 1904 Finot cited a stanza in translation from the *Cpāp' Bāky Cās'* in connection with proverbs. Versions of short passages from the old *Cpāp'* appeared in general works such as Dhingra 1958 and 1959. However, no full translation was ever forthcoming (until Pou and Jenner; see below) if for no other reason than that the *Cpāp'*, for all their simplicity, contain difficult passages.

See Bibliography for the following:

Chau-Seng and Kong-Huot, Dhingra, Finot 1904, Jacob and Morgan, Jenner (see under 'Studies'), Khing Hoc Dy 1990: 78–90 and 91–2 (by Thay Sok), Khing Hoc Dy and Jacqueline Khing (see under 'Studies'), Martini 1949*b*, Pou (see under 'Studies').

Studies

An explanation of the *Cpāp' Kram* was published in Cambodian (Nheuk-Nou 1944) but it still left much unexplained to the Cambodian as well as to the foreigner. There were studies of the *Cpāp'* by Bernard-Thierry (1955*b*) and by Thierry (1968). However, a thorough study of the old *Cpāp'*, investigating the vocabulary and background of each text, had to wait until the work of Pou and Jenner, whose excellent editions, with texts and translations, of *Cpāp' Kerti Kāl*, *Cpāp' Prus*, *Cpāp' Kūn Cau*, *Cpāp' Rājaneti*, *Cpāp' Kram* and *Cpāp' Trīneti* were published by *BEFEO* between 1975 and 1981. Jenner studied the rhyming coefficients (1976) and published a later *Cpāp'* (1978). Khing Hoc Dy and Jacqueline Khing published in 1978 and 1981 the text, with notes and translation, of a later *Cpāp'*, *Paṇṭāṃ Kram N̈uy*, Les Recommandations de Kram Ngoy. Pou wrote two articles (1979*b* and 1981*b*) on the *Cpāp'* and, with Kuoch Haksrea, prepared a list of texts of the *Cpāp'* (1981). In 1988 she published eleven *Cpāp'* with texts in orthography and transcription, translation and notes.

See Bibliography for the following:

Bernard-Thierry 1955*b*, Chap-Pin 1959 (in Khmer), Jenner 1976, 1978 (with text and version), Jenner and Pou 1976 (with text and version), Khing Hoc Dy 1990: 77, 90, Khing Hoc Dy and Jacqueline Khing 1978 and 1981, Nheuk-Nou 1944, Pou 1979*b*, 1981*b*, 1988, Pou and Haksrea 1981, Pou and Jenner 1975–81, Srey-Ou 1958 (in Khmer), Thay Sok, Thierry 1968.

G.6. *Rāmakert(i)* (Reamker) and *Lpoek Aṅgar Vat*

The form of the five texts here discussed varies from poetry to prose. The classical Reamker is a long narrative poem which might, given the form alone, simply be included with the G.7 narrative poetry texts. However, in the first place there have been many ways in which the Reamker has been celebrated through the centuries: in sculpture at Angkor, in art in the monasteries, in the shadow-play, the popular dance-drama, and the Ballet Royal. Then, the veneration which has been accorded to the hero, *Rām*, who is equated to the Buddha by Khmers and Thais, casts the poem in the epic mould. The *Lpoek Aṅgar Vat*, The Poem of Angkor Wat, a poem closely associated with the Reamker in style, age (dated 1620 by Pou), and subject-matter, is included in this section, although the Rāma story is told not as a narrative but bit by bit, through descriptions of the sculptured scenes at Angkor. Mi Chak's narrative is written in prose but it is a rhythmical prose with many simple rhymes. It broadly follows the story given in the classical text and, unlike that text, does not lack, for example, the death of *Rāb* (Rāvana).

The fourth text is a study by Daniel (1982) of a passage, recited by *Tā Krūṭ*, from a popular performance. The fifth is part of a long prose version of the *Rāmakerti* compiled by *Vijjādhar* and edited by Dik-Kéam. The version in *Kambujasuriyā* consists of only twelve of the 107 parts.

The texts will now be discussed in greater detail.

(i) The classical text

The fascicules of the manuscripts of this text are numbered 1–10 and 75–80. Although some of the Rāma story is lacking it is not sufficient to account for the gap in the numeration. There are in fact two compositions, numbered 1–10 and 75–80 respectively, which Pou has dated sixteenth to seventeenth century (1979*a*) and the other seventeenth to eighteenth century (1982*b*). They have been very carefully researched by Pou, who has called them *Rāmakerti I* and *Rāmakerti II*. The first composition tells the main story of *Rām*, who is the god Nārāyaṇa born on earth to overcome evil in the form of *Rāb* (Rāvana), king of the *yaks* (ogres). *Rām* raises the magic bow and thus gains *Sītā* as his wife. She is abducted by *Rāb* and taken to *Laṅkā*. *Rām* and his brother, *Laks*, set off to find her and are helped by *Hanumān*, a white monkey with many magic powers, *Sugrīb*, and a host of brave monkeys. They build a causeway across to the island of *Laṅkā*. *Hanumān* flies over and gives the captive *Sītā Rām*'s ring. He sets fire to *Laṅkā*. *Rāb* parades *Sītā* in a carriage in the sky. *Laks* is mortally wounded but *Hanumān* goes to the *Hemavant* (Himalayas) for remedies. In a series of awesome battles *Rāb* loses his sons one by one and a brother. The poem ends before the death of *Rāb*. In *Rāmakerti II Sītā*, now restored to *Rām*, is tempted by a demon to draw a picture of *Rāb*. *Rām*, also affected by the demon, finds out and tells *Laks* to execute her in the forest. He spares her and she lives in the *āsram* of a hermit and bears *Rām*'s son. The hermit creates a twin brother and teaches the boys the arts of war. They come into conflict with *Rām*'s army. One boy is captured and freed by his brother. All is discovered and *Sītā* is asked to go back to the city. She refuses and is brought back only by being falsely told that *Rām* is dead. She runs away and takes refuge in the Underworld.

The metres in *Rāmakerti I* are the old ones (*Kākagati*, *Baṃnol*, and *Brahmagīti*) plus the metre *Pad Bol*, which seems only to be used in this poem. *Rāmakerti II* is written in the *Pad Bāky Prāṃmuoy*.

(ii) Lpoek Aṅgar Vat

The poem begins with a comparatively short narration of the story of King *Ketumālā*'s visit to his father Indra, after which Angkor was built by Indra's architect to resemble the stables of heaven. It is followed by a series of descriptions of the sculpted panels at Angkor which, when taken in order, relate the Rāma story incident by incident. Bizot (1980) says that the *Lpoek Aṅgar Vat* was intended as a guide for those who showed people round Angkor.

The metres used are *Kākagati*, *Baṃnol*, and *Brahmagīti*.

(iii) Rīoeṅ Rāmakerti nai Tā Cak'

This is a version of the popular Reamker, a text which would be recited by heart by a narrator at countryside productions of the epic, accompanied by mime, dance, and music. The text would be kept with great care by the narrator until he became old and passed it on to his son and pupil. Bizot (1973 and 1980) was able to record the recital of this text by Mi Chak (*Tā Cak'*), an elderly performer. The narrative is firmly in the Khmer (and Thai) Rāma tradition although details are different. For example, when the golden deer calls out with the voice of *Rām* that he, *Rām*, is being attacked, *Hanumān* is there to go with *Laks* to *Rām*'s aid. In the classical text *Hanumān* has not yet entered the story. Then the popular text contains certain incidents which have been very popular with audiences such as the seduction of *Macchānabv*, the sea princess, in her palace by *Hanumān*, who persuades her to tell the fish to return the stones to the causeway, and the impersonation of *Sītā* by *Puññakāy*, who floats as if dead down the river for *Rām* to see. The version has a happy ending. Brahma and Indra engineer the reconciliation of *Sītā* and *Rām*.

The text is written in prose but with a great number of rhymes based on open /ā/ and /ī/.

(iv) Recitation by Tā Krūṭ

The text of a prose recitation by *Tā Krūṭ* of part of the Reamker. This was the subject of a thesis by Daniel (1982). In volume 1 he discussed the presentation of the scenes and gave a translation. Volume 2 contains the text and a detailed translation, phrase by phrase, with a commentary on certain key words.

(v) Rāmakerti *by* Grū Vijjādhar

A text compiled by *Grū Vijjādhar* and partly edited and published by Dik-Kéam (1964–7 and 1964–5). We have only twelve of the 107 parts but the work is entitled '*Rāmakerti*' and not 'Rāmāyaṇa' and it begins with what seems like the full Khmer narrative in prose: the creation of the magic bow and coat of mail, thrown into Mithilā by Çiva; the story of Nandaka who was killed because he became too powerful with his boon from Çiva and was reborn as Rāvana; the births of *Bibhek*, *Hanumān*, and *Maṇḍogiri*. It proceeds with the tale of *Rām*. The beginning is not the same as Valmiki's text.

Work on the classical text, which is, particularly towards the beginning of the work, full of obsolete and misspelt words, was absolutely nonexistent until 1938, one year after the Bibliothèque Royale published the first edition of the text. Martini then produced the first of many articles (1938, 1947, 1950, 1952, and 1961) on the Cambodian version of the Rāmāyaṇa. His translated passages were published in *France-Asie* in 1949 and 1955 and formed part of some articles but, after many years of work, a full translation was published posthumously (1978). Martini had the field to himself until the mid-1960s when one or two articles in Khmer and a glossary were published. In 1977, one year before Martini's translation came out, Pou began her publications with the *Études sur le Rāmakerti (XVIe–XVIIe)*. This was followed by the text, translation, and notes for *Rāmakerti I* and *Rāmakerti II* (1977*c*, 1979*a*, and 1982*b*). The four publications form a monumental work which has made the Reamker available not only to Western readers but to the Khmers themselves. Pou had prepared herself for a study of a Middle Khmer text by editing the Inscriptions Modernes d'Angkor (in BEFEO Lewitz 1970–3, Pou 1974–5) and, with Jenner, the *Cpap'* (1975–81). In establishing her text for the *Rāmakerti* she used two manuscripts from the Bibliothèque Nationale, Paris. Pou resolved many difficulties of the text published by the Bibliothèque Royale and later the Institut Bouddhique.

BIBLIOGRAPHIC REFERENCES
For details see Bibliography.

(i) The classical text

Texts
Bibliothèque Royale 1937, Huffman and Proum 1977, Institut Bouddhique 1959–68, Pou 1979*a*, 1982*b*, Pierres d'Angkor 1982.

Versions
Jacob 1986, Jacob and Morgan 1979, Khing Hoc Dy 1990: 129–43, Martini 1938, 1949*a* and *b*, 1950, 1955, 1978, Pou 1977*a*, *c*, 1982*b*.

Studies
Bernard 1949, Bernard-Thierry 1955, Bizot 1981, Brunet 1974, Khing Hoc Dy 1990, Kosikov 1971, Krasem 1966, Leang Hap An n.d. and 1966–7, Martini 1938, 1947, 1949*a*, 1950, 1952, 1961, Moura 1883, *Paṇṇāgār pradīp khmaer* 1960, Pou 1975*b*, 1977*b*, *c*, 1980, 1981*a*, *c*, 1982*b*, 1983*b*, *c*, 1986, Pou, Lan Sunnary, and Kuoch Haksrea 1981, Singaravelu 1982.

(ii) Lpoek Aṅgar Vat

Texts
Aymonier 1878, Corbet 19—, Pierres d'Angkor 1985.

Versions
Aymonier 1878, Khing Hoc Dy 1990 (**V** by Moura), Moura 1882–3, Pou 1977*b*.

Studies

Om Ṇāgrī 1964 (in Khmer), Pic Bun Nil 1971 (in Khmer), Pou 1975*a*, Khing Hoc Dy 1990: 122–3.

(iii) Mi Chak's text

Text

Bizot 1973, 1980.

Version and *Study*

Bizot 1989.

(iv) Recitation by Tā Krūṭ

Daniel 1982.

(v) Rāmakerti by Grū Vijjādhar

Text of Vijjadhar's compilation

Dik-Kéam 1964–7, 1964–5.

General Cambodian Rāmāyaṇa Studies

Bizot 1983, 1989, Chap-Pin 1958*a*, Deydier 1952, Dik-Kéam 1971*a*, Kambujā 1969, Khing Hoc Dy (forthcoming), Leang-Hap An 1966*a*, 1966–7, n.d., Mâm 1972, Porée-Maspero 1983, Pou 1987, Raghavan 1975, Sarkar, H. B. 19—, Université Royale des Beaux Arts 1968.

G.7. *Lpaeṅ, Sātrā Lpaeṅ*: NARRATIVE POETRY

The *lpaeṅ*, 'works for pleasure', has been a popular genre.[2] French travellers in the nineteenth century would gather round in the village *sālā* in the evenings, for the reading of a *lpaeṅ*. The term 'verse-novel' has often been used for this genre. Many of the compositions, for example *Laksanavaṅs* and *Jinavaṅs**, were later adapted for performance as dance-dramas.

The majority of works in this genre are, but they sometimes only purport to be, *jātak*, tales of the previous lives of the Buddha, when he was a Bodhisatva. Most of the stories have a Buddhist association. However, there is a small number of *lpaeṅ*, notably *Duṃ Dāv*, Tum Teav*, but also some folktales retold in verse and some long secular travel-tales, known as *Nirās* ('journey; regretting absence from home'), which have no connection with the Buddha. The link with Buddhism

[2] Narrative poems which are told in full in Ch. 7, 'Narrative Poetry Summaries', are marked with an asterisk.

is very slight, in any case. Sometimes the *lpaeṅ* are animal stories, like *Cau Kaṅkaep*, 'The frog'* and *Cau Krabat*, 'The tetradon'*, which belong to the early lives of the Buddha. More often they tell of the Bodhisatva in his later life, when he was further on the road to Nirvāṇa and was born as a prince. Of the last ten lives of the Buddha, only the favourite, the *Vessantarajātak* or *Mahājāt(k)* as it is called, escaped being retold as a *lpaeṅ*. Vying with the ten in popularity were the 'Fifty', the *Paññāsajātak*, a collection of *jātak* written in Pali by a Laotian monk several centuries ago which has spread, with slightly different content, to Burma, Siam, and Cambodia. Authors would find these *jātak* among the *samrāy*, the roughly translated Pali texts, though Mok translated his extra-canonical *Devand* direct from the Pali before turning it into a verse-novel. Some of the verse-novels, for example *Jinavaṅs*, which was popular at the turn of the century, were written in the style of the real *jātak*, with the usual dedication in Pali to the Buddha, the Dhamma, and the Saṅgha at the beginning and the statement at the end as to the future lives of the characters, without actually being a part of the Buddhist Canon.*Varavaṅs Sūravaṅs** is based on a folktale which arose near Kompong Speu. There is a *Varavaṅs Sūravaṅs* Hill and a local spirit (*Anak Tā*) which is, like *Nāṅ Mikhā* in the story, headless.

A typical story involves the birth of a Bodhisatva (future Buddha) as a prince. Then, either a jealous second wife or a concubine accuses the boy of some mean act or the king is offended by some 'defect' in the young prince (for example *Săṅkh Silp Jăy** was born with a shell, which would later prove to be magical, attached to him). Mother and son are sent to the jungle with the executioners. They, moved by the pleading of the mother, leave the two in the jungle, quite helpless. They survive, however, often helped by a hermit who educates the prince, particularly in the magic arts. Later the prince has many adventures, fighting with *yaks* (ogres), going on long journeys to the *Hemavant* (the Himalayas), rescuing princesses from the Underworld, gaining wives and kingdoms by doing brave deeds. (Cambodian law did allow a man to have four wives.) Eventually he goes back with an army to the kingdom where he was born and is reconciled with his father. The interest for the reader, or listener, is in the exploits of the hero, the horror of their situations, and the romance of the remote setting.

If one expects the hero to be an example of virtue who can advise others about the way to Buddhahood, one is disapppointed. He is a stereotyped figure, handsome, brave, and clever. When he fights with *yaks* he uses magic devices. The *yaks* shoots an arrow which turns into fire but he sends an arrow which turns into water to quench the fire. The *yaks* sends *nāg* (snakes) but the hero sends *gruḍ* (garuḍas, mythical birds) to attack and eat them. Sometimes he travels through the air in a flying carriage, though these conveyances are not reliable. They often deposit him in the sea in a thunderstorm.

Heroines are by no means the colourless, frightened, protected daughters of the king that one might expect. Kangrei (*Kaṅrī*) in *Buddhisaen** marches off at the head of her army to prevent *Buddhisaen* from leaving her. Various princesses whom *Jinavaṅs* has collected as wives on his travels set out to other kingdoms to find him. In *Săṅkh Silp Jăy*, *Sumand* adapted to being the wife of a *yaks* and grew quite fond of him, while her daughter, *Subarṇadevī*, was heart-broken at leaving her husband, the king of the Underworld, when she was rescued. 'How long are you going to go on weeping?', *Săṅkh Silp Jăy* asked her. 'Think of your mother' (who had sent him to save her). She went back, as they were leaving, on the pretext of fetching a hairpin. 'Remember this', she said as if to her husband, 'My grief at leaving you will never change.' In *Sudhan** the heroine is a *kinnarī*, a mythical half-bird half-woman. In the absence of her husband she is about to be sacrificed but, using her wits, she asks for her wings, which have been taken from her, to dance one last dance. When she has them she flies away home.

The astrologers are indispensable. They are of course consulted about the proper day and time of day for weddings but it is in their interpretation of dreams that they really wield power. In *Sudhan* the astrologer wants his own daughter to marry the prince so, when the prince is away, he declares that a danger threatens the kingdom and that it will only be averted if *Manoharā* is sacrificed. It is the astrologer in *Rājakul** who tells the king that his horse wants to marry one of his daughters and that it would be advisable to go along with it! The youngest daughter obeys her parents' wishes. The horse is really a handsome prince.

The *yaks*, ogres, are not entirely the cruel, man-eating, princess-stealing wild beasts of the jungle. There are kings with handsome palaces. They can be kind and earn the love of those who stay with them. The childless *yaksiṇī*, *Bhandaraparipūrṇ*, in *Khyaṅ Săṅkh**, looks after the hero like a true mother, except that she goes off on trips to hunt for animals and humans to eat. When he leaves her, she is sad. 'You used to run to meet me, when I came back home.' When she is persuaded that he does indeed mean to go away in search of his real mother, she gives him three magic gifts, parts sadly from him, and dies.

Similarly the *nāg*, king of the Underworld, has a fine city and a beautifully decorated palace. He offers a permanent home to *Sītā* at the end of the Reamker (*Rāmakerti II*) and it is accepted. Princess *Subarṇadevī* in *Săṅkh Silp Jăy* is his wife. The executioners lower *Jinavaṅs** into deep water in a cage but he is rescued and brought up by the king of the Underworld.

The king of the *gruḍ* (garuḍas) has a home, *Simbalī* (the silk-cotton tree) in the forest of the Hemavant. He is able to change his bird-like form into that of a handsome young man. In *Kākī** he comes regularly in that form to play chess with the king of Benares. He falls in love with the queen and takes her to *Simbalī*.

Magic is encountered at every turn. Executioners raise their weapons to kill and they are turned into flowers. Baby girls are found in flowers. The sage at whose hermitage the hero has been educated makes a bow and a sword of magic power for him when he is grown up. Sometimes the sage raises the hero or even a helpful *yaks* from the dead. *Racanā* in *Khyaṅ Săṅkh* has the magic power to see, what no one else can see, that beneath his unprepossessing disguise, there is a handsome prince. In *Khyaṅ Săṅkh* too, the hero flies in the air to play *ghlị* (a sort of billiards or polo) against Indra. The kingdom is at stake but Indra lets him win. Indra pities *Bhogakulakumār**, in the verse-novel of that name; he works in the field all day and lives alone at night. He gives him a bag, which he puts in his room. It contains a princess who comes out by day when he is away and sweeps and cooks for him.

Various narrative devices are repeated frequently. Indra often helps a royal heroine, abandoned in the forest, pregnant and destitute. He produces by magic just what she needs: an old woman to look after her and a cottage where she can stay. Or when the hero is lost he produces an old man who can show him the way. A much-repeated scene is the pool in the forest outside the palace grounds to which the princess and her maidens go to refresh themselves and sport and from which the princess is sometimes stolen away by a *yaks*. When a king dies and there is no successor it was usual to let a royal elephant or a king's carriage go of its own free will. It would come to rest near someone who would be the new king. This was the case in *Kruṅ Subhamitr**, when the hero, journeying sadly along, having lost his wife and family, was approached by the elephant and chosen to be king of that land. Then there is the device of the ring which proves to one character that another has been or is nearby. *Manoharā* leaves her ring with a hermit on her journey home and later *Sudhan* stays with the same hermit and is given the ring. Later, outside the palace where she lives, he lets

Manoharā know that he has arrived by putting the ring in a pitcher of water which will be taken to her for bathing. The ring slips on to her finger. Another means of bringing members of a family together again is by having a series of pictures of their early life painted on the walls of a building.

Animals make loyal and at times admonitory companions. When he is dallying in a *yaks* kingdom with his wife, *Añcan Bicitr*, *Jinavaṅs* is reminded by the monkey which accompanies him that he left his wife *Padumkriyā* in the forest in the care of the *kinnarī*. It is time he went back for her. In *Buddhisaen* the horse impatiently tells the tarrying hero that if he does not set off back home with the medicine and the eyes of the twelve girls, he, the horse, will go without him.

The narratives are extended by quite long descriptions of certain items: the palace with its carvings, its decorative thrones and high towers; the army with its different sections, their weapons, the elephants and their trappings; a feast, probably at the time of a wedding, with games, acrobatics, competitions, and superb food and drink; and lastly, when princes go on journeys in the forest, nature. This last-named subject is treated in a totally artificial way. It is the sound of the words, their alliteration and assonance, which is considered and not to any extent the appearance of the flowers and plants. There is no attempt to recognize which trees would be in flower together or what animals would be found in the same habitat. The whole aim of the poet, as he produces more or less a series of names, first of plants, then of animals, sometimes of birds and finally of fish, is to create a pleasant sound—and to show off his verbal skill. In the Reamker (*Rāmakerti I* and *II*), which is kept separate as Genre 6 but is in fact in form a verse-novel, the three nature passages are restrained. There are no more than three stanzas in which alliterative words for plants are placed in conjunction. In the earliest dated *Sātrā Lpaeṅ*, *Khyaṅ Săṅkh*, dated AD 1729, there is almost a page (pp. 220–1) of 'nature description'. In *Sradap Cek**, written in 1889, there are three pages (pp. 11–14) which are nearly filled with names of plants, etc. However, there are whole sentences intermingled about the characters. 'Look at the *Pandanus*, so fresh and white.' 'They picked flowers and took them to the rich man.' In *Duṃ Dāv*, written in 1915, Som has long passages in which trees, flowers, birds, and animals are enumerated but he does relate the natural phenomena to *Duṃ*'s or *Dāv*'s feelings. 'I see the darkened sky where clouds drift apart, separated, as I am, from you.' 'I am not like the *Combretum*, *Dipterocarpus* or *Nauclea*' (all useful for wood or medicine). 'I am like the Strychnine or the *Datura*' (both poisonous) 'growing near the fig.'

Buddhism is certainly in the background of the verse-novels, although many of the so-called *jātak* are apocryphal and it must be admitted that the heroes are not presented as the devout holy characters we might have imagined! When a calamity occurs and the hero and heroine are separated or when someone is gravely ill, the reason is attributed to *karma*, a past act, probably in a past life. They bewail the fact but nothing can be done about it except to grin and bear it. Kings are often praised by the poets for their devotion to the ten kingly attributes, for the peaceful nature of their reign, and for their almsgiving. This last Buddhist virtue, frequently mentioned in the literature, is practised by kings in a grand way, by building a *sālā* or many *sālā* where huge amounts are given away to the poor.

Poets in the eighteenth and nineteenth centuries used the four early metres, the *Baṃnol*, the *Bhujuṅlīlā*, the *Brahmagīti*, and the *Kākagati*, changing from one to the other for different sections of the narrative. Although the association of the metres with particular moods of the characters or with the nature of the narrative was not strictly adhered to, laments or the description of sad separations were usually written in the *Brahmagīti* metre and lively action in the *Kākagati*. However, Nong wrote *Samudr** almost entirely in the *Bāky* 7 (seven syllables) metre, which was to become very popular towards the end of the century and in the twentieth century. He included some *Bāky* 9 (nine syllables) metre, also popular later. Mok was criticized for writing *Devaṇd* and *Siṅhanād* entirely in the *Kākagati* metre. In 1897 *Sai Tan'* and *Ân-Vāt* used *Bāky* 7 and *Bāky* 8 in writing *Jāv Gun*.

BIBLIOGRAPHIC REFERENCES
For details see Bibliography.

The first publications in connection with the *lpaeṅ* were in the form of résumés. Bastian, who travelled through mainland South-East Asia and published in 1868, gave very short summaries of a number of verse-novels which were popular at the time. Feer published Dr Hennecart's papers in 1877; these included translations of Bastian's résumés and a full-length résumé of *Laksanavaṅs*. Then Moura edited *Le Royaume du Cambodge* in 1883, giving a version of a different text, *Vimān Cand*. Leclère published a version of *Săṅkh Silp Jăy* in 1895. Between 1900 and 1903 Plon-Nourrit in Paris published the texts of twelve verse-novels, different again from previous choices. Pavie, in 1898, 1903, and 1921*a* and *b*, published versions of *Varavaṅs Sūravaṅs*, *Săṅkh Silp Jăy*, *Rathasenajātak* (= *Buddhisaen*), and *Mā Yoeṅ**. Guesdon published many texts, none of which seems to be available now. He also published a version of part of *Puññasā Sirasā** and a summary and study of *Rājakul* in 1906. Monod in 1943 (reprinted in 1985) gave versions of *Maraṇamātā**, *Kākī*, and *Stec Kmeṅ**. Versions of extracts will be found in Aymonier 1878, Mathers 1929, and Martini 1949*b*. *Kambujasuriyā* in the 1940s and IB in the 1950s have between them published the texts of many verse-novels. Léang-Hap An published a study of *Haṅs Yant** in 1965. Khing Hoc Dy has published many articles (1976, 1977*a* and *b*, 1979, 1980, 1981*a*) on the verse-novels and in 1987 produced an excellent book, a study and translation of *Bhogakulakumār* with much helpful information which applies to all verse-novels of the *jātak* type. This was followed in 1988 by a study, text, and translation of *Khun Cūv Cau Thuk*. In his two volumes on Khmer literature (1990 and 1993) he deals with the verse-novel in general.

Texts

Chhung-Nguon Huot and Ching-Nguon Huot 1959, Guesdon n.d., Huffman 1977 (excerpts), Institut Bouddhique, *Kambujasuriyā* II *Jātak. Sātrā Lpaeṅ*, Khing Hoc Dy 1988, Kim-Ky 1955, 1965, Kim-Seng 1949, 1953, Plon-Nourrit, Tieng-Khen.

Versions

Aymonier 1878, Bastian 1868, Bharati 1949, Collard 1925, Feer 1877, Guesdon 1906, Karpelès 1956, Khing Hoc Dy 1987, 1988, 1990, Kong-Huot and Chau-Seng 1970, Leclère 1895, Martini 1949*b* (extract), Mathers 1929, Monod 1943*a*, *b*, 1985, Moura 1883, Pavie 1898, 1903, 1921*a*, *b*, 1949, 1969, 1988.

Studies

Bernard-Thierry 1955*a*, *b*, *c*, *e*, Guesdon 1906, Khing Hoc Dy 1974, 1976, 1977*a*, 1977*b*, 1979, 1980, 1987, 1988, 1990, Leang-Hap An 1965*a*, 1966*b*, *d*, Ly-Théam Teng 1970*c*, Nhok-Thaem 1948, Taupin 1886*a*, Terral 1956, 1958, Terral-Martini 1959, Thong-Phan 1976.

Works concerning *jātak* which were not necessarily turned into verse-novels

Bitard 1955*a*, Feer 1875, Finot 1917, Khing Hoc Dy 1981*a*, 1982.

G.8. *Kaṃṇāby or Bāky Kāby*: NON-NARRATIVE POETRY

All non-narrative poetry, apart from that which is already accounted for in the *Cpāp'* (G.5) or in the *Daṃnuk Caṃrīeṅ* Songs (G.2) is included here. G.8 covers lyrics of three different Khmer categories:

(*a*) The short *Rīoeṅ Nirās*, 'Separation poems', a term which might be given to many poems discussed below. It became a convention, however, in imitation of the Thais, to write very lengthy *Rīoeṅ Nirās*, when a long (in those days) journey with the king and dignitaries was made to Angkor or when the Royal Ballet went to France (see Chapter 5 on 'Works': *Kāby Nirās Aṅgar* and *Aṃbī ṭaṃṇoer dau kruṅ pārāṃṅses*). Such poems consist almost entirely of the account of the voyage and are assigned to G.7 'Narrative poetry'.

(*b*) The second category of lyrics is *Kaṃṇāby saṅvās*, 'Love poems', all of which are G.8.

(*c*) Then there are some poems entitled *Lpoek*. Many *Lpoek*, for example *(Lpoek) Kākī* and *(Lpoek) Juc niṅ Trī*, are quite clearly narrative and have been included in G.7. A few of them, however, such as *Lpoek Rīoeṅ Tā Ĥīṅ*, which gives an amusing picture of *Tā Ĥīṅ*'s illness and all that had to be done for him, or Nong's *Lpoek Sīl Prāṃ* 'The five precepts' have only a trace of narrative if any; they are included here in non-narrative poetry.

In comparison with the *Cpāp'* and with the Songs, the language of the *Kaṃṇāby* is less simple. King Srī Dhammarājā wrote delightful lyrics, showing a skilful command of language. He used alliterative pairs of words, some of which, having occurred in the Reamker (*Rāmāyaṇa*), were already part of the poetic language of the day. Occasionally four words in succession begin with the same initial consonant. He did not overdo the alliteration, however, as did (according to my taste) the poets of the second half of the nineteenth century (Pou's Basse Époque; see above, Introduction: 'The Literature'). Like a good Buddhist of the Middle Period, he expressed his wish that his sweetheart should be born again to be the wife of the returning Buddha. The lyrics were written to *M̈ae Yuor Vatī* (or *M̈ae Yuor Pupphāvatī*). In *Braliṅ Mās oey*, 'O my precious darling', he describes the natural scene at each time of evening and night, bewailing that his sweetheart does not come. Birds perch and wait for their mates at sunset; then the breeze rises and makes the clouds float by; next it is dark and the moon and stars come out. But she has not come to share his pillow. At dawn the birds preen themselves and fly off and still he is alone. In *O p-ūn sṅuon beñ saṃḷāñ' sniddh*, 'O sweetheart, so close to me', he asks what *karma* he has incurred that she never comes. What god has led him to fall in love? Another poem, a happy one, *Kanlaṅ' mās maṅgal thlai*, 'Dear fortunate bee', tells how he goes directly to his love, like the bee flying straight towards his objective, the flower or the scent. The poem *Sarsoer Hemantamās* 'In praise of the cool season' is almost entirely a wistful description of natural phenomena, the birds, the bees, the flowers, the deserted mountainous region, a walk in the forest, all of which he enjoyed with his love—but this is now past.

King Ang Duong has been most famous for writing *(Rīoeṅ Nāṅ) Kākī* (G.7) but has also written a *Cpāp' (Cpāp' Srī)* and many plays. There is a delightful short lyric, however, by him, to *Ken Ḷuṅ*, whose love he has lost. It is in the 'new' metre, the nine-syllabled, and is given entire in Chapter 3 'Versification' as the example of 11: *Pad Bāky Prāṃpuon*. Mok also has a pleasing poem two stanzas long in the nine-syllable metre.

Some of the lyricists are princes, Yukanthor and Surivangs; some are women of the court. It is probable that most of the poems were not intended to be printed. 'L.N.', in *Dukh khñuṃ jāti neḥ loes as' srī*, 'My sorrow in this life is greater than any woman's', likens her wretchedness to that of *Kaṅrī* (Kangrei) in the *Rathasenajātak* but notes that *Kaṅrī's* suffering was soon over in death whereas hers goes on. For her, as for other poets, it is an old *karma* which now causes unhappiness. *Cam Srī Deb Apsar*, parted for many years from her lover, turns to the Buddha for strength and help, her sorrow being as great as Mount Sumeru (the mythical central mountain of the Hemavant or Himalayas). *Anak Mnāṅ Kuḷāp* regrets being born as a woman and prays that in the next life she will be an important, clever man.

Uong wrote several quite long poems. When he discerns a strange scent, he seems to feel the presence of his loved one, stretching out her arms towards him, but he is mistaken. Having no news of her, he is troubled, as when sky, water, and mist confuse one's orientation. In his case, both partners are at first eager to meet each other again but are prevented by circumstances. However, in the middle of the long poem he does doubt her; she has proved to be inconsistent. Nevertheless he swears, when he has to go away on duty, that, even with a hundred women to tempt him, it is at her feet only that he lays his life. He wants, like the crow, to go nowhere, if it is away from her. He is like a fledgling which has left the nest and been in a thunderstorm. His love is his life.

References to love are extremely restrained. Hearts break, the anger of the rejected lover is like fire. *Ghun Ŝī Manomai* says lovers are always troubled. He compares them with fish in the sea; if there is a slight change of temperature, they are unhappy. He pictures animals and people going to their partners at dusk while he is alone. Where is she now? Is she thinking of him? There is very little description of the loved one; she is sometimes called 'white, fair'. The most usual references are to her scent and golden skin-colour. In one anonymous poem, *O saen sraṇoḥ campā khaek*, 'O how I miss the frangipani!', the poet asks the gods to help him obtain that flower to wear.

The major part of the poetry in this genre consists of love poems but there are four poems written as elegies to King Norodom (*Pad yaṃ yām Braḥ Karuṇā Braḥ Pād Saṃtec Braḥ Narottaṃ*), 'Songs of mourning for King Norodom'. There is a poem dedicated to a mother, *Sarsoer guṇ mātā*, 'In praise of a mother's goodness'; a poem describing memories of farm-work, *Broḥ Srūv*, 'Sow the rice'; and a well-known invitation to the *grū* to start to cure a sick person, *Pad añjoeñ grū*, 'Invitation to the *guru*'.

King Srī Dhammarājā used the traditional *Kākagati*, *Brahmagīti*, and *Bhujuṅlīlā* metres but also used the metre borrowed from the Thais, the *Bāky* 7 (seven-syllable metre) which was to become the metre *par excellence* of the nineteenth century. The court poets of the nineteenth century used *Bāky* 7 more than any other metre but used *Bāky* 9 too (also borrowed from the Thais), though one poet used the old metres, *Kākagati*, *Brahmagīti*, and *Bhujuṅlīlā*. The elegy for King Norodom is written as a song (four times four syllables). Uong has many pages of *Bāky* 9 but uses in the last poem the old *Kākagati* and *Brahmagīti* and a metre associated chiefly with the *Rāmakerti II* (Reamker), the *Bāky* 6.

Unfortunately, the number of lyrical poems of which we have the manuscripts or texts is extremely small. They tended, like the innumerable songs which have been composed and lost, to be the expression of private emotions and, as such, not preserved. Luckily the manuscripts of the lyrics of King Srī Dhammarājā were arranged for publication in *Kambujasuriyā (KS)* by Princess Malika and, continuing with the court poets of the nineteenth century, Princess Malika published the love poetry which poets such as Prince Yukanthor and Uong, mentioned above, wrote to ladies of the court. There are some poetic replies from 'L.A.N.' and 'Sr. A.' The publication was printed as a book, *Prajuṃ Bāky Kāby*, in 1968.

BIBLIOGRAPHIC REFERENCES

For texts and studies (in Khmer) of non-narrative poetry, see the following in the Bibliography: Huffman and Proum 1977 (texts with vocabulary of *Braliṅ mās oey* and *Pad añjoeñ grū*). Ly-Théam Teng 1960: 65 (part of L.N.'s poem, *Dukh khñuṃ jāti neḥ loes as' srī*; small extracts from well-known poems plus a few stanzas each by Mok and Ngoy). Léang-Hap An 1966*a* (*Braḥ Rāj Sambhār*: texts of poems of King Srī Dhammarājā); and in *KS* 1968 12: 1322–30 (S. and extracts of poems). Malika 1938–41 in *Kambujasuriyā* (texts of *Kaṃṇāby* or *Bāky Kāby*: for the lyrics of King Srī Dhammarājā and of the nineteenth-century court poets); and 1968 id. in book form. Menkence 1973 'Au sujet de la valeur du poème cambodgien au moyen âge: Prah Raj Sambha (et la Princesse Ang Vodi)' (Russian text).

G.9. *Baṅsāvatār*: CHRONICLES

Although much of the Chronicles might be called not literary but purely historical, in that the dates of coronations or of births of sons of the king and the details of expeditions against the Siamese and so on are given, nevertheless the early legendary part and many passages of the later historical part should be regarded as literature. Many historical incidents have themselves become legendary and have been recounted as stories of daring deeds or terrible suffering.

The first king of Cambodia, according to the Chronicles, *Braḥ Thoṅ*, married the daughter of the king of the *Nāgas*. The king had the water, which covered the earth, pumped away, thus creating Cambodia. *Braḥ Thoṅ* had been looking for a place to build a palace. He had rested under a *dhlak* tree—the kingdom was called *Gok Dhlak* or Kok Thlok '*Terra firma* of the *dhlak* tree'—and water had marooned him and made him stay the night there. *Dhāravatī*, daughter of the *Nāga* king, came with her women and he fell in love with her. She said he must come again in seven days, with presents, and they would be married. Angkor was said to have been founded in the reign of *Ketumālā* (Jayavarman II), who was the son of the god Indra and the queen. As a boy, *Ketumālā* was permitted to see heaven and was taught by Indra how to protect Buddhism and make Cambodia prosperous. In one version of the story he is asked if he would like to have a city built like heaven. He modestly asked for it to be like the stables of heaven. Indra sent his architect, *Vishnukār*, down to earth to build Angkor.

Legends surrounded other kings of Cambodia. King Baksei Camkrong *Paksī Cāṃ Kruṅ* was adopted by an oxherd, who risked his life again and again to save the child but was executed at the order of Baksei Camkrong when he became king. Trasak Ph-aem *Trasak' Ph-aem* had a garden of excellent cucumbers. The king gave him a sword to defend the garden from intrusion but then was so foolish as to enter it himself and be slain. The populace made Trasak Ph-aem king. The foundation of Phnom Penh was due to Don (Grandmother) Penh, who lived near the river at the Catumukh (the four arms of the Mekong and the Tonle at Phnom Penh). During the rainy season, when the river was at its height, she saw a tree trunk (a *gagī* of which the wood is good for building) floating down. With the help of neighbours she drew it to the bank and lifted it out. In a niche were four bronze statues of the Buddha and a stone statue of a Brahmanic god. They added height to a small natural hill and built two sanctuaries for the statues. The hill (Phnom), the statues, and the sanctuaries are still there, in Phnom Penh.

The legendary love-story of the monk *Dum* (or *Ek*) and *Dāv* is founded on fact and included in the Chronicles (see Chapter 7, 'Narrative Poetry Summaries'). They tell too, though it redounds to the credit of the Siamese and not the Khmers, of how the enemy at last ended the siege of Longvek; in the bamboos which surrounded Longvek on three sides they organized a slow-burning fire, which lasted three days, forcing those inside the citadel to surrender. The story of King Srī Dhammarājā's unwise romance with his uncle's wife (who had been betrothed to him) is told by many Chronicles (see Srī Dhammarājā in Chapter 4, 'Authors'). The tale of the king Stec Kan has been given a miraculous beginning, for as a new-born babe he was swallowed by a big fish and was still alive when the fish was caught and cut open. He was handsome and likeable and grew in the esteem of the King Srī Sugandhapad until a dream showed the king that Stec Kan would take up arms against him. The king planned that they would go fishing and would pretend that the nets were entangled down below. Stec Kan would be asked to go down to look and the king's men would throw more nets into the water, leaving no room for him to escape. Having been warned of his danger by his sister, Stec Kan did swim away and escape and went on to form an army and rebel against the king.

Some of the Chronicles were kept by a family or in a monastery while other accounts were authorized by the king and written by a monk or palace official. Thus one, *Sīevbhau Baṅsāvatār*, tells the history of a mandarin family from the reign of Srī Sopar at the beginning of the seventeenth century to that of Ang Chan at the beginning of the nineteenth century. The manuscripts of *Vatt Kok Kāk*, *Vatt Sitpur*, or *Vatt Dịk Vil* were the property of those monasteries. Some manuscripts, like *Ampāl khsatr*, give a list of all the kings from Nipvān Pad in the fourteenth century to Norodom in the nineteenth. The reigning king would have the Chronicles rewritten so as to present him in a good light. In 1815 King Ang Duong asked Nong, who was a poet and a monk, to bring the Chronicle up to date. The work, *Rapāl ksatr*, was finished in 1818 and dealt with the years from 1713. This document was translated into Thai in 1855 (as Phoṅsāvadān khamen) and published again in 1914 in *Collection des Annales Siamoises*. It was translated into Vietnamese in 1836 (as Caomen lu'oc) and into French (by Doudart de Lagrée, published by Garnier in 1871–2). The oldest fragment of a Chronicle as presented by King Ang Eng to the King of Siam in 1796; it was translated into Siamese. The most recent is an update in 1941 of the Veang Chuon (*Vāṃṅ Juon*) Chronicle of 1903, which was the most complete account.

Despite their simple language (apart, that is, from the royal terminology) and the straightforward narrative style, the Chronicles present many problems. One simple reason for this is that the dates, though often given liberally according to three systems (the Great Era, the Little Era, and the Christian Era!) are grossly inaccurate, particularly towards the beginning. After the interest shown by Aymonier, Leclère, Maspero, and Moura, French scholars turned for reliability to the absorbing and rewarding task of interpreting the inscriptions on stone, which in any case recorded a more glorious part of Cambodian history. The Chronicles came to be despised as a dubious account of a period when Cambodia was troubled by the Siamese and the Vietnamese. However in more recent times attention has been turned again to the Chronicles, with a new translation by Piat and works by Osborne and Wyatt, Vickery, and Tranet. Excerpts were published in Khmer (Eng-Soth) and new history books were produced in Khmer. Above all, however, we have the works of two Cambodians in Paris, Khin Sok and Mak Phœun. Dividing the whole period covered by the Chronicles between them and comparing the different accounts of events as recorded in the various documents, they have produced excellent studies and translations.

BIBLIOGRAPHIC REFERENCES

For details see Bibliography.

Texts of Chronicles

Dik-Kéam 1968, 1975 (the MS of *Vatt Sit Pūr*). Eng-Soth 1966 (the elephant fight between Laos and Cambodia; subsequent defeat of Cambodia); and 1969 (various extracts from the Chronicles of the monastery of *Vatt Dịk Vil* and *Vāṃṅ Juon*). Huffman and Im Proum 1977 (they give extracts, with vocabulary, from Eng-Soth 1969). *Samāgam Samtec Juon-Ṇāt* 1975 (Chronicle of Vatt Sitpur). Tranet 1983, 1987 (text of a chronicle belonging to Leclère).

Versions and Studies and Texts

VS Aymonier 1880, 1883, 1904. **V** Cœdès 1918 (earliest fragment of AD 1796); and **V** 1949 (foundation of Phnom Penh). **S** Dik-Kéam 1968, 1971*c* (in Khmer). **S** *Gaṅ Sambhār* and *Sūr Hāy* 1972. **VS** Garnier 1871–2 (translation by Doudart de Lagrée of Nong's *Rapāl ksatr* DL/2). **S** *Gīm Sā Ûl* 1971 (historical texts from the south of Cambodia). **S** Govid 1965 (history for schools; in Khmer). **VS** Khin Sok 1975 (thesis), 1976, 1977*a*, *b*, 1985, 1986, 1988 (translation of Chronicles AD 1417–1595 with study of different MSS and translation of parts of them). **VS** Khing Hoc Dy 1990: 57–62. **V** Lagrée, Doudart de (his translation was published by Garnier, q.v.). **VS** Leclère 1914. **S** Ly-Théam Teng 1959*a* and *b*. **VS** Mak Phœun 1973 (thesis), 1976, 1980, 1981 (translation of Chronicles AD 1594–1677 with study of different MSS and translation of parts of them), 1984 (translation of Legendary Chronicles to Paramarājā I). **VS** Maspero 1904. **VS** Moura 1883 (vol. II, chapter 1). **S** Osborne and Wyatt 1968. **V** Piat 1974. **V** Svay Muoy 1972. **STV** Tranet 1983. **S** Vickery 1977. **V** de Villemereuil 1883.

G.10. *Samrāy*: POPULAR BUDDHIST LITERATURE

Much of the literature included in the Genres 1–9, especially that in G.5, *Cpāp'*, is clearly very Buddhist in character, bearing witness to the devotion of the Khmer people, but the works which are regarded as belonging to this final genre are based directly on the religious texts, translated from Pali to Khmer. The *samrāy* are rough translations into Khmer from Pali with explanations or commentary. They are often interspersed with the passages of Pali, the 'translation' or 'explanation' usually being much longer than the original. During the centuries of decline, when Cambodia was barely held together, the care of religious documents was neglected. Afterwards the Cambodians turned to Siam for help with many texts. The *Trai Bhūm* had been lost. This was a Brahman, not a Buddhist, text but it gave the cosmology in which Buddhists had believed and which forms an integral part of the literature. In the middle of the nineteenth century King Ang Duong asked the Siamese for this text and had it translated into Khmer. The *Patham Sambodhi*, a poem about the Enlightenment of the Buddha, was written in Bangkok in the eighteenth century, supervised by Phra Paramanuxit Xinarot. It was translated into Khmer and made into a poem by In. The *Milindapañhā*, in which many Buddhist questions are explained by Nāgasena in answer to King Milinda, also came to Cambodia from Thailand.

Most of the works in this genre are prose versions of *jātak*, which were never turned into verse-novels or dance-dramas. They remained in the *samrāy* form. Manuscripts were kept in monasteries throughout Cambodia and, after its foundation in 1930, in the Institut Bouddhique in Phnom Penh. At festivals the texts were read, expounded, and often altered a little. The manuscripts were copied over and over again. Thus when the Institut Bouddhique came to publish the texts of the favourite *jātak* in the 1960s, the task of editing was phenomenal. This was particularly the case with the most well loved of all *jātak*, the *Mahāvessantarajātak* or *Mahajāt(k)*, which tells how *Vessantar* gave as alms his own children and his wife. The *jātak* was the subject of a festival which took place at the end of the retreat in almost every monastery. Nhok-Thaem edited the text in 1960. In some of the manuscripts there was no Pali, or Pali which was faulty, and he had to supply the correct Pali. All manuscripts had been altered and expanded locally in each monastery. Two sections of this story have been written up as separate texts. The one (*Lpoek Jūjak*) is the amusing story of how *Jūjak* ate until he burst and died; the other (*Lpoek Medrī*) is the sad tale of *Medrī*, *Vessantar*'s wife, who fails to find her children and asks her husband over and over where they are; he does not answer, because he has given them away. A manuscript, the *Ānisaṅ Mahājātak*, explaining the merit to be gained from various activities in connection with the *Mahāvessantarajātak*, has been translated by Khing Hoc Dy.

The *Mahosathajātak*, like the *Vessantarajātak*, is one of the Ten, the birth-stories of the last ten lives of the Buddha. The Buddha was born as a wise man who could solve all riddles and problems. By a clever trick he helped 101 kings to escape punishment. He made a plan to help King *Videharāj* to free himself from the power of King *Cullaṇi Brahmadatt*. A verse-novel, *Sek Sārikā*, 'The parrot and the Myna bird', narrates the love-story of these two 'characters' who meet when the parrot is on a mission to help Mahosath (see Chapter 7, 'Narrative Poetry Summaries'). Translations of excerpts of the *Mahosathajātak* were given in *Le Royaume du Cambodge* by Moura. The *Kumbhajātak*, which is concerned with the effects of alcohol, was translated from the Pali by Chhim-Soum, whose aim it was to help his Pali students to progress. *Ŝī Sau(r)*, the *Sisorajātak*, was edited in the *Kambujasuriyā* by Peung-Pam but not published separately.

The *Surabbhajātak*, published in 1960 from a *samrāy*, is one of the 'Fifty *jātak*', an extra-canonical collection of *jātak* written in Pali, probably by a Laotian monk, between the fifteenth and seventeenth centuries. The collection is known in Burma as well as Cambodia and Laos and the Laotian text was translated into Thai. Finot discovered this connection between the countries in 1917 when he was studying Laotian manuscripts. The Burmese, Laotian, and Cambodian texts are now very different in composition with only fifteen *jātak* which are the same in all three countries and four others which are the same in Laos and Cambodia. The Institut Bouddhique began its publication of the Fifty in 1961 in both Pali and Khmer. Twenty-five *jātak* in Khmer were produced by 1962 in five volumes.

Shortened versions of the *jātak* were published, such as the Ten by Ou Chev, a variety of fifty-one items from the Dhammapadaṭṭhakathā by Chhim-Soum, and the Fifty by Nhok-Thaem.

Some of the *jātak* which were popular at the turn of the century and were constantly read aloud at festivals, such as *Mahājanakajātak*, *Nimirājajātak*, and *Temiyajātak*, are available in translation in Leclère (1906). *Temiyajātak* and *Mahājanakajātak* were told by means of sets of pictures published by the Institut Bouddhique.

The *Hitopades* was a Pali work which was translated first from the French into Khmer in the *Kambujasuriyā* by Choum-Mau and Krasem and then was published as *Srīhitopades* in a translation directly from the Pali by Pang-Khat.

In's *Gatilok* is a very different kind of work. It is a collection of stories and poems, some Buddhist, some from French. It has been attributed to three genres. Those of Folktales and Songs go without saying; it is mentioned here on the strength of the translations from Pali which it contains.

During the vast labour of translating the Tripitaka into Khmer, a text published in 110 volumes in 1969 after more than thirty years of work by many Pali specialists, *Kambujasuriyā* printed a number of 'new' *jātak* which had recently been translated by scholars such as Em, Oum-Sou, Him, Long, Hong-Chea, Chhim-Soum, You-Ponn, You-Oun.

BIBLIOGRAPHIC REFERENCES

For details see Bibliography.

Texts translated from Pali (or Thai) into Khmer Prose

Chhim-Soum 1939 (51 *jātak* from the *Dhammapadaṭṭhakathā*); 1942 *Kumbhajātak*; 1966*b* (the Ten *jātak* abridged); 1968 in *Kambujasuriyā*, *Lpoek Mahārājapārb*. Em *et al.* 1944 (25 of the Fifty). Huffman and Proum 1977 (Excerpts from *Gatilok* and *Mahāvessantarajātak*). In 1933 *Patham Sambodhi*; 1927–30 *Gatilok* in *Kambujasuriyā* and 1936. Institut Bouddhique 1960 *Surabbhajātak*; 1962 *Mahosathajātak*. Krasem: see Choum-Mau below. Nhok-Thaem 1960, 1962 *Mahāvessantarajātak*; 1963 (the Fifty abridged). Ou-Chev 1951 (the Ten *jātak*). Oum-Sou 1930–2 *Milindapañhā* in *Kambujasuriyā*; 1942 *Milindapañhā* as a separate publication. Pang-Khat 1971–2 and (Cedoreck) 1981

Srīhitopades. Peung-Pam 1954–6 *Sisorajātak* in *Kambujasuriyā*. Song-Siv 1953 *Prajuṃ nidān jātak*. Terral 1956 (one of the Fifty, *Samuddaghosajātak*); 1958 (several *jātak*). Terral-Martini 1959 (*jātak* of Indochina).

Pali Texts translated from the French

Choum-Mau 1933–4, then Krasem 1938 *Hitopades*.

Versions into French

Bitard 1955*a*; Leclère 1895 (Chéa-Ly. *Jālī*); 1902 (*Vessantarajātak*); 1906 (*Patham Sambodhi*, *Satrā Devadatt*, *Mahājanakajātak*, *Nimirāj*). Moura 1883 (parts of *Mahosathajātak*).

Version into English

Carrison 1987 (part of the *Gatilok*).

Studies

Finot 1917 (*re* the Fifty *jātak*). Khing Hoc Dy 1982 *Mahāvessantarajātak*, 1990: 26–56. Léang-Hap An 1967*a* (in Khmer). Nhok-Thaem 1982 (in Khmer). *Saem Sūr* 1967 (in Khmer). Terral 1956 (study of the Fifty in Pali).

3

VERSIFICATION

Khmer versification is bound by the strict rules of certain metres. So far as I know, no one has felt it desirable to abandon the syllable-patterns or the rhyme schemes of the metres and write free verse. The metres (*pad*) are determined by the number of syllables (*byāṅg*) to the verse (*ghlā*) and of verses to the stanza (*lbaḥ* or *vagg*). Short, unstressed open syllables, in words of Sanskrit and Pali derivation and at the beginning of Khmer words, may be counted with an adjacent syllable as one, not two syllables. Rhymes (*cuṅ cuon*) occur at predetermined places, some at the end of a verse, some within it. One rule which applies to all metres (though with lapses in the metre used mainly for songs) is that the last syllable of a stanza rhymes with the end syllable of a particular verse (usually the second) of the next stanza. Rhymes occur between the vowels and final consonants of the syllables, as one would expect, but rhymes of two further categories are acceptable to the Khmers. The first category comprises rhymes which are 'across register', that is rhymes which the writing supports but the pronunciation now denies. They are still found in modern poetry. The other category comprises rhymes which are nearly perfect but not quite. To give a few examples, *it* (pronounced /ɤt/ or /µ t/) with *āt*' (/at/ or /ɔət/) and *ak* (pronounced /ɔːk/ or /oːk/) with *ok* (/aok/ or /oːk/). These imperfect rhymes are in some cases the result of a development in pronunciation but in other cases seem to be near-rhymes which are allowed. They have been discussed in Jacob 1966.

The Khmers have been very conservative in using the metres which they have inherited from the past. Metres found in the earliest poetry were still being used in the 1950s, 1960s, and 1980s. In addition to the required rhymes, there is an abundance of alliterative words, a feature much loved by the Khmers. Cambodians have an instinctive gift for words. One of their amusements has been a kind of street theatre where spontaneous questions and answers are given, amusingly, about topical matters. The whole discourse is interlarded with puns and Spoonerisms, produced at a rapid rate.

Poems may simply be read but each metre has an air with which it may be recited. A feature of all the recitation tunes is that, when a syllable ending in a plosive or aspirate is to be sung on a long note or series of notes, a humming sound follows the syllable. The nasal consonant used for the humming is phonetically appropriate to the consonant. (See Jacob 1966 *re* tunes and humming.)

The metre known as *Pad Bol* (Narrating Metre), occurs only, so far as I know, in short passages in the first part of the Reamker (*Rāmakerti I*). This may substantiate other evidence that this is the oldest extant poem. Apart from these occurrences, the *Rāmakerti I* and the *Lpoek Aṅgar Vat* (The raising of Angkor Wat), which is dated AD 1620 (see Pou 1975*a*), are entirely written in the three metres, *Pad Baṃnol* (Narration Metre) and its variation *Pad Mahājăy* (Victory Metre), *Pad Kākagati* (Crow's Gait Metre), and *Pad Brahmagīti* (Brahma's Song Metre). The old *Cpāp'* (Codes), which may well be as old as the *Rāmakerti I*, do not have the *Pad Baṃnol* because they are not narrative poems and this metre is used for narration; they are entirely written in the two other metres. A poem written on one of the Inscriptions Modernes d'Angkor, No. 38, and dated AD 1702 is also written in the *Kākagati* and *Brahmagīti* metres plus the *Pad Bhujuṅlīlā*. This last metre was used by King Srī Dhammarājā who died in AD 1731. *Pad Pandol Kāk* (or *Pad Maṇḍukgati*) is first evidenced in 1882 in *Săṅkh Silp Jăy*.

In addition to these metres, there are metres with a set number of syllables in each of four verses. *Pad Bāky Puon* (four-syllable metre) must be very old as it is the main metre occurring in songs. *Pad Bāky Prāṃmuoy* (six-syllable metre) was used to write *Rāmakerti II* (probably eighteenth century) and a nineteenth-century court poet, Uong, used it too. *Pad Bāky Prāṃbīr* (seven-syllable metre) and *Pad Bāky Prāṃpuon* (nine-syllable metre) were used by Nong in 1808 in the poem, *Samuddh*, and were very popular with the court poets of the nineteenth century. Metres of this kind (particularly with seven and eight syllables, but also with nine, and even ten, twelve, and fourteen) continued to be used in the twentieth century.

The metres were associated with certain moods. *Pad Baṃnol* was used for the description of fights, quarrels, storms, and threats. *Pad Kākagati* was used for the beginning of a story, conversation, and the reporting of events. *Pad Brahmagīti* was for lamentation. *Pad Bhujuṅlīlā* was for descriptions of pleasant scenes or activities such as the countryside or the hero bathing in a pool. *Pad Pandol Kāk* was used for amusing passages particularly for repartee between animal characters.

THE METRES, WITH EXAMPLES IN TRANSLITERATION, TRANSLATION, AND TRANSCRIPTION

1. *Pad Bol* (Narrating Metre) 4–9: 4–9: 4–9: 4–9
Example from Reamker, 4. 24–5 (*Rāmakerti I*, stanzas 1758–9), 16th–17th century.

paṅ cāṃ kesī pī khmau ñāp'	I recall your hair, black and thick,
p-ūn krasop cāp caṅ nūv phkā	And you, your arms up round it, braiding it with flowers,
kaem cuot pruot mālā	Adding further garlands,
as' phkā sāraboe bhñī	All kinds of flowers round it.
paṅ cāṃ nā thṅās	I recall your forehead
pī ṭūc babil mās mān nai rasmī	Shining like the gold of a candle-holder,
ṭūc braḥ candr beñ ťa pūrṇami	Like the full moon
lok yal' banlį krai.	Whose brilliance is visible to the whole world.

/bɔːŋ cam keːsei bei khmau ɲɔəp/	_ _ _ _ _ _ _x
/p′oːn krəsaop cap cɔːŋ nɤu phkaː/	_ _ _ x_ _ _ _A
/kaem cuːət pruːə t miːəliːə/	_ _ _ _ _A
/ɔh phkaː saːrəpɤː phɲiː/	_ _ _ _ _ _B
/bɔːŋ cam niːə thŋaːh/	_ _ _ _y
/bei doːc pəpɯl miːəh miːən nei rasmei/	_ _ _ _ _y _ _ _ _B
/doːc prɛəh can peɲ dɔː boːnəmei/	_ _ _ _ _ _ _ _B
/loːk yuəl puənlɯː krai/	_ _ _ _ _C

The vowels are spelt the same but pronounced differently in the rhymes: /ɔəp/ with /cap/, /phkaː/ with /miːəliːə/, /phɲiː/ with /rasmei/ and /boːnəmei/, /thŋaːh/ with /miːəh/.

2. *Pad Baṃnol* (Narration Metre) and its variation *Pad Mahājǎy* (Victory Metre) 6:4:6
Example from *Lpoek Aṅgar Vat* by Pang in Aymonier 1878, p. 278, AD 1620.

khlaḥ jā nāg nūv mkar	Some were *nāgas* and dragons.
khlaḥ jā gruddhā	Some were *garuḍas*
ǩa cāp' nāgā chak' ŝī	Who grabbed at the *nāgas* and ate them.
chlau chlāk' caṃḷāk' as' ktī	Any and everything was sculpted.
klaep klāy jā bhñī	They became part of the pattern
hāk' mān viññāṇ rūp ras'.	And were just like conscious, live beings.

/khlah ciːə niːək nɤu məkɔː/	_ _ _ _ _ _A
/khlah ciːə kruthiːə/	_ _ _ _A
/kɔː cap niːəkiːə chɔk siː/	_ _ _ _ _ _B
/chlau chlak cɔmlak ɔh kdei/	_ _ _ _ _ _B
/klaep klaːy ciːə phɲiː/	_ _ _ _B
/hak miːən viɲɲiːən ruːp ruəh/	_ _ _ _ _ _C

The vowels are spelt the same but pronounced differently in the rhyme: /siː/ with /kdei/; /məkɔː/ is a near-rhyme with /kruthiːə/. The short neutral vowel in məkɔː is here counted as a whole syllable: cf. srənɔh in No. 5 and prənei in No. 11.

In *Buddhisaen* a few stanzas of *Pad Mahājǎy* occur on pp. 57–8 of the IB edition. The word *jǎy* 'victory' occurs frequently.

3. *Pad Kākagati* (The Crow's Gait Metre)
Cpāp' Kūn Cau, stanzas 9 and 10, 17th century or earlier.

lok thā bhloeṅ bhlī̤	The sage says that fire is bright.
maen bit moḥ rī̤	Is that not so?
buṃ smoe suriyā	But it is not the equal of the sun.
lok thā sūry saeṅ	He says the sun's rays
bhlī̤ caeṅ vehā	Are resplendent in the heavens
moḥ buṃ smoe nā	But are not equal to
braḥ dharm braḥ buddh	The Dharma of the Lord Buddha.
bhloeṅ bhlī̤ as' citt	The fire blazes with all its might
as' kāl hoey pāt'	But at the end of its time it is gone,
ralāy ralat'	Used up, extinguished.
braḥ sūry bhlī̤ ḷoeṅ	The sun is brilliant,
thkoṃ thkoeṅ prākaṭ	Magnificent, it is true
āp' astaṅgat	But, when it sets, it is dimmed.
buṃ yal' rasmī	You cannot see its light.

/loːk thaː phlɤːŋ phlɯː/	_ _ _ _A
/mɛːn pɯt muəh rɯː/	_ _ _ _A

/pum smaə *soriya*ː/	_ _ _ _B
/loːk thaː soː saeŋ/	_ _ _ _x
/phlɯː caeŋ veːhaː/	_ _x _ _B
/muəh pum smaə niːə/	_ _ _ _B
/prɛəh thɔə prɛəh put/	_ _ _ _C
/phlɤːŋ phlɯː ɔh cɤt/	_ _ _ _D
/ɔh kaːl haəy bat/	_ _ _ _D
/rəliːəy rəluət/	_ _ _ _C
/prɛəh soː phlɯ: laəŋ/	_ _ _ _y
/thkom thkaəŋ praːkɔt/	_ _y _ _C
/ap asdɔŋkuət/	_ _ _ _C
/pum yuəl rasmei/	_ _ _ _E

The vowels are spelt the same but pronounced differently in the rhymes: /veːhaː/ with /niːə/. Near-rhymes are (1) /cɤt/ with /bat/ and (2) /put/ with /luət/ /praːkɔt/ and /kuət/.

The two short vowels in open syllables which are italicized count as one syllable.

4. *Pad Brahmagīti* (Brahma's Song Metre) 5:6:5:6
Example from *Cpāp' Kerti Kāl*, stanzas 18 and 19, 17th century or earlier.

gṛhā oy phcit phcaṅ'	Let your house be spick and span
kuṃ oy phaṅ' phuy dhūlī	With no dust rising.
jaṃraḥ pār pos ṭī	Clean, rake and sweep the ground
oy hmat' hmaṅ koet sukhā.	So that its neatness will cause content.
añjulī duk oy gaṅ'	Put your needles away safely
prāk' knuṅ thaṅ' duk oy jā	And keep carefully the money in your purse.
proe khñuṃ moel mukh vā	When you give orders to your slaves, look at their faces
doḥ kāc jā moel oy staeṅ.	To see whether they are good or ill-natured.

/krɯhaː aoy phcɤt phcɔŋ/	_ _ _ _ _x
/kom aoy phɔŋ phoy thuːliː/	_ _ _ x_ _ _A
/cumrɛəh baː baoh dei/	_ _ _ _ _A
/aoy mɔt mɔːŋ kaət sokhaː/	_ _ _(A) _ _ _B
/aɲculiː tuk aoy kuəŋ/	_ _ _ _ _y
/prak knoŋ thɔŋ tuk aoy ciːə/	_ _ _ y_ _ _B

/praə khɲom mɤːl muk viːə/	_ _ _ _ _B
/tuəh kaːc ciːə mɤːl aoy sdaeŋ/	_ _ _(B) _ _ _C

The vowels are spelt the same but pronounced differently in the rhymes: /thuːliː/ and /dei/, /sokhaː/, /ciːə/, and /viːə/ and /kuəŋ/ and /thɔŋ/.

5. *Pad Bhujuṅlīlā* (Serpent's Movement Metre) 6:4:4
Example from *Khyaṅ Săṅkh*, AD 1729, p. 24 in the IB edition.

sraṇoḥ āloḥ grap' gnā	They were all regretful
ānit anā(th)	Pitying the defenceless one,
anāth bek krai	Too defenceless.
mahesī devī prabai	The good queen
sịṅ sok ālăy	Bewailed utterly and thought
āloḥ dau mak	Wistfully of this and that.

/srənɔh aːlɔh krup kniːə/	_ _x _ _x_ _A
/aːnɯt anaː/	_ _ _ _A
/anaːt peːk krai/	_ _ _ _B
/məhaesei teːviː prəpey/	_ _y_ _y _ _B
/sɤŋ saok aːlai/	_ _ _ _B
/aːlɔh tɤu mɔːk/	_ _ _ _C

The vowels are spelt the same but pronounced differently in the rhymes: /kniːə/ with /anaː/ and /prəpey/ with /aːlai/.

The short open syllable, counted with the next syllable as one, is italicized.

6. *Pad Pandol* (or *Pando) Kāk* (Let out the defecation?), called *Pad Pandol Kākagati* by Ing-Yeng (1972), or *Pad Maṇḍukgati* (Frog's Gait Metre) 4:6:4:6
Example from *Săṅkh Silp Jăy*, p. 231 of the IB edition.

doep khñuṃ trāc' car	So I went forth,
chlās' chlaṅ sāgar jalasā	Crossing the oceans,
ḷoeṅ loe pabvatā	Climbing mountains,
sịṅ tae prāṃbīr jān' jāk'.	Seven ranges of them.
pradaḥ satrūv	I met with enemies,
rīeṅ rīep ṭoy phlūv croen thnāk'	Of all kinds, ranked along my way.
sịṅ bas' sịṅ yaks	There were snakes and *yaksas* everywhere,
gajasār vidyādhar phaṅ.	Elephants and Himalayan deities.

/tɤːp khɲom trac cɔː/	_ _ _ _x
/chlah chlɔːŋ saːkɔː culəsaː/	_ _ _ _x_ _A
/laəŋ lɤː bɔpəta:/	_ _ _ _A
/sɤŋ tae prampɯl cɔən cɛək/	_ _(A) _(A) _(A) _ _B
/prətɛəh satrɤu/	_ _ _ _y
/riəŋ riːəp daoy phlɤu craen thnak/	_ _ _ _y _ _B
/sɤŋ puəh sɤŋ yɛək/	_ _ _ _B
/kɛəcəsaː vityiːəthɔː phɔːŋ/	_ _(B) _(B) _(B) _ _C

The vowels are spelt the same but pronounced differently in the rhyme: /cɛək/ with /thnak/ and /yɛək/.

Where two short vowels in open syllables are counted as one syllable they are italicized.

7. *Pad Bāky Puon* (four-syllable metre) 4:4:4:4
This metre is used chiefly for songs. It is the only metre for which the rhyme link between the last syllable of a stanza and the end syllable of the second verse of the next stanza is not obligatory.
Example from a well-known song.

anak cau brāhm(ṇ) oey	Oh Brahmin,
mịn ṭael ṭoe ṭī	You never walk along the ground.
dhlāp' jiḥ ṭaṃrī	You usually ride an elephant
kañcaeṅ rāy phkāy	Its howda decorated with flowers.
anak cau brāhm(ṇ) oey	Oh Brahmin,
cau ṭoe tāṃṅ2	Your feet tap as you walk along.
panlā krasāṃṅ	The thorns of the *Feronia*
mut joeṅ cau brāhm(ṇ).	Cut your feet.

/nɛək cau priːəm aəy/	_ _ _ _
/mɯn dael daə dei/	_ _ _ _A
/thlɔəp cih dɔmrei/	_ _ _ _A
/kaɲcaeŋ riːəy phkaːy/	_ _ _ _[B]
/nɛək cau priːəm aəy/	_ _ _ _
/cau daə taŋ-taŋ/	_ _ _ _B
/bɔnlaː krəsaŋ/	_ _ _ _B
/mut cɤːŋ cau priːəm/	_ _ _ _[C]

8*a*. *Pad Bāky Prāṃmuoy* (six-syllable metre) 6:6:6:6
Example from the Reamker, 75. 2 (*Rāmakerti II*, stanzas 40–1).

doep nāṅ mān braḥ savanī	So the queen spoke
thlā thlaeṅ prāp' bī asurā	Describing the godless creature,

mukh ṭap' ṭai ṭap' phaṅ nā	His ten faces and ten arms.
maen mān ṛddhī jok jăy	Truly he had overwhelming power.
thā poe gāt' niṅ kālā	If he wanted to transform himself
oy ṭūc anak ae ṇā muoy nai	To resemble someone,
sakti sādh it ṭadai	He achieved the likeness to that person and no other.
as' deb sñap' sñaeṅ cestā.	All the gods were astounded at his prowess.

/tɤːp niːəŋ miːən prɛəh *savə*niː/	_ _ _ _ _ _x
/thlaː thlaeŋ prap piː *asu*raː/	_ _ _ _x _ _A
/muk dɔp day dɔp phɔːŋ naː/	_ _ _ _ _ _A
/mɛːn miːən rɯtthiː coːk cey/	_ _ _ _ _ _B
/thaː baə kɔət nɯŋ kaːlaː/	_ _ _ _ _ _y
/aoy doːc nɛək ae naː muːəy ney/	_ _ _ _y _ _B
/sakdei saːt ɤt dɔːtey/	_ _ _ _ _ _B
/ɔh teːp sɲɔp sɲaeŋ ceːsdaː/.	_ _ _ _ _ _C

Where two short vowels in open syllables count as one syllable, they are italicized.

8*b*. A variation of this metre occurs *passim* in the Reamker, 75–80 (*Rāmakerti II*) when a new section starts with a short first verse of four syllables consisting of the words *kāl oey kāl noḥ,* 'Oh at that time': 4:6:6:6

8*c*. *Pad Taṃṇak'* (Accumulative Metre) 5:6:6:6
This is a variation of the six-syllable metre in which the first verse has only five syllables. Reamker, 75. 2 (*Rāmakerti II,* stanza 9).

/ruət aəy riːəc ruət rɔət/	Oh the bejewelled royal carriage!
/kam kɔŋ picɤt thlay thlaː/	With the wheel spokes richly decorated,
/prədap sɤŋ pec *ra*cənaː/	Embellished all over with patterns of gems,
/phlɯː phleːk l'ɔː l'ah craːl cray/	Its brightness dazzled with flashing glints.

The rhyme /rɔət/ with /picɤt/ is a near-rhyme.
The two short vowels in open syllables, counted as one syllable, are italicized.

9. *Pad Bāky Prāṃbīr* (seven-syllable metre) 7:7:7:7
Example from King Srī Dhammarājā's '*O p-ūn beñ saṃḷāñ' snit*' in *Kambujasuriyā* 1939. 1, p. 41.

o p-ūn sṅuon beñ saṃḷāñ snit	O my sweetheart, all I could desire,
bī ṭuoc prās brāt' dau thṅai ṇā	From the moment that we separated on that day
rīem drāṃ dukkh mneñ knuṅ dăyā	I have been broken-hearted,
ktau phsā gmān sukh rāl' rātrī	Feverish and wretched, every night.
bel ṭael niyāy cāṃ vācā	I remember what was said, when we spoke
bel ṭael snehā cāṃ metrī	I remember our closeness when we made love.
o dhvoe kamm avī ṭūcneḥ nai	O what is this fate you have caused
min oy haṛdăy pān sukh soḥ	It allows no peace in my heart.

/ao p′oːn sŋuːən peɲ sɔmlaɲ snɤt/	_ _ _ _ _ _ _x
/piː duːəc prah prɔət tɤu thŋai naː/	_ _x _ or _x _ _ _A
/riəm trɔəm tuk mneɲ knoŋ teyiːə/	_ _ _ _ _ _ _A
/kdau phsaː kmiːən sok rɔəl riːətrei/	_ _A _ or _ A_ _ _B
/peːl dael niyiːəy cam viːəcaː/	_ _ _ _ _ _ _y
/peːl dael snaehaː cam metrei/	_ _y _ or _ y_ _ _B
/ao thvɤː kam əvei doːcneh ney/	_ _ _ _ _ _ _B
/muɯn aoy haruɯtey baːn sok sɔh/	_ _B _ or _B _ _ _ C

The vowels in the rhymes between /snɤt/ and /prɔət/ are near-rhymes. Those in the rhymes /naː/ with /teyiːə/ and in /riːətrei/ and /metrei/ with /ney/ are spelt the same but pronounced differently.

10. *Pad Bāky Prāṃpī* (eight-syllable metre) 8:8:8:8
Nou-Kan *Dāv Ek* Kim-Seng, Phnom Penh, 1950, p.106.

khana: noḥ cās' duṃ krum ak(r) yāy	Just then the group of elderly court ladies
siṅ nāṃ gnā roḥ rāy oy nāṅ smoḥ	Came all together cordially and sincerely,
hoey aṅvar oy nāṅ bhlāṅ phlās ṭoḥ	And pleaded with her immediately to change

grīoeṅ dāṃṅ as' ṭael cās' phlās' grīoeṅ thmī.	All her old clothes for new.
nāṅ buṃ bram tām soḥ ceh tae yuṃ	Refusing to do as they said, she wept constantly
dīep kraḷā panduṃ ghlāt caṃṇī	In the bedroom, refraining from food.
buok ak(r) yāy rāy gnā suor dukkh srī	The elderly ladies asked what was the matter.
nāṅ sraṭī thā dukkh raḷk mtāy.	She said she was sad without her mother.

/khana′ nuh cah tum krom ɔːk yiːəy/	_ _ _ _ _ _ _ _ _x
/sɤŋ nɔəm kniːə ruəh riːəy aoy niːəŋ smɔh/	_ _ _x _or _x or_ x_ _A
/haəy ɔŋvɔː aoy niːəŋ phliːəŋ phlah dɔh/	_ _ _ _ _ _ _ _ _A
/krɯəŋ tɛəŋ ɔh dael cah phlah krɯəŋ thmei/	_ _ _ A_ or_ A_or A_ _B

/niːəŋ pum prɔːm taːm sɔh ceh tae yum/	_ _ _ _ _ _ _ _ _y
/tiəp krəlaː bɔntum khliːət cɔmnei/	_ _ _y or_ _y or_y _ _B
/puːək ɔːk yiːəy riːəy kniːə suːə tuk srei/	_ _ _ _ _ _ _ _ _B
/niːəŋ srədei thaː tuk rəlɯk mdaːy/	_ _ _B_ or _B or_B _ _C

11. *Pad Bāky Prāṃpuon* (nine-syllable metre) 9:9:9:9
King Ang Duong, a poem printed in *Kambujasuriyā* 1939, part 5, p. 106.

o saṃḷāñ añ raḷk ṭek min lak'	O my love, I miss you and am sleepless.
saen jā dukkh mukh jā dīep hīep maraṇā	My distress overwhelms me. Surely I am on the point of death?
drāṃ raḷk nịk ralaṅ' hūr netra:	I endure your absence but tears flow, glistening
sūm devā juoy jīvit git praṇī.	May the gods take pity and help me to live.

dhvoe mtec ge luoc pān thlai varamit	What can I do? You have been stolen, my dearest,
mās mak phtit mitr mak phtuol mūl metrī	You who were close to me, united with me.

doḥ ge kāp' slāp' paṅ' dau sūv pān srī	Even if they killed me, cast me away, dead, I would rather have you.
ptūr jīvit phtāc' jīvā min stāy loey.	I would risk my life, cut off my life with no regret.

/ao sɔmlaɲ aɲ rəlɯk deːk mɯn luək/	_ _ _p _p _ _ q _q _ _r
/saen ciːə tuk muk ciːə tiəp hiəp mɔrənaː/	_ _ _ r _r _ _ s _ s _ _A
/trɔəm rəlɯk nɯk rəluəŋ hoː neːtraː/	_ _ _t _ t_ _ _ _ _ _ A
/soːm teːviːə cuːəy ciːvɯt kɯt prənei/.	_ _ _ A _ _ _ u _u _ _ B
/thvɤː mədec keː luːəc baːn praːn thlai vɔrəmɯt/	_ _ _ _ _ _ v _v _ _ w
/miːəh mɔːk phdɤt mɯt mɔːk phduːəl muːl meːtrei/	_ _ _w _w_ _ x _ x_ _ B
/tuəh keː kap slap bɔŋ tɤu sɤu baːn srei/	_ _ _y _y_ _z _z_ _B
/pdoː ciːvɯt phdac ciːvaː mɯn sdaːy laəy/.	_ _ _ _ _ _ _ _ _C

Rhymes for which the spelling is correct but the pronunciation wrong are /teːviːə/ with /naː/ and /neːtraː/ and /mɯt/ with /phdɤt/. Near-rhymes are /rəlɯk/ with /deːk/ and /luək/ with /tuk/ and /muk/. Italicized short open syllables have to be taken as one syllable or, in the case of vɔrəmɯt with the next vowel as one syllable, if one reads so as to allow the rhyme between /baːn/ and /praːn/.

The rhyme scheme is given for these stanzas only because the variations are very numerous.

12. *Pad Bāky 10* (ten-syllable Metre) 10:10:10:10
Pad Bāky 11 (eleven-syllable Metre) 11:11:11:11
Pad Bāky 14 (fourteen-syllable Metre) 14:14:14:14

Mr Nhoung-Sœung of the Institut Bouddhique wrote to me long ago saying that these metres existed but were not really used and I have never found them, except for the examples given in Ing-Yeng (1972) and Huffman (1977) (10- and 11-syllable metres).

Roeské (1913: 671–87) described Khmer versification using the two manuscript treatises: Kraysar Sorivong. *Paep kaṃṇāby*. 'Les modèles de vers'; Moha Meas. *Paep kalapad*. 'Les modèles de Kalabat'.

Ing-Yeng gives no references. Huffman (1977: 79–103) cites Roeské and uses Chim-Peov 1959, Ieng Say 1966, and Léang Hap-An 1971.

Roeské divides rhymes into (1) long, (2) medium, and (3) cut short depending on whether the syllable ends with (1) an open vowel, (2) a diphthong, nasal consonant, or semi-vowel, or (3) a plosive consonant, sibilant, or aspirate. This division does not seem to be significant in relation to Khmer versification.

Roeské, Chhim-Soum (1966*c*), Ing-Yeng, and Huffman describe the metres given above, except that only Roeské includes the oldest, *Pad Bol.* They also describe, with slight differences from each other, nearly thirty *Kalapad* or Artificial Metres, which are variations of the *Pad Kākagati* or of the 4-, 6-, 7-, 8-, or 9-syllable metres. They involve the following kinds of feature:

1. Alliteration. The metre may require that the initial consonants of every two syllables throughout the poem should be the same; or the consonants of the syllabary are used one by one as the initial consonant of the verse.

2. Repetition of a word. The word at the end of a verse is repeated at the beginning of the next all through; or the words of the second half of the stanza repeat in reverse order the words of the first half!

3. Rhymes. An excessive number of rhymes is required between specific syllables, for example between the first two syllables of every verse.

These metres are for fun really. The examples given are not attributed to anyone and probably arose from one of the treatises. I have only met one of these *kalapad*, a poem by Tan, *Sāralikhit nịk khīṅ citt likhit sār*, in which the first and last words of each verse are the same. I refer the reader to Roeské, Chhim-Soum, Ing-Yeng, and Huffman.

BIBLIOGRAPHIC REFERENCES

For details see Bibliography.

Chhim-Soum 1966*c*, Chim-Peov 1959, Huffman 1977: 79–103 (vocabulary: 103–5) (Khmer), Ieng-Say 1966, In n.d., Ing-Yeng 1972, Jacob 1966, Kraysar Sorivoṅ n.d., Léang-Hap An 1963 (Russian with English summary), 1964*b* (Khmer), 1971 (Khmer), Roeské 1913, Spiriagina 1973 (Russian), Vor Pou n.d. (Khmer). The application of Pali rules of versification to Khmer verse is discussed by In 1947.

4

AUTHORS

This is a list of the authors of works of traditional Khmer literature. Where a French transcription of a name is known this is the form which appears first, followed by a transliteration of the Khmer orthography in italics. It does not normally include translators of Pali works except where the form or content of the original was changed.

Translators of French or Chinese works and modern narrators of folktales are not included.

Details of MSS, **T** Texts, **V** Versions, and **S** Studies of the works and translations of the Khmer titles will be found in Chapter 5, 'Works'.

Am-Dīoek. Work: *Ovād mātā*. G.5.

Anak Mātā Phay̆am (Mother of *Phay̆am*). 19th-century court poet.
Works: *saen dukkh domanass as' saṅghịm*. G.8.
pad yaṃ yām Braḥ Karuṇā Braḥ Pād Saṃtec Braḥ Narottam jā aṃmcās' phaen ṭī krom Kambujā. G.8.

Anak Srī Siddhi. See Seth.

Anak Ukñā Braḥ Ghlāṃṅ Naṅ. See Nong.

Ang Chand, King Ang Chand, *Aṅg Cand, Braḥ Pād Aṅg Cand*. Listed by Ly-Théam Teng 1960: 78 as a Mid-Khmer writer.

Ang Duong *Aṅg Ḍuoṅ, Braḥ Pād Aṅg Ḍuoṅ*. Also called *Braḥ Pād Hariraksarāmādhipatī Aṅg Ḍuoṅ*. b. AD 1796, d. AD 1860. He was the youngest son of King Ang Eng, who reigned AD 1779–96 and whose capital was at Udong Méan Chey. He was educated in Siam, where he wrote some of his works. He reigned 1841–60, a troubled period during which Cambodia had enemies on both sides. He hated war but was firm in not ceding territories to Siam. He was a good ruler, doing what he could for the people: he gave alms, built a monastery and a road from Udong to Kampot; he controlled usury and punished immorality. Ang Duong was himself a distinguished scholar and poet; he gathered round him scholars of Buddhism and literature and encouraged them to write, to teach those who wanted to learn, and to revise and update texts. He personally trained monks and laymen and was very strict about the correct use of words and careful handwriting for government documents. He made education at the local monastery compulsory for boys and sent young men to Singapore at his own expense for linguistic studies. King Ang Duong was a strong, healthy man with clear eyes, curved eyebrows joining the bridge of his nose, a high forehead, and large face. Ly-Théam Teng describes him as 'our greatest poet'. (Information from Chap-Pin (prefaces) 1959 and 1962, Ly-Théam Teng 1960: 146–8, and Léang-Hap An in *KS* 1968. 12: 1356–9.)

Works: *(Rīoeṅ) Nāṅ Kākī* or *(Sāstrā) Lpoek Kākī* AD 1813 (see Ly-Théam Teng 1960: 117), or AD 1815 (see Ray-Buc 1956: 936 and Léang-Hap An 1968. 12: 1359) or AD 1818 (see Chap-Pin 1962: i). G.7.

Cpāp' Srī Braḥ Aṅg Ḍuoṅ AD 1837. G.5.

O saṃḷāñ' añ raḷk ṭek min lak'. G.8.

Pad bol rīoeṅ lkhon phseṅ2. Various plays (according to Ly-Théam Teng 1960: 148).

(Roeské 1913: 670 attributes *Iṇāv* G.7 to Ang Duong and both Roeské and Léang-Hap An attribute *Champ̈ā Thoṇ* G.7 to him. It is possible that he wrote *Mahāvessantarajātak.*)

Ariyagāminī Ĥīṅ (or *Bhịṅ), Braḥ Ariyagāminī Ĥīṅ.* See *Hing*.

Ariyasatthā, Braḥ Ariyasatthā (probably this is the title rather than the name of the poet).

Works: *(Sāstrā Secktī) Ariyasatthā.* G.5.

(Sāstrā) Cpāp' Dharm Aniccā. G.5.

Ālakkh(ṇ)-P̈aen. See P̈aen.

Ân-Vāt (Ân Vat). See *Sai Tan'* and *Ân-Vāt.*

Ban-Teng, *Pān Teṅ.* b. AD 1882 in Phnom Penh, d. AD 1950. His father was a palace official. Ban-Teng went to a state school and was then a novice, from the age of 14 to 15, at the *Vatt Padumvatī.* He studied Khmer versification with *Lok Braḥ Grū P̈āt* in Udong and also with *Lok Ukñā Suttantaprījā Ind.* He became a palace official, then secretary to the Treasury. He taught in *Koḥ Kuṅ* 1921–6 after which he returned to Phnom Penh to teach at *Vatt Svāy Babae*. Ban-Teng was very much involved in the preparation of textbooks for teaching. His own poetry was very easy to understand. (Information from Ly-Théam Teng 1966: 179–81. See also Vandy-Kaonn 1981: 51.)

Works: *Sappurisadharm 7 prakār. Bāky kāby.* G.10.

Ovād Nārī. Bāky kāby ghloṅ. G.5? AD 1946.

Lokadhammatthacariyā. Bāky kāby. G.10.

Nāṅ Hsān ṭāk (Jeanne d'Arc). *Bāky kāby.*

(Rīoeṅ) Chandant. G.7.

(Rīoeṅ) Dibv Saṅvār. G.7.

(Rīoeṅ) Bimbābilāp. G.7.

Manuss yoeṅ neḥ uttam ṭoy kaṃnoet. G.7.

Vandy-Kaonn tells us (1981: 51) that Ban-Teng translated many stories and poems from French.

Bañā Tū, Braḥ Bañā Tū. See *Srī Dhammarājā.*

Bañā Vicitr Srī. Work: *Lpoek Srīvijăy.* AD 1858 (see Ly-Théam Teng 1960: 119). G.7.

Bejr, Braḥ Padumapāramī Bejr. Religious chief of the district of Baray, Kompong Thom, probably after AD 1835.

Works: *(Rīoeṅ) Rapā ksatr sruk khmaer* AD 1815 or 1818. G.7.

Lpoek rapār ksatr phaendī Udaya rājā Aṅg Cand. AD 1855. G.7.

Bhịṅ, Āriyagāmunī Bhịṅ. See Hing.

Bhiramy N̈uy. See Ngoy.

Bhiramy Bhāsā N̈uy. See Ngoy.

Binity. See *Sandhar Binity.*

Bodhirām. Work: *Lpoek Braḥ Dhamm trās'.* 1897? G.7.

Braḥ with the exception of *Braḥ Srī Añjit Srī* and *Braḥ Rāj Sambhār*, if the name begins with any of the following titles, please see under the next word.

Braḥ Preah

Braḥ Aṅg Preah Ang

Braḥ Aṅg Mcās' Preah Ang Mcas

Braḥ Aṅg Mcās' Ksatrī Preah Ang Mcas Ksatrey

Braḥ Bañā Preah Ponhea

Braḥ Bhikkhu Preah Bhikkhu

Braḥ Cakrī Preah Cakrey

Braḥ Ghlāṃṅ Preah Khleang

Braḥ Nāṅ Preah Neang

Braḥ Pād Preah Bat

Braḥ Pād Srī Preah Bat Srey
Braḥ Pālāt Preah Balat

Braḥ Rāj Sambhār. See *Srī Dhammarājā.*

Braḥ Srī Añjit Srī. See *Dīeṅ.*

Brahm Pavar Bhaktī or *Pavar Bhaktī Brahm.*
Works: *(Sāstrā) Bodhivaṅs.* AD 1881. G.7.

Buddher, Lok Buddher.
Work: *Cpāp' dūnmān khluon.* 2. Traité de morale individuelle. See G.5.

Cakrī Kaev. See *Kaev, Anak Ukñ̈ā Cakrī Kaev.*

Cam Srī Deb Apsar, Braḥ Nāṅ Cam Srī Deb Apsar. 19th-century court poetess.
Works (1st lines): *akkharā sā săbd cāp' nidān.* G.8.
khluon oey koet mak knuṅ sāsanā. G.8.

Camd(n). Work: *(Sāstrā) Namo* or *Na-mo.* AD 1858. G.5.

Cand, Anak Ukñ̈ā Dhammādhipatī Cand. Work: *(Sāstrā) Sukh Mānab.* G.7.

Cand, Kavī nām Cand. fl. first half of 19th century.
Work: *Bhin Suvaṇṇ.* G.7.

Cănd Vaṅs, Braḥ Aṅg Mcās' Cănd Vaṅs. 19th-century court poet.
Work (1st line): *Aṅg añ jāti jāk' jā trakūl.* G.8.

Cau Adhikār Vatt Braek Praṇāk. See *Īem.*

Cau Bañā Jaṃnit Ksatrī. See under *Cau Bañā Rājābhaktī.*

Cau Bañā Kraisar Srī. Work: *(Sāstrā) Kram Vaṅs.* G.5.

Cau Bañā Rājābhaktī. Work (with *Cau Bañā Jaṃnit Ksatrī* and *Cau Bañā Srī Añjit)*: *(Sāstrā) Cand Ghāt.* AD 1858 according to Léang-Hap An *KS* 1968. 12: 1340. G.7.

Cau Bañā Srī Añjit. See last entry.

Cau Yam Puṇy Bhaktr. According to a stanza on p. 1 of *Haṅs Yant* as published by Kim-Ky, 1965 (which does not occur in the IB edition) *Cau Yam Puṇy Bhaktr* is the author of *Haṅs Yant.* Khuon Sokhamphu refers to the stanza in an article (1971*b*). He claims (1976: 204) that this author wrote *Haṅs Yant* in 1668; he gives this information also elsewhere (1973: 2), referring to his thesis (1970) as the source.

Chap-Pin, *Cāp-Bin.* Work: *(Rīoeṅ) Braḥ Caṅkūm Kaev.* G.7.

Chey Chettha, King Chey Chettha II, *Braḥ Pād Jăy Jeṭṭhā* (or *Jăyacestā) dī bīr.* Reigned AD 1618–28. Mentioned by Princess Malika (*KS* 1939. 5: 105) and by Ly-Théam Teng (1960: 115) as a renowned author.

Work: *Braḥ Rāj Krity Kram phseṅ2.*

Chhim-Soum. Works: *Nānajātak knuṅ Dhammapadaṭṭhakathā.* 1939. G.10.

Kumbhajātak. Translation from Pali. 1942. G.10.

Karaṇiyakicc rapas' bal raṭṭh phnaek siksādhikār jāt(i) (song). 1951. G.2.

Dasajātak saṅkhep. 1966. G.10.

Chong, *Cuṅ, Ācāry Cuṅ,* son of Ngoy, q.v.

Works: *Cpāp' ṭaṃpūnmān pabbajit grahasth.* 1958. G.5.

Cpāp' gorab mātā pitā. 1967. G.5.

Cuṅ, Ācāry Cuṅ. See Chong.

Dadim, Nāy Dadim Krum Hāt' Ḷik. A 19th-century court poet.

Work: *niṅ thlaeṅ vitakk duk knuṅ prāṇ.* G.8.

Das' Ṅin. See Ngin.

Dhammapaññā M̈aen. See *M̈aen.*

Dhammapaññā Ûk. See *Ûk* 1.

Dhammarājā. See *Srī Dhammarājā.*

Dhipatī Ÿaem, Ukñā Dhipatī Ÿaem. See *Ÿaem.*

Dīeṅ, Cau Bañā Rājāmāty Dīeṅ.

Work (together with *Braḥ Srī Añjit Srī*): *Suvaṇṇ phalā* AD 1804. G.7.

Din-Huot. See Tin-Huot.

Dit, Braḥ Grū Visuddhiraṅsī Dit. See Toet.

Eṅ-Lī. Work: *K-aek ṭap'.* G.7.

Ghun Ŝī Manomai (perhaps the same person as *(Ŝī Manomai) Ṗaen* ?). A 19th-century court poet.

Work (1st line): *ktī sne(h) neḥ niṅ prīep upamā.*

Gīm-Hāk'. See Kim-Hak.

Hāk'-Gīm. See Kim-Hak.

Hak-Kim. See Kim-Hak.

Hang-Kéo, *Haṅs-Kaev.* Work: *Praṭau citt.* G.5.

Hariraksarāmādhipatī Braḥ Aṅg Ḍuoṅ. See Ang Duong.

Him, *Ĥim.* Works: *Nītisāstr (bāky kāby).* G.5.

Hing, *Ĥīṅ, Braḥ Ariyagāminī Ĥīṅ* (Ly-Théam Teng (1960: 118) gives the name as *Ariyagāmunī Bhịṅ* in connection with the authorship of *Jinavaṅs*). A mid-19th-century poet.

Work: *Jinavaṅs.* AD 1856. G.7.

Īem, Prajñādhipati Īem. Work: *Laksanavaṅs* (see Au Chhieng 1953: 261). The work was translated from the Siamese. Roeské (1913: 670) and Ly-Théam Teng (1960: 163) attribute the work to *Cau Adhikār Vatt Braek Praṇāk*, the abbot of the monastery of *Braek Praṇāk*.

In, *Ind, Anak Ukñā Suttantaprījā Ind.* b. AD 1859 at *Rakā Koṅ, Sruk Mukh Kaṃbūl*, province of Kandal, d. 1924. He was educated from the age of 10 in the village monastery and later was a novice there. At the age of 20 he went to Siam for seven years to continue his education. He left the religious life at the age of 37, married and had a family, and lived in Battambang. He was a very industrious writer of prose and poetry. (At his death forty-four works, of which only a small proportion had been published, were found in his house.) He was given the title *Dī Luoṅ Vohār* (Master of Eloquence). When he was 55 he was asked by the government to go to Phnom Penh to work on manuscripts at the Institut Bouddhique and help in the preparation of the first all-Khmer dictionary. Ten years later he asked to leave the government service and retire to Battambang, where he died almost immediately of bronchitis. In was well liked. He enjoyed using his command of language to amuse people. He had no interest, however, in purely frivolous matters. Comments made on his personal appearance include the observation that he had a 'pointed' mouth, as of one who talks a great deal. He was always to be seen wearing a mandarin-collared shirt, with his sarong tucked up breeches-fashion, carrying a silver walking-stick, wearing a hat and loose-fitting shoes. As he walked along he would look upwards. He was, Ly-Théam Teng wrote (1960: 171), the most famous Khmer poet of the 20th century. (Information from Ly-Théam Teng 1960: 169–74. See also Khing Hoc Dy: 1985*c*.)

Works: *Kābyasār Vilāsinī.* AD 1889. G.8.
Aṃpaeṅ paek. AD 1901. G.7.
Gatilok. 1–10. AD 1921. G.1, 2, and 10.
Krāṃṅ Ācāry Ind dī 1–7 (MS of works published as *Gatilok*).
Kāby Nirās Aṅgar or *Nirās Nagar vatt. Bāky Kāby.* 1926. G.7.
Lokanītipakar(ṇ).
(Rīoeṅ) Patham sambodhi. Bāky Kāby. Pad lkhon. G.7.
Subhāsit Cpāp' Srī. G.5.
Juc niṅ Trī (according to Ing-Yeng only).
In wrote two works on versification: *Kpuon me kāby* (Treatise on

versification) and *Kap pakasini* (*kāby pakasanī*. Explanation of versification).

Ing-Kheng, *Îṅ-Kheṅ*. Work: *Lpoek dūnmān kūn cau cin*. G.5.

Jăyacestā. See Chey Chettha.

Jăy Jeṭṭhā. See Chey Chettha.

Kaep. Work: *Kūn Cau*. Reference from Roeské 1913: 671.

Kaev, Anak Okñā Prājñādhipatī or *Paññādhipatī Kaev*.
Work: *(Braḥ) Samuddaghosa*. AD 1818. G.7.
Sekkh Somm Mundit (Sek Som Paṇḍit. Mahosathajātak). G.7.

Kaev, Anak Ukñā Cakrī Kaev.
Work: *(Sāstrā) Ṭāv Rīoeṅ* (with help of *Bañā Ratn Kosā* (*Kaev*)). AD 1837. G.7.

Kaev, Bañā Ratn Kosā (Kaev). Assisted *(Anak Ukña Cakrī) Kaev* in the writing of (*Sāstrā) Ṭāv Rīoeṅ*. AD 1837. G.7.

Kan, Lok Vipul Kan. See Nou-Kan.

Kao, *Kau, Ukñā Kosādhipatī Kau*. Was the chief poet in the reign of King Ang Chand II. He was well versed in Khmer literature and Pali language. His thorough knowledge of the law gained him the palace position of Keeper of the royal treasure *(Cau Hvāy Ghlāṃṅ Maṇīratn)* and legal adviser to the king. In his one extant work he is regarded as having used vocabulary and rhyme in an exemplary way demonstrating the metres usual in verse-novels.
Work: *Kruṅ Subhamitr*. AD 1798. G.7.

Kéo-Hang. See Hang-Kéo.

Kesarā. See *Ketasarā*.

Ketasarā (Kesarā). Son of King Norodom. 19th-century poet said by Princess Yukanthor to have been a clever poet. See introduction to the collection of works of court poets published in *Kambujasuriyā* (1939. 5: 106).

Khaek, Anak Ukñā Sodas Khaek. Son of *Anak Ukñā Yamarāj*.
Work: *Lpoek Jetaban*. AD 1822 (according to Nhok-Thaem 1965–8. 1967. 11: 1172). Ly-Théam Teng gives the date as 1815 (1960: 118). G.7?

Kheṅ-Îṅ. See Ing-Kheng.

Khīev, Bhikkhu Paṇḍit Khīev, Paṇḍit Khīev.
Works: *Candalīvaṅs*. Assigned by Nhok-Thaem to the end of the 19th century on language grounds. G.7.

Balakkhandh. Said by Léang-Hap An to be a folktale.

Kim-Hak, *Gīm Hāk'*. 20th-century poet and novelist. b. AD 1905 and educated at the Lycée Sisowath. At the end of his career in the government service, in various ministries, in provincial administration in Takeo, and in the palace, he had attained the rank of Secretary of State. He was married with six children. (Information from Khuon Sokhamphu 1973: 17–19.)

Works: *Sek Som Paṇḍit.* 1933. G.5.

Muoy ray hā-sip muoy thṅai nau māt' Jhūṅ Samudd Sīem. 1932. G.7.

Articles on religion, morals, etc. for *Kambujasuriyā.*

(Kim-Hak's prose novel, written in the modern style, *Dịk Danle Sāp*, 'The Waters of the Tonle Sap' was serialized in *Kambujasuriyā* in 1938.)

Kim-Samon, *Gīm-Saṃ-un.* Work: *Supin.* G.8.

Ko, Paṇḍit Ko. Work: *Jăy datt.* AD 1754. G.7.

Kor, Paṇḍit Kor. Mid-19th century poet (according to Nhok Thaem 1965: 960–1).

Work: *Sūvăt, Braḥ Sūvăt.* G.7.

Kosādhipatī Kau. See *Kau.*

Kraisar Sūravaṅs, Kraisar Sūrivaṅs. See *Sūravaṅs.*

Kram Ngoy. See Ngoy.

Kuḷāp, Anak Mnāṅ Kuḷāp. A 19th-century court poetess.

Work (1st line): *ahaṃ seṭṭho seṭṭha trek so.* G.8.

L.A.N., Stec ksatrī L.A.N. A 19th-century court poetess.

Work (1st line): *aniccā citt oey saen caṃpaeṅ.* G.8.

L.N., Braḥ Aṅg Mcās' Ksatrī L.N. A 19th-century court poetess.

Work (1st line): *dukkh khñuṃ jāti neḥ loes as' srī.* G.8.

Lok Pamroe Udăy. See Ngin.

Mai. Also known as *Meyyapaṇḍit.* Poet of the late 18th to mid-19th centuries.

Works: *Cpāp' Prus* (known also as *Cpāp' Thmī).* G.5.

Cpāp' Srī. G.5.

Méas *Mās* 1. Roeské (1913: 671) gives his title and name as *Mahā Mās, Ukñā Vipul Rāj Senā.*

Work: *Paṇṭāṃ Bālī.* G.5.

Roeské (1913: 671) attributes *(Rīoeṅ) Dibv Saṅvār* to *Mās.*

Méas, *Mās* 2. Known as *Tā Mās.* Work: *(Rīoeṅ) Paṇṭāṃ Tā Mās.* G.5.

Meun, *Mịn.* See Tan 3.

Mīec, Ukñā Cau Hvāy Ghlāṃṅ Mīec.

Work: *Varanuj Varanetr.* AD 1806. G.7. (See Ray-Buc 1956: 936 for authorship and date. Usually attributed to Nong.)

Mok. *M̈uk, Sandhar M̈uk, Ukñā Sandhar M̈uk, Amṛtaksatrī M̈uk,* a 19th-century court poet b. *circa* AD 1834, d. (according to his great-grandson) AD 1908. He lived at Udong. When he was 11 years old his father, a palace official, and his mother were arrested by the Vietnamese. He was brought up as an orphan, through the kindness of the abbot, An, at the royal monastery at Udong in a culturally excellent environment. He was a very studious pupil and later became a monk. Being very poor, he wrote his literary works with charcoal on fragments of brick or tile. On leaving the priesthood, he was presented to the mother of King Ang Duong. He became an official in her service and was given by her the title *Amṛtaksatrī*. In AD 1859 she asked him to translate from the Pali the extra-canonical *jātak*, Devand. He translated it into classical verse and it was written down by his secretary. He similarly translated at her request in AD 1863 the extra-canonical *jātak, Siṅhanād.* He married and had four sons and one daughter. In AD 1869, after the death of Ang Duong's mother, he went to the court of King Norodom in Phnom Penh. The king put him in charge of the library section of the royal secretariat, with the title *Uk̈ñā Paññādhipatī.* He showed an excellent command of legal matters and was therefore put in charge of the law department, where he taught other officials. Before he died he became Minister of Finance.

The king took him on journeys and outings because Mok could instantly produce very amusing poems about what they had been doing. The literary works of which we have texts are more serious. Ly-Théam Teng comments (1960: 152 ff.) that *(Rīoeṅ) Devand* is characterized by the use of very high language while *(Rīoeṅ) Dum Dāv* makes easier reading. In AD 1877 Mok began to write *Vimān Cand.* Towards the end of the 19th century the king gave him the title *Ukñā Sundhar Vohār,* and asked him to write a new version of the Royal Chronicles. Smallpox left Mok with marks on face and body and a twisted arm. He was nicknamed *M̈uk Kraṅaeṅ*, 'Mok with the twisted arm'. (Information from Collard 1925: 29–39, Nhok-Thaem 1957: 154–8 and 1967: 287 n. 1, Ly-Théam Teng 1960: 152–4, and Khing Hoc Dy 1981: 137–45.)

Works: *Lpoek Cacak.* AD 1859 (according to Ly-Théam Teng 1960: 119). G.7.

(Rīoeṅ) Devand. AD 1859. G.7.

(Rīoeṅ) Dum Dāv. AD 1859. G.7.

(Sāstrā) Siṅhanād. AD 1863. G.7?

Braḥ rāj baṅs sauvaṭār braḥ mahākrasatr soy rāj saṃpatti knuṅ kruṅ kambujādhiptī jā laṃtāp rīeṅ mak (title of the royal chronicles as given by Khing Hoc Dy 1981: 145. Mok wrote the legendary part). G.9.

(Rīoeṅ) Vimān cand. AD 1858 (see Khing Hoc Dy 1981: 140 n. 12). G.7.

Cpāp' Khmaer (according to Roeské 1913: 671). G.5.

(1st line of non-narrative poem) *M̈oṅ prāṃ puon juon raḷk niḳ dau ṭal.* G.8.

(1 stanza) *Voey nai ā cik chā muoy kāk'.* G.8.

(1 stanza) *Satv cīem dāṃṅ bīr cuḥ ŝī smau.* G.8.

(1 stanza) *Kaṃbat kaṃbīṅ p̈oḥ.* G.8.

(1 stanza) *Kaṃbat kaṃbīṅ buoy.* G.8.

(1 stanza) *Pārāṃṅ pāro cor upalakkh(ṇ).* G.8.

(1st line) *Sralāñ' srī tūc.* G.8.

(1st line) *Car cūl ta tāṃṅ.* G.8.

(Roeské 1913 says Mok wrote *Jinavaṅs* but on what authority?)

M̈aen, Bhikkhu Dhammapaññā M̈aen.
Work: *Bejjatā.* 1858 (Nhok-Thaem in *KS* 1967. 8: 832) (1859 according to Léang-Hap An (1968. 12: 1342) and 1857 according to Ly-Théam Teng (1960: 118)). G.7.

M̈ā. Nhok-Thaem (*KS* 1968. 3: 301) gives details of his authorship.
Work: *(Sāstrā) Sīl ṭap'.* G.8.

M̈īn, or *M̈īn Bhaktī Aksar Tan'.* See *Tan* 3.

M̈uk Saṃ-ok. b. AD 1880 in Phnom Penh, son of *Sandhar Vohār M̈uk (Lok Sandhar M̈uk),* a palace official. d. 1931. He went through all available stages of education and read manuscripts, especially *sāstrā lpaeṅ,* at the monastery. From the age of 23, he became a civil servant. Then he taught in Kampong Cham and Phnom Penh and wrote school books. He received honours. His poems were scattered and torn. They were almost all collected by Dik-Kéam and published in *Kambujasuriyā* 1970. He married and had one daughter.
Works: Short poems published in *Kambujasuriyā* 1970. 6: 630–48.

Nab Ratn, Braḥ Aṅg Mcās' Nab Ratn. 19th-century court poet.
Work (1st line): *Knuṅ sār thā Braḥ Cam Mkuṭ Bhab.* G.8.

Naṅ. See Nong.

Ngin, *Ṅin, Paṇḍit Ṅin.* Also known as Yos Ngin, *Yas' Ṅin* and Tos Ngin, *Das' Ṅin.* Was a maker of tinsel for King Norodom.

Works: *(Rīoeṅ) Sradap Cek* or *(Rīoeṅ) Devaṅs* (or more correctly *Devavaṅs) Kumār.* AD 1889 (according to Chhim-Soum 1968: 343). G.7.

(Sāstrā) Ak (2nd part, following *Lpoek Ak*). G.7. Chhim-Soum (1968: 342) suggests that Ngin added the 2nd part of *(Sāstrā) Ak,* using the name *Pamroe Udăy.*

Ngoy, *N̈uy.* Known as Kram Ngoy, *Kram N̈uy,* as Ou, *Ū̂* (his given names being *Ūk Ū̂),* as *Bhiramy N̈uy* and as *Bhiramy Bhāsā N̈uy,* Phirom Phéasa Ngoy. Also known as *Bhiramy Bhāsā Ū̂,* Phirom Phéasa Ou, or Ou Ngoy. b. AD 1865 in the village of *Kaṃpūl* near Phnom Penh. d. AD 1936. He was educated in the monastery not far away from *Kaṃpūl,* where his father had been taught. Ordained at the age of 21, he lived at various monasteries, studying and translating the Tripitaka, before leaving the priesthood, marrying, and leading the life of a farmer. His knowledge and verbal skill earned him respect far and wide and, though he was now a layman, he was often invited to preach at ceremonies. He was also very gifted at composing impromptu poetry, at singing, and at playing the guitar. With a partner, *Jandap' Sān'*, he performed a very amusing and popular 'act'. Underlying the aim to entertain was a serious purpose: to urge his fellow countrymen to use their gifts and their wits and not to be lazy. Presents of fruit, money, and other goods were given to him at these performances. Ngoy had the title Kram as assistant to the village chief (who was in fact his father). He did this work well but was once reprimanded by the Résident of Kompung Speu for being slow at taking in the taxes. This was because he was so sympathetic towards the people.

When Ngoy's renown reached Phnom Penh he was brought before King Munivong, who heard him perform and granted him the title Phirom or Phirom Pheasa 'Pleasant to hear' or 'Of pleasing eloquence'. M. Georges Coedès took Ngoy to Bangkok to sing for the king, who rewarded him with money. In 1930 M. Coedès took Ngoy to sing for Mademoiselle Suzanne Karpelès and various Khmer scholars at the Bibliothèque Royale in Phnom Penh. It was arranged that Ngoy should sing and that the words should be written down as he performed. This was the first time his works were recorded. Four *Cpāp'* were thus made available for later publication.

Ngoy usually put on his sarong breeches fashion and wore slippers and a white shirt with a mandarin collar. He had a broad forehead and a very short haircut. He was sturdily built and pot-bellied. When he travelled about he had the sounding box of his guitar wrapped round with his clothes in a bundle and carried the stem of the guitar on one shoulder.

Ngoy was never rich but nor was he ever really poor. One of his six sons, Acar Chong, *Cuṅ*, was renowned as a good preacher and was the author of two *Cpāp'*. Chong's nephew, grandson of Ngoy, known as *Nāy Sḷik* 'Mr Leaf' because of his thinness, was a singer of the kind of song known as Ayai, *Āÿai* (see 'Genre 2. Songs', p. 21). He is said to have been very clever and amusing but never vulgar. Another of Ngoy's grandsons, *Juoṅ Yān,* was both a singer of Ayai and a performer of old songs on the radio. Ngoy's eldest son, *Juoṅ*, was the source of information for Ly-Théam Teng's 1966 account of Ngoy.

(Information chiefly from Ly-Théam Teng 1966 but also from Khing Hoc Dy and Jacqueline Khing 1981. See also San Sarin 1971 (French translation of part of Ly-Théam Teng 1966), Khuon Sokhamphu 1973: 1–3, and Khing Hoc Dy 1985*c*.)

Works: *Bāky Kāby praṭau jan prus srī.* G.5. Ly-Théam Teng (1966: 62–3) gives the title as *Cpāp' Raṃḷik jan prus srī* when citing stanzas from pp. 11–12 of IB's edition of *Bāky Kāby praṭau jan prus srī.*

Lpoek Cpāp' Saṅgh. G.5. A different version of *Bāky Kāby praṭau jan prus srī.*

Cpāp' dūnmān jan prus srī. G.5.

Cpāp' praṭau jan prus srī. G.5.

Cpāp' Kir Kāl thmī. G.5.

Cpāp' Lpoek Thmī. G.5.

Secktī raṃḷik ṭās' tīoen. G.5.

Cpāp' ṭās' tīoen kūn cau. G.5. This may be the same as *Secktī raṃlik ṭās' tīoen.*

Paṇṭāṃ Kram N̈̆uy. G.5.

Saṃ-āt phcit phcaṅ'. G.8.

Nhok-Thaem, *N̆uk Thaem,* Lok Nhok-Thaem. b. 1903 in the province of Battambang. His father was a goldsmith who later turned to farming and was poor. From the age of 10 to 15, Nhok-Thaem was educated in monasteries and learned Pali. When he was 15 he went to Bangkok where he stayed twelve years, continuing his education, taking several examinations, and teaching Pali. He wrote a number of works in Bangkok and had them printed there. These activities were interrupted by illness in 1929. Returning to Cambodia in 1930, he was called to Phnom Penh by the government to take part in the translation of the Tripitaka into Khmer under the direction of Louis Em.

Nhok-Thaem left the priesthood in 1936, married, and had seven sons and four daughters. In 1938 he became editor of the journal *Kambujasuriyā*, and was involved in the publications of the Bibliothèque Royale. He was a member of a delegation which helped to found Buddhist Institutes in Laos and Cochinchina. In the 1940s he was partly occupied with teaching Khmer in schools and Pali at the Pali School but was also involved in diplomatic missions to reclaim Khmer territory lost to Siam during World War II. From 1950 to 1956 he taught only at the Lycée Sisowath (later a state school). Then, after a two-year period of teaching in Battambang, he returned to teach in Phnom Penh schools and to do research on the Khmer literary manuscripts at the Institut Bouddhique.

Nhok-Thaem's works consisted chiefly in (1) publishing collected proverbs, (2) editing *(Bhogakulakumār, Devand,* with notes on the author, and *Mahāvessantarajātak)*, (3) translating the 50 *jātak* and (4) researching into the literary manuscripts of the Institut Bouddhique. This work will be found under his name in the Bibliography.

Works: *Cpāp' Kram Sāmaṇer.* AD 1949. G.5.

Paññāsajātak Saṅkhep. Published 1963. G.10.

He published the following works in Thai or in both Pali and Thai: *Namokathā, Nānājātak Vaṇṇanā, Dhammaniddes* Parts 1 and 2, *Devatābhāsit,* and *Buddhabhāsit.* Later in Cambodia he wrote two modern prose novels (*Pisāc Snehā,* 'The Amorous Demon' AD 1942 and *Kūlāp Pailin,* 'The Rose of Pailin' AD 1943). He translated, in collaboration with Ray-Buc and using the French and Thai versions, a Mahāyāna Buddhist text, giving it the title *Banlị Āsīdvīp.* He also translated from the French version some parts of the 'Arabian Nights' and from Pali the *Cūḷavedallasūtra.* He wrote two lives of the Buddha and two works on the practice of Buddhism. (Information from Nhok-Thaem 1969 and Khuon Sokhamphu 1973: 14–16. See also Gorgoniev 1968*a* (Russian) and Khing Hoc Dy 1985*c*.)

Nhoung-Sœung, *Ñūṅ Sīoeṅ*. Work: *Camrīeṅ pañcasikhagandhabv devaputr*. G.7. See also under Srey-Ou.

Nong, *Naṅ, Ukñā Braḥ Ghlāṃṅ Naṅ.* Also referred to as *Ukñā Vaṅs Sārabejñ Naṅ*. d. AD 1858. Nong was a scholar of Khmer, Thai, and Pali. He was the outstanding poet of the reigns of King Ang Eng and King Ang Chand, though he did not achieve renown until the reign of King Ang Duong. He was a monk at the *Catudis* monastery, Udong, where he later became the Abbot and was given the title *Mahābrahmamunī*. He was tutor to the four sons of King Ang Eng (Ang Chand, Ang Snguon, Ang Em, and Ang Duong). In AD 1810 he officiated at the initiation of Ang Duong as a novice and in 1811 he accompanied Ang Duong and Ang Em to Bangkok for their further education. On his return he taught at Mongkolborei before leaving the priesthood. He married and had two sons and four daughters. Later Ang Duong gave him a second wife, *Anak Mnāṅ Tūc*, by whom he had two sons and a daughter. All his sons were to become high officials. He now had the title *Ukñā Vaṅsāksatrī*. In 1860 he was sent to Bangkok with two other officials to convey to the Siamese king the news of the death of Ang Duong.

Nong held the following further offices as a layman: *Ukñā Dhirāj Mantrī, Ukñā Braḥ Ghlāṃṅ,* and *Ukñā Vaṅs Sārabejñ*. The last of these titles was given to him in recognition of his knowledge of the Tripitaka and of literature. He was asked to rewrite and update the Chronicles and was put in charge of both lay and religious education.

King Ang Duong made Nong his personal adviser and secretary, employed him as royal tutor, and gave him the territory (and taxes) of *Koḥ Sūdin*. Nong's niece became the wife of Norodom.

(Information from Chhim Krasem 1951; Nhok Thaem 1965–8 (37): 827 n. and 966–7; Ly-Théam Teng 1966: 141–2; Dik-Kéam 1967*b*; Léang-Hap An 1968: 1346–56; Khing Hoc Dy 1976; Mak Phœun 1980. See also Khing Hoc Dy 1985*c*.) Vickery (1982) argues very forcibly that there may have been two (or even three) Nongs; the Chronicles at one point indicate the presence of a *Braḥ Ghlāṃṅ Naṅ* and of a *Brahmmunī Naṅ* at the same function. The information below is given as though for one Nong. For an evaluation of Nong as a poet, see Khing Hoc Dy 1974 and 1976.

Works: *Cpāp' Subhāsit*. AD 1790 or 1809. G.5.

Lokanayapakar(ṇ) or *Lokaneyyajātak*. AD 1794. G.5 and 7.

(Sāstrā) Puññasār Sirasār. AD 1797. G.7.

(Rīoeṅ) Bhogakulakumār. AD 1802 or 1804 G.7. (According to Vickery 1982 the text of *Bhogakulakumār* says that it was written in the reign of Ang Duong, 1841–60. I cannot find this statement.)

(Rīoeṅ) Varanuj Varanetr. AD 1806. G.7.

(Rīoeṅ) Braḥ) Samuddh or *(Rīoeṅ Braḥ) Samudr* AD 1808. G.7.

Rapāl Ksatr (Chronique Royale). AD 1813–18. G.9.

Lpoek Sil Prāṃ. G.8.

(Rīoeṅ) Īṇāv. Nong is said to have had a hand in the preparation of the Khmer version of this story.

Cpāp' Srī (according to Léang-Hap An 1968. 12: 1348).

Norodom, King Norodom, *Braḥ Pād Samtec Narottam.* b. ? d. AD 1904. Reigned 1860–1904.

Work: *Pad Uṃ Dūk.* (Song, of which the text is given in Dik-Kéam 1964: 1088–99). G.2.

Nou, *Nau.* Work: *Subhāsit rājanīti (bāky kāby)* or *Subhāsit rājanītisātth.* G.5.

Nou-Kan, *Ukñā Vipul Rāj Senā Nū Kan.* b. AD 1874 at Angtassom, Takeo. d. AD 1950. Educated from the age of 9 at the local monastery, where he later was a novice for a year. At the age of 17 he went into government service, as a secretary and as a tax collector. In 1902 he passed an examination in Khmer literature with distinction and was then appointed Lieutenant-Governor of the province of Kompung Siem by the French administration. His first temporary appointment as a provincial governor was combined with the duties of teaching law and Khmer customs. After a nine-month visit to France to observe government organization, he was appointed to a series of posts as governor in various provinces. In 1936 he retired from government service and devoted himself to writing and translation. In 1946 he was elected as a Democratic Party delegate in the first Cambodian parliamentary elections. Nou-Kan is described as having a round face and curved beard and the round, clear eyes of a reflective person. Though he was always eager to talk, his speech was hesitant and slow, but very distinct.

Works: *(Rīoeṅ) Dāv Ek. Bāky Kāby.* 1942. G.7. (Gained 1st place in a literary contest.)

(Rīoeṅ) Īṇāv. Kaṃṇāby. G.7.

Nou Kan also wrote two religious works in verse (*Bimbānibvān* 1923 and *Anusāsanī* 1926) and two in prose (*Pakiṇṇakakathā gorab*

7 prakār and *Mahāsupassītāpas*). He translated the Chinese story, Sam Kok (perhaps from the Thai version rather than directly from the Chinese), published at least two modern novels (*Rīoeṅ Tuṅ Jhīn* 1942 and *Rīoeṅ Sumudajeṭṭhā* 1952). His unpublished works included a further novel, a version of *Rīoeṅ Tuṅ Jhīn* in verse, and a versified presentation of some Khmer proverbs.

(Information from Ly-Théam Teng 1966: 174–7 and Khuon Sokhamphu 1973: 4–6.)

N̈uy. See Ngoy.
N̈uk Thaem. See Nhok-Thaem.
Ñūṅ Sīoeṅ. See Nhoung-Sœung.

Ou or Ou Ngoy. See Ngoy.
Ou-Srey. See Srey-Ou.
Ouk. See *Ûk* 1 and 2.
Ouk, *Ûk* 3. Work: *Aṃbī ṭaṃṇoer dau Kruṅ Pārāṃṅses.* 1929. G.7.

Padumapāramī Bejr. See *Bejr.*
Padumather Som, Braḥ Padumather Som. See *Som.*
Pamroe Udăy, Lok Pamroe Udăy. See Ngin.
Pang, *P̈āṅ, Anak P̈āṅ.* Work: *Lpoek Aṅgar Vat.* AD 1620. G.6.
Pang-Khat, *P̈āṅ Khāt', Braḥ Bhikkhu P̈āṅ Khāt'.*
Work: Translation from Pali. *Srīhitopades.* G.10.
Paṇḍit Ṅin. See Ngin.
Pavar Bhaktī Brahm. See *Brahm Pavar Bhaktī.*
Pāl, Cau Bañ̈ā Bhaktī Saṅgrām Pāl. Work: *(Sāstrā) Subhog.* G.7.
Pān-Teṅ. See Ban-Teng.
Phaÿam, Anak Mnāṅ Phaÿam. A 19th-century court poetess.
Works (1st lines): *yap' yūr braḥ candr dāp sradan'.* G.8.
e phkāy kraboe paer sirasā. G.8.
Phirum Ou /Ngoy, Phirum Phéasa Ou/ Ngoy. See Ngoy.
Prāk'. See *Suor* (or *Sūr*).
Preah Réach Samphéar. See *Srī Dhammarājā.*

P̈aen, Ālakkh(ṇ)-P̈aen. It is not clear whether this author and the next *P̈aen* are the same person. Ly-Théam Teng cites one stanza of an unnamed work by *Ālakkh(ṇ)-P̈aen* as an example of an amusing passage.

P̈aen, Ŝī Manomai P̈aen. A 19th-century court poet.
Work (1st line): *aniccā citt oey ī ṭal' m̈leḥ.* G.8.

P̈ān, Samtec Braḥ Sugandh, Saṃtec Braḥ Sugandhādhipatī.
Works: *Braḥ Rāj Baṅsāvatār.* Annales royales. G.9.
Lpoek Aṅgar Vatt paep cās'. G.7?
See Roeské (1913: 671), who refers also to another work by *P̈ān*: *Panṭāṃ Seṭṭhī.* Manuel d'économie domestique et rurale.
P̈āṅ. See Pang.
P̈āṅ-Khāt'. See Pang-Khat.

Rāj Sambhār, Braḥ Rāj Sambhār. See *Srī Dhammarājā.*
Ras-Ûc. See Ros-Ouch.
Ratn Kosā, Bañā Ratn Kosa (Kaev). *See Kaev, Bañā Ratn Kosā.*
Ros-Ouch, *Ras-Ûc.* Work: *Cpāp' Bāl-Paṇḍit.* G.5.

S-āt or *Saṃ-āt.* Work: *Mucalind (Cand Gorab).* AD 1833.
Sai Tan' (Hok Kīen) and *Ân Vāt (Ân-Vat).* Work: *Jāv Gun* AD 1897. G.7.
Saṃ-āt. See *S-āt.*
Sambhār, Braḥ Rāj Sambhār. See *Srī Dhammarājā.*
Sandhar Binity, Ghun Sandhar Binity. Work: *(Rīoeṅ) Cau Mās* AD 1887. G.7.
Sandhar M̈uk. See Mok.
Satthā, Braḥ Aṅg. Work: *(Sāstrā) Cpāp cās'.* AD 1723. (See Ray-Buc 1956: 935.)
Seth or Soeth, Mme Sou Seth, *Anak Srī Sū Siddhi.* b. AD 1881 in Phnom Penh, the daughter of a palace official. d. 1963. She was brought up in a devoutly Buddhist home and educated by her parents. She learned to read and write Thai with the help of people she knew. She was trained to chant with the palace chorus. She married an official in the judiciary but was separated from him when their daughter was 3 years old. After this Mme Seth became even more involved in Buddhism. However, because of her linguistic and literary gifts and her pleasant voice, King Sisowath appointed her secretary of the Royal Ballet company, leader of the women's chorus in the palace, and manager of the royal orchestra. She carried out these duties until the reign of Sihanouk (AD 1945) and also taught the dancers to read and write.
Mme Seth's literary works included prose and poetry. Some were published but some were put on one side by the author and never published. Mme Seth carried out many good works as a Buddhist of great piety. She was remembered by Ly-Théam Teng as an

elderly lady, formally dressed and wearing long earrings and a gold necklace. She had a long face with strong jaw, rather thick eyebrows and clear eyes. Her speaking voice and manner were gentle and pleasing.

(Information from Ly-Théam Teng 1960: 184–7 and 1970*a* and from Khuon Sokhamphu 1973: 7–9. See also Nguon Kamy 1981 (French translation of Ly-Théam Teng 1970*a*) and Khing Hoc Dy 1985*c*.)

Works: *Paep poek Sakravā(d).* Published AD 1932 S (?).

Bimbābilāp. Written in 1900 according to Khing Hoc Dy 1979*a*: 796. Published AD 1941. G.7.

Mahāsammativaṅs. Poem.

Apart from the above works Mme Seth wrote many short poems and two novels (*Rīoeṅ gū sāṅ mitt min drust mitt* 'A couple who build up a friendship and do not betray it', published in 1940, and *Rīoeṅ Citt Satyā* 'A true heart', published in 1952).

Sodas Khaek, Ukñā Sodas Khaek. See *Khaek.*

Soeth, Neak Srey Soeth. See Seth.

Som, Braḥ Bhikkhu Som or *Braḥ Padumather Som.*

Work: *Duṃ Dāv.* AD 1915. *Som* composed the poem with Mok's *Tum Teav*, too dog-eared to publish, in front of him.

Sou Seth. See Seth.

Sraûk, Braḥ Aṅg Mcās' Ksatrī Sraûk. A 19th-century court poet.

Work (1st line): *phkāy seḥ raḥ krom phkāy kūn mān'* G.8.

mtec ḷoey̯ raḥ krom boḥ antoek, G.8.

Srey-Ou, *Srī-Û.* A 20th-century writer and poet.

Works (songs): *Namaskār.*

Ārambhakathā.

—— and Nhoung-Sœung, *Sāvatār jāt.* G.2.

Srī Dhammarājā, Braḥ Pād Srī Dhammarājā, Braḥ Srī Dhammarājā, Braḥ Rāj Sambhār, King Srī Dhammarājā, Preah Réach Samphéar. Also known as a young man as *Braḥ Bañā Tū,* Preah Ponhea To. He was the eldest son of King Chey Chettha (*Jăy Jeṭṭhā).* He was a monk for several years before succeeding his father as king. He disappointed his father when he led a military expedition to reclaim Khmer territory from the Siamese; he returned with many prisoners but had not advanced to take Ayudhya as his father had hoped. When he became king he did not enjoy administration; he left his uncle, Utey *(Udăy),* the *Uparāj* (second king), to carry out his duties while he lived at Koh Khlok *(Koḥ Ghlok),* at a distance from Udong, the capital, and wrote poetry and history, much more of both than is now extant. He was very well educated and could write verse in Pali as well as in Khmer.

While he remained a monk his young step-sister, *Pupphāvatī*, later called *Aṅg Vatī* or *Yuor Vatī,* to whom his father had betrothed him, was taken as wife by his Uncle Utey. His uncle was once ill at Udong. Srī Dhammarājā went to see him and stayed for a while. Yuor Vatī had to attend to his food and they were thus in each other's company for some time. After this he became a regular visitor there. On another occasion, Srī Dhammarājā was at Angkor when his uncle brought a family party there. Srī Dhammarājā and *Yuor Vatī* met secretly. One account tells that he disguised himself as a Chinese and mingled with the musicians in order to arrange a meeting with her. Eventually Yuor Vatī took leave of her husband 'for a few days' and in fact went to live at Srī Dhammarājā's palace at Koh Khlok. Public opinion was divided: some blamed the uncle for taking Yuor Vatī away when she was intended for Srī Dhammarājā and sympathized with her, a young girl married to an old man; others blamed Srī Dhammarājā who, as king, should have had the highest standards of behaviour.

The uncle set off in pursuit of Srī Dhammarājā with a military force which included foreign, probably Portuguese, troops. Srī Dhammarājā's escort included four Chinese officers. Some accounts say that both Srī Dhammarājā and Yuor Vatī were shot in the province of *Kañjar* (now Kratie, *Kraceh*). The Chronicles tell us that he alone fled ahead of his pursuers; when they closed on him, he climbed a sugar-palm, broke off its top and sat there writing a poem about the dangerous situation in which he found himself until they caught up with him and shot him. Yuor Vatī was subsequently condemned to death.

The dates of Srī Dhammarājā's reign are uncertain. The Chronicles give a number of dates between AD 1627–8 and 1651 as the beginning of his reign and various dates between AD 1631 and 1658–9 as the end. Mak Phœun's main text VJ (Mak Phœun 1981) gives his reign as 1627–31 and his age when he died as 30.

Works: *Rājasabd Bāky Kāby* written in AD 1630.
Likhit phñoe dau thvāy Braḥ M̈ae Yuorvattī. G.8.
Kaṃṇāpy Sarsoer Hemantamās. AD 1634. G.8.
Kaṃnāby kanlaṅ' mās maṅgal thlai G.8.
Kaṃṇāp Braliṅ mās oey. G.8.

Bāky Kāby cār ai t̆a kaṃbūl tnot mun bel sugat' ṭoy dāhān pārāṃṅ pāñ'. G.8.
Devatā oey caṅ-īet citt. G.8.
O p-ụn sṅuon beñ saṃlāñ' snịt. G.8.
Sraṇoḥ p-ūn sṅuon. G.8.
Léang-Hap An (1966: 23) attributes several *Cpāp'* to Sri Dhammarājā. Pou and Jenner (1978: 362–6) regard his authorship of *Cpāp' Rājaneti* as possible but reserve judgement.

Sugandh, Samtec Braḥ Sugandh. Known as *P̈ān*, q.v.

Sugandh mān puṇy, Braḥ Sugandh mān puṇy. Work: *(Sāstrā) Mahāneti.* G.5.

Sunthor Chea, *Sundhar Jā.*
Work: *Lpoek Madrī.* G.7.

Suor (or *Sūr*), *Cau Bañā Gajendranassakār Suor* (or *Sūr*). Also called *(Lok Grū Vinăyadhar) Prāk' (nām Chāyā Suvannapaññā).*
Work: *Paṭhamakakā* or *Braḥ Dharmakakā* (Poem on Buddhist theme). G.8?

Suvaṇṇapaññā Chāyā.
Work: *Kumārāṇ.* G.7. MS not perfect but poem not well prepared. Middle part not like a *jātak*; deals with customs, festivals, and beliefs. Not finished; just stops. (Nhok-Thaem). This could be the same person as the previous entry.

Sūr. (Could be same as *Suor~Sūr.*)
Work: *(Sāstrā) Ā Khil Ā Khūc.* Folktale retold as a poem. G.7.

Sūravaṅs (or *Sūrivaṅs*), *Braḥ Aṅg Mcās' Kraisar Sūravaṅs* (or *Sūrivaṅs*), Prince Surivangs. A 19th-century poet, son of King Norodom, an official of secretarial grade, mentioned individually as being a clever poet by Princess Malika in her introduction (1939. 5: 105–6) to the collection of poems by royalty published in *Kambujasuriyā* 1938–41.
Work (1st line): *gị aṃp̈oet koet aṃbī jal' ravit.* G.8.

Sūt, Anak Bhikkhu Munīkesar nām ṭoem Sūt.
Work: *Ktān' jāp' andāk'.* Folktale retold as short poem. G.7.

Ŝīm, Bhikkhu Ŝīm. Work: *(Sāstrā) Cpāp' Prus nịṅ Cpāp' Srī.* G.5.

Tan 1. *Tan', Braḥ Pād Nārāy(ṇ) Rājā (Braḥ Aṅg Tan').* King Nārāy Rājā (Preah Ang Tan) is said to have been a good poet by Princess Malika in her introduction (1939. 5: 105–6) to the collection of poems by royalty published in *Kambujasuriyā* 1938–41.

Tan 2. *Tan', Okñā Narāksatr Tan'.* A 19th-century court poet.
Work (1st line): *Sāralikhit nịk khịṅ citt likhit sār.* G.8.

Tan 3. *Tan', M̈ịn Bhaktī Aksar Tan',* Meun Pheakdei Aksar Tan.
Work: *(Rīoeṅ) Sabvasiddhi.* AD 1899 (see Ma Lay Khem 1970, Vandy Kaonn 1981: 37). G.7.

Thau Kae. Son of a *Yamarāj* (Minister of Justice). Was a goldsmith in the service of the king and had the title *Ghun Racanā.*
Work: *Dibv Saṅvār.* G.7.

Tin-Huot, *Din-Huot.* Work: *Karaṇiyakicc rapas' bal raṭṭh.* G.2.

To, Ponhea To, *Tū, Bañā Tū, Braḥ Bañā Tū.* See *Srī Dhammarājā.*

Toet, *Dit, Braḥ Grū Visuddhiraṅsī Dit.*
Work: *Lpoek Cpāp' Krity kram.* G.5.

Ṭūṅ, Lok Vises Ṭūṅ. b. *circa* AD 1807 d. AD 1897. *Ṭūṅ* became a monk and studied Pali at the *Guk* monastery, Udong, where he knew the much younger poet, Mok. *Ṭūṅ* had an impatient nature. He wanted the reading of Pali to be taken faster but was refused. He declared he would go to Bangkok to study but was not allowed to go. He moved to Battambang where he revised the Khmer version of the *Vessantarajātak*, eliminating the Thai vocabulary in it, enlivening the narrative style and making it more Khmer in character. His teacher reproved him severely for this and threw the manuscript at him.

He kept it as a gift and went back with it to his own district of *Gaṅ Bisī*, where he became well known as an excellent preacher of the *Vessantarajātak.* He became abbot of a monastery at which the elderly monk, *Ĥīṅ*, was resident. Later, when *Ĥīṅ* became ill, he retired with him to the country and looked after him.

Leaving the priesthood, *Ṭūṅ* married and had a son and a daughter. He was a farmer of a class known as *Anak ṅār bal braḥ*, who supplied rice to the monasteries in a scheme organized by the king. During this time *Ṭūṅ* spent two months each year teaching in monasteries. He also received visitors and gave advice—hence much of the poetry which he wrote for individuals and gave to them personally. Both laymen and monks brought him gifts. *Ṭūṅ* was very sensitive about social status. He would not let his daughter marry her suitor until the latter, after working for *Ṭūṅ* for four years, finally agreed to step down from his own position as a *Anak brai ṅār*, a class of workers one degree more elevated than *Ṭūṅ's.* King Norodom gave an audience to *Ṭūṅ* and was intending to confer on him the full rank of *Mantrī sakti Ĥū bān'* with the title *Hluoṅ Vises Akkharā*. However, *Ṭūṅ* asked the king to raise all the peasants of his class to the class above. It was possibly as a result of this too-eager request that *Ṭūṅ* never became a full *Mantrī*, though he did receive his title.

Ṭūṅ had a clear, light-coloured complexion. He was very tall and thin. His speech was rapid, his voice high-pitched but smooth. (Information from Chhim-Soum: 1968.)

Works: *Lpoek Ak*. Probably AD 1837. G.7.

Cpāp' On Aṅg. G.5.

(*Gambīr) Mahājāt(k)*. (*Ṭūṅ's* revised version of the Battambang text). G.10.

Juc niṇ trī or *Lpoek Juc*. G.7.

Lpoek Jūjak. G.10.

Lpoek Rīoeṅ Tā Ĥīn. G.8.

Nen Mās or *Suvaṇṇ bilāp*. G.8.

(Sātrā) Ktām, (Sāstrā) or *(Lpoek) Phgar phtāṃ ktām khcaṅ*. or *Ph-ūk Phgar*. G.8.

Sabd Phgar. G.8.

(*(Rīoeṅ) Sek Sārikā*. G.7.)

Various short poems for people who explained their troubles to him.

(Chhim-Soum claims that *Ṭūṅ* wrote all the above works. He was known to have preached the *Mahājkāt(k)* and *Lpoek Jūjak* many times and to have altered them. In some cases (*Cpāp' On Aṅg* and *Sabd Phgar*), Chhim-Soum or someone else remembered stanzas, in another (*Juc niṇ trī*) *Ṭūṅ*'s grandson was certain that he had written the verses. The two stanzas of *(Rīoeṅ) Sek Sārikā,* quoted from memory by Chhim-Soum, however, are very nearly the same as those given by Au Chhieng (1953: 185) for the MS of *Sekkh Somm Mundit* by Kaev.)

Udăy, Lok Pamroe Udăy. See Ngin.

Uden, Anak Ukñā Uden.

Work: *(Sāstrā) Māgh Mānab*. MS copied in AD 1927. G.8?

Ûk 1. *Dhammapaññā Ûk* or *Ukñā Vaṅsādhipatī Ûk*. Also known as *Indapaññā* to his superior in the monastery.

Works: *(Rīoeṅ) Maraṇamātā*. AD 1877. G.7.

(Rīoeṅ) Saṅkh Silp Jăy? AD 1882. G.7.

Ûk 2. *Mīṇ Ûk*. Khuon Sokhamphu, using *Ekasār Mahāpuras khmaer* and the Royal Cambodian Chronicle, argues (*Dassanavaṭṭi Mahāvidyālăy Aksarsāstr Manussāstr* 1971: 8), that *Mīn Ûk* was the name of the person whom King Chey Chettha commissioned to write *(Rīoeṅ) Khyaṅ Saṅkh.*

Uk 3. See Ouk.

Û. See Ngoy.

Û N̈uy. See Ngoy.

Ukñ̈ā Vaṅs Sārabejñ Naṅ. See Nong.

Uong, Rak-Phirom Uong, *Uoṅ, Raksabhiramy (Uoṅ) Ĥum Brae Mahātaḷik.* The son of a district governor, Uong was himself in government service under King Norodom. He fell in love with a princess referred to as 'Sr. A.', was sent away on duty and killed on his return by order of a palace official. King Norodom never learned of this.

Works (1st lines): *sandhiyā nā knuṅ thṅai ādity.* G.8.

jeṭṭhā tāṃṅ tae koet kaliyug. G.8.

bhlec khlāc aṃnāc braḥ bhuvanaiy. G.8.

oḥ o kamm aniccā. G.8.

V.N.R. A 19th-century court poet.

Work (1st line): *luḥ pān ghoeñ lāy vād ūn ṭal'.*

Varapaññā (known only by this title). Work: *Rājakul.* G.7.

Vijjādhar. d. *circa* 1960. Compiled *Braḥ rāj nibandh rāmakert(i).* G.6.

Vo Banhâ. See *Varapaññā.*

V̈ān', Yodhāranind V̈ān' wrote *Sek Sārikā*, according to Ing-Yeng (1972).

Yas' Ṅin, Yos Ngin. See Ngin, *Ṅin.*

Yukanthor, *Yugandhar, Braḥ Aṅg Mcās' Yugandhar,* Prince Yukanthor. A 19th-century court poet.

Works: *sārānusār jeṭṭhā anak.* G.8.

neḥ sārāsūrivaṅs baṅs trai căkr (in reply to *L.A.N.*). G.8.

Ÿaem, Ukñ̈ā Dhipatī Ÿaem or Ukñ̈ā Paññādhipatī Ÿaem.

Work: *(Sāstrā) Vimān cand* or *(Rīoeṅ) Vimān Cand.* AD 1858 (by *Ÿaem* according to Ray-Buc 1956: 936, Léang-Hap An 1965: 67, and Nhok-Thaem in *KS* 1965. 9: 964 n. but this is generally accepted as being by Mok. See Khing Hoc Dy 1981*b*: 140 n.).

Braḥ rāj baṅs sauvatār braḥ mahākrasatr soy rāj sampatti knuṅ kruṅ kambujādhipatī jā laṃṭāp' rīeṅ mak (with Mok, according to Ray-Buc 1956: 936).

5

WORKS

Titles of Works are translated (except where there is a French translation or the whole title is a person's entitlement and/or name). References to works cited in the Bibliography are given under the headings Texts **T**, Versions **V**, and Studies **S**. The reader will remember that *sāstrā* and *krāṃṅ* mean respectively palm-leaf or folded paper manuscripts and that names may be preceded by various phrases, listed under *Braḥ* in Authors, beginning with *Braḥ*. The following abbreviations are used:

AC	Au Chhieng
B.	*Baṃnol* metre
B.6, B.7, B.8, B.9	*Bāky 6*, *Bāky* 7, *Bāky* 8, *Bāky* 9. 6-, 7-, 8-, or 9-syllable metres
Bh.	*Bhujuṅlīlā* metre
BN	Bibliothèque Nationale, Paris
BR	Bibliothèque Royale, Phnom Penh
Br.	*Brahmagīti* metre
Cl.	Classical
Cp.	*Cpāp'*
EFEO	École Française d'Extrême Orient
G.	Genre
Gén.	Géneral
I.	Indrajit. Metre said by Nhok-Thaem to have been used in the work *Kumārāṇ*. No details are given by him.
IB	Institut Bouddhique
K.	*Kākagati* metre
KS	*Kambujasuriyā*

LN	*Lom Nāṅ* 'cajole the young lady(?)' metre (which the note on *KS* 1967. 8: 832 mentions, but of which I know nothing else)
M.	*Maṇḍukgati* metre
MJ	*Mahājăy* metre
MS	Manuscript
ne.	Concerning royal politics
PK	*Pandol Kāk = Maṇḍukgati* metre
PRBK	*Prajuṃ Rīoeṅ Breṅ Khmaer* or Recueil des contes et légendes cambodgiens. Since different editions had different page numbers, all references are to the number, not the page, of the story
SA	Société Asiatique
4 × 4	4 verses, each of 4 syllables. A metre for songs

* indicates that there is a résumé either in Ch. 6, 'Folktales Summaries' for G.1 or Ch. 7, 'Narrative Poetry Summaries' for G.7

Imprimerie du Gouvernement, Imprimerie Nouvelle, and Imprimerie Royale were in Phnom Penh

Plon-Nourrit and Imprimerie cambodgienne were in Paris

*Abhimani (Aphaimani)** G.7 (B.7). MS AC 328.2 (in difficult transcription). **V** Bastian 1868: 343–4. Feer 1877: 169. Au Chhieng 1953: 264.

Abhinarājā, Abhinarājjā. See *Cint Kumār*.

Aham seṭṭho seṭṭh trek so (I rejoice in the supreme being) by *(Anak Mnāṅ) Kulāp*. G.8 (Bh. Br. K.). **T** *KS* 1939. 10–12: 247–59.

Ak, Sāstrā Ak (The fish-eagle). This may be by *Ṭūṅ* or, as Chhim-Soum argues (*KS* 1968. 3: 336 ff.), the first part, equivalent to the *Lpoek Ak*, q.v., is by *Ṭūṅ* but the second part is by Ngin, using the name *Lok Pamroe Udăy*. G.7 (B.7, B.9). **T** Ly-Théam Teng 1969*b*. (The second part is in *KS* 1969: 1249–59.)

Akkharā sā săbd cāp' nidān (My letter begins by telling) by *(Braḥ Nāṅ) Cam Srī Deb Apsar*, a 19th-century court poetess. G.8 (B.7). **T** *KS* 1939. 7–9: 208–9.

Aṃbī ṭaṃṇoer dau kruṅ pārāṃṅses, Souvenirs d'un voyage en France en l'an 1923,* by Ouk *Ûk*. G.7 (B.7). **T** Ouk 1929.

Aṃpaeṅ paek, La poêle cassée,* by In, AD 1901 (or AD 1889 according to Ly-Théam Teng 1960: 163). G.7. **T** In (n.d.).

Aṃpāl Ksatr (All the kings). MS BN DL/1. Among the papers of

Doudart de Lagrée in BN. Gives list of kings from Nibvān Pad (14th century). G.9. MS DL/1.

Aniccā citt oey ī ṭal' mleḥ (Poor heart! How could it arrive at such a state?) by *(Sī Manomai) P̈aen.* G.8 (B.7). **T** *KS* 1939. 4–6: 181–2.

Aniccā citt oey saen caṃpaeṅ (Poor heart—so worried!) by *(Stec ksatrī) L.A.N.* G.8 (B.7). **T** *KS* 1939. 4–6: 108–9.

Anuruddh, Krāṃṅ Braḥ Anuruddh Saṅkhep (Pad caṅ' kinnarī) (King Anuruddh abbreviated). ('Wooing the kinnarī'). Metre not known. A short *sātrā lpaeṅ* about *Jăy Dat*, q.v. Nhok-Thaem suggests (*KS* 1965. 10: 1071) that it may be by the same author as *(Braḥ) Padumasuriyavaṅs*, *(Braḥ) Samudr*, *Dibv Saṅvār*, and *(Braḥ) Cakravaṅs*, since all works are on the same *krāṃṅ*. G.7 (B.7). MS IB 1261.

Aṅg añ jāti jāk' jā trakūl (I was certainly born of a family) by *(Braḥ Aṅg Mcās') Cănd Vaṅs.* G.8 (B.7). **T** *KS* 1939. 4–6: 112.

Aphaimani. See *Abhimani.*

Ariyasatthā, Sāstrā/Secktī Ariyasatthā by *(Braḥ) Ariyasatthā* (?) G.5 (K.). (Pou and Haksrea 'Cl.') MS IB 667. **T** *KS* 1942. 19–20: 26–30.

Ā Dhuṅ Ā Sāñ', Rīoeṅ Ā Dhuṅ Ā Sāñ', or *Cau Dhuṅ Cau Sāñ'* (*Dhuṅ* and *Sāñ*') Folktale retold in verse.* G.7 (B. Br. K. M.). MS IB 683. **T** *KS* 1943. 4: 223–5; 5: 285–300. *PRBK* 2, No. 19.

Ā Khil Ā Khūc, Sāstrā Ā Khil Ā Khūc (The Mischievous one and the bad one) by *Sūr.* Folktale retold in verse. G.7 (PK). MS IB 634.

Ā Khvāk' Ā Khvin, Rīoeṅ Ā Khvāk' Ā Khvin (The blind man and the cripple).* G.1. **T** Aymonier 1878. 2: 1–8. Corbet 19—: 2–5. *KS* 1935. 4–6: 113–14. *PRBK* 2, No. 2. **V** Aymonier 1878. 1: 1–3. Gorgoniev 1973: 78–88. Laporte 1971*a*. Velder 1971: 204–24.

Ā Ḷev Rīoeṅ Ā Ḷev (A Lev)* G.1. **T** Aymonier 1878. 2: 9–29. Corbet 19—: 6–9. Huffman 1972: 141–88 (pp. 164 ff. contain vocabulary). *KS* 1935. 6: 179–81 and 1941. 1: 31–3; 2: 32–5; 3: 32–4; 5: 21–6; 6: 25–6; 7: 24–6; 9: 25–66; 10: 24–6; 11: 24–6; 12: 23–6. *PRBK* 2, No. 15. **V** Aymonier 1878. 1: 3–8. Gorgoniev 1973: 202–24. Hu'o'ng 1969: 341–4; Laporte 1971.

Ācāry Ind dī 1–7, Krāṃṅ Ācāry Ind dī 1–7 (MS of Teacher In) by In. See *Gatilok.*

Ānisaṅs Mahājātak, Sāstrā Ānisaṅs Mahājātak (The benefit arising from (the recitation of) the *Mahāvessantarajātak*). G.10. MSS AC 27, 28. IB 796, 1013. **S.** Khing Hoc Dy 1982.

Ārambhakathā (Preface). Song by Srey-Ou. G.2. **T** See IB 1951.

Balakkhandh (The Section on Might) by *Khiev*. A tale of woe told in verse. G.7 (B.7). MS IB 1371 (last fifth missing).

Baṅsāvatār khmaer ṭoem (Chronicle of the original Khmers). G.9. A copy of the MS of *Vat Padum Vattī*, Phnom Penh. At Service Pédagogique, Phnom Penh. (Similar to the MS of *Vat Kok Kāk*.)

Baṅsāvatār prades kambujā (Chronicle of Cambodia from the beginning to the 17th century). G.9. MS DV (from *Vatt Dịk Vil*). Original dates back to 1901.

Baṅsāvatār Sruk Sampuk (Chronicle of *Sampuk* (Kratie)). G.9. MS EFEO P6.

Baṅ'sāvatār hluoṅ braḥ poṅ (Chronicle of the king and elder). G.9. MS EFEO 114.

Baṅ'sāvatār rāmker (Chronicle of the Reamker). G.6. MS EFEO 112.

Baṅ'sāvatār sruk lāv (Chronicle of Laos). G.9. MS EFEO 113.

Bāky Breṅ Pradau (Old admonitions). G.5 (B.7). (Pou and Haksrea '*Cp*. Gén.'). **T** Chéa-Kang 1935. Corbet 19—: 116–17.

Bāky cās', Sātrā Bāky cās'. See *Cpāp' Bāky Cās'*.

Bāky kāby cār loe (or *ai ṭa) kaṃbūl tnot mun bel sugat ṭoy dāhān pārāṃṅ pāñ'* (Poem written on top of a sugar-palm before being shot by French soldiers) by Srī Dhammarājā. G.8 (B.7. K.). **T** *KS* 1939. 1–3: 43–4 (and **S** 45–7). Léang-Hap An 1966: 50–1 (and **S** 51–2). Small amount of **T**, **V**, and **S** in Léang-Hap An 1968. 12: 1326–7 (in Khmer). **V** Mak Phœun 1981: 174–5.

Bāky kāby praṭau jan prus srī (Poem. Advice to men and women) by Ngoy. (Also called by Ly-ThéamTeng 1966: 62–3 *Cpāp' raṃlịk jan prus srī*.) (Pou and Haksrea '*Cp*. Gén.'). G.5 (B.7). **T** IB 1935, 1940, 1961, [1972]. This is a different version of the *Lpoek cpāp' saṅgh*, q.v.

Bāky Lpoek (A tale). G.7? MS SA Fonds Aymonier B.39, t. I.

Bāky subhāsit purāṇ (Old sayings). Fragmentary from ruined MS. G.5 (Br. K.). **T** *KS* 1944. 10: 505–7.

Bej mkut (written *Bej mkut'*) G.7 (B. B.6. Bh. Br. K.). MS EFEO 43. **T** Plon-Nourrit 1902.

*Bejjatā, Rīoeṅ Bejjatā, Sāstrā Bejjatā,** AD 1858, by *Dhammapaññā M̈aen*. G.7 (B. Bh. Br. K. LN). MS IB 612 **V** (very short and in Khmer) *KS* 1967. 8: 832 n. 1.

Bhin Suvaṇṇ by *(Kavī nām) Cand*. Source: the 50 jātak.* G.7 (B. Bh. Br. K.). MSS IB 675, 676. AC 52. EFEO 75. **V** Au Chhieng 1953: 35–6.

Bhinavaṅs. G.7. Cited by Ly Théam-Teng 1960: 120.

Bhlec khlāc aṃṇāc braḥ bhuvanaiy (I forgot to fear the power of the lord of the earth) by Uong. G.8 (B.7). **T** *KS* 1940. 10: 59–67; 11: 63–5.

Bhogakulakumār, Sāstrā Bhogakulakumār, AD 1804 (Ray-Buc 1956: 936; Léang-Hap An *KS* 1968. 12: 1352), AD 1802 (Dik-Kéam 1967: 6; Khing Hoc Dy 1987: 52 n. 1) but Vickery (1982: 8 n. 5) claims the text itself shows that it was written in the reign of Ang Duong, AD 1841–60. By Nong.* G.7 (B. Bh. Br. K.). Not a *jātak* of the 50 or the 500. MSS IB 637 (has date *Mahāsakrāj* 1726 = AD 1804), 638. **T** Nong 1948–50 in *KS*. IB 1961. Rasmei Kampuchea 1965. Khing Hoc Dy 1980 (excerpt): 46–7. **V** (in Khmer) Ly-Théam Teng 1960: 142–4; Dik-Kéam 1967*b*: 30–2 (in French); Khing Hoc Dy 1974: 40–237; 1976: 95–7; 1980 (excerpt): 48–9; 1987; and 1990: 175–7. **S** Nhok-Thaem 1948; Ray-Buc 1956: 936; Dik-Kéam 1967*b*: 28–30; Khing Hoc Dy 1974, 1976, 1987 **V S** 1990: 177–8.

Bhuoṅ Mālǎy, Rīoeṅ Bhuoṅ Mālǎy (A garland of flowers). G.7. Ly-Théam Teng (1960: 120) cites the work among those written between the 17th and 19th centuries.

Bhūridattajātak (Birth story of *Bhūridatt*), also written *Bhuridāt, Bhūridātt', Bhūradātth, Boridāt.* MSS AC 181, 273 (same text), 193 (very similar). EFEO 31. G.10.

Bimbābilāp (Bimbā weeps).

(1) By (Sou) Seth. Written in 1900 according to Khing Hoc Dy 1979: 796.* G.7 (B.7). MS EFEO 144 Bimbābhīlāp. **T** Seth 1941.

(2) By Ban-Teng. G.7 (B.7). **T** (excerpt) Tieng-Teng 1950: 344–5.

Bimbānibvān (Bimbā in Nirvāna(?))

(1) By *Kan, Lok Vipul Kan,* or Nou Kan. 1920, according to Ly-Théam Teng, 1923 according to Khuon Sokhamphu. Poem about the wife of the Buddha. G.7. Reference from Ly-Théam Teng 1960: 164.

(2) A *Pimpéa nirpéan* is mentioned in Guesdon 1906: 92 which could be the same poem as (1).

Bimbātherī lpoek, Sāstrā Bimbātherī lpoek (Story of the nun, Bimbā). Buddhist poem. About the wife of the Buddha? G.7 or 8 (Br.). MS IB 625.

Bīdhur, Bīdhūr, Bīy dhur, Bīy dhūr. See *Vidhurapaṇḍitajātak.*

Bodhivaṅs, Sāstrā Bodhivaṅs, written in AD 1881 by *Brahma Pavar*

Bhaktī or *Pavar Bhaktī Brahm.* Source: 500 *jātak.* G.7 (B. Br. Bh. K.). MSS IB 547, 548. EFEO 82.

Bons conseils aux sino-cambodgiens. See *Lpoek dūnmān kūn cau cin.*

Bons conseils (pour les femmes). See *Cpāp' Srī.*

Boridāt. See *Bhūridattajātak.*

Braḥ (Holy). If the name begins with or is *Braḥ Cand, Braḥ Dhammajāti, Braḥ Dharm, Braḥ Dharmakakā, Braḥ Khān*, or *Braḥ rāj*, see under these words but otherwise look under the next word. The transcriptions Préah, Préas, Réach should be similarly treated.

Braḥ Cand gorab Nāṅ Mujalīn (gorab not *goram)* (*Braḥ Cand* pays his respects to *Nāṅ Muccalind*). See *Mucalind.*

Braḥ Dhammajāti, Sāstrā Braḥ Dhammajāti. Subject: Buddhist tradition. G.8? (B. Bh. Br. K.). MS IB 627. Poorly written according to Nhok-Thaem; rhymes lacking.

Braḥ Dharm Aniccā. Lpoek. G.10. Poem (K). **T** from an old palm-leaf MS by Bou-Po in *KS* (39) 1967. 1: 13–22.

Braḥ Dharmakakā. See *Paṭhamakakā.*

Braḥ khān (The sacred sword) G.5. (Pou and Haksrea '*Cp. ne.*: Parodie du *Vidhur paṇḍit* Cl.') MS EFEO 326.

Braḥ rāj baṅs sauvatār braḥ mahākrasatr soy rāj sampatti knuṅ kruṅ kambujādhiptī jā laṃṭāp' rīeṅ mak (Royal Chronicles. List in order of the kings who ruled Cambodia) by Mok. G.9. King Norodom set up a Commission, chaired by the *Mahāsaṅgharāj*, to write them. They go to the end of Ang Sur's reign (AD 1672). Leclère used them for *Histoire du Cambodge.* Khing Hoc Dy (1981: 145) lists them among the works of Mok. Ray-Buc (1956: 936) says *Ÿaem* helped Mok. G.9. MS EFEO P. 58.

Braḥ rāj baṅs sāvaṭā (Royal Chronicles). G.9. Written in AD 1869 by order of King Norodom. MS Library of Société Asiatique. B 39/12/A.

Braḥ rāj baṅs sovatā khemmara ḷek oṅkār (Royal Chronicles. Number of pages (?)). G.9. Written by a Commission set up in 1903 under Norodom, then under Sisowath. MS EFEO P. 63.

Braḥ rāj baṅsāvatār (Royal Chronicles).

(1) A copy of the original of *Vat Dịk Vil, Baṅsāvatār prades kambujā.* G.9. Made in 1941. At IB.

(2) Royal Chronicles by Nong (historical part) and Prince Nabvratn. G.9. MSS EFEO P. 48 (a copy of the MS at *Vat Sitpūr* at Saang, Kandal). Two copies on palm-leaf at IB and palace. IB also has a close copy, that of *Vat Braek Tā Mak.* **T** Dik-Kéam 1975.

(3) Royal Chronicles. In two parts, one from AD 1557 to the middle of the reign of *Paramarājā (Srī Suriyobarṇ)*, and the other from the death of *Srī Dhammarājā* to 1802. G.9. MS EFEO P. 57.

Braḥ rāj baṅsāvatār kruṅ kambujā (Royal Chronicles of Cambodia). AD 1966. G.9. MS at IB (*Vāṃṅ Juon*'s version with the addition of the reigns of Monivong, Sihanouk, and Suramrit and the government of Sihanouk until 1966).

Braḥ rāj baṅsāvatār kruṅ kambujādhīptī (Royal Chronicles of Cambodia). Complete. G.9. MS EFEO P. 3. (A copy with Institut de Civilisation Indienne, Paris.)

Braḥ rāj baṅsāvatār mahākhsatr khmaer (Royal Chronicles of Khmer Kings) or *Braḥ rāj baṅsāvatār kruṅ kambujādhipatī* (Royal Chronicles of Cambodia) by *Vāṃṅ Juon,* a Minister. A letter proves that it was finished by 1934. G.9. MS IB G.53 (copy at the palace).

Braḥ rāj baṅsāvatār nagar khmaer (Royal Chronicles of the kingdom of Cambodia). G.9. Known as Vat Kok Kak's, Kandal Stung, Kandal (KK). Written by order of Norodom in 1869. MSS IB 1403. A close copy was in Phnom Penh at the Direction du Service Pédagogique.

Braḥ rāj baṅsāvatār rajjakāl param koṭṭh (Royal Chronicles of the reign of Paramakoṭṭh (Ang Duong)). G.9. (A fragment. Reigns of Ang-Duong, Norodom, and the beginning of Sisowath's.) MS IB 28.

Braḥ rāj baṅsāvaṭār (Royal Chronicles) by *P̈ān.* G.9. (MS? From Roeské 1913: 671.)

Braḥ rāj krity kram phseṅ2 (Various royal acts). Written in one of the reigns of Chey Chettha by him according to Ly-Théam Teng.

Braḥ rāj nibandh rāmakerti (Royal narration of the Rāmāyaṇa) compiled by *Vijjādhar*. G.6. **T** Dik-Kéam ed. 1964–7 in *KS* and 1964–5.

Braḥ Rāj Sambhār. See *Cpāp' Rājaneti.*

Brahmajāti. See Tamra Prohm Cheat, *Tamrā Brahmajāti.*

Braliṅ mās oey (O my darling).

(1) See *Kaṃṇāby braliṅ mās oey.*

(2) A different text with the same title. **T** Plon-Nourrit 1902 and corrected 1902. Poem (K.).

Breṅ brit, Sātrā breṅ brit (An old *sātrā*) G.5. (Pou and Haksrea 'Même texte que *Cpāp' kūn cau.* "Cl."'). MS EFEO 4.

Breṅ vāsanā (Destiny). Astrological text. See Tamra Preng Veasana, *Tamrā Breṅ Vāsanā.*

Broḥ srūv, Sāstrā broḥ srūv (Sowing paddy). Poem on memories of farm work. G.8 (Bh.). MS IB 646.

Buddhisen. See *Rathasenajātak.*

But Bāl, Sāstrā But Bāl (Telling lies and being bad). The avoidance of vices. G.5 (Bh.). MS IB 1376.

Cacak, Rīoeṅ Cacak. See *Lpoek Cacak.*

Cakravaṅs, Krāṃṅ Cakravaṅs or *Braḥ Cakravaṅs* (MS of Cakravaṅs). Based on folktale. G.7 (B.7). MS IB 1261. Nhok-Thaem suggests (in *KS* 1965. 10: 1071) that it may be written by the same poet as *(Braḥ) Padumasuriyavaṅs, (Braḥ) Samudr, Dibv Saṅvār*, and *(Braḥ) Anuruddh saṅkhep,* all of which are on the same *krāṃṅ.*

Campā Thoṅ, Rīoeṅ Campā Thoṅ, Sāstrā Campā Thoṅ jātak. Roeské (1913: 670), Ly-Théam Teng ([1957]: 115) and Léang-Hap An (*KS* 1968. 12: 1360) name Ang Duong as the author. AD 1816. Source: 500 *jātak.* G.7 (B. Bh. Br. K.). MSS IB 557, 1629 (slightly different texts according to Léang-Hap An). EFEO 79.

Camrīeṅ Yuvasālā (Song of the Hall of Youth). G.8 (B.7). **T** *KS* 1939 (11) 9: 188.

Cand Ghāt, Sāstrā Cand Ghāt (also spelt *Cānd, Cănd, Ghāṭ* and *Ghāt(k)*) by *Cau Bañā Rājābhaktī, Cau Bañā Jaṃnit Ksatrī*, and *Cau Bañā Srī Añjit.* AD 1858. Source: 50 *jātak.* G.7 (B. Bh. Br. K.). MSS IB (number omitted), AC 261 Cānd Ghāt. EFEO 80. Nhok Thaem says (*KS* 1967. 7: 734 n. 1) that the word in the title should be *Grāḥ* because the hero was born when *Rāhu* seized the Moon (*Cand*).

Cand Gorab, Cand Goram, Cand Gorap, Cănd Gorabbh, Cand Gurop. See *Mucalind.*

Cand kūmmā, Cănd kūṁār, *Cand Kumār.* See *Khaṇḍahālajātak.*

Candalīvaṅs, Sāstrā Candalīvaṅs by *(Bhikkhu Paṇḍit) Khīev.* Language suggests end of 19th century (Nhok-Thaem in *KS* 1965. 9: 957). Source: 50 *jātak.* G.7 (B. Bh. Br. K.). MS IB 673.

Caṅkūm Kaev, Rīoeṅ Braḥ Caṅkūm Kaev, La Dent sacrée, by Chap-Pin. 1934. G.7 (B. B.7. Bh. Br. K. M.). **T** Chap-Pin 1934, 1969.

Car cūl ta tāṃṅ (Go into the fight). 1st line of a stanza by Mok. G.8. **T** Ly-Théam Teng 1960: 66.

Cau Bal Ek, Sāstrā Cau Bal Ek (Mr Outstanding Strength). G.7 (B. Bh. Br. K.). MS IB 636.

Cau Dhuṅ Cau Sāñ'. See *Ā Dhuṅ Ā Sāñ'.*

Cau Kambrā, Sāstrā Cau Kambrā (An orphan). G.5. MSS IB 615. AC Cau kuṃbrāh 331 (5).

Cau Kāṃpit Pandoḥ, Rīoeṅ Cau Kāṃpit Pandoḥ (Mr Whittling Knife).* G.1. **T** Plon-Nourit Cau Kuṃpit 1901. Corbet 19—: 10–19 (excerpts). *KS* 1939. 1–3: 63–77 (not complete), 1944 (from the beginning) 1–6: 88–93, 145–9, 261–70, 314–21; *PRBK* 2, No. 7. **V** Martini and Bernard 1946: 33–72; Milne 1972: 27–46.

Cau Kaṅkaep, Rīoeṅ (Mr Frog) (title of a *jātak* listed as 'Chau Kângkêp' in Guesdon 1906: 91).* G.7. **T** Plon-Nourrit 1900, corrected 1901.

Cau Krabat (Mr Tetradon) (title of a *jātak* listed as 'Chau Krâpot' in Guesdon 1906: 92).* G.7 (K.). MSS AC 18, 22. Cor Krabat (same texts). EFEO 73. **T** Plon-Nourrit 1903. **V** Khing Hoc Dy 1977: 24–5.

Cau ktāṃṅ pāy (Mr Crusty rice). G.1. **T** Plon-Nourrit (spelt *kḍāṃṅ*) 1901. Long-Chim 1954.

Cau kuṃpit. See *Cau Kāṃpit Pandoḥ.*

Cau Kūpāl (or *Gopāl), Sāstrā Cau Kūpāl* (or *Gopāl*). Advice to women through the story of *Cau Kūpāl.* G.5 or 7 (K.). MS IB 645.

Cau Mās (Mr Gold). 1887 by *(Ghun) Sundhar Binity.* Source: 50 *jātak.* G.7 (B. Bh. Br. K.). MS IB 1370.

Cau Ṅoḥ (Mr Disguise). The MS IB 623 is the first scene of a play about *Cau Ṅoḥ* or *Khyaṅ Săṅkh.* G.7 (B.7). See *Khyaṅ Săṅkh* for story.

*Cau Om.** G.7. MSS AC 329. EFEO 77. **V** Au Chhieng 1953: 265.

Cau Sradap Cek. See *Sradap Cek.*

Cau Taṃpau Sirasā (Mr Head-wound).* G.7. MS AC 59 Cau taṃmpau sirasā. **V** Au Chhieng 1953: 39.

Cau Thuk. See *Khuṅ Cūv Cau Thuk.*

Cānd Ghātt. See *Cand Ghāt.*

Cand Kumār. See *Khaṇḍahālajātak.*

Chan kurop, Préas Chan Kurop *(Cand Gurop).* See Mucalind.

Chandant, Rīoeṅ Chandant by Ban-Teng. MS EFEO 49 Chātdān'. G.7 (Br. PK). **T** Tieng-Teng (2 excerpts) 1950.

Chandantajātak. See *Chandant.*

Chbab. See *Cpāp* and *Cpāp'*. For Chbab Srei, Sophéaset, Pros, and Treinet, see *Cpāp' Srī, Cpāp' Subhāsit, Cpāp' Prus,* and *Cpāp' Trīneti.*

Chén kâuma. See *Cint kumār.*

Chinavong. See *Jinavaṅs.*

Chpāb srīy. MS SA (E 17). Same text as *Cpāp' Srī* Cl.2 (Pou and Haksrea).

Chronique royale du Cambodge (1340–1868). Begins with *Nibvān Pād*

(14th century). G.9. MS EFEO P 65 (a copy of a *krāṃṅ* which is with the Archives Royales in Phnom Penh).

Chronique royale du Cambodge (1590–1729). Begins with *KaevĤvā* I (*Cau Bañā N̈om*). G.9. MS EFEO P 64/2 (a copy of a *krāṃṅ* which is in the Archives Royales in Phnom Penh).

Chronique royale du Cambodge commençant au règne de Nippân Bat. Written in 1869 by order of Norodom. G.9. MS EFEO Exercise book (a copy of a *krāṃṅ* which is in the Archives Royales in Phnom Penh). Incomplete.

Chronique royale du Cambodge ou Pongsa Voda (succession de rois). **V** Moura 1883. (Not known from which text the translation was made.)

Chronique royale commençant à l'an 1554 de notre ère et finissant vers l'an 1773. G.9. MS P 53/9 (Exercise book at EFEO).

Chroniques royales khmères. G.9. MS belonging to the Mission étrangère, Paris. **V** Piat 1974.

Cint Kumār, Rīoeṅ Braḥ Cint Kumār (also written Chén Kaûma) or *Abhinarājā.** G.7. MS AC 34 Cin Kūmār ou Abhinarājjā. End of a verse-novel. EFEO 53 Cin Kūṁār. **V** Au Chhieng 1953: 21.

Cov Krabat. See *Cau Krabat.*

Cpāp Boddhisatv. See *Cpāp' Boddhisatv.*

Cpāp cuṅ (Code of conduct (by Chong?)) G.5(?) MS AC 66.2.

Cpāp dūnmān khluon. See *Cpāp' dūnmān khluon.*

Cpāp mahārap̈athān. See *Cpāp' Mahāpaṭṭhān.*

Cpāp paṇḍit (Code of conduct of the learned man). (Pou and Haksrea '*Cp.* Gén.'). G.5. MS SA E. 18d.

Cpāpp grupp pandūl grup kāṃbīy (All Codes of conduct, all treatises). (Pou and Haksrea '*Cp.* Gén.') G.5. MS AC 159.

Cpāp' Ariyasatthā (Code of conduct of Ariyasatthā). (Pou and Haksrea '*Cp.* Cl.') G.5 (K.). (MS IB 667 *Sāstrā seckṭī ariyasatthā* has some slight differences.) **T** *KS* 1942. 19–20: 26–30. IB *Cpāp' phseṅ2* 1942–59. 2: 21–5; 1967–73: 143–50 and Cedoreck 1980: 113–19. **T V S** Pou 1988.

Cpāp' Bāky Cās' (Code of conduct. Old sayings) (Pou and Haksrea '*Cp.* Cl.') G.5 (Br.). MSS EFEO 9, 16. *Satrā bāk cās'*. **T** Finot 1904 (one stanza). Kambujavarokās 1911. IB *Cpāp' phseṅ2* 1942–59. 1: 12–14; 1967–73: 139–42. *KS* 1942. 1: 41–3. Ching-Nguon Huot 1959. Cedoreck *Cpāp' Phseṅ2* 1980: 109–12. Corbet 19—: 104–5 (excerpts). Huffman and Proum 1977: 167–9 (vocab. 169–72). **V** Finot 1904: 71–3. **T V S** Pou 1988.

Cpāp' Bāl-paṇḍit (Code of conduct of Bāl, the learned) by Ros-Ouch (Pou and Haksrea '*Cp.* Gén.') G.5. **T** Ros-Ouch 1951.

Cpāp' Boddhisatv (Code of conduct of the Bodhisatva). Incomplete collection of legal tales. G.1. MS AC 73. Cpāp Boddhisatv.

Cpāp' Braḥ Bidhūr, Sāstrā Cpāp' Braḥ Bidhūr (Code of conduct of *Vidhūr*) Father advises child. G.5 (Br.). MS IB 642.

Cpāp' Braḥ Pandūl caeṅ. See *Cpāp' paṇṭāṃ pitā.*

Cpāp' Braḥ Rājasambhār. See *Cpāp' Rājaneti.*

Cpāp' Cās', Sāstrā Cpāp' Cās' (Old Code of conduct) by *(Braḥ Aṅg) Satthā.* AD 1723 (according to Ray-Buc 1956: 935). G.5 (?) (K.) MS IB 639.

Cpāp' Dhammapāl. See *Dharmapāl.*

Cpāp' Dharm Aniccā, Sāstrā Cpāp' Dharm Aniccā (Code of the impermanent Dhamma (Death)) by *Braḥ Ariyasatthā* (?) G.5 (K.). MS IB 625.

Cpāp' dūnmān jan prus srī, Préceptes pour l'instruction des hommes et des femmes, by Ngoy. G.5. **T** IB 19—.

Cpāp' dūnmān khluon (Code for advising oneself).

(1) (Pou and Haksrea '*Cp.* Cl.') G.5 (Br.). MSS EFEO 329 and 343 **T**. Plon-Nourrit 1900, corrected 1901. *KS* 1942. 4: 10–11; 5: 8–10. IB *Cpāp' Phseṅ2* 1942–59. 1: 7–11; 1967–73: 121–7. Cedoreck 1980: 95–100. Tec Hong 1958. Ching-Nguon Huot 1959. **T V S** Pou 1988.

(2) By *Buddher*. G.5 (?). (Reference from Roeské 1913: 671, who lists Buddher with other poets said to be post Ang-Duong.)

Cpāp' gorab mātā pitā (Code for paying respects to one's parents) by Chong. (Pou and Haksrea '*Cp.* Gén.') G.5. **T** Chong 1967.

Cpāp' Hai Mahājan (Code of conduct (beginning) 'O people'). (Pou and Haksrea 'Cl.') G.5. **T** *KS* 1942. 21–2: 24–31. IB *Cpāp' Phseṅ2* 1967–73: 31–43 and Cedoreck 1980: 23–32. **T V S** Pou 1988.

Cpāp' Hai Sādhujan (Code of conduct (beginning) 'O good people'). Nhok-Thaem says this MS (IB 633) is the same as *Trīneti* (MS IB 105) at the beginning but different at the end. See *Cpāp' Rājaneti* (= *Trīneti* 2). The MS AC 315 (Pou and Haksrea ' = *Rājaneti* Cl.') is entitled *Hai sādh jun phoṅ.*

Cpāp' Kerti Kāl (Code of the heritage of (past) time). (Pou and Haksrea 'Cl.') G.5 (Br.). MSS (*Kerti* is variously spelt *Ke, Ker, Kir* on MSS) IB 644. EFEO 2, 16, and 346. AC 44, 296A, 331, 8. **T** Plon-Nourrit. Kel Kal 1901, corrected 1901. Kambujavarokās 1911. BR 1941. Corbet 19— (extracts): 103–4. IB *Cpāp' Phseṅ2* 1942–59.

3: 5–7; 1967–73: 85–9. Ching-Nguon Huot 1959. Seng-Nguon Huot 1963: 9–14. Cedoreck 1980: 65–8. Pou and Jenner 1975: (orthography) 375–8, (transliteration) 379–81. Huffman and Proum 1977: 60–3 (vocabulary 163–6). **V** Martini 1949: (extracts) 961–2. Dhingra 1958 (extract): 138. Pou and Jenner 1975: 382–90. **S** Srey Ou (*Û Srī*) 1958. Pou and Jenner 1975: 369–74; (word index) 391–4.

Cpāp' Khmer (A Khmer Code of conduct). Title of a work attributed by Roeské (1913: 670) to Mok. No other evidence of the work has been found.

Cpāp' Kir Kāl Thmī (New Code of the heritage of (past) time) by Ngoy. (Pou and Haksrea '*Cp.* Gén.') G.5 (Br.). **T** *KS* 1932. 3–6: 181–95. Imprimerie Nouvelle 1932. IB 1940, 1960, 1964, [1972]. Ly-Théam Teng mentions (1966: 6) a publication for schools (Grade 6) of the 4 *Cpāp'* of Ngoy (or possibly selections from them?) with the overall title *Cpāp' Paṇṭāṃ Kram N̈uy.*

Cpāp' Kịṅ Kantrai or *Satrā Kịṅ Kantrai* (The *Kịṅ Kantrai* Code of conduct) Judicial stories.* G.1. **T** Aymonier 1878. 1: 170–254. *KS* 1939. 10–12: 283–6; 1941. 13: 27–8; 15: 27; 17: 28; 18: 27; 19: 26–7; 21: 25–7; 22: 24–5; 23: 25–7; 24: 25–6. 1942. 1: 49–50; 2: 51–4; 3: 26–8; 4: 24–8; 6: 24–6; 11–12: 54–6; 13–14: 61–3; 15–16: 59–60; 17–18: 62–4. Corbet 19—: 124–59. Kim-Ky 1955. *PRBK*, vol. 3 (whole volume. 53 tales). **V** Aymonier 1878: 43–64. Taupin 1886. Tvear 1969 (one tale).

Cpāp' Kram, Sāstrā Cpāp' Kram, Sāstrā Kram Cpāp' (Code of principles). (Pou and Haksrea '*Cp.* Cl'). G.5 (K.). MSS (*Cpāp'* is spelt *Cpāp* and *Cpāb; Kram* is spelt *Kraṃ* and *Kraṃm* on MSS) IB 645. EFEO 1 and 336. AC 75, 78A, 186, 225, 318, 330 (16). A MS with no catalogue number (Bibliothèque municipale de Narbonne) and a MS belonging to Monsieur Jan des Prez. **T** Plon-Nourrit 1900, corrected 1901. Kambujavarokās 1911. BR 1941. *KS* 1944 (with commentary) 6: 305–10; 7: 365–72; 8: 430–6; 9: 477–82; 10: 530–47. Corbet 19— (extract): 102–3. IB *Cpāp' Phseṅ2* 1942–59. 3: 1–4; 1967–73: 77–83 and Cedoreck 1980: 59–64. Ching-Nguon Huot 1959. Bouth Néang 1961. Huffman and Proum 1977: 149–54 (vocab. 154–9). Pou and Jenner 1979: (orthography) 134–41; (transliteration) 142–6. **V** Pou and Jenner 1979: 147–57. **S** Nheuk-Nou 1944 and 1964. Pou and Jenner 1979: 129–33 and (index of vocab.) 158–60.

Cpāp' Kram Baṃnol, Sāstrā Cpāp' Kram Baṃnol (Code of principles for narration (?)). Gnomic style. Prose. G.10. MS IB 983 (MS dated AD 1693).

Cpāp' Kram Dhaṃ, Sāstrā Cpāp' Kram Dhaṃ (The great Code of principles). G.5 (Br. K.). MS IB 1405.

Cpāp' Kram sakravā (Songs for the King when he was on his house floating on the river). G.2. **T** Plon-Nourrit 1900.

Cpāp' Kram Sāmaṇer (Code of principles for novices) by Nhok-Thaem. (Pou and Haksrea '*Cp.* Gén.') G.5 (K.). **T** *KS* 1949. 12: 940–7.

Cpāp' Kūn Cau, Sāstrā Cpāp' Kūn Cau (Code of conduct for children).

(1) (Pou and Haksrea 'Cl.') G.5 (K.). MSS EFEO 3 and (with title *Satrā breṅ brit)* 4. IB 644 (Nhok-Thaem says end faulty). **T** Plon-Nourrit 1901. Kambujavarokās 1911. BR 1941. Corbet 19— (extract): 105–10. IB *Cpāp' Phseṅ2* 1942–59. 3: 8–15; 1967, 1970: 91–104. Ching-Nguon Huot 1959. Cedoreck 1980: 69–80. Pou and Jenner 1977: (orthography) 171–82; (transliteration) 83–90. **V** Dhingra 1958 (extract): 126. Pou and Jenner 1977: 191–206. **S** Pou and Jenner 1977: (introduction) 167–70; (grammatical appendix) 207–9; (index of vocabulary) 210–15.

(2) By Ngoy. (Pou and Haksrea '*Cp.* Gén.') G.5 (Br.). **T** Ngoy in *KS* 1937. 4–6: 111–22.

Cpāp' Kūn Cau Lpoek (Code of conduct for children for their edification). The beginning is the same as that of *Cpāp' paṇṭāṃ pitā* and the end is the same as that of *Cpāp' Bāky Cās'*. G.5. **T** IB *Cpāp' Phseṅ2* 1967–73: 59–76. Cedoreck 1980: 45–58.

Cpāp' Kūn Gambīr, Sāstrā Cpāp' Kūn Gambīr (Code of conduct for children. A treatise). G.5 (K.). MS IB 644.

Cpāp' lpoek thmī, Préceptes nouveaux pour l'édification, by Ngoy. (Pou and Haksrea '*Cp.* Gén.') G.5 (K.). **T** Ngoy in *KS* 1932. 3–6: 149–80. Imprimerie du Gouvernement 1932. Imprimerie Nouvelle 1932. IB 1940, 1960, 1964, [1972].

Cpāp' Mahāneti Rājasuostī (also *Mahānet Rājasvasti),* cf. *Dharmapāl.* (Pou and Haksrea '*Cp.* ne.') G.5 (K.). **T**. Kambujavarokās 1911. *KS* 1942. 23–4: 10–26.

Cpāp' Mahāpaṭṭhān (Pou and Haksrea '*Cp.* Gén.') G.5. MS EFEO 8 Mahārap̈athān **T V S** Pou 1988.

Cpāp' Meyyapaṇḍit, Cpāp' Meyyapaṇḍit (taeṅ). See *Cpāp' Prus* Cl.

Cpāp' On Aṅg (Code of conduct. Bowing down) by *Ṭūṅ.* G.5. **T** (5 stanzas, as remembered by *Lok Grū Tup-Kịṅ* and noted down by Chhim-Soum) *KS* 1968. 7: 759–60. **S**. *KS* 1968. 7: 758–67.

Cpāp' paṇṭāṃ kram N̈uy. See *Paṇṭāṃ Kram N̈uy.*

Cpāp' paṇṭāṃ pitā (Recommendations of a father). (Pou and Haksrea '*Cp.* Cl.') G.5 (K.). **T**. *KS* 1942. 21–2: 17–23. (Same text, with title *Cpāp' braḥ pandūl caeṅ* (Code of conduct. Clear recommendations), in *KS* 1945. 1: 25–32). IB *Cpāp' Phseṅ2* 1967–73: 45–57. Cedoreck 1980: 33–44. **T V S** Pou 1988.

Cpāp' praṭau cau kram, Sāstrā Cpāp' praṭau cau kram (Code of conduct to advise a magistrate). Prose. Gnomic. G.10. MS IB 943 (of AD 1693).

Cpāp' praṭau jan prus srī (Code of advice to men and women) by Ngoy. (Pou and Haksrea '*Cp.* Gén.') G.5 (B.7). **T**. *KS* 1937. 7–9: 205–20. IB 1961.

Cpāp' praṭau khluon, Sāstrā Cpāp' praṭau khluon (Code of advice to oneself). G.5 (K.). MS IB 1376.

Cpāp' Prus (Code of conduct for boys).

(1) Also called *Cpāp' Thmī* (A new code of conduct) and *Cpāp' Meyyapaṇḍit, Cpāp' Meyyapaṇḍit (taeṅ)* (Code of conduct by *Mai*, the learned). By *Mai.* (Pou and Haksrea '*Cp.* Cl.') G.5 (Br.). MSS EFEO 6, 11, 16, 339 *(Satrā Cpāp' Thmīy).* SA (E 18b). **T** Plon-Nourrit 1901. Kambujavarokās 1911. *KS* 1937. 4–6: 155–64; 1942: 17–18: 12–19. IB *Cpāp' Phseṅ2* 1942–59. 2: 1–8; 1967–73: 1–13. Cedoreck 1980: 1–10. Tec-Hong 1957. Bouth-Néang 1959. Seng-Nguon Huot 1965. Pou and Jenner 1976: (orthography) 317–25, (transliteration) 326–30. Huffman and Proum 1977: 173–81 (vocabulary 181–8). **V** Pou and Jenner 1976: 331–43. **S** Pou and Jenner 1976: 313–16, (index of vocabulary) 344–50.

(2) (Pou and Haksrea '*Cp.* Gén.'). G.5. MS AC 296 B.

Cpāp' Prus niṅ Cpāp' Srī, Sāstrā Cpāp' Prus niṅ Cpāp' Srī (Code of conduct for boys and girls) by *Bhikkhu Sīm.* G.5 (B.7). MS IB 1405.

Cpāp' raṃlịk jan prus srī. See *Bāky kāby praṭau jan prus srī.*

Cpāp' Rājaneti (Code for a king's conduct of affairs) or *Braḥ Rāj Sambhār* (King (he who has accumulated merit)) or *Trīneti 2* (Threefold propositions) or *Hai sādh jan phoṅ* (O all good people) or *Sātrā haisān* by a king, but which one is uncertain (Pou and Jenner 1978: 362–6). (Pou and Haksrea 'Cl.') G.5 (K.). MSS IB 622 EFEO 10. AC 76 (1); 315. **T** Plon-Nourrit 1903. Kambujavarokās 1911. *KS* 1939. 4–6: 43–54 and 1943. 21–2: 11–16. IB 1941. *Mitt Sālā Pālī* 1951. IB (Mālikā) 1968. IB *Cpāp' Phseṅ2*

1967–73: 151–61. Cedoreck 1980: 121–9. Pou and Jenner 1978: (orthography) 369–77; (transliteration) 377–83. **V** Léang-Hap An (in Khmer) 1966: 25–37. IB 1969 (English translation of bits of *Sātrā Braḥ Rāj Sambhār*). Pou and Jenner 1978: 383–97. **S** Pou and Jenner 1978: 361–8; (index of vocabulary) 398–402.

Cpāp' Rājapaṇḍit, Sāstrā Cpāp' Rājapaṇḍit (Code of a learned king). G.5 (Br.). MS IB 1738.

Cpāp' Srī (Code of conduct for women).

(1) By *Mai* (Pou and Haksrea 'Cl. 1') G.5 (Bh.). MSS EFEO 7,330 (a) Cpāp srīy. IB 644, 667 *Cpāp' Srī dhaṃ* (Great code for women). **T**. Plon-Nourrit Cpāp Srī 1901 and corrected 1901. Kambujavarokās 1911. *KS* 1942. 19–20: 14–25. IB *Cpāp' Phseṅ2* 1942–59. 2: 9–20; 1967–73: 15–29; Cedoreck 1980: 11–22. **T V S** Pou 1988.

(2) (Pou and Haksrea 'Cl. 2') G.5 (K.). MSS EFEO 330 (b) Cpāp Srīy. AC 164. SA A 18a Cpāb srīy. **T** Jenner 1978: 116–26 (even-numbered pages). **V** *id.*: 117–27 (odd-numbered pages). **S** *id.*: 111–15.

(3) By Ang Duong. G.5 (K.). **T** IB 1962. **S** Léang-Hap An 1965*b*: 91–107. **T** and **S** Chap-Pin in *KS* 1959. 1: 39–52; 2: 169–89. Léang-Hap An (*KS* 1968. 12: 1348) attributes a *Cpāp' Srī* to Nong. Possibly there was confusion between the work of Ang Duong and Nong, as in the case of the Chronicles?

Cpāp' Srī dhaṃ. See *Cpāp' Srī* 1.

Cpāp' Subhāsit (Code of sayings) by Nong. AD 1790 (according to Ray-Buc 1956: 935 and Ly-Théam Teng 1960: 117 but AD 1809 according to Léang-Hap An 1965*b*: 67). G.5 (Br. K.). (Pou and Haksrea '*Cp.* Gén.') MSS IB 613, 632. SA B39 (vol. 1, fasc. 1) and EFEO 15. **T** Nong in *KS* 1941. 1: 12–15; 2: 23–6; 3: 13–17; 4: 23–6; 5: 11–14; 6: 15–18; 7: 13–16; 8: 13–17. IB *Cpāp' Phseṅ2* 1942–59. BR 1942. Khing Hoc Dy 1976 (two stanzas) 93. **T** and **S** Dik-Kéam 1967*b*: 7–11. **T V S** Pou 1988.

Cpāp' svaḥ svaeṅ (Code for those who search). G.5 (K.). MS IB 640.

Cpāp' Thmī.

(1) See *Cpāp' Prus*.

(2) *Sāstrā Cpāp' Thmī* (A new Code of conduct). G.5 (Br.). MS IB 1405.

Cpāp' Trīneti (Threefold code for the conduct of affairs).

(1) Also called *Pūbit* (or *Pabitr*) *Mahārāj* (O great king!). (Pou and Haksrea '*Cp.* Cl.') G.5 (K.). MS EFEO 338 **T** Plon-Nourrit

1901. Corbet 19—: 110–13 (called *Trīneti Thmī (A new Trineti)*). IB 1941. BR 1941. IB *Cpāp' Phseṅ2* 1942–59. 3: 16–24; 1967–73: 105–19. Cedoreck 1980: 81–94. Ching-Nguon Huot 1959. **S T V**. Pou and Jenner 1981: (orthography) 144–57; (transliteration) 158–66; (translation) 167–87; introduction 135–43; (index of vocabulary) 188–93.

(2) See *Cpāp' Rājaneti*.

Cpāp' trūv dharm, Sāstrā Cpāp' trūv dharm (Code adhering to the Dhamma) or, as Nhok-Thaem suggests (*KS* 1968. 4: 425 n. 1), should possibly be read *Cpāp' grū dhaṃ* (Code of the great teacher). G.5 (K.). MS IB 1376.

Cpāp' ṭaṃpūnmān pabbajit grahasth, Préceptes pour l'instruction des religieux et des laïcs by Chong. G.5. **T** Chong 1958.

Cpāp' ṭās' tīoen kūn cau (Code for motivating the children). Title of a work which may be the same text as *Secktī raṃlịk ṭās' tīoen* (A poem for motivation), by Ngoy. G.5. **T** Kim-Seng 19—. *Paṇṭāṃ kram N̈uy* and *Cpāp' ṭās' tīoen kūn cau.*

Cpāp' Vidhūr paṇḍit (Code of the learned Vidhūr). (Pou and Haksrea '*Cp.* Cl.') G.5 (Br.). **T** Kambujavarokās 1911. *KS* 1942. 2: 42–4; 3: 10–12. IB *Cpāp' Phseṅ2* 1942–59. 1: 1–6; 1967–73: 129–37. Ching-Nguon Huot 1959. Cedoreck 1980: 101–8. **T V S** Pou 1988.

Cray-Thong. See *Krāy Thoṅ.*

Daṃbaek puon nāk', Rīoeṅ daṃbaek puon nāk', Daṃbaek dāṃṅ puon (The four bald men). *Manuss chot 4 nāk'* (Four stupid men).*

(1) G.1. MS EFEO 23. T Main story in Plon-Nourrit 1900, corrected 1901. *KS* 1937. 10–12: 327–32; 1938. 10–12: 261–8; and in *PRBK* 4, No. 12. Individual episodes in *PRBK* 1, No. 9; 2, Nos. 3 and 17. **V** Martini and Bernard 1946: 186–93 (the full story). Martini 1949: 1020–6. Bernard 1949: 1018–19. Bernard-Thierry 1953: 23–4; 1955*f*: 541–2. Dik-Kéam 1962: 108–9. Hu'o'ng 1969: 356–9. IB 1970: 65–9. Laporte 1970 (translation of *PRBK* 4, No. 12). Velder 1971: 57–67. Chandler 1976: 5–6. **S** Bernard-Thierry 1953: 22–3.

(2) MS An episode in the collection of tales. G.7 (Br. PK. K). IB 613. Nhok-Thaem suggests that the MS was written in late 18th or early 19th century.

Dansāy crūt srūv, Sāstrā dansāy crūt srūv (The rabbit cuts paddy). G.7. Folktale (not the same as *Subhā Dansāy (bāky kāby)*). (PK and B) MS IB 628.

Dansāy ŝī cek, Sāstrā dansāy ŝī cek (The rabbit eats bananas). G.7 (PK). Folktale (not the same as *Subhā Dansāy (bāky kāby)*). MS IB 667.

Dasajātak, Rīoeṅ dasajātak (The 10 *jātak*). G.10. MS of 18th–19th centuries mentioned by Ray-Buc 1956: 937. **T** (retold) Ou-Chev 1951.

Dāv Ek or *Duṃ Dāv* (*Dāv* and Ek) or (*Duṃ* and *Dāv*).

(1) *Duṃ Dāv* by Mok. G.7 (B. Bh. Br. K). MS said to be very tattered. Nhok-Thaem had not seen it (*KS* 1965: 1055 n. 1). **T** Mok 1961 (edited from the MS). **V** (a few stanzas) Collard 1925.

(2) *Duṃ Dāv* by *Som* 1915.* G.7 (B.7). MS IB 664. **T** IB 1962, 1966. Rasmei Kampuchea 1963. *Samāgam Juon Ṇāt* 1974. Huffman and Proum 1977: 189–99 (vocabulary 200–7). Cedoreck 1980. **V** Khing Hoc Dy 1980: (two stanzas) 66. **S**. Léang-Hap An 1962, 1966*d*. **S V** Huffman and Proum 1977: 189.

(3) *Dāv Ek* by Nou-Kan 1942. G.7 (B.8). **T** Nou-Kan 1949, 1953. Ly-Théam Teng 1960: (excerpt) 177–8.

(4) Nhok-Thaem also describes MSS IB (no number) *Dāv Ek* (B. B.7 K.) (different beginning and end from Som's work). IB 1263 (B.7) (not precisely same as Som's work).

(5) The story in general. **V** Kong-Huot and Chau Seng 1970. **S** Ly-Théam Teng 1960: 54–5. Khing Hoc Dy 1979: 796.

(La) Dent sacrée. See *(Rīoeṅ Braḥ) Caṅkūm Kaev.*

Devadatt. Le Satra de Ṭévaṭat. G.10? **V** and **S** Leclère 1906: 125–44 and 121–3.

Devand by Mok. 1859. One of the 50 *jātak.** G.7 (K.). MS IB 1383. **T** Mok 1957–8 in *KS*. Ly-Théam Teng 1960: (excerpt) 155. Khing Hoc Dy 1981: (excerpt) 146–8. **V** Khing Hoc Dy, ibid. 149–53.

Devaṅs kumār, Devavaṅs kumār. See *Sradap Cek*.

Devatā juṃnuṃ ktīy (The gods decide the case) or *Tamrāp lokkanaiy* (Imitating the leader of the world (?)). Four wise men answer the king's questions. The best is *Dhneñjaiy paṇḍit* (The learned *Dhanañjăy*). Au Chhieng says (1953: 31) that it recalls the *Mahaummaggajātak*. G.10. MS AC 42 (part 3 only) **V** Au Chhieng 1953: 30–1.

Devatā oey caṅ-īet citt (O gods! I am unhappy) by Srī Dhammarājā. G.8 (B.7). **T** *KS* 1939. 1: 44–5.

Dhammapad. See *Mahādhammapadajātak*.

Dhanañjay. See *Dhmeñ Jăy*.

Dharmapāl. (Pou and Haksrea '*Cp*. Ne. (politics of the king)'. G.5. MS EFEO 12, 280. SA B 39, vol. 1, fasc. 2. Variant with the title, *Hai pā put cpaṅ*. **T V S** Pou 1988.

Dhmeñ Jăy or *Dhanañjăy* or *Dhneñ Jăy*.

(1) Known as *Sāstrā Dhmeñ Jăy Anak prājñ* (*Dhmeñ Jăy*, the clever man) or as *Rīoeṅ Dhanañjăy Paṇḍit* (*Dhanañjăy* the learned)* G.1. **T** Aymonier 1878. 2: 67–115. *KS* 1936. 4–6; 1938. 4–6. Corbet 19—: 20–30. Khemarak 1952. Kim-Ky 1958. Komar Pech 1959. IB 1964, 1972. *PRBK* 3, No. 13. **V** Aymonier 1878. 1: 20–30. Monod 1932: 452–7 and 467–72; 1944: 49–97; 1985: 49–97. Bitard 1956: 591–7. Khing Hoc Dy 1977: 32–3. **S** Bitard 1951 and 1956*b*: 588–90. *Ḷāy-Grī* in *KS* 1965: 755.

(2) *Sāstrā Dhmeñ Jăy Anak prājñ*. 1909. G.7 (B. Bh. Br. K.). MS IB 684.

Dhneñ Jăy. See *Dhmeñ Jăy*.

Dibv Saṅvār.

(1) *Rīoeṅ Dibv Saṅvār* by *Thau Kae*. Translated from Thai into verse.* G.7 (B.8). **T** IB 1963. Huffman and Proum 1977: (two extracts) 236–44 (vocabulary 244–50).

(2) *Dibv Saṅvār* by Ban-Teng (Ly-Théam Teng 1960: 181. Vandy-Kaonn 1981: 51) G.7.

(3) *Dibv Saṅvār*. Roeské (1913: 671) attributes a work of this name to Méas 1.

(4) *Krāṃṅ Dibv Saṅvār*. G.7 (B.7). MS IB 1261.

Dịk Danle Sāp (The waters of the Tonle Sap) by Kim-Hak. The first modern novel. **T** *KS* 1939 (11).

Dịk rāṃ phkā rāṃ, Rīoeṅ dịk rāṃ phkā rāṃ (The water and the flowers dance). AD 1911. Cited by Ly-Théam Teng 1960: 120; Khing Hoc Dy 1979: 796. G.7. **T** Seng-Nguon Huot 1963.

Dime Cheadak, (Préas) Dime Cheadak. See *Temiyajātak*.

Douze jeunes filles, Les. See *Rathasenajātak*.

Dukkammamāṇab. Story similar to that of the *Dummānika*: (one of the 50 *jātak*) but this may have been taken from the 500 (Nhok-Thaem in *KS* 1967: 1184). G.7 (B. Bh. Br. K.). MS IB 635. EFEO 54 Duk kaṃ mānab'.

Dukkh khñuṃ jāti neḥ loes as' srī (My sorrow in this life exceeds that of all women) by *(Braḥ Aṅg Mcās' Ksatrī) L.N.* G.8 (B.7). **T** *KS* 1939. 7–9: 207–8.

Duṃ Dāv. See *Dāv Ek*.

E phkāy kraboe paer sirasā (The Great Bear turns his head) by *(Anak Mnāṅ) Phaÿam*. G.8 (B.7). **T** *KS* 1939. 7–9: 210.

Eṇāv. See *Îṇāv*.

Gambīr. See under next word of title.

Gatilok rī̤ Cpāp' dūnmān khluon, 'L'Art de bien se conduire dans la vie' by In. Written in 1921. Stories of Buddhist or Indian or European origin, songs and translations from Pali. G.1, 2, and 10. MS (*krāṃṅ*) IB 1264 *Krāṃṅ Ācāry Ind dī 1–7*. **T** In in *KS* 1927, 1928, and 1930–1. In (various BR and IB reprints) 1936–64. Corbet 19—: 160–96 (15 stories). Cedoreck 1981. **V** Carrison 1987.

Gāṃ bāky rāmakiyerti bhāsā khmaer (Khmer text of the Reamker in Siamese orthography), ed. Tāṃraṅ Rājanubhāb. Bangkok 2471 BE (AD 1928).

Ghun Chāṅ Ghun Phaen. G.7. MS AC 340 (incomplete). **S** *M̈aen-Dan'* 1969.

Gī̤ aṃp̈oet koet aṃbī jal' ravit (Meaning not clear) by *(Braḥ Aṅg Mcās' Kraisar) Sūravaṅs*. G.8 (B.9). **T** *KS* 1939. 4–6: 110–11.

Glorification du Triple Joyau, Poêmes consacrés au Triple Joyau. See *Secktī raṃlịk ṭās' tīoen*.

Hai Mahājan. See *Cpāp' Hai Mahājan*.

Hai pā put cpaṅ. See *Dharmapāl*.

Hai sādh(u) jan phaṅ. See *Cpāp' Rājaneti*.

Hai Saṅkh. See *Khyaṅ Săṅkh*.

Haisān, Sātrā Haisān. See *Cpāp' Rājaneti*.

Hang-Yon. See *Haṅs Yant*.

Haṅs Yant (Swan-machine).* Written in the style of a *jātak*, adapted from a Siamese version. G.7. (B. Br. K. MJ). MS EFEO 52. **T** Im-Phon 1959. Chhung-Nguon Huot 1959. Tec-Hong 1959. IB 1964, 1966. Kim-Ky 1965. Huffman and Proum 1977 (extract): 227–31 (vocabulary 231–5). **V** ibid. 227. Khing Hoc Dy 1979: 95–100, 1980 (part only): 64–5; **V S** 1990 (full story): 188–92. **S** Léang-Hap An 1965. Khing Hoc Dy 1990: 192. Sokhamphu (1976: 204) says that *Haṅs Yant* was the first *Sātrā Lbaeṅ*, written in 1668 by *Cau Yam Puṇy Bhăktr*.

A popular version of this story, called *Suvaṇṇahaṅs*, was recorded by E. Porée-Maspero 1964. 2: 500.

Histoire d'un centenaire: roi du Cambodge au XVIIe siècle. G.9. MS AC 3 (5). **V** Aymonier (in de Villemereuil 1883).

Hitopades, translated from French into Khmer by (1) Choum-Mau and (2) Krasem. G.10. Prose. **T** in *KS* (1) 1933–4 and (2) 1938–40. See also *Srīhitopades*.

Hora Sastr. See Tamra Prohm Cheat.

Huoy, Sāstrā Huoy. G.5 (K). MS IB 1395.

Iṇāv (or *Î̂ṇāv* or *Eṇāv), Rīoeṅ Î̂ṇāv* The Khmer version of this Malay story, of which the title was Raden Panji, was attributed by Roeské (1913: 670) to Ang Duong. Coedès is reported by Dik-Kéam (1967*a*: 57) as having said that Nong had a hand in its preparation. Nou-Kan wrote a work entitled *Î̂ṇāv* which is probably not published. (Ly-Théam Teng 1966: 177). The story had long been turned into a dance-drama by the Thais. G.7 (B.7). MSS IB (*krāṃṅ*) 1258, 1259. AC 16 (incomplete). EFEO 146. **T** Māṇavī 1957 (partial, with prose narrative in between). Was this the work of Ang Duong with Nong's help? **V** Bastian 1868: 345–6. Moura 1883: 416–45.

Jai Dātt', Jaiy Dāt. See *Jăy Dat*.

Jambūpatither. Prose. G.10. MS AC 234. Mahājaṃbūradhipatithera. AC 222. Same text as 234. MS EFEO 61 Mahājuṃmbūr. **V** Finot 1917: 66 (résumé of Laotian version).

Jăy Dat, Sāstrā Jăy Dat (also spelt *Jaiy, dāt, dātth*).

(1) By *Ko*, AD 1758. G.7 (B. Bh. Br. K.). Source: 500 *jātak* (Nhok-Thaem's suggestion.) MSS IB 363, 364, 365. AC 50, 174, 265, 331, 4. **V** Au Chhieng 1953: 211 (brief résumé, as on the MS, of each fascicule).

(2) Short 'drama' (i.e. divided into scenes). G.7 (B.7). MS (*krāṃṅ*) IB 1261 (2 MSS) Krāṃṅ Braḥ Anuruddh saṅkhep. **T** Plon-Nourrit Jai dāt' 1902, corrected 1902. Source: 50 *jātak* (Nhok-Thaem's suggestion).

Jāv Gun by *Sai Tan' (Hok Kīen)* and *Â̂n Vāt' (Â̂n-Vat)* in 1897. Source: Chinese folktale. G.7 (B.7 and 8). MS IB 1381.

Jeṭṭhā tāṃṅ tae koet kaliyug (I am now in turmoil) by Uong. G.8 (B.7). **T** *KS* 1940. 8: 70–1; 9: 51–8.

Jinavaṅs, Sāstrā Jinavaṅs* by Hing AD 1856. (Name given as *Bhịṅ* by Ly-Théam Teng 1960: 118.) By Mok according to Roeské (1913: 670). G.7 (B. Bh. Br. K.). MSS IB 560, 561. EFEO 45. **T** *Lī Eṅ*

Hīek 1957. Seng-Nguon Huot 1961. IB 1964, 1966, 1977. **V** Khing Hoc Dy 1979 (excerpt): 94–5. See Jacq 1982 *re* illustration in painting. Vandy-Kaonn (1981: 27) says it is popular still; was performed, in adapted form, in 1975.

Jīntaṇavaṅs. G.7. MS AC 286. Beginning only. Khmer résumé (AC 1953: 227) tells of yaksas falling asleep, of nurses therefore riding off into the thorns, and of male and female nurses enjoying each other's company.

Jīnuk. See *Mahājanakajātak.*

Jhmuoñ cāk' smugr, Sāstrā Jhmuoñ cāk' smugr. See *Daṃbaek puon nāk'.* 2.

Juc nịṅ trī, Rīoeṅ Juc nịṅ trī (The fish-trap and the fish)* or *Lpoek Juc, Sāstrā Lpoek Juc* (The tale of the fish-trap) by *Ṭūṅ*? Although there is no date or name on the MS, *Ṭūṅ's* grandson and others are convinced that he wrote it (Chhim-Soum in *KS* 1968. 6: 652). Ing-Yeng, however (1972: 46), attributes the work to In. G.7 (PK). MS IB 640. EFEO 16, 19. **T**. Aymonier 1878: 163–9. *Juc Trī bāky kāby* (The fish-trap and the fish. Poem) Corbet19— (Selection of passages): 58–61. Ly-Théam Teng in *KS* 1971. 4: 358–69. **V**. Aymonier 1878: 41–2 Le poisson et la nasse. **S**. Chhim-Soum in *KS* 1968. 6: 652–74.

K-aek nịṅ Krasā (The crow and the heron). Folktale told in verse with Buddhist moral. G.7 (K.). MS IB 1446.

K-aek ṭap' (Ten crows) by *Eṅ-Lī.* Source: a Khmer folktale. G.7 (Br.). MS IB 669.

Kaṃbat kaṃbīṅ buoy (The tetradon, the huge tetradon (?)) by Mok (1 stanza, improvised). G.8 (Br.). **T** Nhok-Thaem in *KS* 1957: 147–8. **T** and **V** Khing Hoc Dy 1981: 141.

Kaṃbat kaṃbīṅ p̈oḥ (The tetradon, the huge tetradon (?)) by Mok (1 stanza improvised). G.8 (Br.). **T** Nhok-Thaem in *KS* 1957: 147. **T** and **V** Khing Hoc Dy 1981: 141.

Kaṃṇāby braliṅ mās oey (Poem. My darling) by Srī Dhammarājā. G.8 (K.). **T** *KS* 1938. 12: 207–16. Slight **T** and **S** in Khmer by Léang-Hap An (*KS* 1968. 12: 1329–30). Similarly in Léang-Hap An 1966: 60.

Kaṃṇāby kanlaṅ' mās maṅgal thlai (Poem. The dear fortunate bee) by Srī Dhammarājā G.8 (Bh.). **T** *KS* 1938. 8: 111–12.

Kaṃṇāby sarsoer hemantamās (Poem in praise of the cool season) by Srī Dhammarājā written (according to Ly-Théam Teng 1960: 116) in AD 1634. G.8 (K.). **T**. *KS* 1938. 7–8: 107–11. Léang-Hap An 1966: 53–6. Ly-Théam Teng 1960 (short passage): 134. **S** Léang-Hap An 1966: 52–3 and 56–7 in *KS* 1968. 12: 1327–8.

Kangrei. See *Rathasenajātak.*

Kaṅ Kap, Rīoeṅ Braḥ Pād Kaṅ Kap. Cited by Ly-Théam Teng (1960: 120) as a work of the Middle period. MS EFEO 44.

Kaṅrī. See *Rathasenajatak.*

Karaṇiyakicc rapas' bal raṭṭh (The duties of citizens) by Tin-Huot. G.2. **T** IB 1951.

Karaṇiyakicc rapas' bal raṭṭh phnaek siksādhikār jāt(i) (The duties of citizens in educating the nation) by Chhim-Soum. G.2. **T** IB 1951.

Katilok. See *Gatilok.*

Kau Hāy. The story of *Kau,* a man, and *Hāy*, a woman. G.7 (K.). **T**. Plon-Nourrit 1902.

Kāby Nirās Aṅgar or *Nirās Nagaravatt Bāky Kāby* (Poem. A journey to Angkor)* composed in 1926 by In. A 'separation' poem, *Nirās*. G.7 (B.8). **T** In in *KS* 1934. 7–9: 5–81. In (excerpt) 1950.

Kābyasār Vilāsinī (A poetic message to prostitutes) composed in 1889 by In. G.8.

Kākī, Rīoeṅ Nāṅ Kākī (Madame *Kākī*) or *Lpoek Kākī* (The story of *Kākī*).

(1) Composed by Ang Duong in 1815, inspired by a Siamese version and using the 500 *jātak* as his source.* G.7 (B. Bh. Br. K.). MSS IB 681. AC 166 Nāṅ Kākīy. EFEO 78. **T** Plon-Nourrit. Nāṅ Kākīy 1902. Corrected 1902. *KS* (incomplete) 1938–9. BR 1940. Ang Duong 1949, 1959, 1966, 1970. Seng-Nguon Huot 1960. Huffman and Proum (2 extracts) 1977: 208–14 (vocabulary 215–19). **V** Monod 1944: 201–46 and 1985: 203–46. Martini (2 short passages) in Khing Hoc Dy 1980: 52–3 and 54 and 1990: 187–8. **S** Léang-Hap An 1965*b*: 70–91 and 111–21; 1966*b*. Vandy-Kaonn 1981: 32–3. **S V** Huffman and Proum 1977 (in Khmer): 208–9. Khing Hoc Dy 1990: 187–8.

(2) Prose version. **T** Pavie 1898: 351–6. **V** Pavie 1898: 155–68. 1903: 70–8.

Kḍān jāp' andāk. See *Ktān' jāp' andāk'.*

Kerti Kāl. See *Cpāp' Kerti Kāl.*

Ket (or *Ketu, Kaetu*) *Mālā, Sātrā Braḥ* (or Preah) *Ket* (or *Ketu, Kaetu*) *Mālā.* See *Lpoek Aṅgar Vat.*

Ket Mealea. See last entry.

Khamā dos, Sāstrā khamā dos (Apology). A plea for mother's pardon considering all she has suffered. G.8 (K.). MS IB 641.

Khaṇḍahālajātak or *Cand Kumār.* Khmer prose version of Pāli *jātak.* G.10. MSS AC 192 Cand kūmmā. AC 264 Candd kūmār. EFEO 32 Cǎnd kūṁār.

Khluon oey koet mak knuṅ sāsanā (Alas that I was born into this faith) by *(Braḥ Nāṅ) Cam Srī Deb Apsar,* a 19th-century court poetess. G.8 (B.7). **T** *KS* 1939. 7–9: 210.

Khñuṃ niṅ cāt' caeṅ taeṅ secktī (I will organize myself to write something). A political poem which was kept secret for a long time. G.8 (B.7). **T** Ly-Théam Teng 1960: 191–2.

Khuṅ Cūv Cau Thuk, Sāstrā (*Khuṅ Cūv* and *Cau Thuk*). Folktale. G.7 (K. B.). MSS IB 620. AC 331 (6). Khing Hoc Dy **T V S** 1988 and 1990 (**V**): 198–202, (**S**): 202–3.

Khyaṅ Sǎṅkh, Sāstrā Khyaṅ Sǎṅkh, Rīoeṅ Khyaṅ Sǎṅkh (Shell shell), or *Hai Sǎṅkh* (O shell). Two very similar poetic versions of the same story.

(1) *Sāstrā Khyaṅ Sǎṅkh.* Commissioned by King Chey Chettha. Written by *Mīn Ûk*, according to Khuon Sokhamphu 1971*b*. Date: AD 1729 (see Pou 1975: 121). Source: *jātak?* G.7* (B. Bh. Br. K.). MSS IB 583, 584, 585. EFEO 89 Khyaṅ sṅaṃ. **T** IB 1961, 1970. **V** (extract) Khing Hoc Dy 1977: 23–4 and (full story) 1990: 156–65 with **S**: 156.

(2) *Hai Sǎṅkh.* **T** Kim-Ky 1955. (This story is the source of a popular dramatic version, *Cau Ṇoḥ* (Mr Disguise) to which reference is made in Thiounn 1956: 91–5.)

Kiṅ Kantrai. See *Cpāp' Kiṅ Kantrai.*

Knuṅ sār thā Braḥ Cam Mkuṭ Bhab (In this letter I call myself *Braḥ Cam Mkuṭ Bhab*) by *(Braḥ Aṅg Mcās') Nab Ratn*, a 19th-century court poet. G.8 (B.7). **T** *KS* 1939. 4–6: 113–14.

Kpuon moel jatā rāsī niṅ gāthā yanta dāṃṅ buoṅ (Treatise considering time of birth, the signs of the zodiac and all the charms). MS IB 466. **S** Khin Sok 1982: 113–19.

Kram Cpāp', Sāstrā Kram Cpāp' (Code of principles).

(1) G.5 (K.). MS IB 667.

(2) G.5 (K.). MS IB 1376.

(3) G.5. Kraṃm cpāp MS AC 317 (Pou and Haksrea '*Cp.* gén.'). (Different from *Cpāp' Kram.*)

Kram vaṅs, Sāstrā Kram vaṅs (Family principles) by *Cau Bañā Kraisar Srī.* G.5 (B.7). MS IB 633.

Krāṃṅ (Folded paper manuscript). See under next word of title.

*Krāy Thoṅ.** Of Thai origin. G.7 (B.7 and ?). MS AC 328 (1) (in transcription). **V** Bastian 1868: 336. Feer 1877: 170.

Krong Sapphamit. See *Kruṅ Subhamitr.*

Kruṅ Malin cot tantiṅ Braḥ Nāggasaen. See *Milindapañhā.*

Kruṅ Sabdamīt, Kruṅ Sabvamit. See next entry.

Kruṅ Subhamitr, Rīoeṅ Kruṅ Subhamitr (King *Subhamitr*)* by Kao, *Kau*, AD 1798. Source: the 50 *jātak.* G.7 (B. Bh. Br. K.). MSS IB 623, 656. EFEO 66. Kruṅ Sabvamit. **T** Plon-Nourrit 1901. BR 1941–2. Kao 1953, 1967, 1970, 1972. Huffman and Proum 1977 (extract): 279–85 (vocabulary 286–8). **V** Khing Hoc Dy 1990: 171–4 and **S**: 174–5. **S** Léang-Hap An in *KS* 1968. 12: 1362.

Ktām, Sātrā ktām, Ktām bāky kāby (The crab. Poetry). *(Sāstrā* or *Lpoek) phgar phtāṃ ktām (khyaṅ)* (The thunder warns the crab), *Phgar ktām* (The thunder and the crab), or *Ph-ūk phgar* (Think of the thunder). The thunder warns the crab after the rainy season to dig a deep hole. According to Chhim-Soum (*KS* 1968. 3: 332), it is by *Ṭūṅ.*

(1) G.5 (K.). (Pou and Haksrea '*Cp.* Gén.') MS AC 331 (7). IB 645. **T** Aymonier 1878: 160–2. Bouth-Néang 1958. Ly-Théam Teng 1971. **V** Aymonier 1878: 41. **S V** Chhim-Soum in *KS* 1968. 3: 332–6. **S** Ly-Théam Teng 1971: 722–4. **T V S** Pou 1988.

(2) *Sātrā Ktām.* G.5. Pou and Haksrea '*Cp.* Cl.' MS EFEO 329.

Ktām sa, Sāstrā Ktām sa (The white crab). Alternative title on MS IB 680 for *(Sāstrā) Suvaṇṇ Ktām sa*, q.v.

Ktān' jāp' andāk', Sāstrā Ktān' jāp' andāk' (The deer is caught in the trap)* by *Sūt.* Theme: a folktale. G.7 (Bh. K. PK). MSS IB 633 **T** Plon-Nourrit Kḍān jāp' andāk' 1900, corrected 1900.

Ktī sne(h) neḥ niṅ prīep upamā (This love may be compared) by *Ghun Ŝī Manomai.* G.8 (B.7, B.9). **T** *KS* 1940. 1: 37–43 and 1941–3 (repeats the poem given in 1940 and extends it) 9: 17–21; 10: 18–20; 11: 20.

Kulukapaṇḍit, Sāstrā Kulukapaṇḍit (Kuluk the wise). Similar to *Mā Yoeṅ*: a story and a proverb (*saṃṇāp yon ṭī*). G.1. MS IB 1018. **T** Plon-Nourrit 1901.

Kumārāṇ by *Suvaṇṇapaññā Chāyā.* Folktale. G.7 (B. Br. M. I. and K.). MS IB 1393. **S** Nhok-Thaem in *KS* 1967. 7: 732 n. 1.

Kumbhajātak. G.10. Prose. **T** Chhim-Soum 1942.

Kūlukapaṇḍit. See *Kulukapaṇḍit.*

Kūn Cau (The children).

(1) See *Cpāp' Kūn Cau.*

(2) By *Kaep* (reference from Roeské 1913: 671).

Kūn Cau bāky cās', Sāstrā Kūn Cau bāky cās' (The children. An old poem). G.5 (Br. K.). MS IB 367. (Different from *Cpāp' Kūn Cau* Cl. and from *Kūn Cau Lpoek.*)

Kūn Cau Lpoek, Sāstrā Kūn Cau Lpoek (The children). 1st 18 stanzas (K.) are the same as those of *Cpāp' paṇṭāṃ pitā*, followed by 48 (K.) stanzas which are not the same, 29 (Br.) stanzas which are the same as those of *Cpāp' Bāky Cās'* and 8 (Br.) stanzas which are not the same. G.5 (K. Br.). MS IB 1405. **T** IB *Cpāp' Phseṅ2* 1967, 1970: 59–76. Cedoreck 1980: 45–55.

Kūn cov khnor nāṃṅ, Satrāh kūn cov khnor nāṃṅ (*Sātrā kūn cau khnor nāṃṅ.* The children. Jackfruit). G.5 (Pou and Haksrea '*Cp.* Gén.') MS AC 344.

Kūn oey kaṃpī (Children, do not . . .). G.5. (Pou and Haksrea '*Cp.* Gén.') MS AC 74 Kūn noey kāṃmbīy.

Laksaṇavaṅs, Rīoeṅ Braḥ Laksaṇavaṅs, written by *Cau Adhikār Vatt Braek Pranāk* in 1890, according to Roeské (1913: 670) and Ly-Théam Teng (1960: 163) but translated from the Siamese by *Prajñādhipati Iem* according to Au Chhieng (1953: 261). G.7 (B.7). MSS IB 675. Complete and partial MSS (in transcription) in Hennecart Collection in BN. AC 2 (parts 1 and 2); 324–7 in roman transcription (Lacsanavong); 148 fragment; 346 (fragment). EFEO 93 Lākkh'sinnavaṅs. **V** MSS AC 331 (10) (résumé of parts 7 and 8) and 331 (14) (résumé of part 18). Bastian 1868: 60–4. Hennecart in Feer 1877: 188–202. Leclère 1911.

Likhit phñoe dau thvāy braḥ M̈ae Yuor Vatī (Letter sent to *Braḥ M̈ae Yuor Vatī*) by Srī Dhammarājā. G.8 (K). **T** *KS* 1938. 8: 103–4. **V** Mak Phœun 1981: 169–71.

Lin Thoṅ, Rīoeṅ or *Sāstrā Lin Thoṅ.* G.7 (B.7). MS IB (no number given by Nhok-Thaem). EFEO 87. Cited by Ray-Buc 1956: 1041 as an old Khmer tale of Buddhist origin and listed by Ly-Théam Teng 1960: 120.

Lokadhammatthacariyā by Ban-Teng. G.10 (poetry). From Ly-Théam Teng 1966: 181.

Lokanăy, Lokanăy bāky kāby (jā rīoeṅ jātak). See *Lokanayapakar(ṇ).*

Lokanăy Dhanañjăy. G.5. (Pou and Haksrea '*Cp.* ne.') MS IB 553.

Lokanayajātak. See *Lokanayapakar(ṇ).*

Lokanayapakar(ṇ), Lokanăy bāky kāby (jā rīoeṅ jātak) (*Lokanăy.* Poem (a *jātak* story)). *Lokanayajātak,* written by Nong in 1794. G.5 (Pou and Haksrea '*Cp.* ne.') and G.7 (B. Bh. Br. K.). MSS IB 142, 553, 1627. **T** Nong 1936–8 and 1942–4 in *KS.* Nong (IB) 1958. **V** Dik-Kéam 1967*b* (in Khmer): 13–17. Khing Hoc Dy 1977*a*: 33–4. **S** Dik-Kéam 1967*b* (in Khmer): 11–13. Khing Hoc Dy 1976: 99.

Lokaneyyajātak. See *Lokanayajātak.*

Lokanītipakar(ṇ) by In. Ly-Théam Teng 1960: 171 is the only source of information on this.

Lokkanaiy, Rīoeṅ Braḥ Lokkanaiy by Nong. G.5 (Pou and Haksrea '*Cp.* ne.'). MS EFEO 113.

Lpoek Ak (The fish-eagle) by *Ṭūṅ*, probably in AD 1837. G.7 (B.7, B.9). This poem ends with the death of the pair of fish-eagles. *Sāstrā Ak*, q.v., uses the *Lpoek Ak* as its beginning but continues with the second female marrying an owl; the second part is almost certainly by *(Yas') Ṅin* or *Lok Pamroe Udăy.* **T** *KS* Ly-Théam Teng ed. 1969: 734–50, 844–60, 970–86, 1249 (1st paragraph). Second part: 1249–59. **S** Chhim-Soum 1968.

Lpoek Aṅgar. See next entry.

Lpoek Aṅgar Vat (The raising (or the story) of Angkor Vat) or *Sātrā Braḥ Ket Mālā.*

(1) Composed by Pang in AD 1620 (as has been argued by Pou 1975: 122–5). G.6 (B. Br. K.). The story of *Rām* told by reference to the friezes at Angkor. MS EFEO 165. SA 39 (12) **T** Aymonier 1878: 267–97. Corbet 19—: 90–100 (abridged). Pierres d'Angkor 1985. **V** Aymonier 1878: 68–84. Moura 1882–3. Pou 1977 (excerpt): 155–66.

(2) *Lpoek Aṅgar Vat paep cās* (An old *Lpoek Aṅgar Vat*) by *Sugandh (Pān. ?)*. G.7? MS SA, Fonds Aymonier 39, vol. IV.

Lpoek ācāry sit (The teacher *Sit*). G.7? MS IB 600.

Lpoek bimbā therī (The nun Bimbā). G.7? MS IB 653.

Lpoek Braḥ Dhamm trās' (The enlightenment) by *(Braḥ Pāḷāt') Bodhirām* possibly in AD 1897. G.7 (B.7). MS IB 1399.

Lpoek Cacak or *Rīoeṅ Cacak* (The jackal)* by Mok. G.7 (B. Br. K.). **T** *PRBK* 4, No. 11. Mok 1970.

Lpoek cpāp' krity kram (Code of principles) by Toet, *Dit.* (Pou and Haksrea '*Cp.* Gén.') G.5 (B.7). **T** Toet in *KS* 1937 and, a separate publication with 86 additional stanzas, in *KS* 1942.

Lpoek cpāp' saṅgh (Code for the Buddhist Community) by Ngoy. G.5 (B.7). **T** *KS* 1937. 7–9: 107–25. This is a different version of *Bāky kāby praṭau jan prus srī*, q.v.

Lpoek doc nịṅ svā (The gibbon and the monkey).* G.7 (B.7). MS IB 1445. **T** and **S** Pruoch-Phoum in *KS* 1967.

Lpoek dūnmān kūn cau cin (Advice to Chinese children) by Ing-Kheng (Pou and Haksrea '*Cp.* Gén.'). G.5 (B.7). **T** Ing-Kheng 1935, 1958.

Lpoek Jetaban, Sāstrā Lpoek Jetaban by *(Anak Ukñā Sodas) Khaek.* Concerns the search for the temple of Jetaban. Written in AD 1815 according to Ly-Théam Teng (1960: 118), in AD 1822 according to Nhok-Thaem (*KS* 1967. 11: 1172). G.7? (K.). MS IB 629.

Lpoek Juc. See *Juc nịṅ Trī.*

Lpoek Jūjak, Sāstrā Lpoek Jūjak. The story of *Jūjak* from the *Vessantarajātak.*

(1) *Lpoek Mahārājapārb* (name of the part of the *Vessantarajātak* which is mainly the story of *Jūjak*) by *Ṭūṅ.* Prose but with rhythm and assonance. The Battambang MS was constantly altered, added to, and made more amusing by the author as he preached it. G.10. **T** Chhim-Soum in *KS* 1968. 8: 877–80 and 9: 990–1007. **S** ibid. 8: 880–2 and 9: 989–90.

(2) MS IB 615. Prose version. G.10. *(Sāstrā) Lpoek Jūjak jān' ṭoem* (original).

(3) MS AC 314 Lpoek Jūjuk. Poetry G.7? Short résumé in Au Chhieng 1953: 257.

Lpoek kaṅ avijjā, Sāstrā Lpoek kaṅ avijjā (Collection against ignorance). Poem on Buddhist theme. G.8 (B.7). MS IB 1399.

Lpoek kābbhyā rīep rāp' brịksā sāt' phaṅ dāṃṅ hlāy (Poem describing all plants and animals). G.7? MS SA Fonds Aymonier B. 39, vol. x.

Lpoek Kākī, Rīoeṅ or *Sāstrā Lpoek Kākī.* See *Kākī.*

Lpoek loṃ vāṃṅ (Surround and enclose or Surround the palace?) MS IB 1635 (5).

Lpoek Madrī. See *Lpoek Medrī.*

Lpoek Madrīparb, Sāstrā. See *Lpoek Medrī.*

Lpoek Mahārājapārb. See *Lpoek Jūjak,* 1.

Lpoek Medrī, Rīoeṅ Lpoek Medrī. The story of *Medrī* from the *Vessantarajātak.*

(1) *(Rīoeṅ) Lpoek Medrī* or *Lpoek Medrīy Pā.* G.7 (B.7). **T** Imprimerie Royale 1930.

(2) *Lpoek Madrīparb, Sāstrā Lpoek Madrīparb* (Section on *Madrī*) G.7 (Br.). MS IB 1376.

(3) *Lpoek Medrīy.* G.7 (K.). MS AC 17.

(4) *Lpoek madrī* by Sunthor Chea. **T** Sunthor Chea 1960.

Lpoek Nāṅ Mān' pāy khum (*Nāṅ Mān'* and Name of a game).* G.7 (B.7). MS IB 641. **T** Pruoch-Phoum 1967.

Lpoek paṭhamasiksā (The first teaching). G.5 (K.). (Pou and Haksrea '*Cp.* Gén.') **T** Héan-Sin in *KS* 1958.

Lpoek phgar lān' (The thunder reverberates). MS IB 643.

Lpoek phgar phtāṃ ktām khyaṅ. See *Ktām.*

Lpoek Pret (The evil spirits) by *Jin P̈ū Huot.* **T** *Jin P̈ū Huot* 1950.

Lpoek rapār ksatr phaendī Uday rāj Aṅg Cand (The king of the land, Udayarāj, Ang Chand) written in AD 1855 by Bejr. The author commemorates the construction of the monastery of Sralau by the lady, Prak, *Prāk'*. G.7. MS 1613.

Lpoek Rīoeṅ Tā Ĥīṅ (Story of Grandfather *Ĥīṅ*) by *Ṭūṅ*. No MS or **T** but Chhim-Soum remembered that it was amusing. *Tūṅ* lived with *Tā Ĥīṅ* in his old age. The poem is a description of all the things that have to be done to deal with *Tā Ĥīṅ's* illness and deformity. G.8. **S** Chhim-Soum 1968.

Lpoek sā săbd, Sāstrā Lpoek sā săbd (Expressions). Theme: pure love. G.8 (B.7, Bh. K.). MS IB 615.

Lpoek Sīl prāṃ (The five precepts) by Nong. G.8 (K.). **T** ed. Ly-Théam Teng 1970.

Lpoek srae vaeṅ (The long ricefield). Song in the form of question and answer between boys and girls about meeting at *Srae Vaeṅ.* Not complete. G.2. MS IB 708.

Lpoek Srīvijăy, composed by *Baññ Vicitr Srī* in 1858, according to Ly-Théam Teng 1960: 119. G.7. MS EFEO 58.

Lpoek stec cām (The Cham king). MS IB 1635 (3).

Lpoek svā, Sāstrā Lpoek svā (The monkey).* G.7 (K.). MS IB 631.

Luḥ pān ghoeñ lāy vād ūn ṭal' (When I saw your letter arrive) by *V.N.R.* G.8 (B.7). **T** in *KS* 1939. 4–6: 111.

Maggaliphal, Rīoeṅ Maggaliphal. G.7. MS EFEO 92. Cited by Ly-Théam Teng 1960: 120.

Maha Chinok. See *Mahājanakajātak.*

Mahābhārat. G.10. Prose. **T** Krasem in *KS* 1929–32. (Translation from Thai version.)

Mahādhammapadajātak. MS AC 281 Dhammapad (incomplete).

Mahājaṃbūradhipatīy. See *Jambūpatither.*

Mahājanakajātak. G.10. MSS AC 270 Mahājinuk. 311 Jīnuk (beginning of 270). **V** Leclère 1906.

Mahājāt. See *Mahāvessantarajātak.*

Mahājāt(k), Gambīr Mahājāt(k) by *Ṭūṅ*. See *Mahāvessantarajātak.*

Mahājinuk. See *Mahājanakajātak.*

Mahājuṃmbūr. See *Jambūpatither.*

Mahānāradakassapajātak. G.10. MSS AC 182 Nārat brahm. AC 191 Nāraddhabraṃhm AC 283 (same as 182) Nāratth braṃmm. **T** You-Oun 1960.

Mahāneti, Sāstrā Mahāneti by *Braḥ Sugandh mān puṇy.* G.5 (K.). MS IB 642.

Mahāsammativaṅs by (Sou) Seth. Unpublished poem. See Khuon Sokhamphu 1973: 9.

Mahāsupassītāpas by Nou-Kan. Work listed by Ly-Théam Teng 1960: 177.

Mahāummaggajātak. See *Mahosathajātak.*

Mahāvessantarajātak, Mahājāt(k) possibly by Ang Duong, as Ly-Théam Teng says (1960: 119), because traditionally known as 'Ang Duong's'. G.10. MSS AC 36, 178, 268, 302, 323 Mahājāt (all same text). AC 37 (different from the others). AC 38, 39 (incomplete). AC 40 Mahārājjapār (only the section so named). EFEO 36, 37 (both only *khsae* 1). The 'Battambang MS' was very much altered by *Ṭūṅ*. He cut out all the Thai words and made the work more entertaining. (See Chhim-Soum in *KS* 1968: 2.) **T** Nhok-Thaem 1960, 1964, 1969. Huffman and Proum 1977 (extract): 298–304 (vocabulary 305–8). **V** Leclère 1895, 1902. Huffman and Proum (in Khmer) 1977: 298. **S** Nhok-Thaem 1960: i–xi. Léang-Hap An 1967*a*. The *Ānisaṅgh Mahājātak* is entered separately.

Mahosathajātak, Mahosut, Mahosuth (also spelt *Mahosuṭṭh).* Pali text called *Mahāummaggajātak.* Popularized with the title, *Sek Sārikā* (The parrot and the Myna bird) or *Sek Som Paṇḍit,* Le perroquet doué de sagesse (The wise *Paloeornis Cyanocephalus*).

(1) *G.10. Prose. MSS AC 200, 269 (same texts). AC 32, 33, 60, 61, 167 are all fragments. EFEO 35 and (*khsae* 1) 105. **T** Im-Phon 1960–3 in *KS*. IB 1962. **V** Moura (extracts) 1883.

(2) *Sek Sārikā, Sātrā /Rīoeṅ Sek Sārikā, Sek Som niṅ Srakā.** G.7 (B.7). *(Rīoeṅ) Sek Sārikā* is said by Chhim-Soum (*KS* 1968. 2: 189–92) to be by *Ṭūṅ* and by Ing-Yeng (1972 preface) to be by *(Yodhāranind) Vän'* but the author's name *(Anak Okñā Prajñādhipatī) Kaev* forms part of the text both in Au Chhieng's MS, Sek Som Mundit, and in the Plon-Nourrit edition. G.7 (B.7). MSS AC 227. EFEO P13. **T** Plon-Nourrit 1900. Kambujavarokās 1912. **S** Chhim-Soum in *KS* 1968. 2: 192–4 and **T** of first two stanzas from memory.

(3) *Sek Som Paṇḍit* by Kim-Hak. The wise parrot is distressed at the poor behaviour of monks and men but is reassured of the worth of the Buddhist way of life by a god. G.5 (Br. K.). (Pou and Haksrea '*Cp.* Gén.') **T** BR 1933, IB 1953, 1965.

Manuel de morale pratique. G.5. (Pou and Haksrea '*Cp.* Gén.') MS AC 76 (2).

Manuss yoeṅ neḥ uttam ṭoy kaṃnoet (We humans are great through our birth) by Ban-Teng. G.7 (B.8). **T** Ly-Théam Teng 1960: 182–3.

Maranamata. See next entry.

Maraṇamātā (Death of a mother)* composed by *Ûk* 1 in AD 1877. Translated from the Pali (Cetanābuddho) G.7 (B. Bh. Br. K.). MS EFEO 86 Maranāk Māṭā. **T** By-Sovann ed. 1959–60 in *KS*. *Ûk* 1959. IB 1961. Govid 19—. Mith Yoeng 19—. **V** Monod 1943: 161–99. Vandy-Kaonn 1981: 35–6. **S** Lay-Kry in *KS* 1965: 748–59.

Mā Yoeṅ (Our uncle)* G.7 (B. Bh. Br. K.). **T** Aymonier 1878: 255–66. Plon-Nourrit 1902. *KS* 1943. 11: 607–15. 1944. 1: 25–45. Corbet 19—: 62–73. *Bejj* 1959: 106–41. *Nuon Nārī* 1960. IB 1961. *PRBK* 4, No. 4, 1963. Seng-Nguon Huot 1965. Huffman and Proum 1977 (2 extracts from IB text: 18–21 and 33–5): 220–4 (vocabulary 224–6). V Aymonier 1878: 64–8. Pavie 1903: 79–94. Khing Hoc Dy 1977: 18–21. Vandy-Kaonn 1981: 75–6.

Māgh Mānab, Sāstrā Māgh Mānab (The young man of Aquarius) by *Uden.* Copied in AD 1927. Buddhist view of Indra, his birth, etc. G.8? (B. Bh. Br. K.) MS IB 650.

Mālaiy debb ther (Mālaiy the divine monk). G.10. MSS AC 199, 301. EFEO 118 Mālai. **V** Au Chhieng 1953: 166.

Mās me sne(h) snaṅ. See *Mitr me sne(h) snaṅ.*

Māyār Srī (The wiles of women).* G.1. **T** *PRBK* 1, No. 6. Chhung-Nguon Huot 1964.

Milindapañhā (The questions of *Milind*). G.10. MSS AC 55 Nāgasen, 204 Kruṅ malin cot tantiṅ braḥ nāggasèn (King *Milind* asks questions of *Nāgasen*). AC 205. Nāggasen chloey (Nāgasen answers). EFEO 134 Kruṅ Milind. **T** BR 1929–34. Oum-Sou in *KS* (3) 1930–2. IB 1942, 1963.

Mitr me sne(h) snaṅ. 1st line of *Likhit phñoe dau thvāy braḥ M̈ae Yuor Vatī*, q.v.

Moha-Chinok. See *Mahājanakajātak.*

Morale pratique. Fragment. G.5. (Pou and Haksrea '*Cp.* gén.') MS AC 162.

Mtec ḷoey raḥ krom boḥ anṭoek (How can it appear beneath the Turtle's Stomach (Name of a star)?) by (*Braḥ Aṅg Mcās' Ksatrī) Sraûk.* G.8 (B.7). **T** *KS* 1939. 7–9: 211.

Mucalind, Muccalind, Muccalin, or *Cand Gorab* (also spelt *Gorap, Gurop,* or *Goram*)* written by *S-āt* or *Saṃ-āt* in AD 1833. G.7 (B. Bh. Br. K.). MSS IB 577. AC 328 (3). E 50. **T** Braḥ Cand gorub. Nāṅ Mucalīn. Plon-Nourrit 1903. **V** Moura (extracts) 1883. Au Chhieng 1953: 264. Vandy-Kaonn 1981: 26–7.

Muoy ray hā-sip muoy thṅai nau māt' Jhūṅ Samudd Sīem (151 days by the Gulf of Siam) by Kim-Hak. G.7 (B.7). **T** *KS* 1932 (4). 7–12: 419–29.

Mūgapakkhajātak. Alternative title for *Temiyajātak,* q.v.

M̈

M̈oṅ prāṃ puon juon raḷik nịk dau ṭal' (9 o'clock! My thoughts go to you) by Mok. G.8 (B.9). **T** *KS* 1939. 5: 112–13.

Na-mo. See *Namo.*

Naen Kaev (Novice *Kaev*). G.7. AC 331 (9) Nèn Kaev.

Namaskār. Song by Srey-Ou. G.2. **T** IB 1951.

Namo (Na-mo), Sāstrā Namo (Na-mo) by *Camt(n),* written in AD 1858. G.5 (Br. K.). MS IB 1424.

Nāgasen, Nāggasena chloey. See *Milindapañhā. Nānajātak knuṅ Dhammapadatthakathā* (Various *jātak* from the Dhammpadatthakathā). Translation from Pali to Khmer prose. G.10. **T** Chhim-Soum 1939, 1953.

Nāṅ Bīrṭanṭap'. See *Rathasenajātak.*

Nāṅ Hsān ṭāk (Jeanne d'arc). *Bāky kāby* by Ban-Teng.

Nāṅ kaev kākī. Beginning of a verse-novel. G.7. MS AC 166.

Nāṅ Kaṅrī. See *Rathasenajātak.*

Nāṅ Kākī. See *Kākī.*

Nāṅ Mān', Sāstrā Nāṅ Mān', or *Nāṅ Mān' pāy khum.* See *Lpoek Nāṅ Mān' pāy khum.*

Nāṅ Raṃsāy sak' (*Nāṅ* Let-her-hair loose).* G.1. **T** *PRBK* 5 *Rīoeṅ Bhnaṃ Saṃbau* (*Saṃbau* Hill): 142–7. **V** Pavie (Néang Roum Say sock) 1898: 1–16. 1903: 25–47. IB 196–

Nāṅ Vimāncand. See *Vimān Cand.*

Nāraddhabraṃhm, Nārat brahm, Nāratth braṃmm. See *Mahānāradakassapajātak.*

Nāvaṇ, Braḥ Pād Nāvaṇ (King *Nāvaṇ*). G.7 (B. Bh. Br. K.). MSS AC Nāvan. 176, 230. EFEO 84 Nāvān'. **T** Plon-Nourrit 1903.

Néavon. See *Nāvaṇ.*

Néang Kakey. See *Kākī.*

Néang Pidandap. See *Rathasenajātak.*

Neang Roum Say Sock. See *Nāṅ Raṃsāy sak'.*

Neḥ sārā sūrivaṅs baṅs trai căkr (This is a letter from *Sūrivaṅs*, scion of the three wheels of power). Written 'In reply to *L.A.N.*' by Prince Yukanthor. G.8 (B.9). **T** *KS* 1939. 4–6: 109–10.

Nen Mās rī Suvaṇṇ bilāp (Novice *Mās* or *Suvaṇṇ* weeps) by *Ṭūṅ.* Description of children's games. G.8 (Br. K.). **T** (2 stanzas) *KS* 1968. 3: 330–1. **S** Chhim-Soum in *KS* 1968. 3: 329–31.

Ngoh, Ngos. See *Khyaṅ Săṅkh.*

Nibvān Pariyāy (Nirvāna explained). On the power of Buddhism. G.8? (Br.) MS IB 669.

Nigrodh Amṛit. (The immortal figtree). Prose preaching style. Based on a *jātak.* G.10. MS IB 1052.

Niméa-réach-chéadak. See *Nimirāj.*

Nimijātak. See *Nimirāj.*

Nimirāj (Nimirājj, Nīmarājj). Prose version of a *jātak.* G.10. MSS AC 263 (313, 349 incomplete). EFEO 30 Nimmarāj. **V** Leclère: 1906: 225–74. **S** ibid. 221–4.

Nirās Nagar vatt, Bāky kāby. See *Kāby Nirās Aṅgar.*

Nirās Hoṅkoṅ (A journey to Hongkong). G.7? MS EFEO 141.

Nītisāstr (bāky kāby) (A book on the law. Poem.) by Him, *Ĥim.* G.5. (Pou and Haksrea '*Cp.* ne.') **T** Him in *KS* 1935. 1–2: 25–36.

Nịṅ thlaeṅ vitakk duk knuṅ prāṇ (I will explain the thoughts which are within me) by *(Nāy) Dadim Krum Hat Lịk.* G.8 (B.7). **T** *KS* 1939. 5: 115–16.

Nouveaux conseils aux enfants. See *Cpāp' lpoek thmī.*

O p-ūn sṅuon beñ saṃlāñ' snit (O my sweetheart, so close to me) by Srī Dhammarājā. G.8 (B.7). **T** *KS* 1939. 1: 41–2.

O saen sranoḥ campā khaek (O how I miss the Malayan *Michelia*) by a 19th-century court poet. G.8 (B.7). **T** *KS* 1939. 5: 116–17.

O saṃlāñ' añ ralk ṭek min lak' (O my love, I miss you and am sleepless) by Ang Duong. G.8 (B.9.). **T** *KS* 1939. 5: 106.

Oḥ o kamm aniccā (O pitiful fate!] by Uong. G.8 (B.6, Br. K.). **T** *KS* 1940. 11: 66–7; 12: 55–62.

On praṇnaṃ (Bow and salute). G.5. (Pou and Haksrea '*Cp*. Gén.') MS SA (E 18c).

L'origine d'Angkor. See *Lpoek Aṅgar Vat.*

Ovād mātā (Advice from a mother) by *Am Ḍīoek.* G.5. (Pou and Haksrea '*Cp.* Gén.') **T** *Am Ḍīoek* in *KS* 1956: 656–60.

Ovād Nārī (Advice to a young lady] by Ban-Teng. G.5? Vandy-Kaonn says it was published in 1946.

Oy bar caṅ taiy (I give my blessing as your hands are joined (with a thread)). Good wishes for a future wife. G.8. MS AC 133.

Pad añjoeñ grū (Poem inviting the guru). Invitation to a mediating spirit to enter a medium. G.8. **T** Huffman and Proum (with vocabulary) 1977: 106–7.

Pad bol rīoeṅ lkhon phseṅ2 (Various plays) by Ang Duong. Ly-Théam Teng includes this title in his list of works by Ang Duong (1960: 148)

Pad Uṃ Dūk (Boat songs) G.2. Various poems have this title. Many were based on the poem by King Norodom. **T** Gironcourt 1941. Dik-Kéam in *KS* 1964. 10 (King Norodom's): 1088–99 and 11 (others): 1163–7. **S** Dik-Kéam in *KS* 1964. 9: 994–8.

Pad yaṃ yām Braḥ Karuṇā Braḥ Pād Saṃtec Braḥ Narottam jā aṃmcās' phaen ṭī kram kambujā (Elegy for King Norodom) by *Anak Mātā Phaÿam.* G.8 (Br. 4 × 4). **T** *KS* 1939. 7–9: 213–20. Corbet 19—: 117–23.

Padumasuriyavaṅs, Krāṃṅ Braḥ Padumasuriyavaṅs. Source: Khmer folktale. G.7 (B.7). MS IB 1261. Nhok-Thaem suggests (*KS* 1965. 10: 1071) that, as they are all on the same *krāṃṅ*, *Braḥ Anuruddh saṅkhep, Dibv Saṅvār* and *Cakravaṅs* may be by the same poet as *Padumasuriyavaṅs.*

Pantūl sārabej (Instruction in divine knowledge). G.5? MS AC 53 Manuel de morale pratique.

Pañasā Sirasā or *Sīrasā.* See *Puññasār Sirsā.*

Paññāsajātak samrāy (Translation and commentary on the 50 *jātak*) by Em, Oum-Sou, and Long. Khmer prose versions. G.10. **T** IB 1944–62 (25 *jātak*). See also Em, Oum-Sou, Long, and Him for individual **V** of *jātak.*

Paññāsajātak saṅkhep (The 50 *jātak* abbreviated). Khmer prose versions by Nhok-Thaem. G.10. **T** Nhok-Thaem 1963.

Paṇṭāṃ bālī (Recommendations of *Bālī*) by Méas 1. G.5. (Pou and Haksrea '*Cp.* Gén.') **T** Méas in *KS* 1943: 309–13.

Paṇṭāṃ Kram N̈uy (Recommendations by Kram Ngoy) (by Ngoy). G.5. (Pou and Haksrea '*Cp.* Gén.') **T** Kim-Seng 19—. BR 1932, 1933. Ly-Théam Teng 1964. Khing Hoc Dy and Jacqueline Khing 1978: 150–74 (even-numbered pp.). **V** ibid. 151–75 (odd-numbered pp.) **S** ibid. 141–9, 176–81. **V S** Cedoreck 1981 (reprint with introduction in Khmer as well as French).

Paṇṭāṃ mātā (Recommendations of a mother). G.5. (Pou and Haksrea '*Cp.* Gén.') **T** Ou-Srey ed. in *KS* 1949. 11.

Paṇṭāṃ seṭṭhī (Recommendations of a wealthy man). Manuel d'économie domestique et rurale, by *(Samtec Braḥ Sugandhādhipatī) P̈ān.* G.9? (From Roeské 1913: 671.)

Paṇṭāṃ tā mās, Rīoeṅ paṇṭāṃ Tā Mās (Recommendations of Grandfather Méas) written AD 1828 by Méas 2. G.5. **T** Méas 1908 (under direction of Leclère).

Patham sambodhi (The beginning of the Enlightenment).

(1) Work composed in Bangkok under the supervision of Phra Paramanuxit Xinarot. (G. Maspero 1929: 298 and Ray-Buc 1956: 937). **V** Leclère 1906: 13–114.

(2) *Patham Sambodhi. Bāky Kāby,* Le grand départ du Bodhisattva pour atteindre la Bodhi (Poem) by In. **T** In in *KS* 1934. 10–12: 5–38. G.10 (B.7).

Paṭhamakakā or *Braḥ Dharmakakā* (*Kathā,* not *kakā*? First discourse or Discourse on the Dhamma) by *(Cau Bañā Gajendranassakār) Suor* (or *Sūr*) or *Lok Grū Vinăyadhar Prāk nām Chāyā. Suvaṇṇ paññā.* On Buddhism. G.8? (K.) MS IB 632 (full of mistakes).

Pārāṃṅ appalakkh(ṇ). See *Bāky kāby cār.*

Pārāṃṅ pāřo cor upalakkh(ṇ) (O Frenchman, wretched thief) by Mok, (1 stanza, improvised) G.8 (B.8). **T** Khing Hoc Dy 1981: 142. **V** ibid. from Collard (1925: 38).

(Le) Perroquet doué de sagesse. See *Mahosathajātak.*

Ph-ūk phgar. See *Ktām.*

Phcañ' Mār (Defeating Māra). Versified account of the Buddha's struggle against Māra. G.10. MS AC 35. EFEO 135 Phceñ mār.

Phgar phtāṃ ktām (khyaṅ). See *Ktām.*

Phkā rāṃ dịk rāṃ. See *Dịk rāṃ phkā rāṃ.*

Phkāy seḥ raḥ krom phkāy kūn mān' (The horse-star shines under the Pleiades) by *(Braḥ Aṅg Mcās' Ksatrī) Sraûk.* G.8 (B.7). **T** *KS* 1939. 7–9: 210.

Phkul oey phkul oey phkul phkā pupphā brai (O Mimusops elengi, O Mimusops elengi, flower of the forest). G.8 (B.9). **T** *KS* 1939. 6: 182–3.

Pịṅ Trapaek, Rīoeṅ Pịṅ Trapaek (Guava Lake). G.9. **T** *PRBK* 1963. 6, No. 17: 127–32 (text is taken from MS of Royal Chronicles in IB).

Poèmes consacrés à la Glorification du Triple Joyau. See *Secktī raṃlịk ṭās'* (or *ṭaḥ*) *tīoen.*

Ponhasa Siresa. See *Puññasār Sirsā.*

Prajuṃ Subhāsit khmaer tām laṃṭāp'aksar, Recueil des proverbes k'mèr par ordre alphabétique, by Nhok-Thaem. G.3. **T** Nhok-Thaem in *KS* 1943 and 1944.

Prasnā Ṭaṅkūv, Sāstrā Prasnā Ṭaṅkūv (Riddles of the worm). Source: possibly 50 *jātak,* says Nhok-Thaem. G.8? (K.) MS IB 627.

Praṭau citt (Educating the heart) by Hang-Kéo. G.5 (B.7). (Pou and Haksrea '*Cp.* Gén.') **T** Hang-Kéo in *KS* 1943.

Pravatti sruk pārāy (The story of Baray). Part of Chronicles. G.9. **T** Eng-Soth in *KS* 1966. 12: 1288–97.

Préah, Préas. See *Braḥ.*

Préceptes nouveaux pour l'édification. See *Cpāp' lpoek thmī.*

Préceptes pour l'instruction des hommes et des femmes. See *Cpāp' dūnmān jan prus srī.*

Puñ sār. See next entry.

*Puññasār Sirsā, Sāstrā Puññasār Sirsā** written by Nong in AD 1797. Source: the 50 *jātak.* G.7 (B. Bh. Br. K.). MSS AC 343. IB 593, 594. EFEO 76. **T** Plon-Nourrit 1905. Guesdon (extract of part 5 only) 1906. **V** Guesdon (extract of part 5 only) 1906. Dik-Kéam (in Khmer) 1967*b*: 24–7. Khing Hoc Dy 1990: 166–70. **S** Dik-Kéam ibid. 18–24. Khing Hoc Dy ibid. 166.

Puras cāk' smugr (The man who wove boxes). Forms part of the tale, *Daṃbaek 4 nāk'* (Four Bald Men). G.1. **T** *KS* 1935. 2: 69–71. *PRBK* 2, No. 17. **V** Martini and Bernard 1946: 190–2.

Purāṇasubhāsit (Old sayings). G.5. (Pou and Haksrea '*Cp.* Gén.') **T** *KS* 1946. 8: 393–5.

Putthisen. See *Rathasenajātak.*

Pūbit mahārāj. See *Cpāp' Trīneti* 1.

Raja Baṅsāvatār Kruṅ Kambujā (*Raxa Phoṅsāvadan Krung Komphuxa*) (Chronicles of Cambodia) G.9. G. Maspero (1929: 301) gives this as title of Mok's recension of the Cambodian Chronicles, published in the Corpus Siamois (Corpus des Annales siamoises?) in Bangkok. He does not say it was a translation into Thai but see *Rapāl ksatr.* Khing Hoc Dy (1981*a*: 143) reminds us that Mok wrote the legendary part.

Rapā ksatr, Rīoeṅ Rapā ksatr (Chronicles of the kings) written by *Braḥ Padum Pāramī Bejr* in AD 1818. G.7. (Ly-Théam Teng 1960: 118.) Is possibly the same work as the next entry.

Rapā ksatr sruk khmaer, Sāstrā rapā ksatr sruk khmaer (Chronicles of the kings of Cambodia) written by *Braḥ Padum Pāramī* (*Bejr*).

Probably afer AD 1835; 1868 is suggested by Nhok-Thaem (in *KS* 1968. 5: 544). Story of Cambodia in the reigns of Ang Eng, Ang Chan, and Ang Duong. G.7 (B. Bh. Br. K.). MS IB 1446.

Rapā ksatr sruk khmaer (Chronicles of Cambodia). Probably after AD 1835. Story of reign of Ang Chan. Poem. MS IB 1049. (May be same as last entry.)

Rapāl ksatr (Chronicles of the kings) by Nong. Written between AD 1813 and 1818. Deals with the period AD 1713–1818. G.9. MSS AC 3, 4. DL/2 Robāl khsăt with Papiers Doudart de Lagrée. In roman. B39/12/B. Rapāl khsāt. 2 texts in exercise books at SA. AC 3.4. **V** DL/2 Garnier 1871–2. de Villemereuil 1883: 21–57. **S** Dik-Kéam 1967*b*: 54–6. He says this was the document translated into Thai (under Mok's supervision), French, and Vietnamese.

Rathasenajātak. One of the 50.*

(1) The full story. *Rīoeṅ Buddhisaen,* Putthisen. G.7 (B. Bh. Br. K. MJ). MS AC 12. EFEO 63. Rattasaen. **T** Plon-Nourrit 1901. IB 1959, 1964, 1966. Rasmei Kampuchea *(Nāṅ Kaṅrī Ṛddhisaen).* 1963.

(2) A prose version of the story known as *Nāṅ Bīrṭaṇṭap'* (The twelve girls) or *Nāṅ Kaṅrī* (Miss Kangrei). G.1. **T** Pavie 1898. 1: 325–34 (difficult script). Corbet 19—: 45–57. *PRBK* 5, No. 16. **V** Pavie 1898. 1: 27–51 and 1969 (IB reprint).

Rājakrity aṃpāl ksatr (Royal decree for all kings). Hymns for the king, partly in verse. G.8, in part. MS AC 57 Rājakrīt aṃpāl khsatr.

Rājakrity kram phseṅ2, Braḥ rājakrity kram phseṅ2 (Various royal decrees). Prose. Law. Written in the reign of King Chey Chettha, 16th century. See Ly-Théam Teng 1960: 119.

*Rājakul** written by *Varapaññā* in the 18th–19th century. Dik-Kéam (1967*b*: 52) says French texts mistakenly attribute this work to Nong G.7. MSS EFEO 88. IB 558. **T** Dik-Kéam in *KS* 1971. 2: 155–70; 3: 237–50; 4: 370–91. **V** Khing Hoc Dy 1977: 26 and 1990: 193-5 **S** Guesdon 1906: 804–16. Dik-Kéam 1967*b*: 52–4. Khing Hoc Dy 1990: 195.

Rājaneti. See *Cpāp' Rājaneti.*

Rājanibandh rāmakerti, Braḥ rājanibandh rāmakerti. See *Rāmakerti* 4.

Rājanīti (The conduct of the king's affairs). G.5. (Pou and Haksrea *'Cp.* ne.'). **T** BR 1941.

Rājanītisātth (*Sāstrā* on the conduct of the king's affairs) by Nau. Mid-19th century.

Rājasabd Bāky kāby, Sāstrā Rājasabd Bāky kāby (Royal language. Poem) written by Srī Dhammarājā in AD 1630. (Nhok-Thaem says that this title is erroneous and that something like *Subhāsit Bāky Kāby* (Sayings. Poem) would be more suitable.) G.5 (K.) with some prose at the end. MS IB 1369.

Rājasuostī, Sāstrā Rājasuostī, or *Rājasuostīy muntriy.* See *Suostī* Cl.

Rājasūbhā (Royal judge). G.5. (Pou and Haksrea '*Cp.* Gén.') **T** Plon-Nourrit 1901.

Rāmaker(ti), Rāmker, Reamker.

(1) The 'classical' text. G.6 (*Rāmakerti* I Bol, B. Br. K. *Rāmakerti* II B.6). MSS AC 49 (parts 3 and 4). 58 (fragment), 172. EFEO 94. Very short MS of *Trabāṃṅ seḥ* Rām Ker 1(*krāṃṅ*). **T** IB 1936–62. Pou 1979 and 1982. **V** Moura (part) 1883. Martini 1938, 1949*a*, *b*, 1950, 1952, 1955, 1961, 1978. Pou 1977, 1977, 1982. Jacob 1986. **S** Martini 1950, 1952. *Om Nāgrī* 1964. Léang-Hap An 1966. Pou 1975, 1977 (both EFEO publications), 1980, 1981, 1983, 1987. Pou, Lan Sunnary, and Haksrea 1981.

(2) A popular text. Prose. G.6. **T** Bizot 1973 (Recorded from memory by Mi Chak *(Tā Cak'))* Piat (review) 1974. Pou (review) 1976. **V** and **S** Bizot 1989.

(3) A popular text recorded orally by *Tā Krūṭ*. Prose. The subject of a thesis by Daniel, 1982.

(4) A long prose text compiled by Vijjādhar. G.6. T Dik-Kéam 1964–7, 1964–5.

(In Genres *Lpoek Aṅgar Vat* is discussed as a *Rāmakert(i)* text too.)

Rīoeṅ. See under next word unless the next word is *Braḥ*, in which case see under the third word.

Roman versifié. G.9. MS AC 300 (*re* revolt of Prince *Vathā*. Incomplete).

Rothisen, Rottisên. See *Rathasenajātak.*

'Royal Annals of the History of Cambodia'. G.9. (Photographed text of the palace chronicle from the earliest days until 1863. Books 1–16.) SOAS MS 78740, M 1045.

Royal Annals, Royal Chronicles. See Chronique(s) royale(s).

Ṛddhisaen. See *Rathasenajātak.*

Sabbasiddhi. See *Sabvasiddhi.*

Sabbhamitt. Extra-canonical *jātak*; one of the '50', *Javasakuṇajātak.* G.10. MS AC 197.

Sabd phgar (The sound of thunder) by *Tūṅ*. When it thunders, the young men watch the girls run for shelter to the huts, hoping that only one girl will be in a hut but they are disappointed; several are there. Composed at the request of one, *Koet,* whose marriage fell through. G.8 (B.7, K.). **T** Chhim-Soum (from memory) in *KS* 1968. 7: 763–6. **S** Chhim-Soum *KS* 1968. 7: 763–7.

*Sabvasiddhi, Rīoeṅ Sabvasiddhi** written in 1899 by Tan (also called *Mīn* from his title *Mīn Bhakti Aksar*). Preface to IB edition says the *jātak* in the 50 of the same title is not the same story. G.7 (B.7, 8, and 9). MS IB 581. **T** Corbet (extract) 19—: 197–204. Bou-Po in *KS* 1959. *Mīn* (ed. Bouth Neang) 1959. *Mīn* (ed. Seng Nguon Huot) 1960. IB 1962, 1966, 1969. Huffman and Proum 1977 (extract): 289–94, vocabulary 295–7. **V** Huffman and Proum 1977 (in Khmer): 289. Vandy-Kaonn 1981: 38–9. **S** Dik-Kéam 1967*b*: 48–52.

Saek som nīñ srakā. See *Mahosathajātak.*

Saen dukkh domanass as' saṅghim (I am melacholy in the extreme and without hope) by *Anak Mātā Phaÿam.* G.8 (B.7). **T** *KS* 1939. 7–9: 211.

Saing Selchey. See *Săṅkh Silp Jăy.*

Sam-āt phcit phcaṅ' (Clean it up and make it spick and span) by Ngoy. Concerns farmwork. G.8 (K.). **T** Ly-Théam Teng 1960: 196–7.

Sammodamānājātak. G.10. **T** Nhéan-Chhin in *KS* 1962. 3: 300–5.

Samuddh, Rīoeṅ Braḥ Samuddh (also spelt *Samudh, Samudr, Sūmutr,* and *Sūputr).*

(1) Written in 1808 by Nong. Source: 50 *jātak.** G.7 (B.7, 9). MSS IB 1373 (date and author given in text). AC 1, 171. **V** and **S** Dik-Kéam 1967*b*: 41–8 and 39–41.

(2) Dik-Kéam says (1967: 40) that the poem was written twice, once with the metres B, Br., and K. and once with metre B.7, as required by King Ang Duong. He suggests that the first may have been written in Ang Chand's reign. However, if the B.7 one is to be thought to be 1. above, the date is not during Ang Duong's reign! G.7.

Samuddhaghos. One of the 50 *jātak.* G.10. MS AC 232. EFEO 40.

Samuddhaghosa, Sāstrā Braḥ Sammudhaghosa: written in AD 1818, by *(Anak Okñā Prajñādhipatī) Kaev.* Source: the 50 *jātak*. G.7 (B. Bh. Br. K.). MS IB 671. Nhok-Thaem praises the vocabulary and rhymes but says the MS is much mutilated.

Samudr, Krāṃṅ Braḥ Samudr. Source: folktale. G.7 (B.7). MS IB 1261. Nhok-Thaem suggests (*KS* 1965: 1071) that, as they are all on the same *krāṃṅ,* the following may be by the same poet as *Braḥ*

Samudr: *Padumasuriyavaṅs*, *Dibv Saṅvār*, *Cakravaṅs*, and *Anuruddh saṅkhep*.

Sandhiyā nā knuṅ thṅai ādity (At dusk on Sunday) by Uong. G.8 (B.7). **T** *KS* 1940. 3: 63–6; 4: 59–63; 5: 85–90; 6: 67–75; 8: 65–70.

Sang, Préas Sang. See *Săṅkh Silp Jăy*.

Sang Thong. See *Săṅkh Silp Jăy*.

*Săṅkh Silp Jăy** written in AD 1882. Ly-Théam Teng (1960: 32) claims that it was by (*Ukñā Vaṅsādhipatī*) *Ûk* but Vandy-Kaonn (1981: 37) expresses his surprise at the claim. G.7 (B. Bh. Br. K. PK). MSS AC 15 (incomplete), 175. EFEO 51 Sṅaṃ Sil Jai. **T** Tec-Hong 19—. IB 1962, 1966. Librairie Phnom Penh 1964. **V** Leclère 1895: 201–93. Pavie 1921. Maspero 1928–30. 3: 305. Mathers 1929 (part).

Saṅvāt, *Rīoeṅ Braḥ Saṅvāt*. G.7. Mentioned by Ly-Théam Teng 1960: 120.

Sappurisadharm 7 prakār. *Bāky kāby* (7 virtues of the sage) translated into verse from the Pali by Ban-Teng. G.10 (B.8). **T** IB 1953. Ban-Teng in *KS* 1969. 9: 1002–12.

Sarsoer Braḥ Pād chveṅ stāṃ, *Sāstrā Sarsoer Braḥ Pād chveṅ stāṃ* (In praise of kings, left and right) Buddhist theme. G.8 (K.). MS IB 1376.

Sarsoer Braḥ Rasmī (In praise of the Light). Old poem. G.10 (Br. B.7). **T** Ith-Hak ed. in *KS* 1943. 7.

Sarsoer Guṇ Mātā, *Sāstrā Sarsoer Guṇ Mātā* (In praise of a mother's goodness). On traditions. G.8 (Br. K.). MS IB 633.

Sarsoer Hemant, *Kāby Nirās Sarsoer Hemant*. See *Kaṃṇāby sarsoer hemantamās*.

Sasoer prathabīy (In praise of the earth). Poésie célébrant la gloire de la terre. G.8. MS AC 83.

Satra du Roi Chea-Ly. See *Mahāvessantarajātak*.

Satra Prèah Ket Méaléa. *See Lpoek Aṅgar Vat*.

Satv cīem dāṃṅ bīr cuḥ ŝī smau (2 sheep came down to eat the grass) by Mok (1 stanza, improvised). G.8 (B.7). **T** Nhok-Thaem in *KS* 1957: 147. **T** and **V** Khing Hoc Dy 1981: 140.

Sāmajātak. G.10. MS AC 272 Sīyāmm. Khmer version in prose. **V** Sunseng Sunkimmeng 1980.

Sārā sā rīem sūm suor citt (May I ask in this letter about your feelings?) by a 19th-century court poet. G.8 (B.7). **T** *KS* 1939. 5: 114–15.

Sārālikhit nịk khịṅ citt likhit sār (Your letter made me angry, your letter) by (*Okñā Narā Ksatr*) Tan. G.8 (B.7, 8, and 9). **T** *KS* 1939. 4–6: 183–96.

Sārānusār jeṭṭhā anak (My letters to you) by Yukanthor. G.8 (B.7). **T** *KS* 1939. 4–6: 107–8.

Sāstrā, Sātrā. See under next word unless this is *Braḥ* or *Braḥ Pād*, in which case, see under following word.

Sāvatār jāti (The story of our race). G.2. Song by Srey-Ou and Nhoung-Sœung. **T** IB 1951.

Sāvatār vatt saṃpuk (The Chronicle of *Saṃpuk* monastery). A family chronicle. G.9. **T** in transcription (and facsimile of MS), **V** and **S** Tranet 1983.

Sdech Khméng. See *Stec Kmeṅ.*

Secktī Ariyasatthā, Sāstrā Secktī Ariyasatthā. See *Cpāp' Ariyasatthā.*

Secktī Cpāp' Kram. See *Cpāp' Kram.*

Secktī Gambīr Cpāp' Kram (On the text of the *Cpāp' Kram*). Text of *Cpāp' Kram*, Cl., G.5 (K.), and prose explanation. MS IB 1377.

Secktī Kram Cpāp' (On principles). G.5 (K.). MS IB 667. (Not *Cpāp' Kram* Cl. according to the beginning and end of the poem given in the description of the MS in *KS* 1967. 7: 744.)

Secktī mātuguṇ thlaeṅ, Sāstrā Secktī mātuguṇ thlaeṅ (About the gratitude due to a mother). G.8? (K.). MS IB 1405.

Secktī raṃlịk ṭās' (or *ṭaḥ*) *tīoen*, Exhortations et recommandations, by Ngoy. (Pou and Haksrea '*Cp.* Gén.') G.5 (B.7). **T** Ngoy in *KS* 1933. 7–12: 97–118. Ou Ngoy in IB 1958. IB (1972).

Sek Sārikā. See *Mahosathajātak.*

Sek Som Mundit, Sek Som Paṇḍit. Sek som niṅ Srakā. See *Mahosathajātak.*

*Sidhnūv.** G.7. MS AC 11 (which lacks beginning and end). EFEO 62 Braḥ Sit Dhnūv.

Siṅhanād, Sāstrā Siṅhanād written by Mok in AD 1863. Source: 50 *jātak*. G.7 (K.). MS IB 1379. EFEO 59 Siṅhanāt.

Sirasā, Sāstrā Braḥ Sirasā. See *Puññasār Sirsā.*

Sisorajātak. See *Ŝī Sau(r).*

Sīevbhau Baṅsāvatār (Book of Chronicles). History of a family from the reign of Srī Sopar (beginning of 17th century) to that of Ang Chand (AD 1806–34). Tells of the rebellion of a Baku (Brahmin priest). G.9. See Maspero 1929: 300.

Sīl Ṭap', Sāstrā Sīl Ṭap' (The ten precepts) by *M̈ā.* G.8 (K.). MS IB 1376.

Sīyāmm. See *Sāmajātak.*

Soben komar. See *Supin kumār.*

Sophea Tonsay. See *Subhā Dansāy.*

Sradap Cek, Rīoeṅ Sradap Cek or *Cau Sradap Cek* or *Sāstrā Devaṅs (Devavaṅs) Kumār,** written in AD 1889 by (Yos)-Ngin. Source: 50 *jātak*. G.7 (B. Bh. Br. K.). MSS IB 575, 576. EFEO 72. **T** (Yos)-Ngin and Choum-Muong 1959 (parts 1 and 2). Nuon-Neary 1960*b*. IB 1962, 1967. Serialized in *Anak Jāti Niyam* 1963. **V** Vandy-Kaonn 1981: 41–3.

Sralāñ' srī tūc (I love the little girl) by Mok. G.8. **T** 3 stanzas cited by Ly-Théam Teng 1960: 156; he says they were taken from *Sruk Khmaer*, Sept. 1927.

Sraṇoḥ p-ūn sṅuon (I miss you, my darling) by Srī Dhammarājā. It is printed following the *Likhit* (Letter) and it is in the same metre as the Letter but there is a break in the rhyme scheme between the last stanza of the letter and the first of this poem. **T** *KS* 1938. 8: 105–7.

Srī kumār. G.7. MS AC 45 (with summary of part 2) Srīy kūmmā.

Srīhitopades translated from Pali to Khmer by Pang-Khat. G.10. Prose. **T** Pang-Khat 1971–2. Cedoreck 1981 (reprint). See also *Hitopades*.

Srīvijăy. See *Lpoek Srīvijăy*.

Stec Kmeṅ, Rīoeṅ Stec Kmeṅ (The young king).* G.7 (B. Bh. Br. K. PK). EFEO 21. **T** Plon-Nourrit 1903. **V** Monod 1943: 247–97.

Subhasiddhi. See *Sabvasiddhi*.

Subhā Dansāy, Rīoeṅ Subhā Dansāy (Judge Rabbit). Various stories of the Rabbit.

(1) *Bāky kāby* (Poetry). Source: folktales* G.7 (B. M.). **T** Aymonier 1878: 119–32. Corbet 19—: 74–89. *KS* 1938. 4–6: 259–65; 7–9: 63–9 and 227–37. *PRBK* 2, No. 11. *Khmaer Samăy* 1967. Cedoreck 1981. **V** Aymonier 1878: 30–3.

(2) *Bāky rāy* (Prose)* G.1. **T** Aymonier 1878: 132–59. Corbet 19—: 31–44. *KS* 1938. 10–12: 173–83. *PRBK* 2, No. 12. Cedoreck 1981. **V** Aymonier 1878: 34–41. Monod 1944: 19–48, 1985: 21–48.

Subhāsit (Proverbs).

(1) G.5. (Pou and Haksrea '*Cp.* Cl.') **T** Plon-Nourrit 1900, corrected 1901.

(2) See *Cpāp' Subhāsit*.

Subhāsit Cpāp' Srī (Proverb. A code for women) by In. G.5 (B.9 but with many verses of 8 syllables). (Pou and Haksrea 'Different from the other *Cpāp' Srī*'.) **T** In in *KS* 1934. 4–6: 46–80. In IB 1959. **V** Chau-Seng and Kong-Huot 1967.

Subhāsit porāṇ (Ancient sayings). G.5. (Pou and Haksrea '*Cp*. Cl. Same text as *Cpāp' Bāky Cās'*.) **T** Chāṃ Dāṅ Gāṃvarrṇ and Yau(v) Lim Pī Nănd 2467 BE (AD 1924).

Subhāsit pratạu jan prus srī (Sayings to educate men and women). G.5 (B.7, B.8). (Pou and Haksrea '*Cp*. Gén.') **T** in *KS* 1957. 1: 50–63; 2: 152–62; 3: 245–54; 4: 324–33.

Subhāsit Rājanīti (bāky kāby) (Sayings on the conduct of the king's affairs) by Nou. G.5. (Pou and Haksrea '*Cp*. ne.') **T** Nou 1955 and in *KS* 1956. 2: 147–52; 3: 247–57; 4: 344–8; 5: 447–55.

Subhāsit Rājanītisātth. Same as last entry.

Subhāsit sạn [sic] *hñin*. G.5. (Pou and Haksrea 'Another *Cpāp' srī*'.) **T** Same as *Subhāsit porāṇ*.

Subhāsit sạn [sic] *putr*. G.5. (Pou and Haksrea ' = *Subhāsit* Cl.') **T** Same as last entry.

Subhāsit sạn tek. G.5. (Pou and Haksrea ' = *Cpāp*' Kertikāl Cl.') **T** Same as last entry.

Subhog, Sāstrā Subhog, Rīoeṅ Braḥ Subhog by *Pāl*. G.7 (B. Bh. Br. K.). MS IB 1375.

Sudhan, Rīoeṅ Braḥ Sudhan.* One of the fifty *jātak*. G.7 (B. Bh. Br. K. PK). MS EFEO 64. **T** IB 1963, 1968. **V** Terral-Martini 1959. Khing Hoc Dy 1977: 29–31 and 1990: 196–8, with **S**: 198.

Sudhanajātak. See last entry.

Sugandh Thoṅ, Sāstrā/Rīoeṅ Sugandh Thoṅ written by *Brahm Pavar Bhaktī* or *Pavar Bhaktī Brahm* in AD 1886 according to Nhok-Thaem, AD 1883 according to Mak Phœun. G.7 (B. Bh. Br. K.). MS IB 1369. EFEO 46, 47.

Sujātajātak. Retold in prose by Mènh-Nakri. G.10. **T** *KS* 1943. 11, 12.

Sukh Mānab, Sāstrā Sukh Mānab by (*Ukñā Dhammādhipati) Cand* in the mid-19th century. Source: *jātak* (with no future lives of characters). G.7 (Br. K.). MS IB 1376 (incomplete).

Sumanagotam, Sāstrā Braḥ Sumanagotam. Source: 50 *jātak* probably. G.7 (B. Bh. Br. K.). MS IB 685. EFEO 90 Sūmannagoṭaṃm.

Suosḍīy, Suostīy, Suostiy. See next entry.

Suostī, Sāstrā/Sātrā Suostī (Greeting, prosperity). G.5 (K.). (Pou and Haksrea 'Cl. *Cp*. ne.') MSS IB 622 *Sāstra Rājasuostī* (King's greeting, prosperity). AC 43, 226 (Rājasuostīy muntriy). EFEO 5, 344 (1st part only). **T** Plon-Nourrit 1903. **T V S** Pou 1988.

Supin by Kim-Samon. G.8 (K.). **T** Kim-Samon 1972: 43–9. Huffman and Proum 1977: 108–9.

Supin kumār (Prince *Supin*) or *Supin tūc* (Little *Supin*).* Source: Khmer folktale. G.7 (B. K.). MS IB 667 Supin tūc. EFEO 20 Sūpin kūmār. **T** IB 1959, 1966. Huffman and Proum 1977: 274–6 (vocabulary 277–8).

Supin sīem, Sāstrā Supin sīem (Siamese *Supin*). On Buddhism and customs. G.8 (B. Bh. Br. K.). MS IB 1405.

Supin tūc. See *Supin kumār*.

Surabajātak, Surabbhajātak. Source: 50 *jātak*. Prose. G.10. **T** Thang-Vong in *KS* 1959. 2–10 (plus 11 and 12?). IB 1960.

Surūpajātak, Braḥ Surūpajātak. Nhok-Thaem suggests (*KS* 1965. 12: 1298) *çirca* AD 1700 as date. Source: 50 *jātak*. Prose. G.10. MS IB 853 (the text does not resemble that of the *Surabbhajātak*, the preceding entry).

Suvaṇṇ bilāp. See *Nen Mās*.

Suvaṇṇ haṅs (The golden swan). Popular story, probably told in verse. MS EFEO 81 Sūvaṇṇahaṅs. **T** Ching-Nguon Huot 1953.

Suvaṇṇ Khyaṅ Saṅkh (The golden shell). Source: 50 *jātak*. Prose. G.10. MS IB 1017.

Suvaṇṇ kinnar, Sāstrā Suvaṇṇ kinnar. See *Suvaṇṇ Ktām Sa*.

Suvaṇṇ Ktām Sa, Sāstrā /Rīoeṅ Suvaṇṇ Ktām Sa or *Sāstrā Ktām Sa* (The golden white crab). Also known as *Sāstrā Suvaṇṇ kinnar* (The golden *kinnar*). Source: old folktale? G.7 (B. B.7, Bh. Br. K.). MS IB 680.

Suvaṇṇ phalā (The golden fruit) written by *Dieṅ* and *Braḥ Srī Añjit Srī* in AD 1804 (Nhok-Thaem in *KS* 1965. 12: 1284). Source: folktale. G.7 (B. Bh. Br. K.). MS IB 1374.

Suvaṇṇ Sirasā sut (Name. Sutra).* Story presented as a *sūtra* in prose. G.10. Au Chhieng points out (1953: 164) that among the 50 *jātak* is one known as the *Sirāsārājakumāra* MS AC 196. BN 165 B/ Camb 87. **V** Au Chhieng 1953: 163–4. Khing Hoc Dy 1977*a*: 22–3.

Suvaṇṇ vaṅs. Cited by Ly-Théam Teng as a poetic work of the Middle Period (17th–19th centuries).

Sūmutr, Braḥ Sūmutr. See *Samuddh*.

Sūputr, Braḥ Sūputr. See *Samuddh*.

Sūvāt, Sāstrā Braḥ Sūvāt (also *Sūvātth*) by *Kor*. Source: 500 *jātak*. G.7 (B. Bh. Br. K.). MS IB 679. AC 19 Sūvātth, 20 (both have only 1st part). EFEO 65. **V** Au Chhieng 1953: 15 (of 1st part).

Svā slūt haṅs slūt, Sāstrā svā slūt haṅs slūt (The nice monkey and the nice swan). Source: Buddhist folktale. G.7 (K.). MS IB 1376.

Ŝī Sau(r), Sāstrā Braḥ Pād Ŝī Sau(r) (Sisorajātak). Written by a monk whose name is illegible. Nhok-Thaem suggests written at end of 19th century. Source: 50 *jātak.* G.7 (B. B.7, Bh. Br. K. MK). MS IB 588. EFEO 84 Sī sau. **T** Peung-Pam in *KS* 1954–6.

Taṃṇaeṅ taṃnoer nā sarsoer grā hemantamās (Narration of a journey in which I praise the time of winter). See *Kaṃṇāby sarsoer hemantamās.*

Tamra Preng Veasana, *Tamrā Breṅ Vāsanā* (Treatise on destiny). Astrological text. **V** Bitard 1954: 51–79 (five excerpts).

Tamra Prohm Cheat or Hora Sastr, *Tamrā Brahmajāti* or *Horāsāstr* (Treatise on Astrology or Soothsaying). Source: astrology. Prose. **T** Bouth-Néang 1953. **V** Bitard 1954: 51–79 (21 excerpts).

Tamrāp lokkanaiy. See *Devatā juṃnuṃ[mm] ktīy.*

Teme, Braḥ Teme. See next entry.

Temiyajātak. Prose version of this *jātak.* G.10. MSS AC 180 Braḥ Teme, 271 Tīmaer and (fragment) Teme 262. EFEO 27. *KS* 1936. 7: 43–54; 8: 121–9. **V** Leclère 1906: 275–340.

Thmenh-Chey, Thnenh-Chey. See *Dhmeñ Jăy.*

Tip-Sangvar. See *Dibv Saṅvār.*

Tīmèr, Tīmaer. See *Temiyajātak.*

Tong Chin, *Tuṅ Jhīn, Rīoeṅ Tuṅ Jhīn* prose novel by Nou-Kan. **V** Vandy-Kaonn 1981: 44–6.

Trai Bhed (The three Vedas). A Brahmanic prose work concerning the cosmogonies dating back possibly to the Angkor period. The IB MS, having this title seems, according to Nhok-Thaem, (*Kambujasuriyā* 1965. 12: 1300), to deal with the births of characters associated with the *Rāmakerti* (Reamker), rather than with the three Vedas. It resembles the *Trai Yuddh* (The three battles) though the MS is longer. Coedès (1931: 182) mentions the 'fragments' of cosmogonies such as the Traiphet (*Trai Bhed*) when discussing what little is left in Cambodian literature of Brahmanism. MSS IB 823. ÉFEO 108, 109, 110.

Trai Bhūm, Traiy Bhum, Tray Bhum (The three worlds). A Brahmanic treatise on cosmic theology. Coedès (1915: 8) says the text is a translation from Thai. This was made by a Commission on the order of King Ang Duong. MSS AC 201, 267, 322. Incomplete, 70, 71. EFEO 111, 156. **V** Feer 1877: 202–15. Roeské 1914: 587–602. **S** Roeské 1914: 602–6.

Trai Lakkh(ṇ), Braḥ Trai Lakkh(ṇ) (The three attributes).

(1) On the Buddhist view of 3 characteristics of life: impermanence, suffering, and unreality. G.8 (K.). MS IB 641.

(2) Old poem with this title. T Pruoch Phoum ed. 1967.

Trai Yuddh (The three battles). A Brahmanic treatise on the births of characters in the *Rāmakerti* (Reamker). MS EFEO 107, Trai Yut.

Triple Joyau. See *Secktī ṭās' tīoen*, Poèmes consacrés à la glorification du Triple Joyau.

Trīneti. See both *Cpāp' Rājaneti* Cl. and *Cpāp' Trīneti*.

Tum Teao. See *Duṃ Dāv*.

Ṭaṃrī Sa, Sāstrā Ṭaṃrī Sa (The white elephant). Folktale. G.7 (B. Br. K.). MS IB 613.

Ṭāv Rīoeṅ, Sāstrā Ṭāv Rīoeṅ (The shining sword) by *(Ukñā Cakrī) Kaev* and *(Baññā Ratn Kosā) Kaev* in AD 1837. Ly-Théam Teng (1960: 118) says AD 1741. A *jātak* brought from Thailand by *Cau Baññā Añjit Srī*. G.7 (B. Bh. Br. K.). MSS IB 549, 550. EFEO 56.

Ṭimaer. See *Temiyajātak*.

Va Net. See Varanuj *Varanetr*.

Va vaṅ. See *Varavaṅs Sūravaṅs*.

Van rājj. See *Vanarāj*.

Vanarāj. G.7. MS AC 86, Van rājj.

Var Nāṭṭh. See *Varanuj Varanetr*.

Varanet, Varanetr. See next entry.

Varanuj Varanetr, Sāstrā Varanuj Varanetr,* composed by Nong in AD 1806. (Ray-Buc 1956: 936 and Ly-Théam Teng [1957]: 115 give the author as *Ukñā Cau Hvāy Ghlāṃṅ Mīec*.) Source: 50 *jātak*. G.7 (B. Bh. Br. K.). MSS IB 563, 564. AC 10 (Ist part only), Va Net. AC 331, 2 (part 6 only) Var Nāṭṭh. EFEO 60, Varanet. **V** Au Chhieng 1953 (part 1 only): 9. Dik-Kéam 1967*b* (in Khmer): 35–9 and **S**: 32–5. Khing Hoc Dy 1990: **V**: 178–86, **S**: 186–7.

Varavaṅs Sūravaṅs, Rīoeṅ Varavaṅs Sūravaṅs. A story told like a *jātak* but in fact probably a local tale. Near Kompung Speu, a hill is known as *Phnuṃ Varavaṅs Sūravaṅs;* a local *Anak Tā Srī* is headless, like *Nāṅ Mikhā*, and two other places are associated with the tale.

(1) * G.7 (B. Bh. Br. I. K.). MSS IB 571, 574. AC 14, Va vaṅs (incomplete) AC 21, Va Vaṅ (incomplete). AC 51, Va Vaṅ (only part 4). AC 177, Var vuṅs. AC 331, 1, Va vaṅ (= 14 but in disorder). EFEO 71. **T** Leroux (n.d.). Pavie 1898: 169–324

(difficult script). Plon-Nourrit 1902. Ly-Théam Teng in *KS* 1970. **V** Pavie 1898: 53–154. 1903, 1949. **S** Ly-ThéamTeng 1970*d*.

(2) G.1. Prose version. **T** *PRBK* 6, No. 14. *Vathā*. Concerns rebellion of Prince Vathā. G.7. MS AC 300 (incomplete).

Vā Vān sūt lā (Prayer to depart from passion). Recitation before entering the religious life. G.8. MS AC 93.

Vesandar, Vessantarajātak. See *Mahāvessantarajātak*.

Vidhurapaṇḍitajātak, Bīdhur, Bīdhūr, Bīy dhur, Bīy dhūr. Khmer prose version of a *jātak*. G.10. MSS AC 183, 190, 282. AC 29 and 30 (two consecutive fragments). EFEO 34.

Vijādhar. See Vijjādhar jātak.

Vijjā guṇ kathā ou les vertus de la science by Chhim-Soum. G.8 (B.7). **T** *KS* 1935. 2–3: 37–58.

Vijjādhar jātak. A prose *jātak*, not in the 50. G.10. MSS IB 1018. AC 41, 280. EFEO 117.

Vijjñādharm. See last entry.

*Vimān Cand, Sāstrā/ Rīoeṅ Vimān Cand** written in AD 1858 by Mok, according to Roeské (1913: 670) and Khing Hoc Dy (1981: 140), but by Yaem, according to Ray-Buc (1956: 936), Ly-Théam Teng ((1957): 115), Léang-Hap An (1965*b*: 67), and Nhok-Thaem, who finds the name in the text (*KS* 1965. 9: 964 n.). Source: 50 *jātak*. G.7 (B. Bh. Br. K.). MSS IB 590, 591, 592. AC 173, 303. BN 69. EFEO 55. **T** Guesdon (n.d.). Khing Hoc Dy 1981 (part): 154–7. **V** Moura 1883: 304–6. Khing Hoc Dy 1981: 158–60. Vandy-Kaonn 1981 (part): 28.

*Vinā, Braḥ Pād Vīnā.** G.7. MSS AC 13 (incomplete), 229. EFEO 69. **V** Taupin 1886: 24–7. Au Chieng 1953: 187.

Voey nae ā cik chā muoy kāk' (Hey, uncle (a Chinese) fries for a dime) by Mok. G.8 (B.7). **T** Ly-Théam Teng 1960: 154 (Ist stanza only).

Vorvong Saurivong. See *Varavaṅs Sūravaṅs*.

Yap' yūr braḥ candr dāp sradan' (It is deep night and the moon is low and gentle) by (*Anak Mnāṅ) Phaẏam*. G.8 (B.7). **T** *KS* 1939. 7–9: 210.

Yasaker(ti), Rīoeṅ Braḥ Pād Yasaker(ti) or *Sāstrā Braḥ Pād Yasaker(ti)*. A *jātak*. G.7 (B. Bh. Br. K.). MS IB 608. EFEO 91, Braḥ Pād Yas' Ker.

6

FOLKTALES SUMMARIES (G.1)

Terms which may be unfamiliar.

āsram	forest dwelling of a hermit
gruḍ, garuḍa,	mythical bird
nāg	supernatural snake
ṛsī	hermit
sālā	open-sided hall where travellers may stay
uparāj	second king
yakkhinī, yaksiṇī	female ogre, giantess
yaks	ogre, giant

Ā DHUṅ SĀÑ'

The story is told in Chapter 7, 'Narrative Poetry Summaries'.

Ā KHVĀK' Ā KHVIN

'Mr Blind man and Mr Cripple' were slaves who wanted to run away. At the first attempt they were in the boat all night but had only gone round in circles because one could not see and one could not row. They set off again, the cripple on the blind man's shoulders. They managed to capture a tiger which ran away when the blind man, thinking it was a cow, tried to put a nose ring on it. They decided to farm and took along some farm implements. They met a man selling 'honey' in a node of bamboo. It was excrement really but it took three attempts to eat it for them to be convinced. They set off to kill the man but pursued a woodpecker by mistake and lost their way.

They came to a country where a *yaks* was about to eat a princess; otherwise he would eat all the men of the country. They reached the *sālā* where she was hidden in a drum. The blind man asked for food and a sword. They would kill the *yaks*. They closed the doors of the *sālā*. The *yaks* arrived and wished to see the liver of the man who was so brave as to close the doors. The blind man threw out a wickerwork tray followed by a turtle representing his fleas and a buffalo-rope for the hair on his feet. The *yaks* went home. Then a *yaksiṇī* came but the blind man beheaded her as she put her head round the door.

When they were sorting out the valuables which people had brought to offer to the *yaks* there was a quarrel, in the course of which the blind man kicked the cripple. After this his limbs were straight. The cripple struck the blind man on the eyes and he could see. The 'Blind' man married the princess and the 'Cripple' became second king.

Ā ḶEV, *A Lev*

This unnaturally adult boy, away from home with his father growing rice beside the Tonle, told his mother, on a visit, that his father was dead and his father that his mother was dead, all because he would enjoy eating the funeral meats! Then he told each one that marriage with someone 'very like their previous partner' would be a good idea and introduced them to each other.

A Lev went to live in a monastery. He tricked a monk and a Chinese into a clandestine meeting at dark at which each thought the other was a beautiful girl. He exacted not a *pād* (piece) of silver but a *pātr* (a begging bowlful) from each of them. (The words are pronounced the same.) He told his parents he got the money by exposing himself in the market. His father went off to do the same and was beaten. A Lev saw his father walking home, followed by a group of Cham merchants. He called out to his father that he was being chased and must run across the fields. Then he told the Chams that the man running was chasing a deer with a broken leg. They must chase it too and all share the deer. When they went off he took their goods and hid them at home.

A Lev helped a grandmother and granddaughter who were loading a boat with their things and preparing to leave. He said his name was 'Grandson-in-law' and he would like to go with them. After a short distance he pretended to have left his knife behind. They rowed back and Grandma went on shore to look for it. He rowed off, leaving her.

'Grandson-in-law is going off with my granddaughter!' It was too late by the time she had explained.

A Lev and his new wife met 500 robbers. He boasted that he had stolen the goods in his boat by means of magic. They should find an island and he would teach them. He made them build a shrine, dig a deep well, shave their heads, and practise diving, without clothes, saying the 'magic' words seven times over. At dusk he told them they must all dive at once and while they were doing that he and his wife sailed away in their junk, towing their own boat. They came to the place where the robbers' wives were. He told them that their husbands would be home soon but first some naked demons, bringing bad luck, would come to their houses. They must beat them off with sticks!

A Lev and his wife returned to Grandma, gave her the goods, built her a house, and settled down with her.

A Lev went off to another region and found a rich man with a marriageable daughter. He served the rich man, accompanying him to court, and soon knew the important people. He picked up scraps of letters and collected the seals of all of them. Then he wrote a note for each mandarin, indicating that he owed A Lev 100 or 200 or 500 *naen* and left them with the rich man's wife. Curiosity overcame her and she read the letters and showed them to her husband. A Lev seemed to belong to a rich family and to be a suitable match for their daughter but people did not know him. The wife suggested a secret marriage until the matter of the debts came out and his prestige increased. The wedding took place. A Lev, poorly dressed, went to the meeting hall, having told his wife to offer him betel there if he summoned her. When his wife came he offered to bet that she would offer betel to him. If he lost he would be their slave for life. If he won, they would give him gold, silver, horses . . . They accepted. With the goods he won in this way, A Lev was established for life.

BAS' KEṄ KAṄ, *The snake*, Keṅ Kaṇ

This story tells of the origin of various kinds of snake from the union of a human with a snake. A girl dropped her chopper down a hole which proved to be the den of a snake. He retrieved it for her on condition that she became his lover. She sent her daughter each time to call him to her house but warned him that when her husband returned home from selling beads she would not send her and he would know not to come. She became pregnant and the husband returned. In revenge he told the daughter to fetch the snake. He killed it and it was cooked and served up to the wife. Its head and tail were displayed so that she would know what she was eating. The husband killed her in the forest and snakes of all varieties were born.

BLIND MAN *and the* CRIPPLE

See *Ā Khvāk' Ā Khvin.*

CAU DHUṄ CAU SĀÑ'

The story is told in Chapter 7, 'Narrative Poetry Summaries', as *Ā Dhuṅ Ā Sāñ'*.

CAU KĀṂPIT PANDOḤ, *'Mr Whittling Knife'*

Two brothers received advice from the abbot when they left the monastery. The elder was told to go to China where he would become rich. The younger, who, the abbot saw, would rule two kingdoms, was given three maxims: not to fall asleep when others do so, not to be in a hurry to eat, and not to talk in bed. The younger brother married and was poor. He left for China in a junk and found his rich brother. Having discovered from a sage that his brother would rule two kingdoms, he merely gave him a piece of rough calico.

On the way home the younger brother was the only one to stay awake on board at night. He defeated a *yaks* and obtained three boons: a rope that ties by itself, a stick that beats on its own, and a cooking pot that cooks unaided. The Captain kept the gifts for him, made him climb a tree to pick figs and sailed away. A pig, which had a crystal with which one might walk on the water, came nightly for figs. The younger brother stole the crystal and caught up the boat. Pretending not to be too angry, he obtained his things and went home over the water.

His wife had a lover, who was under the house at night and heard about the gifts hidden under the steps. The husband remembered the maxim but trusted his wife. In the morning he took the steps to court and accused them. He gained the attention of the king, who gave him a piece of cloth. He gave it to his wife who in turn gave it to her lover. Then at a feast the lover wore the cloth and was recognized as the thief. The young man gave his treasures to the king, who offered him his daughter and the kingdom. He refused and asked for a whittling knife.

He went to serve a rich man and guarded the palace in his place. Where others ate a meal and fell asleep, he refrained and stayed awake. The king came in disguise and *Cau Kāṃpit Pandoḥ* chased him round the pillars and struck at them until the king said who he was. Next day the pillars gave way. The king found out who he was and he demonstrated the power of his whittling knife by cutting through seven planks of wood in an instant. The rich man gave him his daughter. The king gave him his daughter and kingdom. He returned to his former home and married the king's daughter and became king of that kingdom. Finally he sent for his brother from China.

DAṂBAEK PUON NĀK', RĪOEṄ DAṂBAEK PUON NĀK', *'The four bald men'*

Ridiculed because of their lack of hair, they set out to acquire some. Told to bathe in a certain pool, they do this once (and obtain hair) but they lose it again when they bathe again to be more beautiful. They set off in their old age to look for wives. As they proceed they are asked to judge a case where a girl, found with a lover, swears that he came as a robber that night. They judge that her protestations are not to be believed and decree that the two should be married. They find five tortoises. Quite unable to divide them into four, they are helped by a passer-by—who keeps the fifth. Before leaving them he teaches them some sayings. Later they stay with a lady and recite the sayings all night, disturbing her. She complains to the judge, who says they must be her slaves. One of them is lost when they see in a pool the reflection of a swarm of bees and he is drowned in the water trying to obtain the honey. They meet another bald man searching for a wife. They come across a widow who takes them all as husbands but the work she gives them to do is too hard. They leave to go and look for a servant. It happened that *Cau Smugr*, a weaver of boxes, had been in the top of a tree, cutting palm and thinking how he would make many boxes, sell them, and make money. He would have servants and kick and hit them. In imagination he kicked and hit and fell through the tree, catching hold of the last branch. An elephant driver came along, stood on the elephant and held his feet. His own feet moved on the back of the elephant and the latter took it as a sign to move on. The four bald men came across the two men suspended from the tree, one below the other. They took a cloth and each tied a corner round their necks. The two men jumped. The four men hit their heads together and died. The two men asked the help of a widow. She pretended her husband had died and gave the corpses one at a time to a burner of corpses and claimed, each time, that he had not burned it well enough. Her husband had 'returned' because he loved her so much and he must take him again and do it thoroughly. Finally, when all were burned, the burner of corpses saw a charcoal-burner, returning from the forest, covered in charcoal, and burned him!

DANSĀY, *'The hare'*

See *Subhā Dansāy*.

FOUR BALD MEN

See *Daṃbaek Puon Nāk'*.

GAṄ' ĤĀN

'Brave Kong' acquired a reputation for courage which was quite unfounded. His wives killed a tiger while he hid in a tree but because mere women could not possibly kill a tiger, he claimed the glory. Later when he was leading his men into battle, through shere terror he urinates and excretes on to the neck of the elephant. Thinking it is a signal to go ahead the elephant rushes against the enemy and routs it. His courage was confirmed. Finally he was asked by the king to kill a crocodile which was terrifying a certain region. He decided that the best thing would be simply to dive into the water and let the crocodile kill him immediately. He dived in and startled the crocodile, which lept up into the fork of a tree and stuck. *Gaṅ' Ĥān* came up and saw this and called out to his friends and relatives to kill it with a lance. Everyone thought *Gaṅ' Ĥān* had caught the crocodile and thrown it into the fork of the tree. His reputation was increased.

KỊṄ KANTRAI, *Sātrā Kịṅ Kantrai*

This is a collection of legal tales, known in other parts of South-East Asia, in which the judge usually proves unable to decide the case satisfactorily and it is referred to the king. There are many repetitions of ideas in the fifty-three stories. A few are summarized here.

Two men were crossing a bridge, carrying rice seed. They collided in the middle and spilled the seed. Who was in the right? The king asked what kind of seed they were transporting and awarded to the man whose seed was of a kind that had to be sown quickly. Three sons quarrelled about their father's legacy. The king decided that two shares went to the son who was a monk and whose mind was on heavenly matters and one share each went to the others, one of whom served the king and hoped for renown, the other of whom was a business man and hoped for worldly goods. In one case two women claimed to be the mother of a child and, rather like Solomon, the king settled the matter by putting the child in the middle and letting them pull it towards them. The real mother would not hurt the child. Another story tells of a poor man who lived near a rich man and moved his house to this side and that, depending on the way the wind was blowing, so as to receive the smell of the food cooked at the rich man's house. The judge said he was in debt to the rich man and must become his slave. The poor man objected and asked to take the case to the king and plead with him to ransom him. The king said the smell of the food was no more than the shadow of money (which he had piled up on a cloth to demonstrate the fact) and the poor man might go free.

Finally, there was the tale of the king's crown. His Majesty was enjoying himself in the forest and had left his crown in a box in the care of a girl. She fell asleep and a monkey stole the crown. The ministers arrested a fisherman found in the area and when they applied torture, he 'confessed' and said he did it for a reward from the rich man. When tortured the rich man 'confessed' that he had had the crown stolen and had given it to the chaplain. The chaplain under pressure 'confessed' that he had taken it and hidden it in the forest. However, it could not be found. The three were put in prison and a secretary listened outside. They all said that they were innocent and that under duress they had said anything to escape from the questioning. Hearing the secretary's report the ministers had a crown made like the original one and repeated all their actions. This time the girl must only pretend to be asleep. The monkey thief was discovered and both crowns retrieved.

MĀ YOEṄ

The story is told in Chapter 7, 'Narrative Poetry Summaries'.

MĀYĀ SRĪ, *'The wiles of women'*

A man, digging for yams, happened to go to the back of a shrine. Just then his wife, who had a lover, came to the front of the shrine to ask for the death of her husband. The husband answered her, as though he was the spirit, 'Cook him a sitting hen with eggs and he will die.' At home he ate, lay down, and pretended to be ill. She went for the lover. The husband called out that he was cold and needed hot water. The surprised lover jumped into a pitcher, while the wife went to boil water. When she brought it the husband said it is too hot. He needed cold as well. She went out and he poured the boiling water into the pitcher. Returning the wife pushed her lover down in the pitcher and realized he was dead. How was she to dispose of the body?

She knew there were four robbers in the area so she borrowed a number of pretty sarongs and hung them outside the house. The robbers came at night and took the pitcher in which they thought she had stored her treasures.

She went to the quay to shop just when a boat was in. The four thieves began to beat her. She said, 'I'm going to claim money from the captain. Come with me. We'll share it.' Leaving them on the bank, she told the captain she was selling four slaves. He must chain them so that they do not run away.

As she walked home, darkness fell and she dared not go on. She climbed a tree and slept there. The four thieves broke their chains and came to sleep in different parts of the same tree. She promised to be like husband and wife with one of them and to share the money. They must lick tongues to show love. She bit off his tongue. The others heard his cries, thought the captain was after them, and fled.

She went home, gave the money to her husband and they lived happily ever after!

MR BASKET KNIFE or *MR WHITTLING KNIFE*

See *Cau Kāṃpit Pandoḥ*.

NĀṄ LAMAṄ RAṂCEK, *'The daughter of the white elephant'*

There was a drought. The women of Phnom Tbeng went to dig tubers at the foot of the mountain, taking water in a bamboo container. Clouds gathered and *Nāṅ Deb* threw away the water but it did not rain! She looked everywhere for water. The king of white elephants came by. He urinated into a stone basin and then withdrew into the shade of a banyan. *Nāṅ Deb* drank deeply of the urine before noticing what it was—and became pregnant.

She had a beautiful, but quick-tempered daughter whose black hair smelt of the flower *raṃcek*. She was called *Lamaṅ Raṃcek*, Pollen of the *Pandanus Odoratissimus.* When she was grown up she set off to find her father. The king elephant believed her tale but locked her up in a tower. A hunter saw her and told the king of *Pandāy Koh Ker* (The citadel of Koh Ker), who marched off with elephants to rescue her and make her his queen. The king elephant found her gone and followed the elephants' footprints to Banteay Koh Ker. He burst through one wall and then the next, calling for his daughter. She came, with her husband and soldiers. The elephant was killed. (At Koh Ker there is a Prasat Damrey, *Prāsād Ṭaṃrī*, Elephant monument.)

NĀṄ RAṂSĀY SAK', *'The girl who lets down her hair'*

A story, with variations, from Battambang. Local hills are named after the heroine, the crocodile, and the boat.

Rājakul's parents had him educated by a sage, who had in his care also *Nāṅ Raṃsāy Sak'* (Miss Let-down-her hair), found by him in a lotus. *Rājakul* took her as wife and the sage gave her a jewel to tie up her hair (or her hair was magic and she stroked it to make things happen).

Rājakul went away on business, met *Mika* (or *Suvaṇṇamasā* or *Macchānab*), daughter of the king, and married her. They had a child. He left her by boat and, watched by *Mika*, changed course to go back to *Nāṅ Raṃsāy Sak'* (whom he was to marry). *Mika* sent her pet crocodile, *Atonn (Ā Dhan)*, after him to eat him. *Nāṅ Raṃsāy Sak'*, looking out for him, sees him being attacked (or is told about it by a servant of Indra), threw the jewel (or stroked her hair) and the sea retreated. *Atonn* died and *Rājakul* ran towards her.

Mika, now ready with troops, called *Nāṅ Raṃsāy Sak'* to combat but the troops hesitated. *Mika* thought of her child and fled, pursued by *Nāṅ*

Raṃsāy Sak'. She was brought back to the base, tortured and killed. *Nāṅ Raṃsāy Sak'* returned to *Rājakul.*

The story of the RABBIT

See *Subhā Dansāy.*

SRĪ BIT, MTĀY BIT, ŪBUK BIT, *'A true girl, a true mother, a true father'*

A poor man was searching for a true girl, a true mother, and a true father. The king who was to hold a festival had a throne-room and a pavilion built near the river. The poor man sat under the bridge and fished. The king's daughter would not walk over the bridge because she would pass over his head.[1] The man heard her say this and decided to tell the king there were no true girls, mothers, or fathers in the kingdom (except the king's daughter). The king decided to travel about as a poor man and find out whether this was true.

He became engaged to one girl who would not clean up after him when he was drunk and sick. Breaking off the engagement, he married another girl who looked after him well. He tested the parents by gambling. They paid his debts. He thought he had found what he was looking for and sent his brother-in-law with a message to his officials to fetch him home. They gave him food and he put some of it away to take home for his brother-in-law.

When the officials came for him, his wife was selling cakes in another village. The family were told, the king and queen were dressed in suitable garments, the parents and brother rode on elephants or horses. Arriving at the palace the king summoned the man who was searching for a true girl, a true mother, and a true father. Are these people true? They were. The man married the king's daughter.

SUBHĀ DANSĀY, '*Judge Rabbit*' (The story told in prose)

This collection of tales is said to be about *Judge* Rabbit but in all of them he is just Brer Rabbit who escapes from death countless times

[1] It is a great insult in Cambodia to pass over a person's head with any part of the body.

by using his wits. Many other individual tales tell of the rabbit as a judge who frees the right man by unorthodox means.

Seeing a woman carrying bananas on her head, Judge Rabbit lay down on her path and pretended to be dead. She put him in the basket and he ate all the bananas, running away when she put the basket down to sell to a customer.

He bet the shellfish in a pond that if they swam and he ran round the pond's edge, he would win the race. They tricked him—in this one case he lost—by forming a line round the pond with the one ahead of him always answering when he called out. He did not dare to drink the water of any pond again.

The rabbit persuaded a crocodile to take him across the river by promising to cure his 'scurvy'. Once across the rabbit called out that the 'scurf' is inherited and incurable. The angry crocodile was determined to eat the rabbit; he behaved as if he was a log floating on the water.

Meanwhile the rabbit found a dead buffalo and went inside it. The sun caused the carcasse to close up. He called out to a man to acquire merit by sprinkling water on the behind of the buffalo to make it open up. He came out and called, 'No merit. You just helped me.'

Turning his attention to the 'log', he called out, 'If you are a crocodile float with the current. If not, go against the current.' The crocodile was beaten and lay on the bank as if dead.

The rabbit entered his mouth and spoke of having this tooth for one purpose and that for another. The crocodile swallowed him. Now he spoke of eating the vitals and the crocodile begged him to come out.

He sat on a tree-stump near the water and stuck to it. A young elephant came to drink and the rabbit said, 'You can't drink here; a god has made me guardian of the place.' The elephant fetched his mother. The rabbit said, 'Don't hit me downwards; I shan't die.' She knocked him upwards off the stump and he was free.

Every day he ate cucumbers in a plantation. A trap was set and he was caught. A toad came by and, as with the crocodile, the rabbit said he would cure the 'scurvy' if the toad released him. When released he said it was incurable.

Returning to the cucumbers he was caught again and the toad would not help this time. The rabbit explained that he did not really know the cure before but now he does. He can tell the toad that at Angkor there are pretty girls two a penny. The toad freed him and he called out that the 'scurvy' was incurable. Angry at being cheated again, the toad set off for Angkor's pretty girls. He met a dung beetle and told him that he was going to Angkor and would be back for breakfast. The dung beetle tried to outdo his statement by saying that he made cartwheel hubs by making two halves first. The toad continued, telling everyone he met that he was going to Angkor for a wife, until he was swallowed by a big fish.

A tiger approached when the rabbit was sitting in a cane bush. The rabbit cleared his throat and said, 'I've eaten five elephants and am still not satisfied. Now an egg-plant has made my throat sore. I need a tiger's liver to soothe it.' A monkey reassured the tiger; the rabbit is a deceiver. But the tiger saw bits of elephant's tusks . . . and he wanted his liver! The monkey suggested tying their waists together. The rabbit called out, 'Good! Monkey is paying his old debts back to me, by bringing the tiger.' The tiger fled. The monkey was dragged on to a log and killed. He had a grin on his face; the tiger saw this, found it very unusual, set himself free and fled.

The rabbit ate seedlings and was caught in a trap. He pretended to be dead and escaped when the man moved the trap. However, he was caught again and taken to the house and a trap was placed over him. The man also had a fish in a tank. The man decided to test the monk's powers of divination. If the monk said they would have something to eat and they had, he would share it with the monk. He was told that they would have no luck that evening. The rabbit meanwhile told the fish to pretend to be dead, floating with its stomach uppermost, and then jump into any water there was, swim about and pretend to be dead again. 'Then they will take the trap from me to put over you.' The fish was taken to the pond to remove its scales and all went according to plan, the wife taking the trap from the rabbit and hurrying out with it and the fish, seeing her do so, swimming away into the water. The rabbit escaped too. The husband and wife believed the monk's prophecies after that.

THMENH CHEY, DHMEÑ JĂY, DHNEÑ JĂY, *or* DHANAÑJĂY

As a boy Thmenh Chey retrieved the distaff of the rich man's wife from under the house where it had fallen but only after requiring a reward of 'many cakes'. Her husband outwitted Thmenh Chey, who was claiming unlimited cakes, by making him say which of two different baskets of cakes had 'many' in it and taking those cakes.

Determined to have his revenge, Thmenh Chey persuaded his mother to borrow money from the rich man and so make him his slave.

He outmanœuvred the rich man in various ways. He ran after him, on his way to the palace with the betel, and arrived late, 'not wishing to drop anything'. Rebuked, next time he arrived without the betel, having dropped it. Told to pick up 'anything which falls', he arrived next time with horse-dirt in the betel bag! He was put to guard the market garden, allowed animals to eat the plants but claimed, 'The garden is still there!' When he looked after the cows he let the bulls in and claimed compensation because they had 'stolen his wives'. When he had to fetch his master, he shouted from the house but, told to speak softly, he whispered when the house was on fire. He brought out the 'lightest things' (a hen's nest) and found the cause of the fire to be the hearth.

Unable to stand having him any more the rich man offered him to the king. Having heard of his lies, the king asked him to tell one. He asked the king to send to his home for his (non-existent) Book of Lies. Given a slow elephant to follow the king to the forest, he arrived with a sail and punting pole to assist the speed. The courtiers dived for eggs (which they had put in the water beforehand). Thmenh Chey came up without an egg and called out, 'cock-a-doodle-doo'.

So it goes on. Thmenh Chey's fame reached China, which sent 500 ships and wise men to test him. He swam in the river considering drowning himself and overheard the answers to the questions. Sent by the king to live near the Mekong, he extracted dues from those who went on or off the river. He also collected taxes. The king was pleased but said, 'Don't take too much. Take a *pād*.' Like others in folktales he interpreted this as a *pātr* (pronounced the same) and took bowlfuls of silver instead of one piece. The king heard the complaints of the people and sent Thmenh Chey off to the executioners. They took him by boat. On the river he asked to dance. His bonds were undone. He asked the crew to sing the refrain while he sang, 'Thmenh Chey has fallen in the water'. He jumped overboard and escaped to a monastery.

Hearing that he was dead the Chinese came again and again he answered their questions but explained his answers differently to two people afterwards and gave a third explanation to the king. He finally baffled the Chinese with 'writing' done on wood by crabs dipped in ink. The king was pleased and offered him a wife—any woman in the palace. He said they were not real women and set out to find one. He found a girl and, after questions and answers which 'prove' that she is a real woman, married her. He acquired money by making a bet with the ministers that he would give orders to the king. He told the king to look behind him before he gave his order. The king did so and it was a *fait accompli.* Thmenh Chey had given an order. He took the money he won back to his parents-in-law.

The king decided to send him to China out of everyone's way. He made vermicelli and sold it successfully. The Chinese king heard of it and sent for him. Showing the king how to eat, with head upturned, he managed to see the king's face. He said it was black, while the Khmer king's face is like the full moon. Thrown into gaol, he made a musical kite and flew it at night. The king had never seen such a 'bird'. His astrologers thought destruction would come to the country unless the clever Cambodian was sent home. The king gave gifts, a 100 ships, men, and food. Thmenh Chey went home and made a kite for the king.

VARAVAṅS SŪRAVAṅS

The story is told in Chapter 7, 'Narrative Poetry Summaries'.

7

NARRATIVE POETRY SUMMARIES (G.7)

ABHIMANI

Two princes, brothers, learned respectively to sing and to fight and were banished by the king. *Abhimanī* sang his brother to sleep and was then stolen by a *Yakkhinī*.

AṂBĪ ṬAṂṆOER DAU KRUṅ PĀRĀṂṄSAES

The true story, told by Ûk, who was in charge of the expedition to France of the Royal Ballet and Orchestra in 1922.

AṂPAEṅ PAEK

Based on the *Sonandarājajātak*. Two feuding families were reconciled by the marriage of the son of the rich family to the daughter of the poor neighbour (Khuon Sokhamphu 1976: 206).

Ā DHUṅ Ā SĀÑ'

Ā Sāñ' ate too much. His poverty-stricken parents decided to kill him. Father and son went to the forest where the father felled a large tree which fell on *Ā Sāñ'*. Thinking he was dead the father left him.

Ā Sāñ' took the tree and wandered through the forest. He came to a country where a *yaks* was demanding daily food and threatening to eat the king if he did not have it.

Ā Dhuṅ saw how strong *Ā Sāñ'* was and thought he must keep on the right side of him. He gave him hospitality (and much food) but sent him to the *sālā* where the *yaks* would come for his daily food with a message for 'his father'. *Ā Sāñ'* killed the *yaks*. When he returned *Ā Dhuṅ*, astonished that he was still alive, pretended that the king would be annoyed at the death of the *yaks*. *Ā Sāñ'* must take the body away and live by day in the forest from then on. *Ā Dhuṅ* told the king that he himself had killed the *yaks* and was promoted.

Ā Sāñ' hid near the nest of an *Indrī* bird. The princess, at leisure in the forest, was captured by the bird and taken there. The king would give her to the man who rescued her. *Ā Dhuṅ*, learning that *Ā Sāñ'* could take him to the nest, told him that if he did so the king would forgive him. With the army, a rope, and a basket, the princess was saved but *Ā Sāñ'*, with whom she had fallen in love while waiting down in the nest, was left there.

Indra dropped a branch of a fig-tree down into the nest and *Sāñ'* climbed out and went to *Ā Dhuṅ's* house. He was put in irons by the angry *Ā Dhuṅ*. Indra, in the guise of an old man with a guitar, came by and persuaded the guards to free him. *Ā Sāñ'* sang about the whole story and was heard by the princess. All ended well.

BEJJATĀ

A forest fire threatened the nest of a pair of birds. The female would stay with her eggs. The male prayed that they might be born again at the same time and jumped into the fire. She was born as a princess who would speak to no male, he as a prince who taught her to speak and married her.

BHIN SUVAṆṆ

Au Chhieng, summarizes the incomplete manuscript of the Bibliothèque Nationale as follows: Prince Bhin Suvaṇṇ, finding no woman worthy to be his wife, leaves home and marries the adoptive daughter of a hermit, *Nāṅ Umūlavannī*. She is carried off by a *yaks* but, guided by a parrot, *Bhin Suvaṇṇ* finds her.

BHOGAKULAKUMĀR

An orphan cultivated a plot of land and had a white dog for company. Indra took pity on his loneliness and decided to give him the divine daughter of the king of *Sattakuṭapurī* as his wife. He put her in a magic bag from which she emerged in *Bhogakulakumār's* absence to do the housework. He surprised her, however, and she discarded the bag. The village head, *Gāmabhojak*, decided to acquire her for the king. *Bhogakulakumār* had to contend in cock and elephant trials against the king and to immerse himself in boiling water; he succeeded by the divine help of his wife but finally the king made him eat eggs which were forbidden him. His wife went back to her father and he decided to follow her. The dog knew the way but died when they had crossed a forest and a sea. The family divinities of *Bhogakulakumār* decided to aid him, descending in the forms of a vulture, which ate the dog, of a crow, which ate the vulture, of a fly and of a glow-worm. He arrived at *Sattakuṭapurī* and slipped a ring into a pitcher of water which the princess recognized. He was taken to the king and had to pass tests: shooting arrows, transferring sesame seeds from one vase to another and recognizing the fingers of his wife. Aided by the gods, he succeeded. They were married.

Bhogakulakumār and his wife returned to Benares to find out what had become of *Gāmabhojak* and the king. He was surrounded by troops but, shooting his magic bow, he killed both *Gāmabhojak* and *Brahmadatt* and all his enemies died. He was invited to be king of Benares and accepted, asking only for a new palace. Indra sent his architect, *Bisnukār*, and overnight a new palace was built.

BIMBĀBILĀP

For eight years the Buddha had been away from the court and his wife and family. Now he returned. His wife, *Bimbā*, asked him why he ever left her and his comfortable home. She complained to the king. 'He disgraces us, associating with riff-raff. Do stop him.' The king, however, impressed with the Buddha's acount of his Enlightenment, invited all in the palace to hear him. The Buddha decides that a miracle is needed to convince them. He flew in the air. There was a storm but the rain divided so as not to wet people and jewels fell to the ground. He reminded his audience of when he was *Vessantar* and gave his own wife and children. His family were much influenced but where was *Bimbā*? She was weeping, with her son. The king sent a servant to summon her. 'I lead the life of a widow', said *Bimbā*. 'What have I done to displease my husband? He left the night our son was born.' The message is conveyed to the Buddha and he goes to see her. He tells her how he and she were once a pair of *kinnarī*. King *Brahmadatt* fell in love with her and shot her husband, the Bodhisatva, but when he expected her to marry him she refused. Indra descended to earth as a Brahmin and brought the Buddha back to life and they were happy.

The Buddha took his son as a disciple and left. *Bimbā* was reconciled.

BUDDHISAEN

See under Rathasenajātak.

CAND GUROP

See *Mucalind.*

CAU KAṄKAEP, *'Mr Frog'*

A poor old couple were fishing. Three times they threw a frog back but eventually they took it home to keep as a pet. The frog, who was really a Bodhisatva, wanted to marry the king's daughter and asked the wife to speak for him. She went to see the king who said, astounded, 'Let him build a silver and a gold bridge in one night and then he may marry my daughter!' With the help of Vishnukar, Indra's architect, the bridges were built and the king had to give him his daughter. That night he appeared to her in the form of a handsome prince. Next day they went to see the king, who decided to hand over the kingdom to him.

CAU KRABAT

As in the story *Suvaṇṇ Sirasā*, the prospective son-in-law had to build a gold and a silver bridge in one night.

CAU OM

The story of a young man who found favour with the king, married the daughter of a minister, divorced her because she lacked good qualities, and married a daughter of the people. He became a king.

CAU TAṂPAU SIRASĀ

A king was ordered by a more powerful king to find the solutions to five problems. After much searching a man 'with a wound on the head' solved his problems.

CINT KUMĀR

He waged war against the king of the *yaks*, was triumphant, and returned to his father's palace.

DĀV EK OR DUṂ DĀV

A Khmer tale based on events in the Longvek period.

Duṃ and his friend *Bejr* were monks; they travelled round selling decorative ceremonial stands and singing and playing the guitar to people. *Duṃ* sang at the house in Thbaung Khmum where *Dāv* lived and they fell in love. *Duṃ* and *Bejr* returned home and asked permission to leave the religious life. There was a delay in giving permission to *Duṃ* because, as the abbot told *Duṃ's* mother, he had consulted the horoscope and seen that *Duṃ* would die. *Duṃ* committed the serious wrong of leaving without permission. They returned to Thbaung Khmum. *Arjūn*, the rich and powerful *Cau Hvāy Sruk* of Thbaung Khmum, planned to marry his son to *Dāv*. *Duṃ*, hearing of this and intending to depart, passed *Dāv*'s house. She saw him and they met. *Dāv*'s mother, hearing that he had come 'to buy some things' asked him to stay. *Duṃ* and *Dāv* became lovers. *Arjūn*'s son, *Ṅuon,* visited every day.

The king heard of *Duṃ* and *Bejr* and their excellent singing and playing and sent for them via *Arjūn*. They soon asked to leave but were refused. The king sent officials to find him a second wife. They found *Dāv*. She came with her mother and was presented to the king. *Duṃ* sang for them. He sang of the love of *Dāv* and himself. The king married them to each other. *Dāv*'s mother was not pleased as *Duṃ* was poor. She planned to marry *Dāv* to *Ṅuon*. She returned home and suggested that *Arjūn* should prepare for a wedding and that *Dāv* should be summoned home as her mother 'was ill'. This was done. *Dāv* sent a letter to *Duṃ*, who told the king about the marriage plans. The king was angry with *Arjūn* and sent ministers with an order. *Duṃ* and *Bejr* journeyed to Thbaung Khmum and mingled with wedding guests. He spoke to *Dāv* and drank some strong alcohol. *Arjūn* and his son attacked *Duṃ* and took him to an open place to die. That night *Dāv* and her confidante went to the same place and cut their own throats. *Bejr* went by boat to tell the king, who set out by boat for Thbaung Khmum. The entire population of the village was buried alive in a pit. (This is a summary of Som's *Duṃ Dāv*.)

DIBV SAṄVĀR

There was once in *Traipurī* near the Hemavant a very powerful king called *Traiputtī*, whose chief queen was *Candaratthā*. They had a son, *Bhiruṇ*.

One day the queen and *Bhiruṇ* were amusing themselves in front of the palace courtyard when an *Indrī* bird [mythological] swooped down and carried off *Bhiruṇ*. Luckily for the prince, the bird flew over the *āsram* of a hermit, who shouted out to frighten the bird. The Indrī dropped the prince and flew on. The hermit picked up the prince and brought him up, educating him in the magic arts. After fifteen years the prince set off home, receiving from the hermit three enchanted possessions: a horse, a monkey, and a bow. On the way, in *Ketujambunagar*, he came across two *yaks*, *Binarāj* and *Vairat*, fighting *Dibv Saṅvār*. He helped her and killed both the *yaks*. She took him to her home where he was given the kingdom and married *Dibv Saṅvār*. That night the brother of the yaks *Binarāj* stole away *Dibv Saṅvār* and put her in an iron dungeon, ready for him to kill her in seven days. When the sun rose *Bhiruṇ* found *Dibv Saṅvār* gone. The horse was able to tell what had happened to *Dibv Saṅvār* and added that *Bhiruṇ* would meet her in three days. *Bhiruṇ* set out with his army to the *yaks* kingdom. At night he put the *yaks* to sleep and entered the palace. He saw *Sugandh*, daughter of *Cittanurāj*, and they fell in love. Then he rescued *Dibv Saṅvār*. They stopped to fight *Cittanurāj*, who had discovered that *Dibv*

Saṅvār had gone and who, with his army and his bird, *Vāyobhaks*, was defeated and killed.

They rested on a hill and even the horse who was to guard them slept. A *yakkhinī*, *Nīlabhaktr*, recently widowed, sadly climbed to the top of the hill. She saw them and, thinking that *Dibv Saṅvār* was a man, carried her off to be her husband. However, *Dibv Saṅvār* was able to kill her. She lost her way, when intending to return to *Bhiruṇ*. She stayed with the same hermit who had brought up *Bhiruṇ* and she had a son, *Suṅ Ŝiṅ*.

When *Suṅ Ŝiṅ* grew up he wanted to go and seek his father, but his mother would not let him go. One day he wrote a note and left. On his way, in the kingdom of *Kruṅ Kāmarāj*, he met *Aruṇarāj* (who, as we shall see, was in fact his half-brother). They fought each other almost to the bitter end and then, through the parents, discovered their relationship. *Suṅ Ŝiṅ* and the king of *Kruṅ Kāmarāj* arranged the wedding of his daughter *Aṃ Phai Bhaktr* with *Aruṇarāj*. There were many fights with *yaks*. Finally they met with their father, *Bhiruṇ*.

Bhiruṇ, resting on the hill from which *Dibv Saṅvār* was stolen, awoke and set off with his companions to find her. They lost their way and came to *Vichāyant*. They saw the *yaks* fighting and flew down to earth. They saw *Nāṅ Uppalavaṇṇā* weeping with her daughter, *Nāṅ Sugandh*. *Bhiruṇ* comforted *Nāṅ Sugandh* and offered to solve her problem by fighting the *yaks* on her behalf. He won and they were married. The kingdom of *Vichāyant* was his. They had a son, *Aruṇarāj*.

After a time, *Bhiruṇ* left *Sugandh* and went to look for *Dibv Saṅvār*. When he found her they went back to her parents' kingdom, *Ketujambū*.[1]

HAṄS YANT

King *Ādityavaṅsā* and Queen *Bimbā* ruled in *Debapurī*. They had no son. *Bimbā* prayed and made offerings to the gods. Indra heard and asked a Bodhisatva to be born as the queen's child. She had a son, a golden child, called *Suvaṇṇakumār*.

When he was 16 the king had 101 kings bring their daughters but none pleased him. He would find his own wife.

There were in the kingdom two artisans. One could build palaces and do decoration; the other could make animal figures on which one could

[1] There follows a long list of the wives and children and kingdoms of the two sons.

fly. The king had ordered them to make a swan-machine *(Haṅs yant)* with a string to control it and had visited the Hemavant.

Suvaṇṇakumār wanted to go and study. His parents gave permission and gave him the swan-machine. He came to Pañcāl and became the pupil of the king's chaplain. The swan-machine was kept on top of a tree. When he had finished his studies he became the godson of the chaplain and went every day with him to see the king.

The king had a beautiful daughter, *Padumakesar*. They fell in love. He came every night to her room in his swan-machine. Then she became pregnant and the king found out. He captured *Suvaṇṇakumār* by a trick and gave him to the executioner. *Suvaṇṇakumār* in turn tricked the executioner into taking him to where the swan-machine was. He jumped into it and flew away to pick up *Padumakesar* from her apartments. Then they were off to *Debapurī*, waving goodbye to the king.

Padumakesar was about to have the baby. They descended to earth. After the baby was born she was shivering. *Suvaṇṇakumār* saw a boat on the sea. He went to it in the swan-machine to bring back fire to warm her but on the way back the fire burnt the control string and he fell into the sea.

Later, *Padumakesar* put a ring on the baby's hand and went to look for her husband but he had been picked up by one boat and the swan-machine by another.

King *Brahmadatt* of Benares, on an expedition to the forest for pleasure, saw the baby. He adopted him and called him *Cau Kṛisṇākumār*, after the tree under which he was found.

Padumakesar returnd and found the baby gone. She followed the footprints of the soldiers who had accompanied the king until she came to the house of an old couple near the city. They made garlands for the king. She stayed with them and helped them.

When *Cau Kṛisṇākumār* was 16 the king sent for the princesses of neighbouring kings and the daughters of rich men for him to choose a wife. He liked none of them. The king heard of the beauty of the flower-weaver. He fell in love with her and they were married. On the wedding night, however, he heard first a cat then a goat then a horse say that whereas animals could marry their mothers, humans could not. Then he thought about how he was picked up in the forest. He told his mother his story and she told him hers. The marriage was dissolved.

Padumakesar had an almshouse built at the edge of the city with pictures relating their story.

Meanwhile the swan-machine had been taken and given to King

Brahmadatt, who gave it to *Cau Kriṣṇākumār* and the boat which saved *Suvaṇṇakumār* also came to Benares. *Suvaṇṇakumār* came to the almshouse, saw the pictures, and was reunited with his wife and son. The three of them flew off in the swan-machine to *Debapurī*.

JINAVAṄS

King *Ādityavaṅs* reigned in *Sobhaṇaṛddhi* and had a son, *Suvaṇṇavaṅs*. The king's brother, *Jinasār*, was *Uparāj* and had a daughter, *Jinapupphā*. The two children were married to each other and had a son, *Jinavaṅs*. The king had three other wives; their sons were *Bisīvaṅs, Nuonvaṅs*, and *Ratnavaṅs*. The king prefered his grandson to his sons and forbade them to play with him. A maidservant tried to poison *Jinavaṅs* but *Jinavaṅs* knew this and did not eat. *Nuonvaṅs* and *Ratnavaṅs* ate the poisoned food and died. The maidservant told the king that *Jinavaṅs* had killed the two brothers; the king ordered the executioners to put *Jinavaṅs* in a cage and throw him into the sea.

Luckily the king of the *Nāgas* saved him. He took him down into the Underworld, broke open the cage, and kept him for three years. The *nāgas* persuaded the king to return *Jinavaṅs* to the human world. He was placed on the shore, where he was seen by a *yakkhinī*, who took him to her cave. He escaped when she was asleep but she followed him and killed him.

A sage brought him back to life and took him in as a pupil. When he had learned all, *Jinavaṅs* set out, with a bow, arrow, and sword created by the sage, to find his parents. He fought with his own brother, *Bisīvaṅs,* through neither recognizing the other, and pursued him back to the palace. His parents rejoiced at his return.

A *yaks*, *Mālivăn*, and his queen, reigned at *Siṅh Koḥ Krai*. They had two daughters, *Padumasuriyā* (whom they took from a flower and brought up) and one of their own, *Suvaṇṇarekhā*. Another *yaks, Dasakaṇḍh*, friend of *Mālivăn*, reigned at *Gandhabv Koḥ Krai*. His son, *Sālikăṇḍh*, asked for the hand in marriage of *Padumasuriyā*. Her parents knew that she was intended for someone special. When *Sālikăṇḍh* came to see her, the servants mixed up the two. He saw *Suvaṇṇarekhā* and was pleased.

Jinavaṅs saw a golden statue of *Padumasuriyā* (made by Indra) when his mother took him to repay an answered prayer at the stupa of his uncle and aunt. He instantly fell in love. Saying goodbye to his parents, he set soff, with *Bisīvaṅs*. They met Indra, who sent *Bisīvaṅs* back home and accompanied *Jinavaṅs* to *Siṅh Koḥ Krai*. Arriving at night, *Jinavaṅs* went straight to the apartments of *Suvaṇṇarekhā* and had already cajoled her when he realized that she was not like the statue. He asked her to take him to *Padumasuriyā*(!)

The *yaks Dasakaṇḍh* had prepared his wedding gifts and was on his way to *Siṅh Koḥ Krai* with his army for his son's marriage. Hearing that *Padumasuriyā* already had a human lover, he persuaded his friend, *Mālivăn*, to fetch *Jinavaṅs* so as to kill him. A battle raged and *Dasakăṇḍh* was defeated by *Jinavaṅs*. *Mālivăn* then gave both daughters to *Jinavaṅs*. Later, *Jinavaṅs* set off on a mechanized swan, leaving *Suvaṇṇarekhā* behind and taking *Padumasuriyā* with him. Half-way across the ocean they were blown down into the sea by a storm. *Jinavaṅs* swam to shore. He slept and was robbed of his bow and arrow and sword by a monkey who took them to the *yaks Citrā*. The *yaks* killed the monkey, kept the goods, and went home. *Jinavaṅs* woke up, met the ghost of the monkey, and brought him back to life. They set off together. They came across *Padumasuriyā*, who was saved by a golden crocodile and was now being looked after by the *kinnarī* (bird men and women). *Jinavaṅs* stayed a while, then set off to regain his bow and arrow and sword from the *yaks Citrā*. The Princess *Añjanbicitr*, daughter of *Citrā*, was bathing with her women, when the monkey, in the form of a sweet little white monkey, went near them. *Jinavaṅs* seduced the princess and was later given her as his queen by the *yaks*. The *yaks* held a sword-pulling contest which the monkey won.

Padumasuriyā was deserted by the bird people when a hunter came. He took her to be his servant. She was pregnant. The hunter and his wife wanted to kill her child but they fell into a stream and died. She wandered through the forest looking for her husband. She met a *mreñ gaṅvāl* (a kind of ghost who takes care of wild animals), who asked her to be his godmother. The two of them met a white elephant, on which she rode, and they arrived at the kingdom of *Sāmal*. The king ordered the people to catch the white elephant but the ghost demanded first that they should look after *Padumasuriyā*. She was treated as one of the king's family.

Jinavaṅs was reminded by the monkey that *Padumasuriyā* was (supposedly) still with the *kinnarī*. He stole away and went to the place. He learned that a hunter stole her but stayed there, fell for a *kinnar* and had a daughter. He left and went to *Sāmal*, where he did a theatrical performance in front of the king and found *Padumasuriyā*.

Meanwhile *Suvaṇṇarekhā* asked her father to take her to *Sobhaṇaṛddhi*.

As to *Añjanbicitr*, she woke up and rushed after her husband all the way to *Sobhaṇaṛddhi*, where she found her parents-in-law. *Citrā* followed his daughter and met *Mālivăn* at the gate of *Sobhaṇaṛddhi*. They were just arguing about whose right of way it was when *Añjan* saw them and called out to *Jinavaṅs* to help. They realized that they both had daughters married to *Jinavaṅs*. They entered *Sobhaṇaṛddhi* but met only *Jinavaṅs'* father.

Añjan and *Suvaṇṇarekhā* soon left to look for their husband. They met a *Viruḷhayaks* whom they vanquished and took captive. A sage, teacher of *Jinavaṅs*, trained the *yaks*. They left the sage, taking the *yaks* as guide.

Jinavaṅs left *Sāmal* with *Padumasuriyā* for *Sobhaṇaṛddhi*. On the way the monkey picked fruit and met the *yaks*. He was defeated by the *yaks* and tied up. He called out for *Jinavaṅs* and the *yaks* realized that his master was the husband of the two girls. They went home to *Sobhaṇaṛddhi*. *Padumasuriyā* and *Suvaṇṇarekhā* went home to *Siṅh Koḥ Krai* and *Añjan* to her home.

Jinavaṅs remembered *Nāgarāj*, the king of the Underworld, who did him a good turn. He found another wife there.

The *yaks Sālikăṇḍh* went to *Sobhaṇaṛddhi* in the form of a parrot and was put in the palace. Returning to *yaks* form, he captured the king, *Suvaṇṇavaṅs*, and *Padumasuriyā* and took them to his kingdom. The king fought with a *kruḍ* (garuḍa), who won and ate him. *Sālikăṇḍh* took his revenge on *Padumasuriyā*, torturing and ill-using her.

The son of *Jinavaṅs* and *Suvaṇṇarekhā*, *Rekhāvaṅs*, stayed with the *yaks, Mālivăn*. In a dream he learned how *Padumasuriyā* was faring and was told to join his father in *Sobhaṇaṛddhi*. He arrived there at night and a fight started among the guards, who thought he was a *yaks*. He proceeded to *Sāmal*, where he fought *Padumavaṅs* until they discovered they were half-brothers. They went to fetch the third half-brother, *Añjanvaṅs*, who was with the ascetic in the *Hemavant*. The three went to the Underworld and defeated the guards, when they were refused entry. *Jinavaṅs* fought them until they discovered their relationship. They all set off to fight *Sālikăṇḍh*. On the way they met the *kruḍ* who ate the king. They learned where the bones were and the king was revived.

The monkey was to go and tell *Padumasuriyā* of the imminent attempted rescue. He changed himself into a young *yaks*, told her and flew back.

Jinavaṅs sent *Padumavaṅs* and *Añjanvaṅs* to *Bejpurī* to *Citrā* to ask for troops and asked the *yaks* and *kruḍ* to bring friends to help. After great preparations the battle took place. *Sālikăṇḍh* was killed. *Jinavaṅs* took home his four wives (*Padumasuriyā, Suvaṇṇarekhā, Añjanbicitr,* and *Kumutnāgī)* and became king of *Sobhaṇarddhi.*

JUC NịṄ TRĪ, *'The fish-trap and the fish.'*

The fish came across the trap, as he swam along. 'Out of my way', he called, 'or I shall go straight through you!' 'Try at your peril!' The fish leaped at the trap and was caught in it. The fish begged to be let free but it was no good; the trap was adamant. As he became weaker the fish called his family to say his last words to them. They had many suggestions as to how he might be freed but it was of no avail. He died and they were left orphans.

The fisherman came in the morning to look at his catch. Some traps were empty but he was pleased with the trap which had the fish in it. The trap told him what had happened and he approved of its behaviour.

KĀBY NIRĀS AṄGAR

This is the true story of the journey made, largely by boat, in 1909 by the king and court to Angkor.

KĀKĪ

King Brahmadatt's queen, *Kākī*, was extremely beautiful. The king played *skā*, a kind of chess, regularly with the king of the Garuḍa birds, who changed into human form for his visits. He fell in love with *Kākī* and showed this by signs not seen by the king. She, neglectful of duty, reciprocated his feelings. One afternoon, when visiting the king, he caused a terrible thunderstorm to arise and, while the palace was in consternation, he visited the queen in her room and persuaded her to come to his kingdom, *Simbalī*, with him. The king, when he realized she was gone, was overcome with distress and sought for her in vain. The Garuḍa came to play chess as usual. A scent of *Kākī* came with him. The king was suspicious and asked his trusted captain, *Kandhăn*, to change himself into a louse and go with the Garuḍa to *Simbalī*. There, when the Garuḍa was away, *Kandhăn*, in human form, persuaded *Kākī* to be his lover. Next day *Kandhăn* returned on the Garuḍa to the king and, while they played chess, played on the harp and sang about the faithlessness of *Kākī*. The Garuḍa was angry with her. He returned to *Simbalī* and brought her back. *Brahmadatt* would not hear her pleas for forgiveness. She was punished by being sent to her death on a raft on the river.

KHYAṄ SĂṄKH

Long ago there was a king who had two queens, *Chandādevī* and *Chandā*, though the former was slightly more important, being in charge of the concubines. The king regretted that he had no son and both queens went to make offerings and pray for a son. Indra invited a Bodhisatva (future Buddha) to be conceived by *Chandādevī* and he accepted. The queens became pregnant and the astrologer told them that *Chandādevī* would have a son who would be king, while *Chandā* would have a daughter. Jealousy led *Chandā* to seek the help of a witch, who cast a spell over the king, making him love her and hate *Chandādevī*. When *Chandā* told the king that if *Chandādevī* stayed she would go to a nunnery, he angrily banished *Chandādevī* and took away all her possessions. *Chandādevī* left sadly and after a day's travel came to a hut where she stayed with an old lady.

Her son, *Khyaṅ Săṅkh*, was born with a shell. After some time she realized that when she was away looking for food, he left his shell and did useful things about the house and garden. *Chandā* heard about them. She persuaded the king to send executioners. Their weapons turned to flowers. Then they threw him, bound, into deep water but the bonds broke. They threw him again, weighted down, and this time he went to the Underworld and persuaded the king to help him. He was sent to live with a childless *yaksinī*, *Bandharas*. She went off hunting for food and he was disturbed by finding human bones. Also, when he acted against her orders and dipped his finger into a pool, it came out stained silver; another pool made it gold. So she was powerful. Finally he went to a palace where there was a *ṅoḥ*, a disreputable-looking magic outfit of cloak, walking-stick, and sandals. He put them on and found he could fly. He set off to go back to his mother. On the way *Bandharas* caught up with him. She was very fond of him and when she saw that he really was leaving she gave him three magic objects and she taught him how to cast a spell to make animals come to his assistance. Then she died.

The king of *Sāmal* had seven daughters. He invited the princes of all the vassal kingdoms to come to the palace. The daughters would choose their own husbands from among them. Six daughters did so. The seventh and youngest, *Racanā*, refused to choose. The king sent for ordinary men, even slaves, and finally for *Khyaṅ Săṅkh*, who had arrived in his kingdom. *Racanā* saw him as he really was and accepted him. The king was angry and made them live in a hut away from the city. At night *Khyaṅ Săṅkh* took off the *ṅoḥ* and was revealed as a handsome prince.

The king decided to kill *Khyaṅ Săṅkh*. He arranged a hunting contest for his sons-in-law. Whoever returned late would die. *Khyaṅ Săṅkh* called all animals to him. The six sons-in-law, finding none, asked for help from *Khyaṅ Săṅkh*, who looked like a god having taken off his *ṅoḥ*. He allowed them one animal each and he demanded that they cut off the ends of their noses. He killed several old animals for himself and flew home. Next the king sent them fishing. Again *Khyaṅ Săṅkh* called the fish to him and let the six have one fish each if they cut a piece off their ears. Finally the king was to hold a contest of *ghlī* (a ball game) on the arena. Anyone who was not dressed properly would be killed. *Racanā* pleaded with her husband to take off the *ṅoḥ*. He did not do this because he still wanted to be able to fly and go and see his mother. She became more and more distressed and ill. Indra told the king that the gods would play *ghlī* against him and that an army was surrouding the city. The king said any of the six who was defeated would be killed. There were games, dances, and acrobats. The people thronged to see the spectacle. The game began and Indra went up into the air. The king needed *Khyaṅ Săṅkh* who could fly. *Khyaṅ Săṅkh* after some persuasion came, looking like a god, and won, beating Indra. He told the six that it was he, seeming like a god, who had made them cut off their noses and ears.

Indra went to see *Khyaṅ Săṅkh's* father and told him all that had happened. *Chandā* tried to bewitch *Chandādevī* again but was caught red-handed and taken to a place of execution. The king persuaded *Chandādevī* with difficulty to come back to him. Then they went and lived as poor people with the gatekeeper of the palace of the king of *Sāmal*. As they never caught sight of their son, the queen went to work in the palace kitchen. She cut vegetables into shapes telling about *Khyaṅ Săṅkh* with the shell, about her banishment by the king, and so on. They were reunited.

Khyaṅ Săṅkh was now king of both his father's and his father-in-law's kingdoms and everyone was happy.

KRĀY THOṄ

The story of a crocodile which eats a man every day. *Krāy Thoṅ* kills it and thus gains the king's daughter.

KRUṄ SUBHAMITR

He was a Bodhisatva who ruled over a kingdom. When his brother, *Asubhamitr*, tried to overthrow him he would not fight. He left the kingdom with his wife and two small sons. They came to a river which *Subhamitr* swam across taking his wife. When he came back for his sons they were gone, taken by a hunter. Returning to his wife, he found she had gone too. The captain of a boat took her on board. *Subhamitr* sadly proceeded and came to *Takkasilā*, where on the death of the king the ministers had let a white elephant go loose to find a new monarch. The elephant knelt before him and he began his reign there. The hunter came and offered the two boys as servants of the king. The captain came to barter goods. The boys were sent with soldiers to guard the goods on the boat. The queen heard them speak of their mother and this led to a reunion. Soldiers saw them embracing the queen, seized them, and took them to the king. They explained, however, and all ended well.

KTĀN' JĀP' ANDĀK'

A deer took her kid out hunting all night. As they neared the edge of the forest she saw an animal trap and warned it to move out of the way. The trap refused and she was caught. She gave advice to her child before being taken away by the owner of the trap.

LPOEK CACAK

A jackal went fishing to feed his pregnant wife. He exclaimed aloud about his desire to be reborn as the sun. A *yaks* overheard and told him to offer himself as food (to the *yaks*) and it would be arranged. The jackal told his wife; he would go and kill himself straight away. She was sad but he said he would come and fetch her to be united with him.

A *yaksinī* came on the scene and was courted and won by the *yaks*. It poured with rain.

The jackal left his wife before she woke up next morning. He saw the *yaksinī* and fled. He fell to the bottom of a ravine and died. The *yaks* fetched the body to eat. The female jackal had followed the male and found his skull. She lamented, grew thin, and died.

The jackal, now reborn as the sun, went through many rebirths as he sought an impregnable position. The sun, covered by clouds, cannot shine. He was reborn as a cloud but the wind blew the clouds to bits. Reborn as the wind, he enjoyed uprooting the trees, etc. One thing, an anthill, resists him. He was reborn as an anthill. A herd of deer came and spoiled and trampled the anthill. Reborn as a deer, he met a big deer and ran away into the forest.

A hunter killed and ate him but not before he had prayed to be reborn as the string of a crossbow. The hunter sang a love song and slept under a tree. A very hungry jackal approached and ate the bowstring. He was reborn as a jackal.

(A note by Mok says that he is retelling the tale of the 'very small dog', *chkae tīoe*.)

LPOEK DOC NIṄ SVĀ

A gibbon persuaded the wife of a monkey to become his lover; the monkey husband had many wives, he had none. They went to a nearby tree but before they became lovers the monkey husband came, fought the gibbon, and took his wife back home. The gibbon came again and the wife went with him much further away. They became lovers. The monkey husband came again and saw them. He was angry and fought the gibbon, who returned and took the wife away from the tree. Neither could fight any more that day. The gibbon fell from a tree and was almost dead. The monkey beat his wife and invited others to join in.

LPOEK NĀṄ PĀY KHUM

Two old ladies quarrelled over the game of *Pāy khum* (a game played by two players with twenty-one counters placed in five containers. The players move the counters one at a time to the next container, left or right.) One lady went away for three years, prospered, and returned. All was forgiven.

LPOEK SVĀ, SĀSTRĀ LPOEK SVĀ

Women are advised to be faithful to their husbands. The point is illustrated by telling the story of the rebirth of the Buddha as a monkey.

MAHOSATHAJĀTAK

See *Sek Sārikā*.

MARAṆAMĀTĀ

King *Vimal Dhammarāj* reigned in *Videhanagar*. Among his servants were *Kulliya*, a village chief, and his wife, *Kaev Kesī*. Their daughter, *Kula Kesī*, and a poor young man, *Kuṭumbī(k)*, fell in love, eloped, and went to live in *Kāsī* among thieves. *Kuṭumbī(k)* was tied up by them but *Kula Kesī* gave the village chief a ring. He became their godfather, set them up with house and servants, and established them in a new village, where they prospered. They had a daughter, *Kumarī*.

A widow, *Kālī*, with two daughters, *Candī* and *Candāsālinī*, came constantly to see *Kulakoṭi Kuṭumbī(k)*, as he was now called. He took her as second wife. Very soon they became poor. *Kuṭumbī(k)* constantly scolded and beat *Kula Kesī*. Finally he took her to cast nets to catch fish and hit her and pushed her into the water where she drowned. She was born again as a fish, an *Oxyellotrismarmorata*, in the same pool. When he returned without her mother, *Kumārī* ran to the place and learned what had happened from a goddess. She called to her mother and talked to her. From then on the daughter was called *Maraṇamātā* (Mother died). She took bran to sprinkle on the water every day. *Kālī* sent her children, ostensibly to provide bran but in fact to kill the mother. A duck came to *Maraṇamātā* with two scales (what was left of her mother). She planted them and two egg-plants with lovely fruit grew there. *Kālī* had the trees brought and pounded in a mortar. A cat brought *Maraṇamātā* two roots from what was left and she planted them. They grew into an *Erythrina indica* and her mother was a goddess looking after them. King *Vimal Dhammarāj* saw it and asked for it. It would only move when *Maraṇamātā* prayed to it. It was planted in a gold trough and called *Rājabriks*. The king made *Maraṇamātā* his chief queen.

When the king was away on an elephant hunt, *Kālī*, who was trying to kill *Maraṇamātā*, prepared a huge pot of boiling oil and covered it over with wood and sent for her urgently, as 'her father was dying'. She was invited to take off her things before seeing her father. She stepped on the wood, fell into the oil and died. *Kālī* dressed her own child in the garments and sent her to the palace. The king returned and was angry. The *Rājabriks* wilted.

A goddess made *Maraṇamātā* live again as a Myna-bird. She went to the palace and lived there, with a golden ring on her foot. She prayed to the tree and it revived.

Candāsālinī was killed by order of the king and was made into a paste and sent to her parents. They realized what it was and fled.

A sentence of death was passed on the woman who had taken *Maraṇamātā* to her death. Her daughter, *Chandā*, one of the king's servants, stole the bird and gave it to a kitchen maid to cook. The maid plucked her and put her down. She fled into a mouse-hole, where she stayed until her feathers had grown again. The mouse bit off *Chandā's* nose and she died. The Myna-bird left the mouse, and met a snake but the snake was killed by a marabou.

Indra descended in the form of a lion which ate the fruit of a fig-tree on one side and turned into a bird. The bird ate figs on another side and turned into a deer. The deer ate and turned into a monkey and the monkey turned into a handsome prince. The Myna-bird saw all this and did likewise, turning finally into a woman. She met a sage, *Mittajin*, and lived in his hermitage. The sage found a boy, born in a lotus, and brought him for her to bring up. He was called *Padumakumār*. When he grew up he went off to look for his father, taking the ring from his mother's foot and the fig.

King *Vimal Dhammarāj* and his mother reigned again. King *Vimal Dhammarāj* always gave offerings to ducks, cats, mice, and the poor.

MĀ YOEṄ, *'Our Uncle'*

When *Brahmadatt* was king in Benares, there was a poor fisherman who had a beautiful, but mean and greedy, wife. She did not even mend the holes in the basket which was used to keep the fish, as her husband caught them. One day a junk appeared. The wife of its captain called out, 'Why don't you mend the holes in your basket? You're losing the fish!' The captain said, 'If you can give orders like that, go and mend the basket and be his wife. I'll have her as mine.'

The exchange was made. The new fisherman's wife mended the basket and looked after everything. They prospered. She was pleasant and was liked by everybody. Eventually she asked a mandarin to present her husband for the king's service, which he did.

One day the king rode ahead of his followers and lost them. He had only the fisherman with him. He called him *Mā Yoeṅ* ('Our uncle') because he faithfully followed his sovereign. The king ate some of *Mā Yoeṅ's* lunch and praised his wife. He would raise *Mā Yoeṅ* to be an important mandarin.

The king said he would tell a tale but he fell asleep. The spirit which lived in the tree under which they were resting was angry that there was no story. He told *Mā Yoeṅ* that he would either drop a branch on the king or cause a lintel to fall on him or, if he escaped these dangers, he would enter his bedroom as a snake and bite him to death. *Mā Yoeṅ* roused the king and they hurried off and escaped the first two dangers but the spirit came as a snake to the king's bedroom. *Mā Yoeṅ* was on duty. He killed the snake but its blood spurted on to the breast of the sleeping queen. *Mā Yoeṅ*, after much thought, decides to lick the blood off. She woke and told the king, who ordered the executioner to take *Mā Yoeṅ* out of the city and kill him immediately.

At all four gates of the city, the guard refused to let them out in the middle of the night for an execution and in three cases told a story about a hasty execution. One was about a woman whose child died of a snake bite in her absence and whose pet weasel, whose job it was to protect the child, had fought the snake bravely. She killed the weasel, thinking it had killed the child, and then saw the dead snake. The second story was of a rich man who had 500 dogs to guard his treasures. 500 thieves dug a tunnel to steal the goods. The dogs chased them back into the tunnel and bit them to death. The owner killed the dogs who, it seemed, had not protected his property. Later, when there was an unexplained stench, he investigated and found the dead robbers and the goods. The third was about a king who killed his innocent pet parrot. The parrot had assured the king that mangoes from a certain tree in the *Hemavant* make people younger. The king had some mango seeds brought by the parrot and planted. Unknown to anyone a serpent lived under the mango tree and its poison seeped into the entire tree. The king had his page try a fruit. He died. In anger the king killed the parrot. Years later, when the snake had died and the poison was gone, an elderly couple who looked after the king's elephant had no strength left for the task. They thought that after all these years they might try the mangoes. They became young. The king regretted his haste. The fourth guard gave a lecture on the duties of guards and on the laws of the land.

The king regretted his order for execution, thinking of all the kindnesses done by *Mā Yoeṅ*. He sent a page off to catch *Mā Yoeṅ* before execution and to bring him to him. *Mā Yoeṅ* was encouraged to explain. The highest rank of mandarin was bestowed upon him.

The captain of the junk and his wife came begging to the house of *Mā Yoeṅ* and his wife gaves them alms.

MUCALIND *(Part only)*

Braḥ Cand Gorab arrived at the place and saw the girl as Indra had prophesied. He told her she was to be his wife. 'I am not educated to belong to your class. Look elsewhere for Mademoiselle Mucalind.' He insisted that she must marry him 'If Indra were here to present you . . .', she said. 'My father, the King of *Rājapurī*, gave me 500 young ladies—not one of them could I want. So I came away to be alone. In the forest, Indra spoke of you.' 'My parents will disagree', she said. 'I insist.' She went behind a screen and said he must go away (but she sounded encouraging); she might call for help, if he continued in this vein.

PUÑÑASĀR SIRSĀ *(from Dik-Kéam 1967; no text available except for Part 5)*

Sirasā, son of King *Bhavadularāj* and Queen *Sāgaradevī* of Benares, and his friend, *Puññasā*, son of a rich man, went about together perpetrating much mischief. They would steal fruit and vegetables or other crops and upset the owners. The people were angry and went to tell the king, who banished them.

In the forest they saw a deer, produced by the gods. A god told them: anyone who swallows its right eye will become a great king while anyone who swallows the left eye will be very rich. The deer died. *Sirasā* cut out the right eye with his knife and swallowed it. *Puññasā* swallowed the left eye. They parted company and moved on.

Sirasā came to a civilized kingdom whose king had just died. The people had met to choose a successor but could think of no one suitable. When they saw *Sirasā* approaching, they liked him and invited him to be king and offered him *Bimbā*, the daughter of the late king, as his queen.

Meanwhile *Puññasā* arrived at *Cittavatī*. The king liked him and treated him as an adopted son. He gave him his daughter, *Sālit*, as wife. Later, however, desiring the eye of the deer, which *Puññasā* had swallowed and kept inside him, the king planned to kill him. He tried two or three times, unsuccessfully because a god helped *Puññasā*. The god told him to fight his father-in-law. He must offer figs from the *Hemavant* to the king and all his entourage, who were in the plot to kill him. When they had eaten the figs they turned into monkeys. *Puññasā* was king.

Later *Puññasā* flew through the air with his queen, looking for *Sirasā*. They found him and the two friends were delighted. *Puññasā* gave many gifts to his friend but *Sirasā* took only the deer's eye and returned the other presents. *Sirasā* urged *Puññasā* to go and amuse himself in the forest while his own attendants went to *Uttakurudvīp*. Indra had his son, *Mātulī*, invite them all to the heaven of the 33. He asked *Sirasā* to reign there jointly with him. *Sirasā* told *Puññasā* and his attendants to return to the world of men where *Puññasā* must observe the ten kingly duties. *Sirasā* stayed to rule in heaven.

RATHASENAJĀTAK (BUDDHISAEN)

The twelve daughters (*nāṅ bīrṭanṭap'*) of a poor woodcutter were abandoned in the forest. They came to the dwelling of a *yaksinī*, *Sandhamār*, who welcomed them, thinking that they would look after her daughter, *Kaṅrī*. They soon discovered, when *Sandhamār* was away hunting, that there were human bones in a storehouse. They took rice and clothes and left in fear.

A crow told *Sandhamār* where they were but when she came for them they hid in the mouth of an ox and then in the stomach of an elephant; finally they were temporarilly swallowed by a mouse-deer.

They bathed in a pool and put on the fine clothes they had brought with them and were discovered by someone from the palace. Thus they were introduced to King *Rathariddhi*. He fell in love with them all and married them. However, *Sandhamār* heard of this and came in the guise of a beautiful young girl to bewitch the king. He married her and made her chief queen over the twelve girls.

Sandhamār pretended to be ill. Only a concoction made from the eyes of the twelve girls would cure her. The king had the eyes of the twelve gouged out and the girls were put in a hole in the ground. They were all pregnant. Eleven ate their babies but the twelfth protected hers. When this child, *Buddhisaen*, was 7 he climbed up out of the hole by means of a golden fig-tree, created by Indra. He played *aṅguñ* (a sort of skittles with the nuts of the tree *aṅguñ*') against boys for rice at first but, acquiring a reputation, he eventually played against the king. The king found out who he was and became fond of him. Now the king needed someone to go to *Sandhamār's* home and ask *Kaṅrī* to mix the medicine! *Buddhisaen* would go if the king gave food to the twelve while he was away. This was agreed and a horse of magic powers was to go with him.

On the way they stayed overnight with a hermit, who read the message they took with them. He saw that *Kaṅrī* was told to kill *Buddhisaen* and the horse. He changed the wording: *Kaṅrī* was to marry *Buddhisaen* and give him an army. The hermit told *Buddhisaen* about this.

Buddhisaen and *Kaṅrī* fell in love and were married. He stayed three years and they had two sons. He was sad one day. *Kaṅrī* planned an expedition to the forest to cheer him up. They passed a storehouse where, *Kaṅrī* told him, the eyes of the twelve were kept together with an ointment which would fit them back. They also passed a gong, which would cause any enemy to die, and three citrus fruits which could turn into a river, a mountain, and a fire.

Buddhisaen made the whole company drunk, while remaining sober himself. He said goodbye to *Kaṅrī* many times, threatened by the horse that if he did not hurry he would go back by himself. He took the eyes, the ointment, and the magic objects and they left. *Kaṅrī* woke up and followed him with the army. They were merely delayed by the fruit which turns into a mountain but the army was wiped out by the gong and *Kaṅrī* was drowned in the river.

Arriving at the palace *Buddhisaen* killed *Sandhamār* with the gong and fitted the eyes on to the twelve. All ended happily with the twelve restored to the king.

RĀJAKUL

King Candarāj and his chief queen, *Nāṅ Candadevī*, had three daughters, *Rājaksatrī, Srīksatrā*, and *Nāṅ Bau*. The youngest was beautiful and had 'all the signs (of good fortune)'.

A poor man *Dūbhī* and his wife *Miñ Durgat Kumārī* had very little money. The man said he would buy tools and seed and they would grow rice. With the money from that they would give alms. Indra saw them looking after their ricefield. He decided to send a heavenly prince, *Rājakul*, to look after them. *Rājakul* saw that *Nāṅ Bau* was his wife in previous lives and thought he ought to join her.

Rājakul was enveloped in the form of a horse and descended to the ricefield and browsed the plants. *Dūbhī* took him home. The king soon learned about the fine horse and ordered it to be brought before him. He kept the horse, compensating the couple with a fortune. Soon afterwards, they turned into a young couple.

The king grew fond of his horse but the horse sighed with love for *Nāṅ Bau*. Consulting his astrologer, the king learned that the horse wished to marry one of his daughters. The king called for his daughters and asked them in turn whether they were willing to marry the horse. The eldest and the second one said no. The youngest said she would do her parents' bidding.

After the wedding *Nāṅ Bau* performed all the duties of a wife. *Rājakul* came out of his horse envelope at night. He was a handsome prince. The king sent for the couple and handed the throne to *Rājakul*.

SABVASIDDHI

The Bodhisatva was born as a small sparrow, living in a forest with his wife and children. One day when he went off to search for food, he perched on a big lotus, and the sun's heat caused the lotus to close over him. He had to stay there until dark and came away with the scent of lotus on him. When he went home, a forest fire had killed his children and his wife was full of accusations against him. How could he be out so late in the day looking for food? Why did he smell of flowers? He had a lover! Let him go to her! Nothing he could say would convince her of the truth. She prayed that in a future life she should have nothing to do with men and he that in a future life he would marry her. Then they both flew into the flames.

The husband was born to a rich man in Benares. His name was *Sabvasiddhi*. When he was 15 he went with a companion to study the magic arts in *Takkasilā*. They both learned how to take over the bodies of dead men and animals and live.

The wife was born as Princess *Suvaṇṇakesar*, daughter of King *Brahmadatt* of Benares. Princess *Suvaṇṇakesar* had never in her life spoken to any man. The king made a proclamation that any man who could make his daughter speak should have her as his wife. Princes and rich men's sons came and tried to persuade her but with no success.

Then *Sabvasiddhi* came back from his studies and was allowed to try. He took the heart from his companion and put it in the door, the lamp, the tray for betel and the curtains and asked them various questions. Their replies were not satisfactory to the princess. She answered instead. The delighted king gave her to *Sabvasiddhi* and made him second king.

One day *Sabvasiddhi* went with his companion to the forest and came across a dead deer. Taking out his heart and putting it into the deer he ran along with the herd. His companion, left guarding his human form, was untrustworthy. He took his own heart and put it into *Sabvasiddhi*'s form. Then he burned his own shape, returned to the capital, and made a fuss of *Suvaṇṇakesar*. She realized he was different, however, and would not speak.

Sabvasiddhi returned at sunset and found his companion and his own human form gone. He went to the garden of an old couple and found a dead Myna-bird, which had been their pet. He put his heart into it, flew to the palace and sat on *Suvaṇṇakesar*'s window-sill, asking for food. *Suvaṇṇakesar* realized that it was *Sabvasiddhi*. They formed a plan. The companion would be asked to demonstrate his strength in front of everyone. A goat would be brought in for the demonstration and *Sabvasiddhi* would be near by in a box.

All went well. When the companion went into the goat *Sabvasiddhi* took up his old form, sent the executioner after the companion-goat, and lived happily ever after with *Suvaṇṇakesar*.

SAMUDDH, SAMUDR *(Résumé by By-Sovann, given by Dik-Kéam, 1967b: 41–8)*

Braḥ Samudr was the son of King *Brahmadatt* and Queen *Say Sumā*, who reigned at Benares. (Three other queens were *Gandhādhar, Sīsumā*, and *Kaṇikār*.) The fourth wife made the chaplain forecast the character of *Braḥ Samudr* in front of the king, predicting that he was accursed and would bring misfortune to the kingdom unless he was banished. *Braḥ Samudr* left the kingdom with a cousin, *Vijjādhar*, and his mother.

They came to the kingdom of *Kanurāj*, a good *yaks* king, who, having no children, adopted *Braḥ Samudr*. He gave *Braḥ Samudr* a diamond walking-stick, which, when shaken, produced whatever the owner wanted.

After some time *Braḥ Samudr* thought he would return to his father. He set off but lost his way and came to the kingdom of a garuḍa, *Sūrikānt*, and eloped with his daughter, *Vimānathān*. They met a *yaksinī*, who took *Braḥ Samudr* away as her husband. *Vimānathān* and *Vijjādhar* went back to the kingdom of *Kanurāj*, where *Vimānathān* bore a son, *Candadatt*.

Braḥ Samudr freed himself from the *yaksinī* and fled to the kingdom of a *yaks*, *Virullacakr*, married his daughter, *Sumālī*, and fled with her to the kingdom of *Kanurāj*.

Vimānathān was jealous and persecuted *Sumālī* until she could endure it no longer and secretly fled from the kingdom. She took shelter with a *ṛsī*. Her son, *Hatthaḍī*, was born there and was educated by the *ṛsī*. When *Sumālī* ran away, *Braḥ Samudr* set out to find her. After many years he met with his two sons, one the son of *Sumālī* and one the son of *Vimānathān*, who were looking for him. They took him to the *āsram* where *Sumālī* (and his mother) was. Having been reunited with *Sumāli*, his sons, and his mother, *Braḥ Samudr* took them all to see his father in Benares.

When they were nearly there, *Braḥ Samudr* said that in order to show the king his might, he would send *Hatthaḍī* to stir up trouble. He did so and the people asked the king to fight. Troops were sent but were captured by *Hatthaḍī*, who said, 'Tell your king to come and fight himself or submit to us.' The king came to submit and *Hatthaḍī* took him to meet his wife, his son, and his other grandson.

Braḥ Samudr reigned in his father's place and sent his two sons to reign in the kingdoms of their grandfathers.

SĂṄKH SILP JĂY

Princess *Kesarasumandā* (or just *Sumandā*), bathing outside the palace grounds, with her brother, King *(Sena)kuttarāj*, and his army to guard her, was nevertheless carried off by a *yaks*, as the astrologer had prophesied she would be. He proved to be a kind husband and they had a daughter, *Suvarṇadevī*. The *yaks* played *skā* (a kind of chess) with the king of the Underworld and one day he wagered his daughter and lost.

When Princess *Kesarasumandā* was stolen away, King *(Sena)kuttarāj* went into a monastery. Near by lived a couple with seven daughters. One day they came to the monastery and he fell in love with them. Leaving the monastery he married them. One of the king's concubines, *Kesarāpupphā*, and the youngest sister of the seven, *Padumā*, gave birth on the same day respectively to a lion and a fine boy, *Săṅkh Silp Jăy*, a Bodhisatva or future Buddha, who held a bow of supernatural power and a shell. The six sisters plotted to be rid of these offspring and bribed the astrologer to prophesy doom to the kingdom if they were not sent away. They were banished and for seven years lived in a palace built for them by *Vishnukār*, Indra's architect.

A hunter came across them and told the six sisters where they were. They sent their six sons with poison. *Săṅkh Silp Jăy* suspected them and said he ate only heavenly food. They sent poisoned betel but he did not swallow it.

The six all seemed unworthy to rule. To test their powers the king sent them to fetch first a bird, then an animal, then a fish from the *Hemavant. Săṅkh Silp Jăy* helped them. He shot an arrow each time and the bird, animal, and fish appeared. Then the king asked them to fetch *Kesarasumandā* from the *yaks* and *Suvarṇadevī* from the king of the Underworld. With *Săṅkh Silp Jăy* they set out. *Săṅkh Silp Jăy* defeated 26,000 *nāg* (supernatural snakes) and left the lion to look after the six—who had run away! Proceeding on his own, he overcame 500 elephants; resisted the blandishments of a *yaksini*; met the *Vidyādhar*, learned demons, who were disputing possession of the fruits which are in the form of women; cut off the head of an ogress, and escaped from the *kinnarī* (bird-women), whom he at first told he was looking for a wife.

At last, using the shell to travel swiftly, he arrived at the palace of *Kesarasumandā* when the *yaks* was out. They exchanged news excitedly and *Săṅkh Silp Jăy* urged her to come back with him. She agreed to ask permission to go home for seven days but the *yaks* refused. In the end she agreed to go and regretfully left. *Săṅkh Silp Jăy* put her in a cave and went back, mounted on the lion, whom he had summoned by shooting an arrow, to fight her husband to the death.

Leaving *Kesarasumandā* in a specially created palace, he used the shell for transport and went to the Underworld. He played *skā* with *nāg*, with ministers, and finally with the king, wagering his sword and shell against the king's wife. He won but the king refused to give her. A tremendous fight took place in which *Săṅkh Silp Jăy* was victorious. *Suvarṇadevī* had to be persuaded to leave.

Now that *Kesarasumandā* and *Suvarṇadevī* were rescued the six sons planned to kill *Săṅkh Silp Jăy*. They went with him to gather fruit, making him leave his sword and shell behind, and pushed him into a gulley. They insisted that he was lost and intended that everyone should now go home but first the women went to the gulley and threw into a stream a piece of cloth, given to *Kesarasumandā* by Çiva, and a hair-pin, given to *Suvarṇadevī* by her father, and prayed that the objects should arrive in *(Sena)kuttarāj*'s kingdom if *Săṅkh Silp Jăy* was alive. They all went home.

The lion looked for *Săṅkh Silp Jăy* and found the sword and shell near the gulley. He flew with them to where the mothers lived. Indra brought *Săṅkh Silp Jăy* to the same place.

A ship's captain found the objects cast into the stream by the women and brought them to the king and soon afterwards *Săṅkh Silp Jăy* himself arrived with the two mothers. The six sons were eventually condemned simply to live as ordinary people. *Săṅkh Silp Jăy* reigned in place of his father.

SEK SĀRIKĀ

In *Mithilā*, where King *Videha* reigned, a marriage between him and the daughter of King *Cullaṇī* of *Uttarapañcāl* was supposed to have been arranged. To verify secretly that this really was so, *Mahosath*, the Bodhisatva, sent his clever parrot to *Uttarapañcāl*. The parrot was to coax and cajole the Myna-bird which was King *Cullaṇī*'s pet and lived in a cage near his bedroom. She was sure to have heard the king's secrets and to know what was happening. The parrot did court the Myna-bird and found out that King *Cullaṇī* was indeed plotting against King *Videha*. Having found out all that was needed, the parrot had to go back to *Mithilā*. Alas, he and the Myna-bird had fallen in love! They were very unhappy at their separation but, after a long time they were reunited.

SIDHNŪV *(Résumé based on that by Au- Chhieng 1953)*

King *Sidhnūv* and Queen *Paripūphphārī* were shipwrecked and separated. The queen arrived in the kingdom of *Caṃmpākapūrī* and requested hospitality of an old lady. She sold her ring for four cartloads of gold and with the money she organized a festival and transferred the merit to her husband, wherever he might be. Divine architects descended to help with the construction of the pavilion for the festival.

Sidhnūv looked in vain for his wife. He met a *yakkhinī* with whom he passed some time.

SRADAP CEK

Two rich men, *Dhan* and *Bhog*, were friends. Both were childless. They offered prayers and declared that their children should be friends or should marry if they were of opposite sexes. *Dhan* had a son and *Bhog* a daughter.

Dhan was soon to depart this life. He gave away all his possessions and died a poor man. His widow went with her son to see *Bhog* but not only had he forgotten his promises to *Dhan*, he even beat her and sent her away. As they walked away, she died, telling her son to study. The son had to sell everything in order to bury her, including his own clothes. He dressed himself in the leaves of the banana tree, which wrap round the trunk *(Sradap Cek)* and went to find a teacher.

Bhog's daughter, *Kesar Mālā*, had become infatuated with *Sradap Cek* when her father was beating his mother. How could she find him again? She persuaded her father to let her have a shop at the market. It would dispel her depression, she said. She met *Sradap Cek* and caused him to be caught as a thief, after which he gave up his studies and sold cakes. He did well at this because *Kesar Mālā* bought all his cakes!

King *Dhammarājā*, having no son, wanted to marry his daughter to the future king. In order to find out who should be king, he let an elephant go of its own free will. Whoever was the person before whom the elephant knelt, would be the king. The elephant knelt before *Sradap Cek*, who was flown to the palace, mounted on the elephant. There was great rejoicing.

Sradap Cek took the name *Devavaṅs*, and married the king's daughter, *Kesar Pupphā*. He also wanted to marry *Kesar Mālā*, however. Three times he asked for her hand, incognito, through the District

Chief. Her father chased him away, beating him. *Sradap Cek* started a law case against the father in which *Kesar Mālā* was a witness. Knowing the whole story now and torn between her father and her lover, she remained silent throughout the trial and so had the right to have the last word. When her father was condemned to death she saved him.

Sradap Cek and *Kesar Mālā* were married and she became chief queen, while *Kesar Pupphā* was second queen.

STEC KMEṄ, *'The youthful king'*

In the realm of King *Brahmadatt* 500 young herdsmen guarded his animals. A tree-god inspired these young men to choose a king and court from among themselves, build a palace with seven circular walls of thorns, make a litter, and finally to go to the monastery and make an invocation. On the day that they went to the monastery only a novice was there. The god made the 'king' draw a beautiful girl, *Nāṅ Krep Samudr*, and leave the drawing at the monastery.

The real king dreamed of a beautiful woman from the Underworld, *Krep Samudr*, but when he stretched out his hand towards her she vanished. Next day he went to the monastery and saw the portrait of her. She must be found. He sent word to the young men; the official was refused entry. An elderly dignitary was told that the young king would give his answer. The youths set out in a dignified procession, ignored the real king, and made obeisance to the dignitary. The real king asked whether the artist knew *Krep Samudr*. If so, he was to fetch her. If he did not do so the youths would all be boiled alive with all seven generations of their families.

The young king asked for a boat and 100 sailors. The king added some fine cloth to this. The parents of the youths were amazed and angry but could do nothing but see them off. After four months they needed more food. They stopped at an island and planted seeds which grew quickly. Monkeys came and took their fruit, however. As they chased them away they heard them say the monkey king would come tomorrow. The young human king set a trap to catch the monkey king: some planks, on which the monkey king would surely sit, over a trench. Sitting in the trench he grasped the monkey's tail, when he sat on the planks. The monkey king had a useful crystal, which took the owner where he wanted and he knew where *Krep Samudr* lived! They must go to a turbulent whirlpool and anchor. Then he must jump into the water with the crystal. The young king was pleased and the monkey king allowed his son to go with him.

All went well and they arrived in the Underworld where Princess *Krep Samudr* lived. He enlisted the help of an old lady who served *Krep Samudr*, telling her that he wanted to marry her. First flowers, then the monkey, and finally the young king came to *Krep Samudr*. He should have approached her parents through an intermediary but he did not. He stayed three months and at the end of that time she was pregnant.

They fled to the boat. When they reached the chain, by which they would be pulled up into the boat she remembered her jewel box. He went back for it but told her not to step on the platform, which would indicate that he was there. She did step on it and was hauled up with the monkey, who lept up and caught hold just in time. The sailors decided to set off for home because food and water were in short supply and the young king had the crystal for travelling. The young king caught up with a merchant ship and acquired a rope which tied by itself, a stick which beat by itself and a cooking pot which cooked by itself.[2] He joined his own ship and soon they were home.

After using his magic treasures to beat the real king and his army he settled down to rule harmoniously with his wife as queen.

SUDHAN

He was the Bodhisatva (future Buddha) born to Queen *Chandādevī*, wife of King *Ādityarāj* of *Pañcār*. When he grew up 101 princes brought their daughters for him to choose a wife. None pleased him. The chaplain offered his own daughter, *Ekānuṃ*, as concubine. *Sudhan* was not particularly pleased but accepted.

There was a kingdom of *kinnar* (bird-people), with its king, *Udumbar*. According to the astrologer some disaster would cause his separation from his seventh daughter, *Manoharā*. One day she persuaded her sisters to go and bathe in a pool near the palace grounds. It happened that a hunter, *Puṇḍarik*, had saved the life of a *nāg* at this pool by shooting the *gruḍ* which had swooped down and caught him. The grateful *nāg* had promised to capture a *kinnari* (bird-lady) for him. Now, when the

[2] Cf. Ch. 6, 'Folktales Summaries': *Cau Kāṃpit Pandoḥ*.

sisters came to bathe, the *nāg* seized the foot of *Manoharā* and the hunter took her away and offered her to *Sudhan*, who delightedly made her his wife. *Ekānuṃ* was not pleased.

Sudhan had to go and fight a rebellious vassal. While he was away the king had a dream which the astrologer interpreted (falsely). In order to avoid danger to the kingdom, the astrologer said, animals, including *Manoharā*, must be sacrificed, by burning alive. *Manoharā* asked to dance before the king, as she had never done so. When she was applauded enthusiastically she asked if she could have her wings, which had been taken away from her, to dance as she danced in front of her own parents. They were given to her and she flew away.

Manoharā descended to leave a ring, handkerchief, ointment for protection, and a note explaining the way to her home with a hermit, in case *Sudhan* came that way. Then she went home to be greeted with rejoicing.

Having subdued the vassal, *Sudhan* returned home. When he heard what had happened in his absence he set off immediately with the hunter as his guide. They came to the hermit's hut. The hunter was sent back with a message to imprison the astrologer until he returned. Then for seven years, seven months, and seven days *Sudhan* journeyed. Finally he was taken by some *Indrī* birds to a pool outside the palace grounds, where girls were drawing water. He secretly put the ring in a pitcher. It was taken up to *Manoharā* and it went on to her finger by itself. The king was delighted with his brave son-in-law, who passed with ease his test of raising and shooting a bow. A splendid wedding ceremony took place in a palace created by Çiva.

Soon *Sudhan* and *Manoharā* went back to *Pañcār*, where they became king and queen. They ruled peacefully and had a son. In later life *Sudhan* became a hermit in the forest of the *Hemavant*.

SUPIN KUMĀR

Supin Kumār was a good, kind boy, who went often to the monastery to help the monks. His father was a fisherman, an angry, ungrateful, mean man who, when he died, became a bad spirit. His mother was devoted to her son but when he grew up he wanted to go away and become a monk. He needed her permission for this and she would not give it. Then one day the king of hell sent his guards out to see what bad people they could catch and bring to hell. They caught his mother.

As she was thrown into the fire she called upon her son to help her. A lotus sprang up and she was saved. She gave in then about his becoming a monk. Later, when she died, she went to heaven.

The father, who was a bad spirit, had had no food for years until *Supin Kumār* became a monk. Now he came to see his son. *Supin Kumār* held a ceremony and made offerings on his father's behalf. As a result his father went to heaven.

SUVAṆṆ SIRASĀ

When *Brahmadatt* reigned in Benares there lived in the village of *Pañcāl* a very poor couple. The wife dreamed that a frog ate the moon and a bit fell on her. The astrologer said she would give birth to a son who had only a head. She did have such a son and named him *Suvaṇṇ Sirasā.*

Later, *Suvaṇṇ Sirasā* left home and went off with merchants to do business. He saw a deserted island, however, and there he cultivated vegetables. Two girls from the Underworld pulled them up for fun but he surprised them in his garden. They acknowledged their guilt and brought him countless treasures from the Underworld.

Now that he was rich, *Suvaṇṇ Sirasā* wanted to marry one of the daughters of King *Brahmadatt* but first he must build a bridge of silver and gold, connecting his house to the palace. With the help of the gods he did this and married one of the princesses.

The people were indignant and demanded his death but Indra helped by asking the king four questions; if he could not answer them he and his kingdom would be destroyed. All the ministers and sages were of no avail. In the end he appealed to *Suvaṇṇ Sirasā*, who went to heaven and obtained the answers. He came out of his 'head' and was seen to be a handsome man. *Brahmadatt* gave him the throne as well as his daughter.

VARANUJ VARANETR *(Part 1 only)*

King *Cetarāj* had two chief queens, *Khemā* and *Subhadr*. *Khemā* had no sons while *Subhadr* had one. Khemā was resentful of this. When a second son was born to *Subhadr Khemā* was tempted. The king was away when he was born and she took her opportunity. She tried to kill the baby by putting him in a cooking pot and floating it down the river. In its place she put a piece of wood. She told the king that *Subhadr* had given birth to a piece of wood and should be banished. A hermit rescued the baby and brought him up, calling him *Varanuj*. She had someone take the elder and abandon him. He was put beneath a Bodhi tree, however, was saved by a god, and was called *Varanetr*. The king had *Subhadr* put on a raft and floated down the river. She reached an island.

When *Varanuj* grew up he wanted to find his parents. Indra told him what had happened and where his mother was. He went to a hermit, who cast a spell over a horse so that he could take him to his mother on the island. They set out and came to a forest, where they stopped. A god carried him off and put him down in the apartments of *Suvaṇṇagandhā*, daughter of a *yaks*. They fell in love. Her father was angry when he heard of this and in the ensuing fight was killed by *Varanuj*. Leaving *Suvaṇṇagandhā*, *Varanuj* flew on to the island and was reunited with his mother. He took her to the Underworld, where he made the king's daughter his chief queen. He then fetched *Suvaṇṇagandhā* and left his wives with his mother.

Varanuj allowed a white elephant to eat grass and was seen by a hunter from *Cetarājanagar* who reported it to the king. When the king came to capture it, *Varanuj* called the elephant to him. The king was angry and a fight followed. But the arrows turned into food, questions were asked, and they discovered they were father and son. The king set his son on the throne and forgave *Khemā*.

VARAVAṅS SŪRAVAṅS

King *Sūriyā* of *Krasaṅ* had two queens. The chief queen, *Vaṅsadhyā* had two sons, *Varavaṅs* and *Sūravaṅs*, while the second queen, *Mandā*, had one son. One day when the boys were playing, *Mandā* hurt *Vaṅsadhyā*'s sons and called out that they were attacking her in an unseemly way. The king called for the executioner but the mother pleaded and they were spared but had to leave. *Vaṅsadhyā* gave them each a ring and told them to return in ten years.

The boys walked on and slept under a tree. Indra sent a white and a black hen. As they pecked, the black hen said, 'Eat me and be a king in seven years.' The white one said, 'Eat me and be a king in seven months.' The hens then quarrelled and died. The boys cooked and ate the hens. *Sūravaṅs* ate the white hen and *Varavaṅs* the black. After seven months they came to a *sālā* in *Gandhapurī*. There, the king having died, an elephant was being sent forth to find a new king. The elephant came to *Sūravaṅs* and, despite *Sūravaṅs*' pleas that his brother should come too, went off with *Sūravaṅs* on his head. *Sūravaṅs* married *Sapupphā,* daughter of the dead king.

Varavaṅs followed the elephant prints to the palace but was refused entry. For five days and nights he walked and came to the kingdom of King *Dharaṇit.* Near the palace an elderly lady let him stay with her but when she saw his ring she thought he was a burglar and told the king. He was cast into gaol.

A *yaks* was at that time devastating the realm of *Jayapurī* and threatening King *Sodatt.* He asked King *Dharaṇit* for help. A boat was to be launched immediately—but no one could push it into the water! A very strong man was needed. *Varavaṅs* offered his help and pushed out the boat with ease. He was freed and given gifts. Then with his daughter, *Kesakesī,* his ministers, and *Varavaṅs,* the king set out for *Jayapurī* to confer with *Sodatt. Kesakesī* and *Varavaṅs* fell in love.

The two kings decided that *Varavaṅs* could tackle the *yaks.* If he failed, he was after all only a prisoner. *Varavaṅs* agreed but asked for a king's sword and garments. He killed the *yaks.* Both kings gave him their daughters and their kingdoms. An *āraks* or spirit who had fled when the *yaks* was there returned and gave him a crystal with which he could fly.

Varavaṅs therefore decided to go home by air. *Kesakesī* would go with him. They flew away and stopped for the night at the *āsram* of a hermit. He stole the crystal, flew with it, crashed in a storm, and died. The crystal fell into *Gandhapurī* and was given to *Sūravaṅs.*

Varavaṅs and *Kesakesī* proceeded on foot but were separated when they had to cross some water in a storm. *Kesakesī* reached land and, leaving a piece of cloth tied up to let *Varavaṅs* know she was not dead, went towards *Gandhapurī,* where she stayed with a hunter and his wife. *Kesakesī,* who was pregnant, worked as a servant but was ill treated by the wife. She was driven out and had the baby in a storm. Indra came down in the form of an old woman. She would look after the baby if she was given some proof that it was *Kesakesī*'s. *Kesakesī* put the ring on a string round the baby's neck and Indra put the baby on a path on which *Sūravaṅs* often passed. *Sūravaṅs* came by and recognized the ring.

Sūravaṅs now built a *sālā* where alms were distributed and put pictures of his and *Varavaṅs*' early life on the walls.

Varavaṅs, who had also reached land safely, came along and saw the cloth left by *Kesakesī.* He heard about the gifts and came to the *sālā.* He recognized the pictures and was taken to his brother, who sent for the baby. Then he went to look for *Kesakesī* and happened to meet her quite soon.

Varavaṅs and *Sūravaṅs* went home with an army to protect them. Their mother was in prison. The second queen's son was now king and suggested a fight on elephant-back. He was defeated and killed. His mother was executed. The king's chief wife, mother of *Varavaṅs* and *Sūravaṅs*, was reinstated. All ended happily.

VIMĀN CAND

Braḥ Cand fell in love with a rich and beautiful girl. He followed her and covered her bed with pieces of gold. He took her away to his planet (the Moon). Jealous women caused her to go back to earth, as follows: The Moon was ravaged by a storm. *Braḥ Cand* had his carriage harnessed for him to go as usual and light the 'fire' (the Moon's light). The women urged her to go with him. In the storm her head was torn off and fell to earth. *Braḥ Cand* took her body to earth, found the head and revived her but left her on earth. She might remarry. She married the seventh son of a powerful king. He was accused of wanting to usurp the throne and he and his family were expelled from the kingdom.They had a son and lived frugally in the forest until Indra built them a palace with all known fruit trees around it. The son was educated by a hermit until he was 20. He then went off and killed his six uncles and won the kingdom from his father.

VINĀ

King *Vinā* sent a delegation by boat to ask for the hand of Princess *Uttami* for his son, *Dasarath*. An agreement was made and *Uttami*, with her entourage, set out on the boat to go to her future husband. Her old nurse planned that her own daughter, *Candā*, should take the place of *Uttami*, since the prince had not seen her. *Uttami* was pushed overboard by them but, with the help of Indra, reached an island. *Uttami*'s clever parrot, left on board, was put in a cage by the nurse in case it thwarted their plans but when they arrived at the palace, he tells everything to King *Vinā*. The king sends him to find *Uttami* and then sends an expedition to bring her to the palace. The nurse and her accomplices are punished and *Dasarath* and *Uttami* are married.

BIBLIOGRAPHY

Where relevant, the abbreviations **T** (Text), **V** (Version), or **S** (Study) are given beside entries.

Am Ḍīoek

T 1956 *Ovād Mātā* in *KS* (28) 7: 656–60.

Anak Jāti Niyam, Le Nationaliste

T 1963 *Sradap Cek* serialized.

Anakota

V 1977 *Contes et légendes khmers I*, Paris. Contains:

pp. 8–27. Le mariage des quatre chauves (F. Martini).

pp. 28–44. Neáng Phim (F. Martini).

pp. 45–58. Le réincarnation (Jeanne Leuba. *RC* Nos. 192–3. Dec. 1959, pp. 19 and 34).

pp. 59–73. Histoire des deux amis qui voulaient tarir la mer (*RC* Nos. 213, 3 June 1968, pp. 20 and 23).

pp. 74–87. L'homme aux trente sapèques (*RC* No. 206, 9 Apr. 1960, p. 18).

pp. 88–103. La Bonne Fortune et la Malchance (*RC* No. 215, 17 June 1960, pp. 15–17).

Ang Duong, *Aṅg Ḍuoṅ* (King Hariraksarāmā)

T 1938–9 *Rīoeṅ Kākī*, Histoire de Kaki or La légende de Kaki, in *KS* (10) 7–9: 35–49. (11) 1–3: 193–212; 7–9: 131–51 (not complete).

T 1949, 1959, 1966 *Rīoeṅ Kākī*, Kaki l'infidèle. From MS of Princess Malika. Phnom Penh, Institut Bouddhique.

T S 1959 *Cpāp' Srī*. Chap-Pin ed. in *KS* (31) 1: 39–52; 2: 169–89 (pp. 40–2. Introduction by Chap-Pin).

T 1962 *Cpāp' Srī*. Phnom Penh, Institut Bouddhique.

T 1977 in Huffman, F. E., and Im Proum (2 extracts of *Rīoeṅ Kākī* from Ang-Duong 1966: 8–10 and 21–6): 209–14 (vocabulary 215–19).

Au Chhieng

1953 *Catalogue du Fonds khmer*. Bibliothèque Nationale. Département des manuscrits. Paris, Imprimerie Nationale.

S 1962 'Études de philologie indo-khmères (I et II)'. *JA* (250) 4:

575–91. (Discussion of the *Brahmagīti* metre with an indication of its use in Angkorian Khmer.)

Aung, Pearl

V *c.*1969 'The lost rod', 'The two neighbours', and 'The talking stone'. Folktales translated for the *Guardian* (Burmese–English daily).

Aymonier, Étienne

T V 1878 *Textes Khmers publiés avec une traduction sommaire.* Saigon (lithographed).

Ière Série: choix de contes populaires; anciens satras khmers.

Première Partie

pp. 1–3. L'aveugle et l'impotent.
pp. 3–8. A Lev.
pp. 8–9. Le menteur (pour manger).
pp. 9–10. Le tigre.
pp. 10–11. Le serpent Kéng Kâng.
p. 11. Sok et Sau.
pp. 11–12. Longhor.
pp. 12–15. Beau-père qui se choisit un gendre.
pp. 15–17. Proverbe du prix de 30 onces d'argent.
pp. 17–19. La fourberie féminine.
pp. 19–20. Kong le brave.
pp. 20–30. Thménh Chéy.
p. 30. Le roi de Chine.
pp. 30–3. Le juge lièvre (partie rimée).
pp. 33–41. Le juge lièvre (partie contée).
p. 41. Le tonnerre et le crabe (poésie).
pp. 41–2. Le poisson et la nasse (poésie).

Deuxième Partie

pp. 43–64. Satra Keng Kantray.
pp. 64–8. Méa Yôeng (fragment).
pp. 64–84. Édification d'Angkor Vat ou Satra de Prea Kêt Mealéa.

Rīoeṅ Khmaer niyāy breṅ.

pp. 1–8. *Ā khvāk'* Ā *khvin.*
pp. 9–29. *Ā Lev.*
pp. 29–32. *Ā Ǩahak' Ŝīy.*
pp. 32–4. *Khlār.*
pp. 34–8. *Bas' Keṅ Kaṅ'.*
pp. 38–40. *Cov Suk Cov Sov.*
p. 40. *Sruk Luṅhor.*
pp. 41–8. *Ā buk kmek roes kūn prasā.*
pp. 49–57. *Bāk damnīem thlai 3 ṭaṃḷiṅ.*
pp. 57–62. *Māyā srī.*
pp. 62–6. *Guṅ Ĥān.*

pp. 67–115. *Dhmeñ Jaiy.*
pp. 116–18. *Kruṅ Cint.*
pp. 119–32. *Subhā Dansāy bāk kāb(y).*
pp. 132–59. *Subhā Dansāy bāk niyāy.*
pp. 160–2. *Ktām bāk kāb(y).*
pp. 163–9. *Juc Trī bāk kāb(y).*

Satrā khmaer pūrāṇ.
pp. 170–254. *Satra Kịṅ Kan traiy.*
pp. 254–66. *Mā Yoeṅ jā saṃkhaep.*
pp. 267–97. *Lpoek Aṅgar Vat.*

S 1880 'Chronique des anciens rois du Cambodge.' *Excursions et Reconnaisances* (4): 149–84.

1883 'Chronique royale du Cambodge.' *Revue de Cochinchine.*

S 1883 'Histoire d'un centenaire, roi du Cambodge au XVIIe siècle.' A. B. de Villemereuil ed. *Explorations et missions*: 320 (from Khmer Chronicles).

T S 1904 *Le Cambodge.* 3 vols. Paris, E. Leroux. Vol. 1: 43–4 'La littérature'.

T 1932 'Histoire du tigre. *Rīoeṅ satv khlā ṭak yak bī rīoeṅ breṅ khmaer knuṅ sievbhau lok Eṁuniñe* [sic]' in *KS* (4) 1: 39–41.

1932 'Contes cambodgiens recueillis par E. Aymonier. "Les trois hommes qui se disputent. *Rīoeṅ puras pī nāk' vivād gnā*" ' in *KS* (4) 2: 37.

Ban Teng

T 1953, 1965 *Sappurisadharm.* Phnom Penh, IB.

Baradat, R.

V 1939 'Sras Banh Dang et sa légende.' *BSEI* NS (14) 1–2: 101–17 (translation of a Chong tale).

T S 1941 'Les Sâmrê ou Péâr. Population primitive de l'ouest du Cambodge.' BEFEO (41): 1–150. Chants et Danses pp. 80–97. **T** in transcription of songs as follows: (Péâr de l'est) 3 songs (on p. 82, p. 83 and pp. 84–5. (Péâr de l'ouest) 2 alternating songs, pp. 86–8 and 89–91. Alternating song of the Samre at Siem Reap, pp. 91–2. A song of Suren (Siam), p. 97.

Bareau, A.

S 1982 'Une représentation du monde selon la tradition bouddhique.' *Seksa Khmer* 5: 11–6. Also 1969 *EC* 17: 31–4.

Baruch, Jacques

S 1968 *Bibliographie des traductions français des littératures du Viet-nam et du Cambodge.* Études Orientales No. 3. Brussels, Thanh Long.

Bastian, Adolf

V S 1868 *Die Voelker des Oestlichen Asien. Studien. Reisen. Reise durch*

Kambodja nach Cochinchina. Jena, Costenoble (contains summaries of Aphaimani, *Abhimani* (343–4), Cray-Thong, *Krāy Thong* (336), Inav, *Īṇāv* (345–6), Lacsanavong, *Laksaṇavaṅs* (60–4)) and Vovong Sosong, *Varavaṅs Sūravaṅs* (128–36).

Bausani, Alessandro

S 1970 'La letteratura cambodgiana (khmer)', in *La letteratura del sud-est asiatico. Enciclopedia universale delle letterature diretta da Riccardo Bacchelli, Giovanni Macchia, Antonio Viscardi.* Milan, Sansoni Academi: 165–94.

Bellan, Charles

V? 1925? 'Fleur de lotus, roman cambodgien.' *RI.* 183–.

Bernard, Solange (see also Bernard-Thierry and Thierry)

V 1949 'Le cambodge à travers sa littérature.' *FA* Nos. 37–8: 910–21.

'Le sens du merveilleux et de l'héroisme dans le Râmâyaṇa cambodgien'. ibid.: 922–7.

'Poèmes populaires'. ibid.: 978–83:

'Barcarolle': 978–9.

'L'air d'Angkor': 979–80.

'Invitation aux génies': 980.

'Chanson triste': 981.

'Tonnerre gronde': 981–2.

'L'écharpe rouge': 982–3.

'La naissance des moustiques'. ibid.: 1003–5.

'Histoire du serpent Ken Kan ou la naissance des serpents'. ibid.: 1006–9.

'Histoire de l'ours et de l'arbre banra (pongro)'. ibid.: 1010.

'Histoire de la marmite longue et de l'anguille longue'. ibid.: 1013.

'Histoire des quatre chauves (épisode des cheveux)'. ibid.: 1018–9.

S 1952 'Quelques aspects de la chance dans les contes populaires du Cambodge.' *BSEI* 27. 3: 251–60.

V 1953 'L'éléphant et les bonzes (Conte cambodgien).' *FA* (9) No. 84: 470–1.

V 1970 'Barcarolle', 'L'air d'Angkor', 'Invitation aux Génies', 'Chanson triste', 'Tonnerre gronde', and 'L'écharpe rouge', in *Chansons populaires. Série de Culture et Civilisation khmères. Tome* 12. Phnom Penh, Institut Bouddhique: 15–17, 17–18, 18–19, 19–20, 21–2, and 22–3.

V 1971 'La naissance des moustiques.' 'Histoire de l'ours et de Banra.' *RC* 751: 26–7.

V 1971(?) 'Histoire des quatre chauves.' 'Histoire de la marmite longue et de l'anguille longue.' *RC* 753: 26–7.

Bernard-Thierry, Solange

S 1953 'Notes de littérature populaire comparée (I Jâtaka et conte siamois. II Conte siamois et conte cambodgien). *BSEI* NS (28) 1: 19–24. See pp. 22–4.

S 1955*a* 'La littérature cambodgienne', in R. Queneau ed. *Histoire des littératures. I Histoires anciennes et orientales et orales.* Paris, Encyclopédie de la Pléiade: 1353–61.

S 1955*b* 'Sagesse du Cambodge'. *FA* (12) Nos. 114–15: 436–9.

S 1955*c* 'Le Cambodge à travers sa littérature'. ibid.: 440–50.

S 1955*d* 'Le sens du merveilleux et de l'héroisme dans le Râmâyana cambodgien'. ibid.: 451–5.

S 1955*e* 'Le roi dans la littérature cambodgienne'. ibid.: 456–9.

V 1955*f* 'Poèmes populaires'. ibid.: 517–22:

'Barcarolle': 517–18.

'L'air d'Angkor': 519.

'Invitation aux Génies': 519–20.

'Chanson triste': 520–1.

'Tonnerre gronde': 521–2.

'L'écharpe rouge': 522.

V 'La naissance des moustiques': 528–30.

V 'La naisance des serpents ou l'histoire du serpent Ken Kan: 531–4.

V 'Histoire de l'ours et de l'arbre banra': 535.

V 'Histoire de la marmite longue et de l'anguille longue': 538.

V 'Histoire des quatre chauves (épisode des cheveux): 541–2.

V 1957 'Le trompeur trompé (légende khmère)'. *FA* (14) Nos. 138–9: 395–8.

S 1958 'Essai sur les proverbes cambodgiens.' *Revue de Psychologie des Peuples* 4: 418–30.

S 1959 'Le bouddhisme d'après les textes Palis.' *FA* (16) Nos. 153–7 and 158–63: 571–632.

Bernon, Olivier de

1991 'Note sur la prosodie khmere'. *Cahiers de l'Asie du Sud-Est* Nos. 29–30: 93–8.

Bharati

V 1949 'Protection maternelle.' Adaptation of a story translated by G. H. Monod in *Contes Khmèrs*, 1944. *FA* Nos. 37–8: 985–992.

Bhatt, G. H.

1960 *The Vālmīki-Rāmāyaṇa* critically edited for the first time. Vols. 1–7. Oriental Institute, Baroda.

Bibliothèque Royale, Phnom Penh

T 1929–34 *Milindapañhā* Vols. I and II (translation from Pali to Khmer, a *Samrāy*).

T 1932–3 *Paṇṭāṃ Kram N̈uy* by Ngoy.

T 1933 *Sek Som Paṇḍit* by Kim-Hak.

T 1938 *Rāmakerti* Reamker. 1–10, 75–80.

T 1940 *Kākī* (by Ang-Duong).

T 1941 *Cpāp' Ker(ti) Kāl.*

T *Cpāp' Kram.*

T *Cpāp' Kūn Cau.*

T *Rājanīti.*

T *Trīneti*

T 1941 *Kruṅ Subhamitr* Vols. I and II.

T 1942 ″ ″Vol. III.

T 1942 *Cpāp' Subhāsit* (by Nong).

Bitard, Pierre

S 1951 'Essai sur la satire sociale dans la littérature du Cambodge.' *BSEI* NS (26) 2: 189–218.

S 1952 'La légende de Mathakut, génie protecteur du village de Vœunsai.' *BSEI* NS (27) 4: 449–52.

V 1954 'Études cambodgiennes. Méthode pour protéger les huit prospérités.' *BSEI* NS (29) 1: 51–79 (translations from Tamra Prohm Cheat or Hora Sastr and from Preng Veasana of various predictions which concern everyday life).

V 1955*a* 'Cinq jâtakas cambodgiens.' *BSEI* NS (30) 2: 121–34 (translation from *Prajuṃ nidān jātak* (*Suṅ Sīv* 1953)]. Avant-propos: 123.

V 'Histoire de la jeune esclave Thûna': 125–7.

V 'Histoire de la jeune fille malheureuse': 127–8.

V 'Histoire du jeune Guttila': 128–30.

V 'Histoire de la vieille femme Chandali': 131.

V 'Histoire de la jeune fille Kesakārī': 132–3.

1955*b* 'Etudes khmères'. *BSEI* NS (30) 2: 135–62 (translation of Tamra Prohm Cheat (*Brahmajāti*)):

Introduction: 137.

'Traité de la construction des maisons': 139–54.

'Manière de voir si les terrains sont propices': 155–6.

'Traité de l'achat des barques': 157–62.

1955*c* 'La littérature cambodgienne moderne.' *FA* (12) Nos. 114–15: 467–79. Includes translation of extracts of modern works, Keng-Vannsak's 'Le cœur Vierge' (pp. 469–70) and 'L'estomac' (470) and a poem by Méas-Yutt (pp. 468–9).

1956*a* 'Études khmères. Le manuscrit 145 du fonds khmèr de la Bibliothèque Nationale de Paris.' *BSEI* (31) 4: 309–424 (translation of treatise on traditional beliefs and interpretation of dreams).

1956*b* 'La merveilleuse histoire de Thmenh Chey l'astucieux.' Conte populaire, traduit et adapté du cambodgien par Pierre Bitard.

FA (12) No. 116: 588–97 (with comment, 588–90), No. 117: 648–62, Nos. 121–2: 25–39.

1959 'Trois contes d'animaux (contes khmers) traduits et adaptés.' *FA* (16) Nos. 162–3: 1300–5:

'Histoire des cinq oiseaux': 1300–2.

'Histoire du tigre et du perroquet': 1302–3.

'Histoire de l'aigrette savante': 1303–5.

Bizot, François

T V S 1973 *Rīoeṅ Rāmakerti nai Tā Cak'* (*Tā Cāk' 's* story of the *Rāmakert(i)*) Compiled by F. Bizot. Phnom Penh EFEO. Contains:

Introduction, 1–6.
Résumé of text in French, 6–27.
Illustrations from the Pagode d'argent, 28–33.
Khmer recitation, taken down by Ung Hok Lay, 33–306.
Commentary by F. Bizot.

T V S 1980 Reprint with different pagination of last entry, Bangkok.

S 1983 'The Reamker.' *Asian Variations in Rāmāyaṇa.* Delhi, Sahitya Akademi: 263–75.

S V 1989 *Rāmaker ou l'Amour Symbolique de Rām et Setā. Recherches sur le Bouddhisme khmer, V.* CLV. Paris, EFEO. Contains **V** of the *Rīoeṅ Rāmakerti nai Tā Cak'*, pp. 65–124, and reproductions of all the 166 illustrations of the Pagode d'Argent, following p. 148.

Bou-Po, *P̂ū-P̈ū*

T S 1951 *'Paññā bhāsit ṭap' bīr.* Douze expressions proverbiales khmères.' *KS* (23) 4: 287–95.

T 1959 ed. *Sabvasiddhi. KS* (31) 1: 53–61; 2: 190–206; 3: 290–310; 4: 404–30; 5: 520–46; 6: 635–41.

T 1959, 1961, and 1968 See *Kambujasuriyā.* III Texts of folktales and legends. (31) 8 and 12; (33) 4, 5, 6, and 7; (40) 7.

Bouth-Neang, *P̂ut-Nāṅ*, Publisher, Phnom Penh

V 1952 ed. *Le roman cambodgien des lièvres* (47 pp.).

T 1953 ed. *Tamrā Brahmajāti* or *Horāsāstr.*

T 1958 ed. *Sāstrā ktām.*

T 1959 ed. *Cpāp' prus ṭoy Paṇḍit Mai.*

T 1959 ed. *Rīoeṅ Sradap Cek.* 2 vols. by 'Yos Ngin and Choum Muong'.

T 1959 ed. *Rīoeṅ Sabvasiddhi.*

T 1960 ed. *Cpāp' bāky cās'.*

T 1961 ed. *Cpāp' Ker(ti) kāl.*

T 1961 ed. *Cpāp' Kram.*

Brebion, A., and Cabaton, A.

S 1935 *Dictionnaire de bio-bibliographie générale, ancienne et moderne.* Paris (Mok is the subject of an article, p. 264).

Brunet, Jacques

S 1974 'Themes and motifs of the Cambodian Ramayana in the shadow theatre.' Osman, M. T. ed. *Traditional drama and music of Southeast Asia.* Kuala Lumpur: 3–4.

S 1974 'The comic element in the Khmer shadow theatre.' Osman, M. T. ed. *Traditional drama and music of Southeast Asia.* Kuala Lumpur: 27–9.

S 1974 'The shadow theatre of Cambodia.' Osman, M. T. ed. *Traditional drama and music of Southeast Asia.* Kuala Lumpur: 52–7.

S 1975 *La musique et les chants dans le mariage cambodgien.* (Thèse de doctorat de IIIe cycle) Paris.

By-Sovann, *P̂ī-Suvaṇṇ*

T 1959–60 ed. *Rīoeṅ Maraṇamātā.* Histoire de Marana Mâtâ (by *Ûk*). From palm-leaf MS. In *KS* (31) 7: 784–92; 8: 878–84; 9: 1050–60; 10: 1156–76; 11: 1294–1300; 12: 1422–3. (32) 1: 51–8; 2: 163–70; 3: 285–96; 4: 423–30; 5: 533–52; 6: 653–72; 7: 777–800; 8: 895–920; 9: 1027–41; 10: 1129–58; 11: 1261–70; 12: 1361–9.

T 1966 See *Kambujasuriyā.* III Texts of folktales and legends. (38) 11.

Cabaton, A.

S 1901 'Rapport sur les littératures cambodgienne et chame'. *Comptes rendus de l'Académie des inscriptions et Belles-Lettres.* Paris: 64–76.

1932 *L'Indochine.* Choix de textes précédés d'une étude. Paris, Laurens (pp. 158–9 Poésie cambodgienne recueillie par M. Collard, 1925).

Cambodge d'Aujourd'hui

V 1958 'La légende du tigre recueilli et traduit par la Commission des Mœurs et Coutumes.' Nos. 4–5, Apr.–May: 39.

V 1958 'Un conte khmer. Les monts Pros et Srei.' No. 6, June: 26.

V 1958 'Conte khmer. L'origine des monts de la province de Battambang.' No. 12, Dec. 26 and 28.

V 1959 'Conte khmer. Le vieux, la vieille et le sorcier.' Nos. 7–8, July–Aug. 38.

Cambodia Today

V 1959 'A Khmer legend. The origin of the three areca palm flowers used in the Cambodian marriage ceremony.' No. 2, Feb. 26.

V 1959 'The legend of the lightening.' (Translation based on French version by S. Bernard-Thierry and F. Martini) No. 5, May 26.

V 1959 'Khmer Tale. The birth of the mosquitoes.' No. 6, June 26–7.

Carrison, Muriel Paskin

V 1987 *Cambodian folkstories from the Gatilok.* Retold from a translation by the Venerable Kong Chhean. Vermont/Tokyo, Tuttle Company.

Cedoreck. Centre de Documentation et de Recherche sur la Civilisation Khmere, Paris

T 1980 *Cpāp' Phseṅ2.* (Various *Cpāp'.* Reprint of the 1973 6th edition by the Institut Bouddhique, Phnom Penh, with a preface by Khing Hoc Dy.)

T 1980 *Duṃ Dāv* by *Som.*

T V 1981 *Paṇṭāṃ Kram N̈uy. Les recommandations de Kram Ngoy* by Khing Hoc Dy and Jacqueline Khing.

1981 *Rīoeṅ Dhanañjăy.*

T 1981 *Gatilok* by In.

T 1981 *Srīhitopades* by Pang-Khat.

T 1981 *Subhā Dansāy.*

T 1982 *Rīoeṅ Mahāvessantarajātak* by Nhok-Thaem. Paris.

T 1983 *Ṭaṃṇoer chboḥ dau dis khāṅ lic niṅ Iṇḍūcin chnāṃ 2000.* Paris.

T 1984 *Laṃnāṃ bhleṅ khmaer.* (Khmer Music) Paris.

T 1985 *Contes Khmers* by G. H. Monod. (Reprint of Feuilles de l'Inde No. 9, Mouans-Sartoux (Alpes-Maritimes), Högman, 1943.) Paris.

Chan-Sok, *Cān'-Sukh.* See Som-Sukh.

Chandler, David

V 1971 'Two Cambodian Folk Stories.' *Look East* 1 No. 3: 50–1.

V 1971 'Two friends who tried to empty the sea.' *Sawaddi*, May–June: 22–3.

V 1971 'How the *koun lok* bird got her feathers.' *Bangkok Standard Magazine*, 12 June: 12–13.

V 1971 'The duplicate husband.' *Bangkok Standard Magazine*, 26 June: 19–20.

V 1971 'Why herons and crows are enemies.' *Sawaddi*, July–Aug. (Translator unable to verify that this appeared in this issue.)

V 1976 '*Two friends who tried to empty the sea: eleven Cambodian folk-tales.*' Monash University Centre of Southeast Asian Studies, Working Paper Number 8.

V 1978 *Favourite stories from Cambodia.* Heinemann Educational Books (Asia) with exercises by Susan Chandler. Heinemann Educational Books (Asia), Hongkong. Contains:

p. 1. The woodcutter and the king of the mice.
pp. 3–5. Why herons and crows are enemies.
pp. 5–7. The hare and the elephant's mother.
pp. 7–10. The kind man and the tiger.
pp. 10–13. The second husband.
pp. 13–16. One thing leads to another.
pp. 17–20. How thunder and lightening began.
pp. 20–4. Si-the-liar.
pp. 24–8. The jackal and the pond full of fish.
pp. 28–32. The friends who tried to empty the sea.
pp. 32–9. How the old man Mei was tricked.
pp. 40–6. How the koun lok bird got its name.

Chap-Pin, *Cāp-Bin*

T 1934 1969 *Rīoeṅ Braḥ Caṅkūm Kaev.* La dent sacrée. Phnom Penh, BR/IB.

T 1944 'Bândau (*Paṇṭau*) (devinettes cambodgiennes)'. *KS* (16) 9: 451–8; 10: 508–15; 11: 582–93 (3 pages of introduction).

T S 1945–6 *'Adhippāy subhāsit khmaer'*. *KS* (17) 3: 126–37; 4: 169–81; 5: 252–63; 6: 316–19; 7: 360–7; 8: 427–30; 9: 483–9; 10: 636–48; 11: 700–4. Last instalment repeated in (18) 2: 742–58. (Explanation of proverbs is in verse except for the first instalment.)

T S 1958*a* *'Adhippāy subhāsit khlaḥ'*. Quelques proverbes expliqués en vers. *KS* (30) 4: 367–72.

S 1958*b* See *Kambujasuriyā*. III Texts of folktales and legends. (30) 7.

S 1958*c* *'Ṭoem kaṃṇoet rīoeṅ rām kerti'*. (Origins of the *Rāmakert(i)*) *KS* (30) 11: 1027–36.

T S 1959 *'Cpāp' Srī. Braḥ rājanibandh ṭoy Braḥ Pād Aṅg Ḍuoṅ.'* 'Chbap Srey Preah Bat Ang Duong revu et corrigé par . . .' in *KS* (31) 1: 39–52; 2: 169–89. (Introduction, text, and commentary.)

S 1959 *Pravatti pad nagar rāj bhleṅ jāti khmaer.* (The *nagar rāj* song. National Khmer Music) Phnom Penh.

T S 1962 *'Cpāp' Srī'* by Ang Duong, edited with introduction, text, and commentary. Phnom Penh, IB.

Chau-Seng, *Cau-Seṅ*, and Kong-Huot, *Gaṅ-Huot*

V S 1967 'Morale aux jeunes-filles de Suttantaprija In. Adapté du poème khmer par . . . A propos de Thmenh Chey et de Maître Lièvre.' (Translation of *Subhāsit Cpāp Srī* by In and discussion of a French film of the stories, Thmenh Chey and Maître Lièvre.) Culture et civilisation khmère. No. 9. Phnom Penh, Université Bouddhique Preah Sihanouk Rāj. 16 + 11 pp.

Chaufea Thiounn. See Thiounn, Samdach Chauféa.

Chāṃ Daṅ Gāṃvarrṇ and Yau(v) Lim Pīnand

T 2467 BE (AD 1924) *Praḥjum subhāsit khmer* (contains text and translation of *Subhāsit porāṇ, Subhāsit sạn tek, Subhāsit sạn putr*, and *Subhāsit sạn hñiṅ*) Bangkok.

Chbap Phseng-Phseng

See Institut Bouddhique, 1967 *Cpāp' Phseṅ2.*

Chéa, *Sundhar Jā*. See *Sunthor Chea*.

Chéa-Kang, *Jā-Kaṅ*, ed.

T 1935 *Bāky breṅ praṭau* (Poem composed at the command of Ang-Duong collected by Chéa-Kang, followed by a poem by Chéa-Kang). *KS* (7) 1–3: 68–70. Chéa-Kang's poem, 70–1.

T 19— See Corbet 19—: 115–23.

Chéa-Paur, *Jā-P̈ūr*

T 1966 See *Kambujasuriyā*. III Texts of folktales and legends. 1966. 10.

Chéon, A.

S 1890 'Note sur la chanson cambodgienne'. *BSEI* (18) 1: 18–21. (Introduction followed by translation of 8 songs.)

1890 'Note sur la chanson cambodgienne: légende tonkinoise'. Saigon. 11 pp.

Chhim-Krasem, *Jhiṃ-Krasem*

S 1947–8 '*Lkhon khol.* La danse masquée'. *KS* (20) 3: 161–70.

S 1951 '[Short biography of Nong]'. Khmer text. *Mitt Sālā Pālī* 2: 57–60. (Reference from Léang-Hap An in *KS* 1968. 12: 1346 n.1.)

—— and Bou-Po, *P̂ū-P̈ū*

V 1956 *Mahābhāratayuddh.* Translated into Khmer. Phnom Penh, *Khemarapaṇṇāgār.*

Chhim-Nak, *Jhiṃ-Ṇāk*

T 1950 See *Kambujasuriyā.* III Texts of folktales and legends. 1950. 1 and 3.

Chhim-Saret, *Jhiṃ-Sāret*

T 1948 See *Kambujasuriyā* Texts of folktales and legends. 1948. 10.

Chhim-Soth, *Jhiṃ-Sut*, and Cambefort, [G].

V 1952 *Lois des temps passés.* Phnom Penh, Kim-Seng. (Translation into French of *Cpāp'*?)

V 1952 *Recueil des règles.* Phnom Penh, Kim-Seng. (Translation into French of *Cpāp'*?)

—— You-Heng, *Yūr-Heṅ*, and Manipoud

V 1959 *Les anciens dits.* Phnom Penh, Bouth-Néang. (Translation into French of *Cpāp' Bāky Cās'*?)

Chhim-Soum, *Jhiṃ-Sum*

T 1935 '*Vijjā Guṇ Kathā* ou Les vertus de la science'. *KS* (7) 2–3: 37–58 (Poem).

T 1939, 1953 *Nānajātak knuṅ dhammapadaṭṭhakathā.* Corrected by Louis-Em. Phnom Penh, IB (Pali and Khmer. 51 *jātak* in prose).

T 1942 *Kumbhajātak.* Phnom Penh, Institut Bouddhique (Pali and Khmer. Prose).

T 1951 '*Āÿai*'. (Text of one song of this style.) *Camrīeṅ Jātiniyam.* ('Patriotic songs') Phnom Penh, Institut Bouddhique I: 64–73. Also reprinted in Huffman and Proum 1977: 134–9 (vocabulary 139–42).

T 1965 '*Dịk trajāk' trī kuṃ. Adhippāy bhāsit*'. *KS* (37) 1: 63–74. (Explanation of the proverb in verse, followed by a translation in verse of a Pali story, touching on the meaning of the proverb.)

S 1966*a* '*Adhippāy bhāsit. Bāky kāby.*' *KS* (38) 1: 36–51; 2: 195–210; 3: 299–314; 4: 397–408; 5: 505–23. (5: 505–16 is a repeat of the 1965 publication with slightly diffferent footnotes. Explanations of some proverbs accompanied by tales retold from the Buddhist Canon and moral advice, all in verse. The proverbs are: *prahaes pāt' prayatn gaṅ'; nāy l-a kra rak pān, nāy klāhān pān srec kās; ūs dūk kuṃ oy l-ān, cāp' trī pān kuṃ oy l-ak' dịk; gnā croen ansam khloc gnā ṭūc sramoc ansam chau; dịk trajāk' trī kuṃ.*)

T 1966*b* '*Dasajātak saṅkhep.*' Phnom Penh.

S 1966*c* '*Secktī adhippāy aṃbī bāky thā kāby-kaṃṇāby.*' *KS* (38) 7: 751–63. (Describes 48 Khmer metres of which he would not use 15.)

S 1968 '*Kār srāv jrāv pravatti Lok Vises Ṭūṅ.*' ('Research into the Biography of *Lok Vises Ṭūṅ.*') *KS* (40) 1: 51–9; 2: 185–94; 3: 329–44; 6: 652–74; 7: 758–67; 8: 875–82; 9: 989–1007.

T The following extracts of works, known by heart to Chhim-Soum or to monks who had known *Ṭūṅ*, are quoted on the pages indicated: *Sāstrā Nen Mās rī Suvaṇṇabilāp* (2 stanzas) 3: 330–1. *Cpāp' on aṅg* (5 stanzas) 7: 759–60. *Sabd phgar* 7: 763–6. *Lpoek Mahārājapārb.* 8: 875–82; 9: 989–1007.

Chhung-Nguon Huot, *Jhuṅ-Ṅuon Huot*, ed.

T 1959 *Histoire de Hang Yun (Haṅs Yant).* Phnom Penh.

T 1964 *Histoire de Méa Yoeung (Mā Yoeṅ).* Phnom Penh.

T 1964 *Histoire de Méayéar Srey (Māyā Srī).* Phnom Penh.

T 1964 *Histoire du serpent Kéng Kang (Bas' Keṅ Kaṅ).*

Chim-Peov

S 1959 *Kābyasāstr.* Poésie: Étude de la versification. Phnom Penh, Vichay Serey.

Ching-Nguon Huot, *Jiṅ-Ṅuon Huot*, publisher, Phnom Penh

T n.d. *Aṃpaeṅ paek* by In.

T 1953 *Suvaṇṇ haṅs.* 4 vols.

T 1959 *Cpāp' dūnmān khluon, Cpāp' bāky cās' niṅ Cpāp' Vidhurpaṇḍit.*

T 1959 *Cpāp' kūn cau, Cpāp' kram, Cpāp' ker kāl, Cpāp' Trīneti.*

T 1959 *Haṅs Yant.*

Ching-Paur, Huot *Jiṅ-P̈ū Huot*

T 1950 *Lpoek Pret* 2 vols.

Chong Ou, *Cuṅ Û*

T 1958 *Cpāp' ṭaṃpūnmān pabbajit grahasth.* Préceptes pour l'instruction des religieux et des laïcs. Phnom Penh.

T 1967 *Cpāp' gorab mātā pitā.* Phnom Penh.

Choum-Mau, *Juṃ-M̈au*

T 1933–4 '*Hitopades*'. *KS* (5) 1–6: 144–60; 7–12: 38–49. (Translation from French into Khmer. Part only. Continued by Krasem, q.v.)

Choum-Muong. See Ngin and Choum-Muong.

Chuon-Nat, *Juon-Ṇāt*

T 1931 '*Kāby thlaeṅ Lokadharm 8 prakār*'. (Poem translating 8 Lokadharm) *KS* (4) 1: 31–8.

Cœdès, Georges

S 1902 'Liste des manuscrits khmèrs.' *BEFEO* (2) 4: 387–400.

V 1913 'La fondation de Phnom Peñ au XVe siècle, d'après la Chronique cambodgienne.' *BEFEO* (13): 6–11.

S 1914 Review of San Antonio, Gabriel 'Brève et véridique relation des événements de Cambodge'. *BEFEO* (14) 9: 44–7.

S 1915 Review of Roeské 'L'enfer cambodgien d'après le Trai Phum' *JA*, 1914: 587–606 in *BEFEO* (15) 4: 8–13. (Severe criticism of Roeské's mistakes.)

S 1918 'Essai de classification des documents historiques cambodgiens conservés à la bibliothèque de l'École Française d'Extrême-Orient. Études cambodgiennes XVI'. *BEFEO* (18) 9: 15–28. (Translation of earliest fragments of chronicle, AD 1796, offered by Ang Eng to King of Siam, 24–8.)

S 1931 'La littérature cambodgienne'. Sylvain Lévi ed. *L'Indochine* I, Paris, Société d'éditions Géographiques, Maritimes et Coloniales: 180–91.

S 1942 *Aṃbī aksarsāstr khmaer. KS* (14) 1: 31–4; 2: 37–41; 6: 3–9. (Translation of last entry.)

V 1949 Reprints of 1913. *FA* 1949 Nos. 37–8: 943–7 and 1955 Nos. 114–15: 499–504.

Collard, Paul

V S 1925 *Cambodge et Cambodgiens.* Paris, Société d'éditions Géographiques, Maritimes et Coloniales. Néang pi ton dop (*Nāṅ bīṭanṭap'*) from Pavie: 18–22. Life of Mok: 29–39, with translation of excerpts of Mok's poem (*Daṃ Dāv*): 33–6 and example of improvised stanza: 38.

Commission des Mœurs et Coutumes

T 1951 *Camrīeṅ jāti niyam.* Chamrieng Cheat Niyum ou Chant patriotique. Fasc. 1. Phnom Penh, IB. (Introduction and 4 sections of songs by 8 authors, intended to stimulate nationalism.)

V 1958 'La légende du tigre recueilli et traduit par la Commission des Mœurs et Coutumes'. *CA* Nos. 4–5, Apr.–May: 39.

V 1958 'Conte Khmer. L'origine des monts de la province de Battambang'. *CA* No. 12, Dec. 26 and 28.

V 1959 'A Khmer legend. The origin of the three areca palm flowers used in the Cambodian marriage ceremony'. *CT* No. 2: 26.

T 1959–74 *Prajuṃ Rīoeṅ Breṅ Khmaer.* Recueil des contes et légendes cambodgiens. 9 Vols. Phnom Penh, IB. Vols 1 and 2 contain:

Vol. 1. 1. *Rīoeṅ manuss bīr nāk' nau phdaḥ jit gnā* (Two neighbours).
2. *Rīoeṅ cacak* (The jackal).
3. *Rīoeṅ Bas' keṅ kaṅ* (The snake Keng Kang).
4. *Rīoeṅ Gaṅ' Ĥān* (*Gaṅ'* the brave).
5. *Rīoeṅ Bāky subhāsit tamlai 30 taṃliṅ* (Maxims worth 30 ounces of silver).
6. *Rīoeṅ Māyā srī* (The wiles of women).
7. *Rīoeṅ Ā kuhak ŝī* (The liar eats).
8. *Rīoeṅ Puras ceḥ thnāṃ bis bas'* (The man who knows of a medicine to cure snake-bite).
9. *Rīoeṅ Manuss chot 4 nāk'* (4 stupid men).
10. *Rīoeṅ K-aek 1 jā k-aek ṭap'* (1 crow becomes 10).
11. *Rīoeṅ Cau Sukr niṅ Cau Sau(r)* (Mr *Sukr* and Mr *Sau(r)*)

12. *Rīoeṅ Grū nīṅ Siss* (Master and pupil).
13. *Rīoeṅ Kamloḥ bīr nāk' caṅ' pān prabandh ge* (Two youths want someone's wife).
14. *Rīoeṅ Jāti khlā dhaṃ* (The origin of the tiger).
15. *Rīoeṅ Cau Citt Jā* (Mr Good Heart).
16. *Rīoeṅ Ūbuk kmek roes kūn prasā* (A father-in-law seeks a son-in law).
17. *Rīoeṅ Ā Sukh Slūt, Ā Sokh Kāc* (Nice *Sukh* and Nasty *Sukh*).
18. *Rīoeṅ Samlāñ' bīr nāk'* (Two friends (who wanted to empty the sea)).
19. *Rīoeṅ Suostī nịṅ Abvamaṅgal* (Good Fortune and Bad Luck).
20. *Rīoeṅ Khlā cāñ' prājñā gīṅgak' nịṅ anṭoek* (The tiger is outwitted by the toad and the turtle).
21. *Rīoeṅ khlā, svā nịṅ dansāy* (The tiger, the monkey and the hare).
22. *Rīoeṅ Anṭoek nịṅ svā* (The turtle and the monkey).
23. *Rīoeṅ Ṭaṅkūv nịṅ k-aek* (The worm and the crow).
24. *Rīoeṅ Paṅ thlai nịṅ p-ūn thlai* (Brothers-in-law, elder and younger).
25. *Rīoeṅ Puras kuhak 4 nāk'* (4 liars).
26. *Rīoeṅ Puras kaṃījil mān prabandh grap' lǎkkh(ṇ)* (A lazy man with a wife marked with the signs of good luck).
27. *Rīoeṅ Puras mān kūn 4 nāk' rīen vijjā 4 pad* (A man with 4 sons, who had studied 4 subjects).
28. *Rīoeṅ Cau āc(m) seḥ* (Mr Horse-dirt).
29. *Rịoeṅ Srī kṅok mās* (The women and the golden peacock).
30. *Rīoeṅ puras kās 30* (The man with 30 coins).

Vol. 2. 1. *Rīoeṅ manuss lobh* (Greedy people).
2. *Ā Khvāk' Ā Khvin* (See Folktales Summaries).
3. *Manuss khboem āc(m) jiḥ ṭaṃrī, khboem ktī, ḷoeṅ cuṅ tnot* (Part of Four Bald men. See Folktales Summaries).
4. *Cāp sruk nịṅ cāp brai* (Tame *versus* wild sparrows).
5. *Puras ṭanṭoem brabandh* (Son-in-law 3 nights in water).
6. *Devatā saek soy* (Good Luck and Bad Luck protect child).
7. *Cau Kampit Pandoḥ* (See Folktales Summaries).
8. *Cau tap' pramal'* (Fisherman catches gold. King wants some).
9. *Cau phkāp' traḷok* (Son-in-law must build house in 1 day).
10. *Taṃlaṅ' 7 santān* (Deaf couple and others shout at each other).
11. *Subhā dansāy (bāky kāby)* (See Narrative poems Summaries).
12. *Subhā Dansāy (bāky rāy)* (See Folktales Summaries).
13. *Srī bit, mtāy bit, ūbik bit* (See Folktales Summaries).
14. *Andaṅ' vaeṅ, chnāṃṅ vaeṅ* (Eel too big for pot).
15. *Ā Ḷev* (See Folktales Summaries).
16. *Srī kanṭur l-oc, gị kanṭur paṃphlāñ* (White mice King and gold).
17. *Puras cāk' smugr* (See Folktales Summaries. 4 Bald men).

18. *Anak ṭaṃṇoer bīr nāk' ṭanṭoem gnā ṭek kantāl* (Animals scared hare, who 'reads' letter from Indra).

19. *Cau Thuṅ Cau Sāñ'* (Poem but see Folktales Summaries *Ā Thuṅ Ā Sāñ'*).

20. *Ā Saṃgam pāñ' lalak* (Mr Thin shoots doves).

21. *Ā P̈āṅ Nāṅ Tī* (*Ā P̈āṅ* and *Nāṅ Tī*).

22. *Hor niṅ tā cās' ṭūn cās'* (The astrologer and the elderly couple).

23. *Kmeṅ kaṃbrā* (The orphan).

Many of the translated tales come from Vols. 1 and 2. For an indication of the contents of Vols. 3–8, see in Genres under G. 1 Folktales. I have not seen Vol. 9.

Commission du Reamker

S 1968 *Rāmker (Rāmāyaṇa Khmer).* Phnom Penh, Université Royale des Beaux-Arts (reproduced in *Kambuja* 1969, Oct. 142–7, Nov. 124–33, Dec. 176–90).

Corbet, Ch.

T 19— *Rīoeṅ breṅ.* (Phnom Penh) Contains:

[I] *Rīoeṅ breṅ*, pp. 1–5. *Ā khvāk Ā khvin* (selection of incidents). 3 proverbs.

pp. 6–9. *Rīoeṅ Ā Ḷev* (selection of incidents). 2 proverbs.

pp. 10–19. *Rīoeṅ Cau Kaṃpit pandoḥ* (selection of incidents).

pp. 20–30. *Dhanañjăy paṇḍit* (selection of incidents). 7 proverbs.

pp. 31–44. *Rīoeṅ Subhā Dansāy* (selection of incidents). pp. 45–57. *Rīoeṅ Nāṅ bīrṭanṭap'.*

[II] *Rīoeṅ bāky kāby.*

pp. 58–61. *Rīoeṅ juc niṅ trī* (selection of passages).

pp. 62–73. *Rīoeṅ Mā Yoeṅ.* 1 proverb.

pp. 74–89. *Rīoeṅ Subhā Dansāy (bāky kāby)* (selection of incidents). 3 proverbs.

pp. 90–100. *Lpoek Nagar Vatt* (abridged). 1 proverb.

[III] *Cpāp' cās'* (selection of passages).

pp. 102–3. *Cpāp' Kram.*

pp. 103–4. *Cpāp' Kerti Kāl.*

pp. 104–5. *Cpāp' Bāky Cās'.*

pp. 105–10. *Cpāp' Kūn Cau.*

pp. 110–13. *Cpāp' Trīneti.*

pp. 113–14. *Vidhur Paṇḍit.*

[IV] *Braḥ rāj nibandh cās'* (*Lok Kramakār Kaṅ-Jā* edited these texts on the order of King Ang Duong).

pp. 116–7. *Bāky breṅ praṭau.*

pp. 117–23. *Pad Yaṃ Yām.* An elegy for King Norodom.

[V] *Cpāp' Kịṅ Kantrai.*

pp. 124–59 (Selected stories, numbered 1–11, 19 (for 12?), 13–16).

p. 159. 1 proverb.

[VI] *Gatilok*.
pp. 160–96 (Selection of stories).
p. 196. 1 proverb.

[VII] *Rīoeṅ Sabvasiddhi*.
pp. 197–204 (Selection of passages).
p. 204. 1 proverb.

T 1947 *Ru'aṅ Samru'aṅ*. Phnom Penh (*Rīoeṅ Samrāṅ'?* Selections?).

Cpāp' Paṇṭāṃ Krum N̈uy

Ly-Théam Teng (1966: 6) gave this as the title of a book published for use in schools (Grade 6). It consisted of Ngoy's 4 *Cpāp'* (or selections from them?). These are:

T *Cpāp' dūnmān jan prus srī.*
T *Cpāp' kir kāl thmī.*
T *Cpāp' Lpoek thmī.*
T *Secktī raṃlịk ṭās' tīoen.*

Culture et Civilisation Khmere

1965 No. 8. *Les élites khmères*. Phnom Penh.

Damas, L. G.

1948 *Poètes d'expression française*. Paris, Éditions du Seuil, Pierre Vives. (Not seen.)

Damnīem

T n.d. *Court recueil de dictons* (Orthography and transcription of 212 numbered proverbs. Resembles Guesdon's but shorter. At EFEO).

Daniel, Alain

T V S 1982 Étude d'un fragment du Rām Ker (Rāmāyaṇa cambodgien) dit par un conteur. Thèse de doctorat de 3e cycle. 2 vols. (The narrator was *Tā Krūṭ*.)

1991 'Un réinterpretation de l'histoire de Chey'. *Cahiers de l'Asie du Sud-Est*, Nos. 29–30: 199–227.

Deydier, H.

S 1952 'L'enlèvement de Sītâ au Pràsàt Khnà Sèn Kév'. *BSEI* (27) 3: 363–6.

Dhingra, Baldoon

V 1958 *L'orient par lui-même. Textes des littératures classiques et populaires arabe, iranienne, chinoise, japonaise, thai, cambodgienne et indonésienne*. Paris and Neuchâtel. Contains:

p. 73. Chant populaire.
p. 75. Chanson populaire.
p. 85. Chant populaire.
p. 126. Sagesse populaire. (The first 8 stanzas of *Cpāp' Kūn Cau*).
p. 127. Proverbes.
p. 138. Chbap Ker Kal (*Cpāp' Ker Kāl*).

V 1959 *Asia through Asian eyes. Parables, poetry, proverbs, stories and epigrams of the Asian peoples.* London, Thames and Hudson. Contains:

pp. 76–7. Cambodian legend (Concerns ogress and human husband turn into two mountains).
pp. 93–4. Snub-nose.
pp. 105–6. The tryst (A poem).

Dik-Kéam, *Ḍīk-Gām*

V 1962*a* *Cambodian Short Stories. Nidān rīoeṅ breṅ khmaer* (with grammatical notes for those learning English). Contents:

pp. 1–2. The rabbit and the palm fruit.
pp. 13–14. The blackbird and the monkey.
pp. 22–3. The female crocodile who wanted to eat the monkey's heart.
pp. 30–1. The crow and the deer.
pp. 36–8. The deer, the crow, and the tortoise.
pp. 50–3. The hungry liar.
pp. 59–62. The two neighbours (they set traps).
pp. 68–70. A dwarfish dog.
pp. 75–6. A long eel and a long cooking pot.
pp. 85–7. Four liars.
pp. 94–5. The fisherman and his wife.
pp. 101–2. The hunter and the birds.
pp. 108–9. Chau chak smok (*Cau cāk' smogr*).
pp. 114–8. One crow to ten crows.
pp. 124–32. The father who was strict in choosing his son-in-law.

S 1962*b* '*Bhāsāsāstr niṅ Aksarsāstr khmaer*' (Le langage et la littérature khmèrs). *KS* (34) 5: 555–65; 6: 667–84; 7: 776–90; 8: 901–14. (Concerns language rather than literature.)

T S 1964 '*Pad Uṃ Dūk.*' (Songs for when in a rowing boat) *KS* (36) 9: 994–8; 10: 1088–99; 11: 1185–93.

T 1964–7 ed. in *KS, Braḥ rājanibandh Rāmakerti*, compiled by *Vijjādhar,* q.v. (incomplete).

T 1964–5 ed. *Braḥ rājanibandh Rāmakerti.* 6 vols. (incomplete).

T 1965 See *Kambujasuriyā* III Texts of folktales and legends. (37) 1–4.

S 1967*a* *Anak nibandh khmaer. Paṇḍit Jayanand. Jīvapravatti niṅ snā ṭai.* (Khmer authors. Chey Nand. Life and works) Phnom Penh, Seng-Nguon-Huot.

V S 1967*b* *Anak nibandh khmaer. Ukñā Braḥ Ghlāṃṅ Naṅ. Jīvapravatti niṅ snā ṭai.* (Khmer authors. Uknha Preah Khleang Nong. Life and works) Phnom Penh, Seng-Nguon Huot. Contains:

pp. i–ii. Preface.
pp. 1–6. Biography.

V S of following:
pp. 7–11. *Cpāp' Subhāsit.*
pp. 11–17. *Lokaneyyajātak.*
pp. 18–27. *Puññasār Sirasā.*
pp. 28–32. *Bhogakulakumār.*
pp. 32–9. *Varanuj Varanetr.*
pp. 39–48. *Braḥ Samudr.*
pp. 48–52. *Sabvasiddhi* and *Rājakul.*
pp. 52–6. Chronicles.
pp. 56–8. *Īṇāv.*

V 1967*c* *Cambodian Proverbs.* (English translation on palm-leaf pages) Phnom Penh, Institut Bouddhique.

T 1967*d* See *Kambujasuriyā* Texts of folktales and legends. 1967 (39) 1.

T 1968 *Sāvatār dāk' daṅ bhūmisāstr khmaer.* (Chronicles connected with Khmer geography) Phnom Penh, Seng-Nguon-Huot.

T S 1970 '*Anak nibandh. M̈uk-Saṃ-ok.*' (Authors. *M̈uk-Saṃ-uk*) *KS* (42) 6: 626–48.

T 1971*a* *Rāmakerti.* Researched by Phnom Penh, IB.

T 1971*b* '*Rīoeṅ Rājakul caṃlaṅ binity phdīeṅ phdāt' ṭoy Lok̂ Ḍīk-Gām.*' (*Rājakul* edited by Dik-Kéam) *KS* (43) 2: 155–70; 3: 237–50; 4: 370–91.

T 1971*c* *Vīrapuras khmaer knuṅ kār paṭivatt(n) niṅ kār kārbār ḍik ṭī khmaer. srāv jrāv tām ekasār bit knuṅ sāstrā sliķ riṭ niṅ baṅsāvatār khmaer.* (Khmer heroes, who were revolutionaries or who defended the country, researched using manuscript documents and chronicles) Phnom Penh, *Banlī vijjā.*

T 1975 *Baṅsāvatār khmaer. Sāstr slo'k ro't vātt sit pūt.* (*Baṅsāvatār khmaer. Sāstr sliķ riṭ vātt Sit Pūt.* Khmer chronicles. The manuscript of *Vatt Sitpūt*) Phnom Penh, *Samāgam Samtec Juon Nāt.*

—— and Pen Sa-Oeun

V 1968 *Preah Reach Samphear.* (Translated into English) Phnom Penh, Institut Bouddhique.

Duong-Ouch, *Ḍuoṅ-Ûc*, and Vann-Chœung, *V̈ān'-Jīoeṅ*

T 1966 See *Kambujasuriyā* III Texts of folktales and legends. 1966 (38) 11.

Dupaigne, Bernard, and Khing Hoc Dy, *Ghīṅ-Huk Ḍī*

S 1981 'Les plus anciennes peintures datées du Cambodge: quatorze épisodes du Vessantara Jataka (1877).' *AA* (36): 26–36.

Ḍuc Ŝī Diṃ

T 1950 *Kaṃraṅ Rīoeṅ Lpoek.* (Collection of *Lpoek*) Phnom Penh, éditions *Ḍuc Ŝī Diṃ.*

Ek, Khun Akkharā, *Ek, Ghun Akkharā*

T 1935 See *Kambujasuriyā* III Texts of folktales and legends. 1935. 4–6.

Ek-Nhim (Acāry Dhammissaro), *Ek-Ñim*

T 1934 *Girimāndasūtra prae jā bāk(ya) kāb(ya).* Phnom Penh, Bibliothèque Royale.

Ellul, Jean

S 1972 'Le traité de la chasse aux éléphants de l'Uknha Maha Pithu Krassem.' *Annales de l'Université des Beaux-Arts Cambodge* (2): 47–76.

S 1980 'Le mythe de Ganésa. Le Ganésa cambodgien, un mythe d'origine de la magie.' *Seksa Khmer* (1–2): 69–153.

Em, Louis, *Lvī-Em*

T 1931 '*Prasnā Dharm. Satv k-aek niṅ ṭaṅkūv. Khsae 1.*' (Riddles from the Dharma. The crow and the grub) *KS* (4) 1: 17–30.

T 1931 '*Prasnā Dharm. Satv kaṇṭūp niṅ gruḍ*'. (Riddles from the Dharma. The grasshopper and the *garuḍa*) *KS* (4) 2: 21–36.

T 1932 '*Prasnā Dharm. Braḥ Indr niṅ Stec Korabyarāj*'. (Riddles from the Dharma. Indra and King Korabyarāj) *KS* (4) 3–6: 86–133.

T 1932 '*Prasnā Dharm. Braḥ Indr dūl suor Braḥ Sammāsambuddh*'. (Riddles from the Dharma. Indra questions the Buddha) *KS* (4) 3–6: 134–48.

T 1932 '*Uppattikathā, Vitakkapañhā niṅ Malatarapañhā.*' Translated into Khmer (from *Lokanayajātak*). *KS* (4) 7–12: 124–213.

—— Oum-Sou, *Ûṃ-Ŝūr*, Long, *Ḷuṅ, et al.*

T 1944, 1958, 1961, 1962 *Paññāsajātak Samrāy* I–V. (25 of the 50 *jātak*, translation and commentary) Phnom Penh, Institut Bouddhique.

Eng-Soth, *Eṅ Sut*

T 1966 '*Pravatti sruk Pārāy*'. *KS* (38) 12: 1288–97. (Chronicle. History of Baray and the elephant fight between Laos and Cambodia.)

T 1969 *Ekasār mahāpuras khmaer.* (Documents on Great Khmer Figures) 2 vols. Phnom Penh, *Antrajīeti*, International Printers. (Extracts from Khmer chronicle of the monastery of Kompung Tralach Krom (*Kaṃbuṅ tralāc krom*).)

T 1977 Extracts from *Ekasār mahāpuras khmaer* in Huffman, F. E., and Proum 1977. They are:

pp. 39–43. *Braḥ Suriyovaṅs.*

pp. 47–51. *Bañā Suorgā lok Mīoeṅ (Ghlāṃṅ Mīoeṅ).*

pp. 54–8. *Braḥ Candarājā.*

pp. 63–7. *Ācāry Lāk'.*

—— Sam-Thang, *Sam Thāṃṅ*, Hang-Thun Hak, *Haṅs Dhan' Hāk'*, and Neang Hou, *Nāṅ Ḣū*

1961 *Duṃ Dāv ṭoy Sandhar M̈uk.* Revised and corrected. (Dum Dāv by Sandhar Mok) Phnom Penh, Kim-Seng.

Fabricius, Pierre

V 1969 'Un conte khmer. Histoire de deux compères'. *EC* No. 17, Jan.–Mar. 36–7.

V 1970 'La légende des tours de la Demoiselle Noire.' *CN* 1, No. 3: 54–5.

Feer, Léon

S 1875 'Études bouddhiques: les jātakas'. *JA* 7e Série. (5): 357–434.

V 1877 'Études cambodgiennes. La collection Hennecart de la Bibliothèque Nationale.' *JA* 7e Série. (9): 161–234 (p. 169, résumé of Aphaimani *(Abhimani)*, taken from Bastian 1868: 343–4; p. 170, résumé of Cray-Thong *(Krāy Thoṅ);* pp. 188–202, summary of *Laksaṇavoṅs*; pp. 202–15, Tray-Bhum *(Trai Bhūm)* (extrait du premier chapitre)).

Filliozat, Jean

S 1937 'Études de démonologie indienne. Le kumāratantra de Rāvana et les textes parallèles indiens, chinois, thibétains, cambodgiens et arabes.' *Cahiers de la Société Asiatique* IV.

Finot, Louis

V 1904 'Proverbes cambodgiens. Dits anciens.' *RI* (2) 30 janv. 71–3. (A translation of *Cpāp' bāky cās'*. 1 stanza quoted in transcription.)

V 1904 'Un almanach cambodgien.' *RI* (3) fév. 138–42. (A translation of the almanach of 1903–4.)

V S 1917 'Recherches sur la littérature laotienne.' *BEFEO* (17) 5: 1–218. pp. 45–6, List of the Khmer '50' jatakas made from 2 MSS with Burmese and Laotian comparisons and concordance. p. 66, summaries of the Laotian stories, Jambūpatithera and Yasandharānīrbbān, which Au Chhieng (1953: Nos. 234 and 202) says are like the Khmer).

Foshko, N. D., and Deopik

S 1981 'Khmerskiemify i legendi' (Khmer. Littérature populaire, mythes, légendes. Recueil traditionnel russe) Moscow.

Gaṅ Sambhār and *Sūr Hāy*

T S 1972 *Braḥ pāḷat ghosanāg Haem Cīev vīr puras jāti. Ekasār pravattisāstr.* ('Balat *Haem Ciev*, national hero. Historical document.') Phnom Penh, *Sahakar(ṇ).*

Garnett, Wilma Leslie, Fleet, Betsy, and Mahin, Jane

V *c.*1965 *Literature of other lands: Asia.* pp. 143–5, 'Legend of the thunder'. pp. 146–7, 'Barcarolle' (Translations from the French).

Garnier, Francis

V 1871–2 'Chronique royale du Cambodge.' *JA* 6e Série. (18): 336–85; (20): 112–44 (Translation of Nong's *Rapāl ksatr*, MS DL/2.)

Gerny-Marchal, Mary

[1908 'Rimes khmères'. *RI* 31 déc. 901–2 (seem like European's impressions of Angkor, etc.)]

V 1913 'Les quatre pattes du chat (conte cambodgien). Adapté par . . .' *BSEI* (65): 43–6.

V 1919 'Contes cambodgiens et laotiens'. *RI* NS (32) 7–8: 71–7. (pp. 71–2, 'Le pari: conte cambodgien.' translated into verse.)

Gīm Sā Ûl

T 1971 *Ṭaen ṭī kambujā krom. Lpaṅ srāv jrāv ekasār pravattisāstr.* (The land of Cambodia. Research into historical documents) Phnom Penh, Apsara.

Gironcourt, Georges de

T V 1941 'Motifs de chants cambodgiens recueillis de LL. AA. la princesse Malika et la princesse Peng-pas Yukanthor'. *BSEI* NS (16) 1: 51–105. 21 songs from Princesses Malika and Peng-pas. 39 from Khmer Loe (tribes). Cambodian text in orthography and transcription, French translation and melody. The 21 Khmer songs are:

Haio-Haia. Salutation enfantine de bienvenue. (*Haiÿū haiÿā*).

On euy dek teov. Fais dodo, petite sœur (*Ūn oey ṭek dau*).

Bang phdam ruoch heuy. Adieux du seigneur à sa dame (*Paṅ phtāṃ ruoc hoey*).

Beuk préah kaut. Ouvre l'urne royale (Ramayana cambodgien). (*Poek braḥ koṭṭh*).

Peantaling. Salutation dansée (Ramayana cambodgien).

Néang Sochada. Le plaisir de faire sa toilette (Ramayana cambodgien) (*Nāṅ Sujaṭā*).

Sarika aou long. Beau merle du papa Long (*Sārikā Ū Ḷuṅ*).

Kon lang. Berceuse royale du roi-poète Pon-héa-to (*Bañā Tū Srī Dhammarāj*) (*Kanlaṅ'*).

Phlom Sleuk. Chanson de la feuille (*Phluṃ sḷik*).

Phuong Malay. Bracelet de fleurs (*Phuoṅ mālǎy*).

Chau préam. Auguste brahme (*Cau brāhm*).

Sorya longeach thngay. Soleil couchant (Pastorale) (*Suriyā lṅāc thṅai*).

Kantek aha. Chant aux étoiles (A Cham title).

Om touk. Promenade sur l'eau (barcarole) (*Uṃ dūk*).

O Chet Yeung. Notre cœur (berceuse triste) (*O citr yoeṅ*).

Luong lous atreat. Vers minuit. (Berceuse royale) (*Laṅ' luḥ adhrātr*).

Prom kit Phou thiong liléa. Deux exemples de lectures chantées (*Brahmagīt, Bhūjaṅ līlā.* Metres which are recited).

Lous ban kheunh lay. Ballade du page (*Luḥ pān ghoeñ ḷāy*).

O chap poukeuy. Le moineau: chant de garde de la récoltemûrissante (*O cāp būk oey*).

Préah barom. Psalmodie: chant des pleureuses royales (*Braḥ param*).

Gorgoniev, Yuri A.

S 1966 'Kambodska Leteratura.' Kratka Literaturia lopedi. 'Littérature cambodgienne.' *Petite Encyclopédie Littéraire.* (3) Moscow (Russian text).

S 1968*a* 'Nhok Thaem.' *Petite Encyclopédie Littéraire.* (5) Moscow (Russian text).

S 1968*b* 'Nou Hac.' *Petite Encyclopédie Littéraire.* (5) Moscow (Russian text).

V 1973 'Pokhozhdeniia khitroumnogo Aleu, i drugie skazki Kambodzhi' (Adventures of the clever A Lev and other Cambodian tales) Hudogestvenneaya literatura. Moscow.

Govid, *Ravivaṅs*

T 19— *Maraṇamātā.* ed. with notes for schools. Pnom Penh.

T 1965 *Saṅkhep baṅsāvatār prades kambujā.* ('Short history of Cambodia.' For schools) Phnom Penh, *Serei Raṭṭh.*

Groslier, Georges

S 1921 *Recherches sur les cambodgiens.* Paris.

Guesdon, Joseph

T n.d. *Domniem (Daṃnīem). Proverbes khmèrs.* No place of publication (Orthography and transcription of 928 proverbs).

T V S 1906 'La littérature khmère et le Bouddhisme'. *A* (1): 91–109; 278–95; 4: 804–17. pp. 278–95. Ponhasa Siresa *(Puññasār Sirsā).* Extract from Vol. V. Orthography, transcription and translation, following two pages of summary of preceding part. (Old-fashioned spelling). pp. 804–16. Réach Kol *(Rājakul),* analyse et critique du poème khmêr'. (Analysis, 804–13, study 813–17).

V *Textes Khmers.* (Various titles published by Plon-Nourrit, q.v.)

Hak Seng Gry, *Hāk' Seṅ Grī*, Publisher

T 1962 *Mahāvessantarajātak.* ed. Nhok-Thaem.

Hang-Kéo, *Haṅs-Kaev*

T 1943 '*Praṭau citt*'. *KS* (15) 1–3: 58–78; 4: 216–22; 5: 270–84.

T 1958 See *Kambujasuriyā* III Texts of folktales and legends. (30) 7.

1966 See *Kambujasuriyā* III Texts of folktales and legends. (38) 10.

Héan-Sin, *Ĥān-Ŝin*

T 1958 ed. *'Lpoek Pathamasiksā'. KS* (31) 8: 637–48.

Heng-Sam-An, *Heṅ-Saṃ-an*

1967 See *Kambujasuriyā* III Texts of folktales and legends. (39) 11.

Heng Yann, *Heṅ-Ÿān'*

T 1951 *Prajuṃ rīoeṅ lpoek.* (Collection of *Lpoek* tales) Phnom Penh, *Roṅ bumbh khmaer.* See also Khuon Sokhamphu and Heng-Yann.

Hennecart, Dr. See under Feer, Léon.

Him, *Ĥim*

T 1934 '*Eka Nipâta jâtaka. I Vedabba jâtaka*'. *KS* (6) 1–3: 46–62 (Translated into Khmer from the Pali).

T 1934 '*Eka Nipāta Jātaka. II Nakkhatta Jātaka*'. *KS* (6) 4–6: 81–92 (Translation into Khmer from Pali).

T 1934 '*Eka-Tripāta Jātaka. III Dumedhi Jātaka*'. *KS* (6) 10–12: 45–55 (Translation into Khmer from Pali).

T 1935 '*Nītisāstr (bāky kāby)*'. *KS* (7) 1–2: 25–36.

T 1935 '*Eka Nipāta Jātaka IV Mahā Sīlava Jātaka*'. *KS* (7) 3: 99–121 (Translation into Khmer from Pali).

T 1936 *Sāsanivād'*. Poem in *KS* 1936 (8) 8: 131–6; 9: 185–93; 10: 43–51.

Hing, *Hīṅ*

T 1964, 1966 *Rīoeṅ Braḥ Jinavaṅs.* L'Histoire de Preah Chinavong. 4 vols. Phnom Penh, IB.

T 1977 '*Rīoeṅ Braḥ Jinavaṅs.* L'histoire de Preah Chinavong.' Extract in Huffman, F. E., and Proum 1977: 251–68 (vocabulary 269–73) from IB 1964 edition 2: 103–19.

Hong-Chhéa, *Huṅ-Jhā*

T 1939 '*Kusulakammapath.*' *KS* (11) 5: 137–46.

Houn-Savi, *Hun-Sāvī*

T 1965 See *Kambujasuriyā* III Texts of folktales and legends. (37) 9.

Huber, E.

S 1903 Review of Leclère, Adhémard *Contes laotiens et Contes cambodgiens. Collection de contes et chansons populaires. BEFEO* (3): 91–2. (Suggests comparison of *(Sātrā) Kịṅ Kantrai* with Burmese *Jugement de la princesse Thudammachari.*)

Huffman, Franklin E. (with the assistance of Im Proum)

T 1972 *Intermediate Cambodian Reader*. Yale University Press. Contains:

pp. 11–13. *Rīoeṅ hor nịṅ tā cās' ṭūn cās'*. ('The astrologer and the old couple.') (Vocabulary 13–15.)

pp. 29–31. *Rīoeṅ Cau Sukr nịṅ Cau Sau(r).* ('Mr *Sokr* and Mr *Sau(r).*') (Vocabulary 31–3.)

pp. 41–3. *Rīoeṅ puras kaṃsat' nau jit phdaḥ seṭṭhī.* ('A poor man lives near the rich man's house.') (Vocabulary 43–4.)

pp. 55–7. *Rīoeṅ puras kaṃjil mān prabandh grap' lăkkh(ṇ).* ('A lazy man whose wife had every virtue.') (Vocabulary 57–60.)

p. 67. *Rīoeṅ andaṅ' vaeṅ chnāṃṅ vaeṅ.* ('A long eel and a long cooking pot.') (Vocabulary 68–9.)

pp. 70–6. *Rīoeṅ puras mān kūn 4 nāk' rīen vijjā 4 pad.* ('A man with 4 sons who learn four subjects.') (Vocabulary 76–83.)

pp. 84–7. *Rīoeṅ bānar luoc braḥ makuṭ.* ('A monkey steals the king's crown.') (Vocabulary 88–91.)

pp. 98–100. *Rīoeṅ srī smoḥ traṅ' nịṅ svāmī.* ('A woman who is faithful to her husband.') (Vocabulary 100–3.)

pp. 104–5. *Rīoeṅ bhnaṃ prus bhnaṃ srī.* ('The Men's Hill and the Women's Hill.') (Vocabulary 106–8.)

pp. 109–19. *Rīoeṅ Subhā Dansāy. Bāky rāy ta bī bāky kāby.* ('The rabbit.' Prose) (Vocabulary 19–31.)

pp. 132–7. *Rīoeṅ braḥ rāj vinicchăy ktī dāṃṅ 4.* ('The king decides 4 cases.') (Vocabulary 138–40.)

pp. 141–63. *Rīoeṅ Ā Lev.* (Vocabulary 164–88.)

Huffman, Franklin E. and Proum, Im
1977 *Cambodian Literary Reader and Glossary.* Yale Linguistic Series. New Haven and London, Yale University Press. Contains, with introductions in Khmer, the following texts:

Extracts from the Chronicle of Kampong Tralach Krom (from Eng Soth 1969):
T pp. 39–43. *Braḥ Suriyovaṅs* (vocabulary 43–6).
T pp. 47–51. *Bañā Suorgālok Mīoeṅ (Ghlāṃṅ Mīoeṅ)* (vocabulary 51–3).
T pp. 54–8. *Braḥ Candarājā* (vocabulary 59–62).
T pp. 63–7. *Ācāry Lāk'* (vocabulary 67–70).
S *Kābyasāstr khmaer* (Khmer prosody pp. 79–103) (vocabulary 103–5).
T pp. 106–7. *Pad añjoeñ grū.* ('Inviting the teacher.') (Vocabulary 107.)
T pp. 108–9. *Supin.* (Vocabulary 109–10) (by Kim Samon 1972: 43–9) (Poem).
T pp. 111–12. *Bhleṅ kār.* ('Wedding music.') (Vocabulary 12). (Identical with the poem entitled *'Poek vāṃṅ nan'* in Pou 1973: 303–4 and taken from Nheuk Nou and Nou 1965: 111.)
T pp. 113–4. *Pad Stec phdaṃ.* ('The king sleeps.') (Vocabulary 114–15) (Also in Pou 1973: 304–5 and taken from Nheuk Nou and Nou 1965: 122–3.)
T pp. 116–21. *Sarsoer hemantamās.* (Vocabulary 121–5). From *KS* 1938.
T pp. 126–9. *Āÿai* by Srey-Ou and Nhoung-Sœung. (Vocabulary 130–3). From IB 1951 (1). 2: 11–24.
T pp. 134–9. *Āÿai* by Chhim-Sum. (Vocabulary 139–42). From IB 1951 (1). 4: 54–80.
T pp. 143–6. *Gatilok* by In, from In (1): 1–6. (Vocabulary 146–8).
T pp. 149–54. *Cpāp' Kram.* (Vocabulary 154–9). From *Cpāp' Kram* 1961.
T pp. 160–3. *Cpāp' Ker(ti) Kāl.* (Vocabulary 163–6). From *Ker(ti) Kāl* 1961.
T pp. 167–9. *Cpāp' Bāky Cās'.* (Vocabulary 169–72). From *Cpāp' Bāky cās'*: (Bouth Néang) 1960.
T pp. 173–81. *Cpāp' Prus.* (Vocabulary 181–8). From *Cpāp' Prus Srī*, n.d.
T pp. 189–99. *Rīoeṅ Duṃ Dāv.* (Vocabulary 200–7). Excerpt from Som 1966.
T pp. 208–14. *Rīoeṅ Kākī.* (Vocabulary 215–19). 2 excerpts from Ang Duong 1966: 8–10 and 21–6.
T pp. 220–4. *Rīoeṅ Mā Yoeṅ.* (Vocabulary 224–6). 2 excerpts from IB 1961: 18–21 and 33–5.
T pp. 227–31. *Rīoeṅ Haṅs Yant.* (Vocabulary 231–5). Excerpt from IB 1966: 21–7.
pp. 236–44. *Rīoeṅ Dibv Saṅvār.* (Vocabulary 244–50). Excerpt from IB 1963 (1): 53–5 and 64–73.

T pp. 251–68. *Rīoeṅ Braḥ Jinavaṅs.* (Vocabulary 269–73). Excerpt from Hing 1964 (2): 103–19.

pp. 274–6. *Rīoeṅ Supin kumār.* (Vocabulary 277–8). Excerpt from IB 1966: 20–2.

pp. 279–85. *Kruṅ Subhamitr.* (Vocabulary 286–8). Excerpt from Kao 1967: 26–36.

pp. 289–94. *Rīoeṅ Sabvasiddhi.* (Vocabulary 295–7). Excerpt from Tan 1966: 7–15.

pp. 298–304. *Mahāvessantarajātak.* (Vocabulary 305–8). Excerpt from Nhok-Thaem 1964: 281–98.

pp. 309–12. *Rāmker(ti).* (Vocabulary 312–14) and pp. 315–17. (Vocabulary 317–19). 2 excerpts from IB 1961 (1): 6–11 and (6): 34–40.

Hu'o'ng, Lê

V 1969 *Truyện cô' cao Miên.* 2 vols. Saigon, Khai Tri (Translation into Vietnamese of 79 folktales).

Ieng-Say, *Īeṅ-Say*

S 1966 *Me kāby* (Versification). Phnom Penh, Mey-Sok.

Im-Phon, *Īm-Bhan*

T 1959 ed. *Rīoeṅ Haṅs Yant.* Histoire de Hang-Yon. *KS* (31) 4: 431–6; 5: 547–56; 6: 647–64; 7: 800–18; 8: 871–7; 9: 994–1009; 10: 1107–20; 11: 1239–56; 12: 1346–67.

T 1960–3 ed. *Mahosathajātak.* *KS* (32) 1: 41–50; 2: 155–62; 3: 275–84; 4: 404–12; 5: 525–32; 6: 645–52; 7: 770–6; 8: 881–94; 9: 1017–26; 10: 1119–28; 11: 1255–60; 12: 1350–60. (33) 1: 39–48; 2: 169–78; 3: 276–83; 4: 406–11; 5: 516–23; 6: 652–60; 7: 766–76; 8: 879–91; 9: 1005–12; 10: 1108–17; 11: 1276–85. (34) 1: 30–7; 2: 166–70; 3: 270–7; 4: 397–409; 5: 523–32; 6: 635–50; 7: 750–62; 8: 899–900; 9: 1006–18; 10: 1123–42; 11: 1236–53; 12: 1369–83. (35) 1: 29–48; 2: 164–76; 3: 260–71; 4: 375–93; 5: 491–506; 6: 582–93; 7: 683–93; 8: 757–74; 9: 921–33; 10: 1016–26; 11: 36–44.

Imprimerie du Gouvernement, Phnom Penh

T 1932 *Cpāp' Lpoek Thmī* by Ngoy.

Imprimerie Nouvelle, Phnom Penh

T 1932 *Cpāp' Kir Kāl Thmī* by Ngoy.

T 1932 *Cpāp' Lpoek Thmī* by Ngoy.

Imprimerie Royale

T 1930 *Lpoek Medrīy Pā.*

T 1932 *Cpāp' Kir Kāl Thmī* by Ngoy.

In, *Ind*, *Ukñā Suttanta Prījā.*

S n.d. *Kap Pakasini.* Règles de Versification. *Mitt Sālā Pālī.*

S n.d. *Kpuon Me Kāby* (Treatise on versification).

T n.d. *Rīoeṅ Aṃpaeṅ paek.* La poêle cassée. Phnom Penh, Ching Nguon Huot.

T 1927–30 '*Gatilok ṛ Cpāp' dūnmān khluon* ou l'Art de bien se conduire dans la vie'. *KS* (1) 1: 45–61; 2: 65–74; 3: 69–85; 5: 57–69; 6: 65–79; 7: 79–93; 8: 61–8; 10: 75–92; 11: 79–97; 12: 57–75. (2) 3: 65–84; 4: 115–35; 6: 89–108; 9: 25–60; 10: 21–58; 11: 57–90; 12: 51–84. (3) 1: 75–94; 2: 37–58; 3: 33–56; 4: 49–66; 5: 39–62; 6: 33–56; 7: 27–46; 8: 29–50.

T 1934 '*Patham Sambodhi. Bāky kāby.*' *KS* (6) 10–12: 5–38.

T 1934 '*Nirās Nagar vatt. Bāky kāby.* Pélerinage à Angkor en 1909.' *KS* (6) 7–9: 5–81.

T 1934 '*Rīoeṅ paṭham sambodhi. Bāky kāby. Pad lkhaon.* Le grand départ du Bodhisattva pour atteindre la Bodhi.' *KS* (6) 10–12: 5–38.

T 1934 '*Subhāsit Cpāp' Srī.*' *KS* (6) 4–6: 46–80.

T 1936, 1961, 1964, 1971 *Gatilok ṛ Cpāp' dūnmān khluon* ou l'Art de bien se conduire dans la vie. Phnom Penh, BR/IB.

S 1947 '*Cpāp' taeṅ chandagaṇa: jā khemarabhāsā niṅ vidhī rāp' khae chnāṃ.*' (Pali rules applied to Khmer verse) *KS* (19) 4: 171–80 and 5: 246–53.

T 1950 '*Secktī sraṅ' bī Nirās Aṅgar. Brai bṛksā. Aniccā to thma. Sbān nāg.*' *Mitt Sālā Pālī.* (1) 1: 26–8 (Selections from *Nirās nagaravatt*).

T 1951, 1959 *Subhāsit Cpāp' Srī.* Phnom Penh, IB.

T 1969 *Nirās Nagar Vat.* Phnom Penh, IB.

Ing-Kheng *Īṅ-Kheṅ*

T 1935, 1958 *Lpoek dūnmān kūn cau cin.* Phnom Penh, IB.

Ing-Yeng, *Iṅ-Yeṅ*

S 1972 *Kābyasāstr khmaer.* (Khmer Versification) Phnom Penh, Mea Yeung.

Institut Bouddhique, Phnom Penh

This list consists of works either with no stated author or of which *the author may not be as well known as the title.* They were published in Phnom Penh by the Institut Bouddhique (or in the 1930s and early 1940s by the Bibliothèque Royale).

T n.d. *Cpāp' dūnmān jan prus srī.* Préceptes pour l'instruction des hommes et des femmes (By Ngoy).

T n.d. *Cpāp' Paṇṭāṃ Kram N̈uy* (Contains 4 *Cpāp'* for schools).

T 1933, 1953, 1965 *Sek Som Paṇḍit* by Kim-Hak.

T 1935, 1958 *Lpoek dūnmān kūn cau cin* by Ing-Kheng.

T 1939, 1953 *Nānajātak knuṅ dhammapadaṭṭhakathā* by Chhim-Soum.

T 1940, 1961 *Bāky kāby praṭau jan prus srī* by Ngoy.

T 1940, 1960, 1964 *Cpāp' Lpoek Thmī. Cpāp' Kir Kāl Thmī* by Ngoy.

T 1941 *Cpāp' Rājaneti. Krasuoṅ Dhammasāstr.* Ministry of religion.

T 1941 *Cpāp' Trīneti.*

T 1942, 1953, 1957, 1959 *Cpāp' Phseṅ2.* Contains the following classical texts:

Vol. 1
pp. 1–6. *Vidhurapaṇḍit.*
pp. 7–11. *Cpāp' dūnmān khluon.*
pp. 12–14. *Cpāp' bāky cās'.*

Vol. 2
pp. 1–8. *Cpāp' Prus.*
pp. 9–20. *Cpāp' Srī.*
pp. 21–5. *Cpāp' Ariyasatthā.*

Vol. 3
pp. 1–4. *Cpāp' Kram.*
pp. 5–7. *Ker Kāl.*
pp. 8–15. *Kūn cau.*
pp. 16–24. *Trīnet.*

T 1942, 1953 *Cpāp' Subhāsit* by Nong.
T 1942, 1958, 1961 *Kumbhajātak.* Translated by Chhim-Soum.
T 1942, 1963 *Milindapañhā.* 2 vols. Translated by Oum-Sou.
T 1944, 1958, 1961, 1962 *Paññāsajātak samrāy,* 1–5, the 50 *jātak* translated by Louis-Em, Oum-Sou, Long, *et al.*
T 1951 *Camrīeṅ jāti niyam.* Chamrieng Cheat Niyum ou Chant Patriotique.

Fasc. 1 contains:
pp. i–xii. Introduction.
Songs pp. 1–3. *Namaskār* (Salutation) by *Srī Û* (Srey-Ou).
pp. 4–10. *Ārambhakathā* (Foreword) by *Srī Û* (Srey-Ou).
pp. 11–24. *Sāratārajāt* by *Srī Û* and *Ñūṅ Sīoeṅ.* (Srey-Ou and Nhoung Sœung).
pp. 25–53. *Karaṇīyakicc rapas' bal raṭṭh* (The duty of citizens) by *Din Huot* (Tin-Huot).
pp. 54–80. *Karaṇīyakicc rapas' bal raṭṭh phnaek siksādhikār jāt(i)* (The duty of citizens towards education) by *Jhịm Sum* (Chhim-Soum).

T 1951 *Cpāp' praṭau jan prus srī* by Ngoy.
T 1951, 1959 *Subhāsit Cpāp' Srī* by In.
T 1953, 1961, 1970 *Kruṅ Subhamitr.* Krungsubhamitra by Kao. 3 vols.
T 1953, 1965 *Sappurisadharm* by Ban-Teng.
T 1958, 1966 *Lokaṇayapakar(ṇ).* Lokanayapakarana by Nong. 2 vols.
T 1958 *Secktī ramḷik ṭās' tīoen* by Ou Ngoy.
T 1959, 1964, 1967 *Rīoeṅ Buddhisaen.* Le Roi Putthisen. (From palm-leaf manuscript.)
T 1959, 1970 *Rīoeṅ Kākī.* Kaki l'infidèle by King Ang-Duong. (From MS of Princess Malika.)

T 1959, 1961, 1964 *Rīoeṅ Rāmakerti.* Reamker. Parts 1–10 and 75–80.

T 1959, 1966 *Rīoeṅ Supin kumār.* Soben Komar. (From palm-leaf MS.)

T 1959–72 *Prajuṃ Rīoeṅ Breṅ Khmaer.* Recueil des contes et légendes cambodgiens. *Krum jaṃnuṃ daṃnīem damlāp' khmaer.* 9 vols.

V 196– *Connaisssance du Cambodge.* Département du Tourisme. (Published translations of folktales (from Pavie 1898, 1903) and songs (from Bernard 1955).)

V 196– Chants de Sakava en Khmer. (In IB booklist, 1969.)

T 1960, 1964 *Cpāp' Lpoek Thmī. Cpāp' Kir Kāl Thmī* by Ou Ngoy. Commission des Mœurs et Coutumes du Cambodge. Vols. 1–8.

T 1960 *Surabbhajātak.*

T 1960, 1964, 1969 *Mahāvessantarajātak.* ed. Nhok-Thaem.

T 1961, 1966 *Rīoeṅ Bhogakulakumār.* Bhogakula kumar by Nong. (From palm-leaf MS.)

T 1961, 1970 *Rīoeṅ Khyaṅ Săṅkh.* Histoire de Khyang-Saing. (From palm-leaf MS.)

T 1961, 1965, 1969 *Rīoeṅ Maraṇamātā* by Ûk.

T 1961 *Rīoeṅ Mā Yoeṅ.* Mea Yœung. (From palm-leaf MS.)

T 1962 *Cpāp' Srī* by Ang Duong.

T 1962, 1964, 1966, 1971 *Rīoeṅ Duṃ Dāv.* Histoire de Tum Teao by Som. (From palm-leaf MS.)

T 1962, 1966, 1969 *Rīoeṅ Sabvasiddhi.* Histoire de Sabbasiddhi by Tan (*Mīn Bhaktī Aksar Tan'*). (From palm-leaf MS.)

T 1962, 1966, 1969 *Rīoeṅ Săṅkh Silp Jăy.* Histoire de Saing Selchey (By Ûk, according to Ly-Théam Teng only. From palm-leaf MS.)

T 1962, 1965, 1967 *Rīoeṅ Sradap Cek.* Histoire de Sratôp Chek by Ngin. (Taken from palm-leaf MS.)

T 1963 *Rīoeṅ Braḥ Sudhan.* Histoire de Preah Sudhana. (Taken from palm-leaf MS.)

T 1963 *Rīoeṅ Dibv Saṅvār.* Histoire de Tip-Sangvar. Translated from Thai by Thau-Kae. (from a MS) 5 vols.

T 1964 *Cpāp' Kram Pariyāy* by Nheuk-Nou. (Text and explanation of *Cpāp' Kram.*)

T 1964, 1966 *Rīoeṅ Braḥ Jinavaṅs.* L'histoire de Preah Chinavong. By Hing. 4 vols.

T 1964, 1972 *Rīoeṅ Dhanañjăy.* Histoire de Thnenh Chey.

T 1964, 1966 *Rīoeṅ Haṅs Yant.* Histoire de Hang-Yon (Hangsa Yonta). (From palm-leaf MS.)

T 1966 *Padānukram Rāmaker(ti)* (Glossary to the Reamker) by Krasem.

T 1967, 1970, 1973 *Cpāp' Phseṅ2.* Chbap divers.

pp. 1–13. *Cpāp' Prus.*
pp. 15–29. *Cpāp' Srī.*
pp. 31–43. *Cpāp' Hai Mahājan.*
pp. 45–57. *Cpāp' Paṇṭāṃ Pitā.*

pp. 59–76. *Cpāp' Kūn Cau Lpoek* (1st part same as *Cpāp' Paṇṭāṃ Pitā*; 2nd part same as *Cpāp' Bāky Cās'*).
pp. 77–83. *Cpāp' Kram.*
pp. 85–9. *Cpāp' Kerti Kāl.*
pp. 91–104. *Cpāp' Kūn Cau.*
pp. 105–19. *Cpāp' Trīneti.*
pp. 121–7. *Cpāp' dūnmān khluon.*
pp. 129–37. *Cpāp' Vidhurapaṇḍit.*
pp. 139–42. *Cpāp' Bāky Cās'.*
pp. 143–50. *Cpāp' Ariyasatthā.*
pp. 151–61. *Cpāp' Rājaneti.*

T 1968 *Prajuṃ bāky kāby. Cpāp' Braḥ Rāj sambhār.* (Collection of poems. *Cpāp' Braḥ rāj sambhār = Cpāp' rājaneti*) Editions Mālikā.

V 1969 *Recueil de contes khmères.* Série de Culture et Civilisation khmères. (From Pavie's translations)

No. 1. Les douze jeunes filles ou l'histoire de Néang Kangrey.
No. 2. Néang Roumsay-Sak.
No. 3. Néang Kakey ou Dame Kakey.

V 1969 *Historique de la traduction et de l'édition du Tripitaka du Pali en cambodgien.* pp. 8.

V 1969 Preah Reach Samphear (*Braḥ Rāj Sambhār.* English translation of a few stanzas of *Cpāp' Rājaneti*).

T 1969 *Traipiṭak.* (Translation of the Tripiṭaka into Khmer in 110 vols.)

S 1970 *Aṃbī lamnāṃ saṅkhep nai bhleṅ khmaer* (Khmer music abridged) by Pech-Sal.

V 1970 *Recueil de contes khmères.* Série de Culture et Civilisation Khmères. 4 (1) Contains:

pp. 1–16. Protection maternelle *(Maraṇamātā).*
pp. 17–20. La légende du Tigre.
pp. 21–4. Légende de la Foudre.
pp. 25–37. L'Homme qui déterrait des crabes.
pp. 38–42. La naissance des Moustiques.
pp. 43–9. Histoire du Serpent Kéng Kâng.
pp. 50–1. Histoire de l'Ours et de l'arbre Banra.
pp. 52–6. Conte du sorcier, du Vieux et de la Vieille.
pp. 57–8. Histoire de la Marmite longue et de l'Anguille longue.
pp. 59–61. Histoire d'un vol de bœuf.
pp. 62–4. Histoire de trois Setthi.
pp. 65–9. Histoire de Quatre Chauves. (From versions by Bernard, Martini, Monod, and Martini and Bernard) Imprimerie Cambodia.

V 1970 *Recueil de contes khmères.* Série de Culture et Civilisation Khmères. *Histoire du juge lièvre.* (Introduction by Midan) 4 (4) Imprimerie Bokor.

V 1970 *Chansons populaires.* Série de Culture et Civilisation Khmères. 12. Reprint from *Connaissance du Cambodge* and *France-Asie* Nos. 37–8. 196– , IB. Contains in French:

pp. 1–15. Introduction with excerpts from songs.
pp. 15–17. Barcarolle.
pp. 17–18. L'air d'Angkor.
pp. 18–19. Invitation aux Génies.
pp. 19–20. Chanson Triste.
pp. 21–2. Tonnerre gronde.
pp. 22–3. L'écharpe rouge.
For guitar:
pp. 25–6. Je vais à la fontaine.
p. 27. Le poitier de Kompong Chhnang.
pp. 28–9. La gare de Sisophon.
p. 31. Si tu me donnes un sou.
p. 32. Ballade du l'île du Pic.
p. 33. La marchande de Kompong Thom.
p. 34. La sirène de Kratie.
p. 35. La forêt de Stung-Treng.

V 1971 *Recueil de contes khmères.* Série de Culture et Civilisation khmères. 4. 5.

pp. 1–14. Le mariage des quatre chauves (Martini).
pp. 15–25. Neang Phim (Martini).
pp. 26–34. La réincarnation (Leuba).
pp. 35–42. Histoire de deux amis qui voulaient tarir la mère. *(RC)*
pp. 43–9. L'homme aux trente sapèques. *(RC)*
pp. 50–8. La Bonne Fortune et la Malchance. *(RC)*

V 1971 *Recueil de contes khmères.* Série de Culture et Civilisation khmères. No. 5. Vorvong et Saurivong. (From Mission Pavie.)

T [1972] *Cpāp' Lpoek Thmī, Cpāp' Ker Kāl, Secktī raṃlịk ṭās' tīoen*, by Ngoy.

S 1973 *Lpoek Aṅgar Vatt. Prakratidīn chnāṃ chlūv pañcasak:* 25–79.

Ith-Hak, *Ît-Hāk'*

T 1943 ed. '*Sarsoer Braḥ Rasmī.* Les six rayons de la puissance bouddhique.' *KS* (15) 7: 369–76.

Jacob, Judith M.

S 1966 'Some features of Khmer versification'. *In memory of J. R. Firth.* London, Longmans: 227–42.

S 1979 'Observations on the uses of reduplication as a poetic device in Khmer'. Theraphan L. Thongkum *et al.* eds. *Studies in Thai and Mon-Khmer Phonetics and Phonology. In honour of Eugénie J. A. Henderson.* Bangkok, Chulalongkorn University Press: 111–30.

S 1982 'The short stories of Cambodian popular tradition'. J. H. C. S. Davidson and H. Cordell eds. *The short story in South East Asia.*

Aspects of a genre. London, School of Oriental and African Studies: 37–61.

V 1986 *Reamker (Cambodian Rāmāyaṇa)* translated with the assistance of Kuoch Haksrea. London, Royal Asiatic Society.

V 1987 'Appendix: The story of the *yakṣa* Nandaka, guardian of the gate of Isvara'. J. H. C. S. Davidson ed. *Laī Sū' Thai. Essays in honour of E. H. S. Simmonds.* London, School of Oriental and African Studies: 140–50.

S 1989 'Some features of modern Khmer literary style'. J. H. C. S. Davidson ed. *South East Asian Linguistics. Essays in honour of Eugénie J. A. Henderson.* London, School of Oriental and African Studies: 23–41.

S 1995 'Cambodia (Kampuchea)'. Alastair Dingwall ed. *Traveller's Literary Companion to South-East Asia.* Brighton: 154–62.

—— and Morgan, Edwin

V 1979 'Reamker' (extract) and 'The code of behaviour for the young' (extract) edited and translated. Keith Bosley ed. *The Elek Book of Oriental verse.* London, Paul Elek: 94–5 and 95–6.

Jacq, Michel

S 1979 Le roman, source d'inspiration de la peinture khmère à la fin du XIXe siècle et au début du XXe siècle. L'histoire de Preah Chinavong et son illustration dans la (sālā) de Vat Kieng Svay Krau. Thèse de 3ème cycle, Etudes Indiennes (option Asie du Sud-Est), Paris.

—— and Hergoualch, Michel

S 1982 *Le roman, source d'inspiration de la peinture khmère à la fin du XIXe et du début du XXe siècle. L'histoire de Preah Chinavong et son illustration dans la (sālā) de Vat Kieng Svay Krau.* Paris, EFEO. 2 vols. (Vol. I. 1. Introduction to khmère literature. 2. How paintings link with the novel. II. The paintings).

Jenner, Philip N.

S 1973 *Southeast Asian literatures in translation: a preliminary bibliography.* Asian Studies at Hawaii, No. 9. Hawaii, University Press.

S 1976 'The relative dating of some Khmer *Cpā'pa**' Philip N. Jenner *et al.* eds. *Austroasiatic Studies* II. Hawaii, University Press 2: 693–710.

T V S 1978 'A minor Khmer ethical text of early date'. *MKS* 7: 111–40. (The text is *Cpāp' Srī* Cl. 2. (Pou and Haksrea, Nos. 95 and 96). **S**, 111–15. Text with parallel translation, 116–27. Notes, 127–33. Word list, 133–40.)

—— and Pou, Saveros

T V S 1976 'Les *Cpāp'* ou "Codes de conduite" khmers. II *Cpāp' Prus.*' *BEFEO* (63): 313–50. (Introduction, 313–16. **T**, 317–25. **V**, **S** 326–43. Word-list, 344–50.)

See under Pou, Saveros, and Philip N. Jenner.

Jivapravatti saṅkhep rapas' anak nibandh samājik nai samāgam
(Short Biographies of Authors, members of the Association) 1970. Phnom Penh.

Kambuja

S 1969 *Rāmker (Rāmāyaṇa khmer)*. Oct. 142–7; Nov. 124–33; Dec. 176–90. (A reprint, in 3 parts, of the book, *Rāmker ou Rāmāyaṇa khmer*, printed in 1968 by the Commission du Reamker.)

Kambujasuriyā

Below are listed I *Cpāp'*, II *Jātak*, III Folktales and legends, and IV Riddles, published in *Kambujasuriyā*.

I *Cpāp'*

T 1932 '*Cpāp' Lpoek thmī*' by Ou Ngoy. See Ngoy.

T 1932 '*Cpāp' Kir kāl thmī*' by Ou Ngoy. See Ngoy.

T 1933 '*Secktī ramlịk ṭaḥ tīoen*. Hommage au Triple Joyau' by Ngoy, q.v.

T 1934 '*Subhāsit cpāp' srī*' by In, q.v.

T 1935 '*Nītisāstr (bāky kāby)*' by Him, q.v.

T 1937 '*Lpoek cpāp' krity kram*' by Toet, q.v.

T 1937 '*Cpāp' Kūn Cau*.' (9) 4–6: 111–22 by Ngoy.

T 1937 '*Cpāp' Thmī*' by Mai, q.v.

T 1937 '*Lpoek Cpāp' Săṅgh*. Paroles de Kram Ngoy.' See Ngoy.

T 1937 '*Cpāp' praṭau jan prus srī*' by Ngoy, q.v.

T 1939 '*Cpāp' Braḥ Rāj Sambhār*. Recueil de poèmes.' (11) 4–6: 43–54. (Same text as *Cpap' Rājaneti* Cl. Pou and Haksrea No. 33.)

T 1941 '*Cpāp' Subhāsit*' by Nong, q.v.

T 1942 '*Cpāp' bāky cās*'. Chbab Péakchas (Bons conseils en vers).' (14) 1: 41–3.

T 1942 '*Cpāp' Vidhurapaṇḍit (bāky kāby)*. Chbab Vidhurapaṇḍit (poème).' (14) 2: 42–6; 3: 10–2.

T 1942 '*Cpāp' dūnmān khluon*. Chbab tounméan khluon (bons conseils en vers).' (14) 4: 10–11; 5: 8–10.

T 1942 '*Cpāp' Prus*. Chbab Pros (Conseils aux fils).' (14) 17–8: 12–19. (By Mai.)

T 1942 '*Cpāp' Srī*. Chbab-srey (Conseils aux filles).' (14) 19–20: 14–25. (By Mai.)

T 1942 '*Cpāp' Ariyasatthā*. Chbab-Ariyasatthā (Conseils aux enfants).' (14) 19–20: 26–30.

T 1942 '*Cpāp' Rājaneti*. Chbab Rājanet.' (14) 21–2: 11–6. (Same as *Cpāp' Braḥ Rāj Sambhār, Hai Sādhujan phaṅ, Satrā hai sān, Trīneti* 2.)

T 1942 '*Cpāp' Paṇṭāṃ pitā*. Chbap Bandaṃ Beida.' (14) 21–2: 17–23. (Same as *Cpāp' Braḥ pandūl caeṅ*.)

T 1942 '*Cpāp' Hai Mahājan*. Chbap Haimahājan.' (14) 21–2: 24–31.

T 1942 '*Cpāp' Mahāneti rājasvastī.* Chbab Mahanet Rājasvasti.' (14) 23–4: 10–26.

T 1942 '*Lpoek Cpāp' Krity kram.* Lbeuk chbab krit-kram' by Toet, q.v.

T 1943 *Praṭau citt* by Hang-Keo, q.v.

T 1943 '*Cpāp' Rājaneti.*' (15) 21–2: 11–6.

T 1943 '*Paṇṭāṃ Bālī*' by Méas 1.

T S 1944 '*Cpāp' Kram Pariyāy*' by Nheuk-Nuv, q.v. (Text with explanation).

T 1944 '*Bāky Subhāsit purāṇ*'. See Kong-Séan, ed.

T 1945 '*Cpāp' Braḥ pandūl caeṅ.* Chbăb preah bântul chèng, poème.' (17) 1: 25–32. (Same text as *Cpāp' paṇṭāṃ pitā* Cl.)

T 1946 '*Purāṇasubhāsit*'. (18) 8: 393–5.

T 1949 '*Cpāp' Kram Sāmaṇer*' by Nhok-Thaem, q.v.

T 1949 '*Paṇṭāṃ mātā*'. See Ou-Srey ed.

T 1956 '*Ovād Mātā*' by *Am Dīoek,* q.v.

T 1956 *Subhāsit rājanīti (bāky kāby).*

T 1957 '*Subhāsit praṭau jan prus srī.*' (29) 1: 50–63; 2: 152–62; 3: 245–54; 4: 324–33.

T 1958 '*Lpoek paṭhamasiksā*'. See Héan-Sin ed.

T 1968 '*Cpāp' On Aṅg*' by *Ṭūn.* (40) 7: 758–67.

II *Jātak. Satrā Lpaeṅ*

T 1936 '*Rīoeṅ Temiyajātak. Secktī Cās*'. Temiyajātaka ou Bouddha dans ses vies antérieueres'. (8) 7: 43–54 and 8: 121–9.

T 1936–8 and 1942–4 '*Lokanaya.*' (Also written *Lokaneya, Lokaneyya, Lokanayapakar(ṇ)*) See Nong.

T 1943–4 '*Mā Yoeṅ bāky kāby.* Méayông, poème ancien'. (15) 11: 607–15. (16) 1: 25–45.

T 1948–50 '*Bhogakulakumār*' by Nong, q.v.

T 1954–6 '*Rīoeṅ Sau(r) Soy* or *Satrā Braḥ Pād Ŝī Sau(r)., Sisorajātak.*' See Peung-Pam ed.

T 1957–8 *'Devand'* by Mok, q.v.

T 1959 '*Sabvasiddhi.*' See Bou-Po ed.

T 1959 '*Surabajātak.*' See Thang-Vong ed.

T 1959–60 '*Maraṇamātā.*' See By-Sovann ed.

T 1960–3 '*Mahosathajātak.*' See Im-Phon ed.

T 1962 '*Sammodanamānajātak.*' See Nhéan-Chhin ed.

T 1964 '*Haṅs Yant.* Histoire de Hang-Yon.' See Im-Phon ed.

T 1969 '*Lpoek Ak.*' See Ly-Théam Teng ed.

III *Rīoeṅ Breṅ.* Folktales and legends

1932 (4) 1

T pp. 39–41. '*Rīoeṅ satv khlā.* Histoire du tigre.' (From Aymonier 1878).

2.

T p. 37. *'Rīoeṅ puras pī nāk' vivād gnā.* Les trois hommes qui se disputent.' (from Aymonier 1878).

1934 (6) 1–3

T pp. 162–73. *'Rīoeṅ Ā cor citt jā.* Ruong A Chor Chett Chéa.' ('The good-natured thief.') ed. Yin.

T pp. 174–88. *'Rīoeṅ Ā Sukh slūt niṅ Ā Sukh kāc.* Ruong A Sok slaut nung A Sok kach.' ('Nice Sok and Nasty Sok') ed. Nop.

T pp. 188–94. *'Rīoeṅ saṃḷāñ' bīr nāk'.* Ruong samlanh pir neak.' ('Two friends.') ed. Nop.

T pp. 195–202. *'Rīoeṅ suostī niṅ abvamaṅgal.* Ruong suosdey nung Appamongol.' ('Good and Bad Fortune.') ed. Nop.

4–6

T pp. 199–200. *'Rīoeṅ khlā cāñ' prājñā gīṅgak' niṅ aṇṭoek.* Un tigre étourdi est dupé par un crapaud et une tortue.' ed. Sugado.

pp. 200–10. *'Rīoeṅ satv khlā, svā niṅ dansāy.* Le tigre, le singe et le lièvre.' ed. Sugado.

7–9

T pp. 152–3. *'Rīoeṅ aṇṭoek niṅ svā.* La tortue et le singe'.

pp. 155–62. *'Rīoeṅ jhmoḥ M̈au cūl sās(n) cām yak prabandh.* Le nommé Mao qui, par amour pour une Malaise, devient musulman'.

T pp. 164–71. *'Rīoeṅ samlāñ' bīr nāk' nau grū jā muoy gnā.* Les deux amis qui font ensemble leurs études et qui ont le même professeur'.

T pp. 173–5. *'Rīoeṅ puras puon nāk', dī muoy kpāl daṃbaek, dī bīr sampor hīer, dī pī babrīek bhnaek, dī puon samdak' joeṅ.* Les quatre amis dont l'un chauve, le deuxième morveux, le troisième atteint de la paupiérité et le quatrième d'éléphantiasis'.

T pp. 176–9. *'Rīoeṅ puras kamjil mān prabandh grap' lakkh(ṇ).* Le paresseux dont la femme est vertueuse'.

10–12

T pp. 134–7. *'Rīoeṅ jāti satv khlā dhaṃ.* Légende sur l'origine des tigres'.

T pp. 138–48. *'Rīoeṅ puras mnāk' mān kūn puon nāk' siksā jaṃnāñ sdāt' nūv ved vijjā puon pad.* Histoire d'un homme qui a quatre enfants possédant chacun une science différente'.

pp. 149–53. *'Rīoeṅ puras mnāk' jhmoḥ cau āc(m) seḥ.* Conte du Cau Ach Sès ou l'homme du crottin de cheval'.

1935 (7) 1

T pp. 24–37. *'Ṭaṃṇiṅ khlaḥ aṃbī Lok G. H. Monod kāl nau dhvoe jā resìṭaṅt knuṅ sruk khmaer niṅ rīoeṅ go ñī ṭael Lok rīep rīeṅ.* Histoire d'une vache racontée par M. G. Monod, ancien Résident de France, précédée de quelques souvenirs relatif à son séjour au Cambodge'. T of story pp. 24–7.

T pp. 71–8. *'Rīoeṅ prājñā saṃnāṅ phal dāṃṅ pī uot ṛddhi tae sabv khluon.* L'intelligence, le bonheur et le mérite d'une existence antérieure se vantent respectivement de leur vertu.'

T pp. 79–81. '*Rīoeṅ srī kṅok mās.* Ruong Srey Kangok Méas ou l'histoire de la femme dénommée "Paon d'or".'

2

T pp. 63–6. '*Rīoeṅ satv ṭaṅkūv niṅ satv k-aek ṭoḥ prasnā gnā.* Dialogue entre le corbeau et la chenille.'

T pp. 67–8. '*Cāp būk prajhloḥ niṅ cāp kpāl daṃbaek.* Histoire de la dispute entre les oiselets Chap Pouk et les oiselets Chap Kbal Tumpèk'.

T pp. 69–71. '*Rīoeṅ puras cāk' smugr.* Conte d'un homme qui tresse une malle en feuilles de palmier à sucre'.

3

T pp. 131–4. '*Rīoeṅ srī māryār ṭak khñī.* Une femme qui trompe son mari'.

T pp. 135–6. '*Lok saṅgh muoy aṅg.* Un bonze qui aime une femme'.

T pp. 137–8. '*Rīoeṅ Ā Khil Ā Khūc.* Le malin et le roublard'.

4–6

T pp. 53–61. *(Rīoeṅ Tā Cān' ruṃlāk').* 'Ruong Tachan rumléak'. Ek ed.

T pp. 62–3. '*Rīoeṅ plaek nau Kaṃbaṅ' Dhaṃ kāl bī chnāṃ 1905.* Ce qui se passait mystérieusement à Kompong-Thom en 1905'.

T pp. 109–12. '*Rīoeṅ manuss lobh.* Conséquence d'une cupidité.'

T pp. 112–13. '*Ambī sruk Kaṃbaṅ' Dhaṃ bī ṭoem.* Histoire du Srok de Kompong Thom.'

T pp. 113–14. '*Rīoeṅ Ā Khvak' niṅ Ā Khvin.* L'Aveugle et le Paralytique.'

T pp. 171–4. '*Rīoeṅ manus bīr nāk', mnāk' khboem āc(m), mnāk' khboem ktī.* Conte de deux hommes, l'un a l'horreur de la saleté et l'autre a l'horreur des procès'.

T pp. 175–8. '*Rīoeṅ ṭael paṅkoet mān hau thā tejo Cau Hvāy Khaetr Kaṃbaṅ' Svāy.* Légende relative au titre Dêcho que porte le Gouverneur de Kompong Svai'.

T pp. 179–81. '*Rīoeṅ Ā Ḷev.* L'histoire d'A-Léo.

7–9

T pp. 71–80. '*Aṃbī kpuon ṭael devatā saek soy.* L'influence des différents dieux qui interviennent pour protéger la même étoile sous laquelle ont lieu les naissances'.

T p. 81. '*Aṃbī pos(t) Kaṃbaṅ' Dhaṃ.* Le poste de Kompong Thom'.

T p. 83. '*Aṃbī khmoc cūl ṭap.* Le diable dans la bouteille'.

10–12

T pp. 41–3. '*Puras pī nāk', mnāk' jak' kañchā, mnāk' jak' aphīen, mnāk'phiḳ srā.* L'opiuman, le fumeur de haschisch et l'alcoolique'.

T pp. 79–80. '*Rīoeṅ khlā ghmuṃ niṅ ṭoem baṅra.* L'ours et l'arbre Pongro'.

T p. 81. '*Rīoeṅ satv brāp, dīduy, graleṅ-graloṅ, ā ūt, mān' dịk, mān' dadā niṅ khlā grūs'*. ('Story of the pigeon, the owl, the *Gracupica Nigricollis*, the pagoda cock, the moorhen, the partridge and the *Khlā Grūs.*')

T pp. 119–26. '*Rīoeṅ k-aek 1 jā k-aek 10.* L'histoire d'un corbeau qui se décuple'.

1936 (8) 1–3

T pp. 43–7. '*Rīoeṅ khlā ā bhed.* Histoire du tigre'.

T pp. 77–81. '*Rīoeṅ Cau Sokh Cau Sau.* Chao Sok Chau Sao'.

T pp. 125–40. '*Rīoeṅ ābuk kmek roes kūn prasā.* Beau-père choisissant un gendre'.

T 1936 (8)–1938 (10)

Rīoeṅ Dhmeñ Jaiy (Dhanañjay) paṇḍit rapas' purāṇ. Histoire de Thmenh Chhey (Thananh-Chaya). (8) 4–6: 181–9; 7–9: 71–7, 139–45, 195–206; 10–12: 53–62. (9) 1–3: 41–51, 133–51; 4–6: 31–43, 75–106. (10) 1–3: 67–75, 149–56; 4–6: 57–66.

10–12

T pp. 143–7. '*Rīoeṅ cacak ṭal' nūv groḥ thnāk'*. Histoire du margouillat'.

T pp. 149–53. '*Rīoeṅ ^{a}nak nau phdaḥ bhūmi jit gnā.* Le voisinage des hommes'.

T pp. 225–8. '*Rīoeṅ proḥ khlā ṅāp'*. Histoire d'un tigre'.

1937 (9) 1–3

T pp. 53–61. '*Rīoeṅ bas' Keṅ Kaṅ.* Le serpent Keng-Kâng'.

T pp. 153–69. '*Subhāsit prakap nidān.* Proverbe du prix de 30 onces d'argent'.

4–6

T pp. 45–53. '*Rīoeṅ Gaṅ Ĥān.* Kong le brave'.

T pp. 123–8. '*Rīoeṅ stec kruṅ cin.* Le roi de Chine'.

T pp. 165–70. '*Rīoeṅ ^{a}nak ṭaṃṇoer bīr nāk'*. Histoire de deux hommes'.

7–9

T pp. 221–7. '*Rīoeṅ kuhak puon nāk'*. Les quatre menteurs'.

T pp. 327–37. '*Rīoeṅ māyā srī.* La fourberie féminine'.

10–12

T pp. 93–100. '*Rīoeṅ Ā Kuhak Ŝī.* Le menteur pour manger'.

T pp. 201–3. '*Rīoeṅ puras ceḥ thnāṃ bis bas'*. Histoire de l'homme connaissant le remède contre le venin des serpents'.

T pp. 327–32. '*Rīoeṅ manuss chot 4 nāk'*. Histoire de quatre niais'.

1938 (10) 4–6 and 7–9

T 4–6 pp. 259–65. '*Rīoeṅ subhā dansāy rapas' purāṇ.* Le juge lièvre'.

7–9 pp. 63–9, 227–37. '*Rīoeṅ subhā dansāy rapas' purāṇ*. Le juge lièvre'.
(In verse).

10–12
T pp. 173–83. '*Ta rīoeṅ subhā dansāy*. Le juge lièvre' (Story continues in prose).
T pp. 261–8. '*Rīoeṅ daṃbaek puon nāk'*. Les quatre chauves'.

1939 (11) 1–3
T pp. 63–7. '*Rīoeṅ Cau Kāṃpit Pandoḥ (mān ta)*. Chau Kombet Bantos ou le couteau miraculeux (à suivre)'. (Not continued. Started again in 1944.)

4–6
T pp. 71–6. '*Grū niṅ siss*. Conte du krôu et de son sœus (le maître et son élève).' (ed. Yin, it is said on p. 76).
T pp. 147–9. '*Puras bīr nāk'*. L'aventure de deux hommes.' (ed. Yin, it is said on p. 149).
T pp. 207–14. '*Puras phkāp' traḷok*. L'homme à la noix de coco renversée. (Boros phkab Tralôk).' (ed. Nop, it is said on p. 213).

7–9
T pp. 99–102. '*Taṃlaṅ 7 santān*. Les sourds héréditaires.' (Told by Nop, it is said on p. 102).
T pp. 257–64. '*Rīoeṅ puras jīk ktām*. L'aventure d'un pêcheur de crabes.' (ed. Yin, it is said on p. 264).

10–12
T pp. 117–22. '*Puras kās 30*. L'homme aux 30 sapèques.' (ed. Yin, it is said on p. 121).
T pp. 175–7. '*Puras rīen silp*. L'homme qui s'instruit'. ed. Yin.
T pp. 179–81. '*Puras mān prabandh l-a*. L'homme qui a une jolie femme'. ed. Yin.
T pp. 283–6. '*Cpāp' Kiṅ Kantrai*. L'enseignement du savant Keng-Kantray'. (See below, 1941. 13–1942. 3 for other tales from the *Cpāp' Kiṅ Kantrai*.)

1940 (12) 1
T pp. 45–7. '*Rīoeṅ puras kaṃsat' ceñ dau juoñ*. Un homme pauvre qui fait le commerce'.

1941 (13) 1
T pp. 24–30. '*Aṃbī* ^{a}*nak tā ghlāṃṅ mīoeṅ*. Le génie Khléang Mœung'.

1–12
T pp. 1: 31–3; 2: 32–5; 3: 32–4; 5: 21–6; 6: 25–6; 7: 24–6; 9: 25–6; 10: 24–6; 11: 24–6; 12: 23–6. '*Ā Ḷev dī 2*. Légende de Alev II.' Yin ed.

13

T pp. 27–8. '*Rīoeṅ puras mān groḥ bīr nāk'*. Les déboires de deux jeunes gens, à l'un, sa mère est morte, à l'autre un incendie s'abat sur la maison.' (From *Cpāp' Kịṅ Kantrai.*)

15

T p. 27. '*Rīoeṅ puras bīr nāk' raek srūv.* Deux hommes portent la semence de paddy.' (From *Cpāp' Kịṅ Kantrai.*)

17

T p. 28. '*Puras bīr nāk' tām khñuṃ rat'*. Querelle entre deux personnes.' (From *Cpāp' Kịṅ Kantrai.*)

18

T p. 27. '*Rīoeṅ puras par radeḥ bīr nāk' dās' daeṅ gnā.* Querelle entre deux cochers'. (From *Cpāp' Kịṅ Kantrai.*)

19

T pp. 26–7. '*Rīoeṅ puras bīr nāk' dās' daeṅ gnā aṃbī kār jīk aṇṭūṅ.* Querelle entre deux personnes creusant un puits'. (From *Cpāp' Kịṅ Kantrai.*)

21

T pp. 25–7. '*Rīoeṅ jhmuoñ mnāk'*. Récit d'un marchand'. (From *Cpāp' Kịṅ Kantrai.*)

22

T pp. 24–5. '*Rīoeṅ puras mnāk' ṭek lak' knuṅ sālā.* L'homme qui dort dans un sâlâ'. (From *Cpāp' Kịṅ Kantrai.*)

23

T pp. 25–7. '*Rīoeṅ cor luoc kraṭās.* Le voleur de papier'. (From *Cpāp'Kịṅ Kantrai.*)

24

T pp. 25–6. '*Rīoeṅ puras bīr nāk' dau par pāñ'*. Histoire de deux chasseurs partant à la chasse'. (From *Cpāp' Kịṅ Kantrai.*)

1942 (14) 1

T pp. 49–50. '*Rīoeṅ srī bīr nāk' ṭaṇṭoem kūn gnā.* Deux femmes se disputent un enfant'. (From *Cpāp' Kịṅ Kantrai.*)

2

T pp. 51–4. '*Rīoeṅ ṭịṅ saṅ ṭịṅ, aṃbaeṅ saṅ aṃbaeṅ.* Tesson pour tesson, herminette pour herminette'. (From *Cpāp' Kịṅ Kantrai.*)

3

T pp. 26–8. '*Rīoeṅ seṭṭhī pī nāk'*. Légende de trois richards.' (From *Cpāp' Kịṅ Kantrai.*)

4

T pp. 24–8. '*Rīoeṅ svā luoc makuṭ stec bānar.* Le singe voleur de la couronne du roi.' (From *Cpāp' Kịṅ Kantrai.*)

6–7

T pp. 24–6 and 30–4. '*Rīoeṅ Braḥ Rāj vinicchăy ktī dāṃṅ 4.* La procédure d'un roi au cour de quatre procès.' (From *Cpāp' Kịṅ Kantrai.*)

11–12

T pp. 54–6. '*Rīoeṅ Cau mcās' phdaḥ nịṅ Cau suṃ saṃcat.* Un maître de maison et son hôte'.

13–14

T pp. 61–3. '*Rīoeṅ puras pāñ' duṅ.* Un chasseur de pélicans'. (From *Cpāp' Kịṅ Kantrai.*)

15–16

T pp. 59–60. '*Rīoeṅ amāty raksā bnau Braḥ rāj draby.* Le gardien de l'orange du Malabar d'un roi'. (From *Cpāp' Kịṅ Kantrai.*)

17–18

T pp. 62–4. '*Rīoeṅ strī smoḥ traṅ' nịṅ svāmī.* Une femme fidèle à son mari'. (From *Cpāp' Kịṅ Kantrai.*)

1943 (15) 8–9

T pp. 489–95 and 524–32. '*Nidān mān' dhnāk'* '. ('The hen which served as a snare'?)

11

T pp. 616–31. '*Rīoeṅ mtāy bit, ābuk bit, srī bit.* Rûong Mdaypit, Apukpit, Sreipit'. ('A true mother, father and daughter.')

12

T p. 673. '*Rīoeṅ me cor s̃ī phaṅ gnā.* Méchor si p'âng knea'. ('The rascals eat all together.')

T p. 674. '*Rīoeṅ chnāṃṅ vaeṅ andaṅ' vaeṅ.* Ch'năng vèng Ântông vèng'. ('A long pot and a long eel.')

1944 (16)

T 2: 88–93; 3: 145–9; 5: 261–70; 6: 314–21.'*Rīoeṅ Cau Kāṃpit Pandoḥ.* Rûong chau kămbi(^)t băntôh'. ('Mr Whittling Knife.')

1946 (19) 3

T pp. 152–4. '*Mitr saṃlāñ' khcī prāk' gnā*' (Friends borrow money from each other) ed. Nhoung-Sœung.

1947 (20) 1

T pp. 27–31. '*Isī sla pāṛat*' ('A hermit cooks with mercury') ed. Sam-Soun.

2

T pp. 89–92. '*Rīoeṅ antarāy riddhi nai satv assatar*' ('The end of the horse's power') ed. Sam-Soun.

3

T pp. 149–55. '*Prabaiṇī nai satv sunakh*' ('Traditions in connection with dogs') ed. Sam-Soun.

4

T pp. 198–204. '*Kicc kal' smā ktī*' ('A lawyer's ruse') ed. Sam-Soun.

6

T pp. 312–16. '*Jamnīoe nāṃ oy samrec prayoj(n)*' ('Faith brings achievement') ed. Sam-Soun.

8

T pp. 419–29. '*Pravatti nai satv ṭaṃrī*' ('The history of the elephant') ed. Sam-Soun.

9

T pp. 483–7. '*Pravatti piṅ duṃlaeṅ*' ('History of Lake *Duṃlaeṅ*') ed. Sak-Khat.

10 and 11

T pp. 543–53 and pp. 594–603. '*Rīoeṅ Ā Jū Jiṅ*' ('Story of *Ā Jū Jiṅ*') ed. Sam-Soun.

12

T pp. 646–55. '*Rīoeṅ bedy saṃnāṅ*' ('A doctor's good fortune') ed. You-Oun.

1948 (21) 6

pp. 409–12. '*Rīoeṅ dāk' jrūk brai (raṅvān' lekh 1)*' ('Catching a wild boar (1st prize)') ed. Thach-Sak.

10

T pp. 754–9. '*Ā saṃgam pāñ' lalak.* Ā sanggom banh lolok' ('Mr Thin shoots a dove') ed. Chhim-Saret.

1950 (22) 1 and 3

T pp. 28–38 and 210–15. '*Rīoeṅ kmeṅ kaṃbrā.* L'enfant orphelin. *(Rīoeṅ breṅ)*'. ed. Chhim-Nak.

2

T p. 136. Folktale told in the middle of an article, '*Kār crūt srūv*' ('Harvesting paddy') ed. Som-Sukh.

9 and 10

T pp. 685–9 and 756–62. '*Sāvatār vatt aṭṭhāras.* Notice historique de Vat Attharasa'. ed. Contesse Norodom Sukhanari.

1956 (28) 1

T pp. 45–9. '*Rīoeṅ Bhnaṃ Saṃbau nau khaetr Pāt'-Ṭaṃpaṅ.* Historique du Phnom Sampeou'. ed. Mme. Saris-Yann.

T pp. 49–52. '*Rīoeṅ Bhnaṃ Mtāy niṅ Kūn*' ('The Mother and Child Hill') ed. Mme Saris-Yann.

1957 (29) 1

T pp. 41–9. '*Rīoeṅ trī mās jā rīoeṅ breṅ*' ('Story of a goldfish, a folktale') ed. Sak-Khat.

12–1958 (30) 1, 2, 3, and 4

T pp. 1088–99 and 65–72, 147–50, 249–54 and 355–8. '*Cau pāy kdāṃṅ*' ('The boy and the rice stuck to the cooking-pot') ed. Tieng-Day Chhoun.

1958 (30) 1

T pp. 44–8; 2: 141–6; 3: 249–54. '*Rīoeṅ Anak gaṅvāl cīem slūt traṅ niṅ braḥ rāj dhītā*' ('The shepherd who is honest with the princess') ed. Pheng-Criv.

T pp. 33–43. '*Rīoeṅ kṅān niṅ kaṃbis*' ('The goose and the shrimp') ed. Léang-Hap An.

2

T pp. 151–62. '*Rīoeṅ Nāṅ Nāy Caṅkrān*' ('Miss In-charge of the Hearth') ed. Léang-Hap An.

3

T pp. 209–24. '*Rīoeṅ Aṅguṭṭh kumār*' ('The boy, *Angkuṭṭh*') ed. Léang-Hap An.

4

T pp. 373–6. '*Rīoeṅ Ek Aṅg ksatr*' ('The Prince Ek Aṅg') ed. Léang-Hap An.

6

T pp. 541–50. '*Rīoeṅ saṃḷāñ' bīr nāk' caṅ' baṅrīṅ dịk samudr*' ('Two friends want to dry up the sea') ed. Tieng-Day Chhoun.

7

T pp. 653–5. '*Rīoeṅ breṅ prārabdh bāky thā 'chkae chmā ǩa oy dau*' ('A folktale which demonstrates the saying, "The dogs and cats allow you to go ahead" ') ed. Chap-Pin. Story by Keo-Hang (elsewhere Hang-Keo).

12

T pp. 1078–83. '*Rīoeṅ kaṃjil mān bhăbv*' ('A lazy person is lucky') ed. Léang-Hap An.

1959 (31) 3

T pp. 311–24. '*Nidān cau kāṃpit jhmol*' ('A man whose knife was male') ed. Mann-Eng.

7

pp. 793–800. '*Rīoeṅ breṅ caeṅ aṃbī ᵃnak proe gaṃnit khus nāṃ oy mān dukkh ṭal' khluon*' ('A folktale about a man who took a wrong decision which caused him distress') ed. Mann-Eng.

8

T pp. 885–9. '*Jăy Suostī*. Légende de Chey Suos' (According to MS of Commission des Moeurs et coutumes) ed. Bou-Po.

11–12

T pp. 1276–93 and 1396–1421. *'Srī grap' lakkh(ṇ)*. La femme vertueuse.' ed. Yok-Vochir, corrected by Pheng-Chriv.

12

T pp. 1368–78. *'Rīoeṅ bas' lep mantrī dhaṃ'* ('Story of a serpent which swallows a high official') ed. Bou-Po.

T pp. 1423–8. *'Rīoeṅ puras pid randh khyal'* ('A man who closes the air way'(?)).

1960 (32) 3

T pp. 304–12. *'Rīoeṅ breṅ satv kūn lok'* (Folktale. The birds known as *Kūn lok* (people).') ed. Thang-Vong.

5

T pp. 553–8. *'Rīoeṅ breṅ Vatt Paññājī''* (Story of Vat *Paññājī*) ed. Meas-Ham.

8

T pp. 921–8. *'Rīoeṅ breṅ dāk' daṅ niṅ damnīem dhvoe bidhī samlāp' manuss ṭoempī phtāc' groḥ'* (Folktale connected with the custom of ceremoniously killing a person to end a dangerous situation') ed. Thang-Vong.

11

T pp. 1271–6. *'Rīoeṅ nāṅ sak' kra-ūp'* (The girl with the perfumed hair) ed. Nhaem-Khim.

T pp. 1277–82. *'Rīoeṅ saṅgrām ravāṅ gīṅgak' niṅ Braḥ Brahm'* ('War between the toad and Brahm'. Not said to be a folktale) ed. Léang-Hap An.

12

T pp. 1386–96. *'Rīoeṅ Stec Pāyaṅkor'* (King *Pāyaṅkor*) ed. Nhaem-Khim.

1961 (33) 1–3

pp. 81–91; 2: 223–5; 3: 304–15. *'Rīoeṅ breṅ dāk' daṅ ṭoy sthāpanā prāsād Aṅgar'* (Folktale concerned with establishing the monument of Angkor) ed. Nhaem-Khim.

4

T pp. 431–7. *'Rīoeṅ srī knuṅ smugr'* ('Story of a woman in a palm-leaf box') Bou-Po ed. (incorporated into a tale of fiction).

T pp. 440–4. *'Rīoeṅ Cau Kaṃjil hau Cau Grịp'* ('Mr Lazy called Mr Bang'. Not stated to be a folktale) ed. Mann-Eng.

T pp. 452–64. *'Rīoeṅ Anak Tā Kraham Ka (nau khaetr Kaṃbaṅ' Dhaṃ)'* ('Old Mr Red-neck (in the province of Kompong Thom)').

5 and 6

T pp. 548–58 and 691–7. *'Rīoeṅ prus s-ap' srī'* ('Story of a man who hated women'). Bou-Po ed. (incorporated into a tale of fiction).

T pp. 567–83. '*Rīoeṅ mānab min ceḥ ṭek prajrīet.* Légende d'un jeune homme qui s'ennuit en dormant'. ed. Nhoung-Sœung.

7

T pp. 808–16. '*Rīoeṅ srī ṭai dan*'' (Story of a woman with soft hands). Bou-Po ed. (incorporated into a tale of fiction).

T pp. 824–8. '*Rīoeṅ breṅ. Bhnaṃ Pāṇan' nau khaetr Pāt' ṭaṃpaṅ*' ('Folktale. The Banan mountain in the province of Battambang').

10

T pp. 1200–1. '*Rīoeṅ breṅ. Ūr jāl mās tām ekasār Damnīem danlāp' Khmaer. Bhūmi Svāy Aṅgol, Bhūmi Srī Paṇḍit knuṅ khaetr Tā Kaev* ('Folktale. The Gold Basket Stream, according to a manuscript of the Commission des mœurs et coutumes cambodgiens. Villages of *Aṅgol* Mango and Learned Women in the province of Takeo').

1962 (34) 2–3

T pp. 216–21 and 340–5. '*Rīoeṅ breṅ prārabdh subhāsit 4 pad*' ('Folktale demonstrating 4 proverbial sayings').

6

T pp. 715–18. '*Rīoeṅ breṅ dāk' daṅ ṭoy bhūmisāstr khmaer. Rīoeṅ Bhnaṃ Subarṇ Kālī nau Khaetr Kraceḥ* ('Folktale concerned with Khmer geography. The story of Phnom *Subarṇ Kālī* in the Province of Kratie').

7

T pp. 812–19. '*Rīoeṅ breṅ dāk' daṅ ṭoy pravattisāstr Kambujā. Rīoeṅ Prāsād Nāṅ Khmau*' ('Folktale concerned with the geography of Cambodia. The story of Prasat Néang Khmau').

11

T pp. 1303–7. '*Rīoeṅ trabāṃṅ lāk' nāṅgal' nau Khaetr Kaṃbaṅ' Chnāṃṅ*' ('The pond which concealed a plough in the Province of Kompong Chhnang').

12

T pp. 1417–19. '*Rīoeṅ Bhnaṃ Prus Bhnaṃ Srī nau Khaetr Kaṃbaṅ' Cām*' ('Phnom Pros Phnom Srey in the Province of Kompong Cham').

1964 (36) 4

T pp. 439–46. '*Rīoeṅ breṅ Piṅ Te*' *(nau Khett Kaṃbaṅ' Sbī)* ('Folktale about Lake *Te*'). ed. Ly-Théam Teng.

10

T pp. 1100–10. '*Prāsād Bhnaṃ Jīsūr*' ('The temple of Chisor'. The folktale is told from pp. 1106 onwards). ed. Ly-Théam Teng.

12

T pp. 1253–60. '*Rīoeṅ Bhnaṃ Srī Vipul Ker(ti)*' (Phnom Srey Vibol Ker).

1965 (37) 1–4

T pp. 56–62, 191–8, 298–302, and 357–66. '*Rīoeṅ Cau Ralā Ṭūṅ*' ('Mr Coconut-shell') ed. Dik-Kéam.

5

T pp. 489–95. '*Rīoeṅ breṅ nau Bhnaṃ Ÿāt nau Pailin*' ('Folktale at Phnom Yat in Pailin') ed. Ly-Théam Teng.

7

T pp. 760–7. '*Rīoeṅ Bhnaṃ Pūrī- Bhnaṃ Ṭā nau Khett Tākaev*' ('Phnom Borei and Phnom Da in the province of Takeo').

9

T pp. 950–3. '*Rīoeṅ Sraḥ Yakkh Ḷom (Khett Ratanagirī)*' ('Story of the Yaksa Lom Pool (Province of Ratanagiri)') ed. Houn-Savi.

1966 (38) 10

T pp. 1069–71. '*Rīoeṅ Bhnaṃ Krom*' (Text from the Department of Traditional Customs. The story of Low Hill') ed. Chea-Paur.

T pp. 1072–4. '*Pravatti sruk Tpūṅ Ghmuṃ niṅ Anak Tā Peṅ*' ('History of Thboung Khmum and Nak Ta Peng') ed. Hang-Keo.

11

T pp. 1140–8. '*Rīoeṅ breṅ. Braḥ Isūr leṅ buon*' ('Isvara plays at hiding'). From palm-leaf MS ed. By-Sovann.

T pp. 1177–84. '*Atthapad phnaek daṃnīem damlāp*'. *Rīoeṅ bhnaṃ purī khett Tā Kaev. (Tām ekasār rapas' Lok Ḍuoṅ-Ûc niṅ V̇ān'-Jīoeṅ, sruk Brai Kappās)*' ('Text of the Commission des mœurs et coutumes. Phnom Borei, province of Takeo. (According to the manuscript of Mr Duong-Ouch and Mr Vann-Chœung)') ed. Duong-Ouch and Vann-Chœung.

12

T pp. 1282–7. '*Pravatti Sruk Pāy Chau*' (The history of Bai Cau') ed. Ly-Nguon.

1967 (39) 1

T pp. 75–82. '*Atthapad phnaek daṃnīem damlāp*'. *Pravatti Ghuṃ Sān Gar, khett Kaṃbaṅ' Dhaṃ*' (Text belonging to the Commission des mœurs et coutumes. History of the village of San Kor, province of Kompong Thom') ed. Dik-Kéam.

2

T pp. 194–202. '*Rīoeṅ breṅ nau knuṅ Ghuṃ Ŝīdhar*' (Folktale in the village of Sithor) ed. Kem-Houy.

11

T pp. 1199–1205. '*Khlā cās' niṅ kūn dansāy*' *(bāky kāby)* ('An old tiger and a young hare'). Folktale retold in verse, ed. Heng-Sam-an.

12

T pp. 1252–7. '*Rīoeṅ Nāṅ Taeṅ An*' ('Mistress Teng-An'), ed. Soung-Phuoy, a Laotian.

1968 (40)

2, 3, and 4

T pp. 195–12, 288–97, 391–412. '*Rīoeṅ Cau Gai Lalak*' (Mr Dove-thief') ed. Pruoch-Phoum.

4

T pp. 441–5. '*Rīoeṅ bis bas' niṅ bis trī*' ('The venom of the snake and of the fish') ed. Ly-Théam Teng.

5

T pp. 535–43. '*Rīoeṅ breṅ dāk' daṅ niṅ dī kanlaeṅ phseṅ2 knuṅ Khett Brai Vaeṅ*' ('Folktales connected with various places in the Province of Prey Veng') ed. Kol-Sary.

7

T pp. 743–7. '*Rīoeṅ breṅ pañjāk' subhāsit thā "Poe trūv slāp' grū min jā, poe gū niṅ gnā gec min ruoc"*' ('A folktale which explains the saying, "If you have to die, your teacher failed to protect you. If you marry, you'll not escape"') Bou-Po ed.

8

T pp. 854–74. '*Pravatti nai Vatt Braḥ Dvār*' ('History of Vat Preah Tvéar') ed. Sou-Sokon, known as Nouch.

pp. 892–6. '*Rīoeṅ Tā cās' niṅ kraboe*' ('The old man and the crocodile') ed. Oum-Chhoum.

9

T pp. 972–8. '*Pravatti Sruk Pāy Chau*' ed. Ly-Nguon. (Repeat from 1966. 12, except that in 1968 it is preceded by an introduction.)

1969 (41) 2

T pp. 182–98. '*Anak Tā Bodhi ārăks*' ('The Nak Ta, spirit of the Bodhi tree') ed. Sdoeng-Chhou.

3

T pp. 273–92. '*Rīoeṅ sūtr sāc', ak kaṃpor prāk*" ('Sew up flesh'?? . . . The tale, *Māyā srī*, told in modern style) ed. Pruoch-Phoum.

7

T pp. 716–26. '*Ekasār: pravatti bhūmi niṅ koḥ nānā nau khett koḥ kuṅ. 6: Pravatti cetiy Ghun Chāṅ*' ('Manuscript: History of various villages and islands in the province of Koh Kong. 6: History of the stupa of Khun Chhang'. Incident from the tale, Khun Chang, Khun Phaeng, is told on pp. 722–3), ed. Maen-Ton.

pp. 727–33. '*Pravatti bhūmi Kpāl Anak ṛ Bhūmi "Pla-Aṅ"*' (The story of the village of Kbal Anak or "Pla-Ang"'. The Kuoy and some words in their speech are involved).

8

T pp. 861–84. '*Ekasār: Pravatti Bhūmi niṅ Koḥ nānā nau Khett Koḥ Kuṅ*' ('Manuscript: Story of various villages and islands in the province of Koh Kong'). The story is connected with the next entry.

T pp. 868–75. '*Pravatti Yāy Ṁau*' ('Old Mrs Mau').

IV Riddles

T 1942 '*Prasnā camroen satipaññā. Suor niṅ chloey aṃbī raṭūv dāṃṅ pī.* Dialogue sur les trois saisons.' (14) 5: 11–13; 6: 21–3; 7: 27–9. *Suor niṅ chloey (i) aṃbī khvāk' niṅ khvin, (ii) aṃbī sak', (iii) aṃbī slā niṅ pārī, (iv) aṃbī buk māt'.* Dialogue (i) sur l'aveugle et le paralytique, (ii) sur les cheveux, (iii) sur la fumée de cigarette et la chique de bétel, (iv) sur les barbes.' 11–12: 51–3; 13–14: 53–60.

T 1968 '*Aṃbī bāky paṇṭau khmaer*' ('Khmer Riddles). (40) 6: 687–90 and 7: 802.

Kambujavarokās, Printing house, Phnom Penh

T 1911 *Cpāp' Bāky Cās'.*

T 1911 *Cpāp' Ker Kāl.*

T 1911 *Cpāp' Kraṃm, Cpāp' Kram.*

T 1911 *Cpāp' Kūn Cau.*

T 1911 *Cpāp' Mahānetti rāj suostī.*

T 1911 *Cpāp' Meyyapaṇḍit (taeṅ)* (= *Cpāp' Prus* by Mai).

T 1911 *Cpāp' Rājanetti (= Cpāp' Rājaneti).*

T 1911 *Cpāp' Srī Meyyapaṇḍit* (=*Cpāp' Srī* by Mai).

T 1911 *Cpāp' Trīnetti.*

T 1911 *Cpāp' Vidhūrapaṇḍity.*

T 1912 *Satrā Sek Sārikā.*

Kao, *Kau*

T 1941–1942 *Kruṅ Subhamitr.* 3 vols. BR.

T 1953, 1967, 1970, 1972 *Kruṅ Subhamitr.* 3 vols. IB.

T 1977 Extract from *Kruṅ Subhamitr* in Huffman and Proum 1977: 279–85 (vocabulary 286–8).

Karpelès, Suzanne

V 1956, 1968 'Histoire du Prince Préas Sang dit Ngos' (A translation of the Khmer version of the Thai drama, Sang Thong (Suvaṇṇasaṅkhajātaka. cf. Khmer *Khyaṅ Saṅkh*)). Thiounn 1956: 91–5.

Kem-Houy, *Kịm-Ĥuy*

T 1967 See *Kambujasuriyā* III Texts of folktales and legends. (39) 2.

Kem-To, *Kim-Tū*

S 1955 '*Ghlok lic aṃpaeṅ aṇṭaet.* Khlouk lich âmbêng ândêt. Proverbe cambodgien' ('The gourd sinks, the pot floats') *KS* (27) 4: 253–60.

Keng-Vannsak, *Keṅ-Ṿān' Sāk'*

T 1954 *Citt kramuṃ. Kaṃṇāby.* Cœur Vierge. Poèmes. Phnom Penh, Henry.

T 1956, 1963 *Guk kām kiles.* Prison de la passion. Phnom Penh. (Poems).

S 1961 *Quelques aspects de la littérature khmère*. Phnom Penh.

S 1967 'Quelques aspects de la littérature khmère.' Phnom Penh, *Annales de la faculté des lettres et des sciences humaines de l'Université Royale:* 39–54.

S 1968 'Réflexions sur la littérature khmère.' *Revue française de l'élite européenne* 206: 31–4.

T 197– *Caṃrīeṅ cāp̄ī khmaer*. Montmorency.

S 1971 Recherche d'un fonds culturel khmer. Thèse de troisième cycle, Paris.

Keo-Hang. See Hang-Kéo.

Khemarak, *Khemara*:, Phnom Penh

T 1952 *Histoire de Thnenh Chey le sage.*

Khemararaṭṭh

T [1963] BE 2506 *Lpoek satv ak.* Phnom Penh.

Khim Sam-Or

1961 *Histoire de la littérature khmère.* Phnom Penh, Yoveak Peanich.

Khin Sok

V S 1975 Les chroniques royales du Cambodge (de Bañā Ÿāt jusqu'à la prise de Laṅvaek). Traduction française avec comparaison des différentes versions et introduction. Thèse de troisième cycle, Paris.

S 1976 'La prise de Laṅvaek en 1594 d'après les chroniques cambodgiennes.' *Asie du Sud-Est continentale.* 1. Actes de XXIXe Congrès internationale des Orientalistes. Paris, Asiathèque: 77–82.

V S 1977*a* 'Les chroniques royales et l'inscription moderne d'Angkor no. 39.' *BEFEO* (64): 225–41.

S 1977*b* 'Les chroniques royales khmères'. *MKS* (6): 191–215.

S 1982 'Essai d'interpretation de formules magiques des cambodgiens'. *ASEMI* (13) 1–4: 111–21.

S 1985 'Quelques documents khmers relatifs aux relations entre le Cambodge et l'Annam.' *BEFEO* (74) 403–21.

S 1986 'Quelques réflexions sur la valeur historique des chroniques royales du Cambodge'. *BEFEO* (75): 197–214.

V S 1988 *Collection de textes et documents sur l'Indochine* 13. *Chroniques royales du Cambodge (de Bañā Ÿat à la prise de Laṅvaek) (de 1417 à 1595).* Traduction française avec comparaison des différentes versions et introduction. Paris, EFEO.

Khing Hoc Dy, *Ghīṅ Huk Ḍī*

V S 1974 L'œuvre littéraire de Naṅ, auteur cambodgien de la fin du 18e siècle et du début du 19e. Thèse de troisième cycle, Paris.

S 1976 'L'œuvre littéraire de Naṅ, auteur cambodgien de la fin du XVIIIe et du début du XIXe siècle'. *ASEMI* (7) 1: 91–100.

V S 1977*a* 'Notes sur le thème de la femme 'marquée de signes' dans la littérature populaire khmère'. *Cah. de l'Asie du Sud-Est* 2: 15–43.

Résumés and translations are on following pp: Histoire du paresseux à la femme vertueuse, 16. Histoire de l'homme qui déterrait les crabes, 16–17. L'histoire des deux amis, 17–18. *Mā Yoeṅ*, 18–21. *Suvaṇṇ Sirasā*, 22–3. *Khyaṅ Saṅkh, Hai Saṅkh*, 23–4. *Cau Krabat*, 25–6. *Cau Kaṅkaep*, 25–6. *Rājakul*, 26. *Bhogakulakumār*, 28. *Braḥ Sudhan*, 29–31. Histoire de la vraie femme, de la vraie mère at du vrai père, 31–2. *Dhanañjaya*, 32–3. *Lokaṇayapakaraṇa*, 33–4. *Mahosathajātaka*, 34–5.

S 1977*b* 'Quelques traits bouddhiques dans Bhogakulakumār, roman cambodgien en vers du début du XIXe siècle'. *Cah. de l'Asie du Sud-Est* 1: 59–78.

S 1979 'Le développement économique et la transformation littéraire dans le Cambodge moderne'. *Mondes en développement* 28: 793–801.

V S 1979 'Note sur le motif du cygne mécanique dans la littérature khmère'. *MKS* (8): 91–101. Résumé of passage of *Jinavaṅs* describing construction of the goose, 94–5. Résumé of *Haṅs Yant*, 95–100.

T V S 1980 'Quelques aspects de la beauté de la femme dans la littérature populaire khmère'. *Seksa Khmer* 1–2: 45–68. Reprint at Shiroku in the publications of Kagashima University. No. 13 1980: 1–20. (Texts and translations of excerpts from *Bhogakulakumār* (**T** 46–7, **V** 48–9); *Kākī* (**T** 50–1, 53 and 61–2, **V** (translated by F. Martini) 52–3, 54 and 62–3); poetry by Mok (translated by P. Collard) 54–5; song (from Tricon and Bellan 1921), 56. *Rāmakerti* (**T** 57 and 59, **V** (by Pou) 58 and 60). *Haṅs Yant* (résumé of part) 64–5. *Duṃ Dāv* (**V** 65, **T** 66).

S 1981*a* 'Les plus anciennes peintures datées du Cambodge: quatorze épisodes du Vessantarajātak'. *Arts Asiatiques* (36): 26–36.

T V S 1981*b* 'Santhor Mok, *Sandhar M̈uk*, poète et chroniqueur du XIXe siècle'. *Seksa Khmer* 3–4: 137–60. Texts and translations of excerpts from *Devand* (**T**, in orthography, 146–8 and **V** 149–53) and from *Vimān Cand* (**T**, in orthography of MS and in modern orthography, 153–7 and **V** 158–60).

T S 1982 *Rīoeṅ Mahāvessantarajātak* ('The story of the Mahāvessantara Jātaka'). Preface by Nhok-Thaem, pp. I–II. Comment by Khing Hoc Dy, pp. III–X. Text of the *Ānisaṅs Mahājātak (Mahāvessantarajāt(k))*, pp. X–XXI. Paris, Association Bouddhique Khmère and Cedoreck.

S 1983 'Note sur le genre *lpoek* dans la littérature khmère'. *Seksa Khmer* 6: 11–8.

S 1983 'Quelques témoignages et expériences de recherche sur la littérature d'expression orale et écrite au Cambodge'. *Objets et Mondes* (3) 3–4: 111–16.

T V 1985*a* *Contes et légendes du pays khmer* recueillis, traduits et illustrés par . . . Fleuve et Flamme. Paris, Conseil international de la langue française (Texts and translation) Contains:

Foreword, pp. 1–11.
Légende du temple d'Angkor-Vat, pp. 13–24.
Légende du temple Prom-Kel, pp. 25–37.
Légende du temple d'Attharoeus, pp. 38–51.
La colline-des-hommes et la colline-des-femmes, pp. 52–6.
Le village de Sdei-Bet-Méas, pp. 57–65.
La pagode de Panhnha-Chi, pp. 66–76.
Histoire du 'Paresseux-se-vautrant-dans-la-cendre', pp. 77–86.
Le vautour qui voulait tromper l'éléphant blanc, pp. 87–90.
Le grand ascète qui avait ressuscité le tigre, pp. 91–8.
Le crocodile et le charretier, pp. 99–110.
Histoire du fantôme en bouteille, pp. 111–15.
Histoire du singe qui vola la couronne royale, pp. 116–27.
La mangue divine, pp. 128–34.
Histoire du lièvre à l'arrière-train collé à une souche résineuse, pp. 135–9.
Histoire de la chenille et du corbeau, pp. 140–5.
Histoire du python qui vomit du venin, pp. 146–51.
Histoire du limule, pp. 152–60.
Histoire du tresseur de boîtes, pp. 161–7.

S 1985*b* 'La poésie cambodgienne de langue khmère et de langue française'. *Lettres et Cultures de langue française.* (8). No. 4: 3–13.

S 1985*c* Chuon Nath (1883–1967), Hell Sumpha (1922–71), Heng Yan (1905–1950), Oknha Sutan Preichea In (1859–1924), Iêv Kœus (1905–1950), Kram Ngoy (1865–1936), Nhok Them (1903–74), Norodom Suramarit (1896–1960), Nong (?–1858), Rim Kin (1911–59), Sisowath Youtevong (1913–47), Sou Seth (1882–1963). *Hommes et Destins* VI Asie. Paris, Académie des Sciences d'Outre-Mer.

V S 1987 *Bhogakulakumār, roman khmer en vers du début du XIXe siècle, traduction, notes, étude, et texte en khmer.* 2 vols. Paris, Pierres d'Angkor.

V S 1988 *Khuṅ Cūv Cau Thuk. L'histoire de Khuṅ Cūv et Cau Thuk, version khmère de l'entrevue entre Confucius et un jeune garçon.* Étude, Texte khmer, Annotations. Paris, Pierre d'Angkor.

S 1990 and 1993 *Contribution à l'histoire de la littérature khmère.* 2 vols. Paris, Harmattan. An excellent introduction to Khmer Literature with many pages of translation.

S 1991 'Le conte historique de *Braḥ Go Braḥ Kaev.' Mélanges offerts à Madame Thierry. Cahiers de l'Asie du Sud-Est* Nos. 29–30: 169–90.

T V S (forthcoming) Un épisode du Rāmakerti. Rāma endormi par les maléfices de Vaiy Rābṇ (Études, traduction, annotation et texte khmer).

Khing Hoc Dy, *Ghīn Huk Ḍī* and Khing, Jacqueline

T V S 1978 'Les Recommandations de Kram Ngoy'. *MKS* 7: 141–81. (Parallel text, in transliteration, on even-numbered pages (150–74) and translation, on odd-numbered pages (151–75), of *Paṇṭāṃ Kram N̈uy*, with notes and introduction.)

T V S 1981 *Paṇṭāṃ Kram N̈uy. Les recommandations de Kram Ngoy Vappadharm khmaer. 5. Aksarsāstr.* Paris, Cedoreck. (Introduction in Khmer and French. Text and parallel translation into French (both on each page), pp. 23–45. Notes, pp. 47–52.)

Khmer Samay, *Khmaer Samăy*, Printing House, Phnom Penh

T 1967 *Rīoeṅ Subhā Dansāy* (Contes du Juge Lièvre).

Khuon Sokhamphu, *Ghuon-Sukhambhu*

S 1963 *Aksarsāstr khmaer paep brahm(ṇ) niyam.* (Brahmanism in Khmer literature) *Cours de littérature khmère.* (Classe de Ier). Phnom Penh, Institut National Pédagogique.

S 1970 Doctoral thesis on the modern Khmer novel. Humboldt.

S 1971*a* *Lpoek Aṅgar Vatt* (Poème d'Angkor Vat) Phnom Penh, Faculté des Lettres.

S 1971*b* *Pañhā anak nibandh. kāl paricched niṅ saṅgam pariyākās knuṅ aksarsilpkhmaer.* (Topics concerning authors. Dates and society in Khmer literature) *Dassanāvaṭṭī Mahāvidyālăy Aksarsāstr Manussasāstr.* (Journal of the Faculté des Lettres et des Sciences Humaines Year 1 No. 2 (Feb.)).

S 1973 *Le roman khmer contemporain.* Phnom Penh, Faculté des Lettres. (Roneotypé.)

S 1976 *Le roman khmer contemporain.* P. B. Lafont, *Asie du Sud Est continentale.* Actes du XXIXème Congrès International des Orientalistes, Paris, Asiathèque: 204–8.

—— *et al.*

S 1971 *Srāv jrāv anak nibandh khmaer.* Recherche des noms des écrivains khmers/Recherche sur les écrivains khmers. Phnom Penh, Faculté des Lettres et des Sciences Humaines. (Roneotypé.)

S 1973 *Jīvapravatti Anak Nibandh Khmaer paccupann* (Biographies of contemporary Khmer authors). Phnom Penh. (Roneotypé).

—— and Heng-Yann

S 1956 *Gol Pravattisāstr nai aksarsāstr khmaer.* Notes sur l'histoire de la littérature khmère. *Paṇṇāgār Bhnaṃ Beñ* (Librairie Phnom Penh).

Kim-Hak, *Gim-Hāk'*

T 1928 '*Kosaj ṛ secktī khjil.* Kosaja ou la Paresse.' *KS* (2) 11: 91–100 (Poem).

T 1928 '*Suvijjā*' ('Knowledge of good things') *KS* (3) 8: 27–36 (Poem).

T 1932 '*Muoy ray hā-sip muoy thṅai nau māt' Jhūṅ Samudd Sīem.*' *KS* (4) 7–12: 419–29 (Poem).

T 1933, 1953, 1965 '*Sek Som Paṇḍit.*' Phnom Penh, BR/IB (Poem).

T 1939 '*Dịk Danle Sāp.* L'eau du Tonlé Sap (premier roman moderne du Cambodge).' *KS* (11) 1: 5–32; 7: 15–34; 10: 15–42.

T 1941 Reprint of 1939. Phnom Penh.

T 1970 '*Kosaj gī secktī khjil cra-ūs.*' (Reprint of 1928*a*) *KS* (41) 4: 458–66.

Kim-Ky, *Gim-Gī*, Publisher, Phnom Penh

T 1955 *Cpāp' Kịṅ Kantrai.* Cbap Keng Kantray. (Reference from Vandy-Kaonn 1981: 82.)

T 1955 *Hai Saṅkh.* 8 vols.

T 1958 *Rīoeṅ dhanañjăy paṇḍit.*

T 1965 *Haṅs Yant.*

Kim-Samon, *Gīm-Saṃ-un*

T 1972 '*Supin*'. In *M̈yāṅ dau ṭaer.* (That's interesting!) Phnom Penh, Kim-Samon: 43–9 and Huffman and Proum 1977: 108–9 (Poem).

Kim-Seng, *Gim-Seṅ* ed., Phnom Penh

T n.d. *Cpāp' Prus Srī.* (=*Cpāp' Prus. Cpāp' Srī*?)

T n.d. *Paṇṭāṃ Kram N̈uy* and *Cpāp' ṭās' tīoen kūn cau.*

T 1949, 1953 *Dāv Ek* (By Nou-Kan).

T 1960 *Lpoek Madrī* by Sunthor Chea.

T 1967 *Cpāp' gorab mātā pitā* by Chong. *Kiriyā ciñcịṃ jīvit ṭoy kram.*

Knosp, Gaston

S 1908 'Le théatre en Indochine'. *Anthropos* 3: 280–93. (Cambodian theatre, pp. 289–93.)

Kol-Sary

T 1968 See *Kambujasuriyā* III Texts of folktales and legends (40) 5.

Komar Pech, *Kumār Bejj*, Printing house, Takeo

T 1959 *Dhanañjăy, Bas' Keṅkaṅ, Māyā Srī, Mā Yoeṅ.* Takeo. (The stories, 'Thmenh Chey', 'The snake *Keṅkaṅ*', 'The wiles of women', and 'Our Uncle' are respectively on pp. 1–84, 85–92, 93–105, 106–41.)

Kong-Bun Chhœun, *Gaṅ-P̂un Jhīoen*

T 1962 *Histoire de néang Rumsay Sâk ou Préah Bat Réach Kol.* (*Nāṅ Raṃsāy sak'* or *Braḥ Pād Rājakul*) Phnom Penh, Sing Hun. (Reference from Vandy-Kaonn 1981: 81.)

Kong-Huot, *Gaṅ-Huot*

V 1963 10 Sept.–12 Oct. (Translation of *Duṃ Dāv*, Tum Teav, in daily excerpts) *La Dépêche du Cambodge*, Phnom Penh.

Kong-Huot, *Gaṅ-Huot* and Chau Seng, *Cau-Seng*

V 1970 *Tum-Teav. Adapté du poème cambodgien par.* Culture et Civilisation Khmères. No. 7. Phnom Penh, Université Bouddhique Preah Sihanouk Raj. (Short account of the story in French.)

Kong Sân (or Sân Kong), *San-Gaṅ'*

T 1944 *Bāky subhāsit purāṇ.* Peak sop'easet boran. *KS* (16) 10: 505–7. (Text from memory.)

Kosikov, I. G.

S 1971 'Les noms propres de personnages dans le poème "Reamker"'. *Ethnologie des noms propres.* Moscow, Institut d'Ethnologie de Moscou: 126–40. (Russian text. Compares names of Reamker and Indian Rāmāyaṇa.)

Kourov, A.

S 1958 'Littérature du Cambodge'. *Littérature et Vie.* Moscow. (Russian text. Reference from Long-Séam and Y. P. Dementiev 1980.)

Krasem, *Braḥ Mahābidūr Krasem*

T 1929–32 *Mahābhārat. KS* 1929–30 (2) 3: 85–111; (3) 1: 95–113; 2: 59–80; 3: 57–79; 4: 67–91; 5: 63–81; 7: 69–86; 8: 71–91; 9: 75–98; 10: 55–69; 11: 57–73; 12: 51–76. (4) 7–12: 430–91. (Translation from Thai.)

T 1938–40 Translation from French of *Hitopades*, continuing from Choum Mau in KS 1933. *KS* (10) 5: 129–36; (11) 2: 101–10; 6: 197–206; 8: 153–60; 10: 107–15; 11: 165–73; 12: 261–70.

S 1966 *Padānukram Rāmakerti* (lexique du Rāmakerti) Phnom Penh, IB.

Kraysar Sorivoṅ, Prince, *Kraisar Sūrivaṅs, Braḥ Aṅg Mcās'*

S n.d. *Paep Kaṃṇāby.* Modèles de vers (A MS used by Roeské (1913: 670 n. 1 and 671)).

Krum Jaṃnuṃ Daṃnīem Daṃlāp' Khmaer. See Commission des Mœurs et Coutumes du Cambodge.

Kumār Bejj. See Komar Pech.

Lagrée, Doudart de

V 1883 'Chronique royale du Cambodge'. A. B. Villemereuil ed. *Explorations et missions de Doudart de Lagrée.* Paris: 21–57.

Laporte, René (also known as Tvear, q.v.)

V 1970 'La légende de la ville d'Oudong (province de Kompong Speu).' *CN* (1) 4: 60–5. (Taken from *Prajuṃ Rīoeṅ Breṅ Khmaer* 5: 47.)

V 1970 'Legend of the Four Bald Men.' *NC* (1) 5: 78–81. (Taken from *Prajuṃ Rīoeṅ Breṅ Khmaer* 4: 122.)

V 1970 'Histoire de la Montagne de Neang Kangrei (province de Kompong Chhnang).' *CN* (1) 6: 78–9. (Taken from *Prajuṃ Rīoeṅ Breṅ Khmaer* 5: 165.)

V 1970 'The two orphans.' *NC* (1) 8: 52–5. (No name of translator. Translated from the French of René Laporte. Taken from *Prajuṃ Rīoeṅ Breṅ Khmaer* 2: 198.)

V 1971 'Histoire du rat blanc qui fut élevé au rang de prince.' *RC* 731: 27–8.

V 1971 'Les quatre chercheurs d'or.' *RC* 731: 28.

V 1971 'Comment les chevaux perdirent leur puissance.' *RC* 750: 26–7.

V 1971 'The story of Alev.' *NC* (2) 10: 82–8. (No name of translator. Translated from the French of René Laporte. Taken from *Prajuṃ Rīoeṅ Breṅ Khmaer* 2: 120.)

Laspeyres, Pierre-Jean

V 1958 'Petites chansons khmères pour une guitare'. *FA* (15) No. 143: 108–14. Contains, in French translation only:

pp. 108–9. 'Je vais à la fontaine.'
pp. 109–10. 'Si tu me donnes un sou.'
pp. 110–11. 'Le potier de Kompong Chhnang.'
pp. 111–12. 'Ballade de l'île du Pic.'
pp. 112–13. 'La marchande de Kompong Thom.'
pp. 113–14. 'La sirène de Kratie.'
p. 114. 'La forêt de Stung-Treng.'

Lay-Kry, *Ḷāy-Grī*

S 1965 '*Rīoeṅ biroḥ choet*'. ('Attractive tales.') *KS* (37) 7: 748–59. (Discusses the likeable characteristics of various stories of Khmer literature.)

Lay-Tek

S 1919 *Moyens de locomotion en pays khmèr. (Dans la légende et dans la réalité.)* Hanoi, Imprimerie Taupin.

Léang-Hap An, *Lāṅ-Hāp' Ān*

S n.d. *Rāmakerti niṅ Rāmāyaṇa (Rāmakerti et Rāmāyaṇa).* Phnom Penh.

T 1958 See *Kambujasuriyā.* III Texts of folktales and legends 1958. 1, 2, 3, 4, and 12. 1960. 11.

S 1959 '*Opinions sur le roman "La rose de Pailin"*.' Phnom Penh, Chhung-Nguon Huot.

S 1962 *Dum Dāv. Banyal'vaekñaek atthā adhippāy.* (*Dum Dāv.* 'Detailed explanation and discussion of its meaning.') Phnom Penh, Subhamitr.

S 1963 'Elements of Khmer Prosody.' *Narodui Azii i Afriki* 6: 130–9. (Russian text. Résumé in English, p. 281.)

S 1964*a* '*Anak nibandh khmaer. Braḥ Pād Aṅg Duoṅ*'. ('Khmer Authors. King Ang Duong.') *Dassanāvaṭṭī Aksarsāstr* (Journal of Literature, Phnom Penh) (pp. not known).

S 1964*b* *Kābyasāstr.* ('Versification.') Vol. 1. Phnom Penh. (Roneotyped).

T S 1964*c* '*Anak nibandh khmaer. Braḥ Rāj Sambhār*'. ('Khmer Authors.

Braḥ Rāj Sambhār.') *Dassanāvaṭṭī Aksarsāstr* (pp. not known). (Phnom Penh). See 1966*e* for details.

S 1965*a* *Atthādhippāyakathā rīoeṅ haṅs yant. Pañhā atthanăy, attharūp niṅ attharas.* (Explanation of Haṅs Yant. Its meaning, form and tenor.) Phnom Penh, Sing Heng.

S 1965*b* Reprint of *Anak nibandh khmaer. Braḥ Pād Aṅg Duoṅ.* Batambang, Librairie Ing-Hun (*Paṇṇāgār Îṅ-Ĥun*).

S 1966*a* *Atthādhippāyakathā rāmakert(i) prīep dhīep niṅ rāmāyaṇa.* ('Explanation of the *Rāmakert(i)*, compared with the Ramayana.') Phnom Penh, *Vijjāsākal.*

T 1966*b* *Atthādhippāyakathā rīoeṅ kākī.* ('Explanation of *Kākī*') Phnom Penh.

T 1966*c* *Bhiram N̈uy.* Phnom Penh, Seng-Nguon-Huot.

T 1966*d* *Duṃ Dāv.* For schools. Phnom Penh, Seng-Nguon-Huot.

T S 1966*e* Reprint of *Anak Nibandh khmaer. Braḥ Rāj Sambhār.* Phnom Penh, Seng-Nguon Huot. Contains:

pp. 1–22. Life of King Srī Dhammarāj, also known as Preah Réach Samphéar.

pp. 23–4. List of works.

S and part or all of **T** of following:

pp. 25–37. *Cpāp' Rājanīti.*

pp. 37–45. *Braḥ Rāj Sambhār.*

pp. 46–9. *Likhit phñoe dau thvāy Braḥ M̈ae Yuor Vaṭṭī.*

pp. 50–2. *Bāky kāby cār niṅ kaṃbūl tnot.*

pp. 52–7. *Kaṃṇāby sarsoer hemantamās.*

pp. 57–9. *Kanlaṅ' mās maṅgal thlai.*

pp. 59–? *Kaṃṇāby braliṅ mās oey* (Faulty copy).

pp. 70–8. *Cpāp' Kram.*

pp. 79–86. *Cpāp' Trīneti.*

S 1966*f* *Etudes de textes,* Vol. 2 Phnom Penh, Sing Héng. (Reference from Vandy-Kaonn 1981: 81.)

S 1966–7 *Siksā Rāmakerti khmaer* (Études du Rāmakerti). Phnom Penh. 2 vols.

T 1967*a* *Atthādhippāyakathā rīoeṅ mahāvessantarajātak.* ('Explanation of the Mahāvessantarajātak.') Phnom Penh, Seng-Nguon-Huot.

S 1967*b* *Histoire de la littérature khmère (du 1er siècle à 1859).* Phnom Penh, Kim Eng.

S 1968 *Siksā atthapad.* ('Explanation of texts') Phnom Penh, *Jhān Hāk' Heṅ.*

S 1968, 1969, and 1971 *'Lpaṅ siksā pravatti aksarsāstr khmaer'.* ('Attempt to teach the history of Khmer literature.') *KS* (40) 1: 89–102; 2: 213–23; 3: 277–87; 4: 381–90; 5: 487–96; 6: 607–20; 7:

733–42; 8: 834–42; 9: 957–71; 10: 1096–1109; 11: 1192–1243; 12: 1321–76. (41) 1: 57–63. (43) 2: 144–54.

S 1969 *Liste d'ouvrages édités par Institut Bouddhique.* Phnom Penh, IB.

S 1971 *Kābyasāstr. Prosodie Khmère.* Part I. Phnom Penh, B. H.

Lebedev, Y.

S 1959 'Contes, proverbes et maximes du Cambodge'. *Littératures Etrangères.* Moscow (Russian text).

Leclère, Adhémard

V 1895 *Cambodge. Contes et légendes recueillis et publiés en français. Introduction par Léon Feer.* Paris, Emile Bouillon. Contains:

1. Légendes Bouddhiques.
i. pp. 1–35 Le satra du roi Chéa-Ly.
ii. pp. 36–8 La graine de moutarde.
2. Histoire locale.
pp. 38–52 Le Déchou Kraham Ka et le Déchou Yat.
3. Contes.
i. pp. 53–69 Le perroquet et la merle.
ii. pp. 70–91 Néang Kantoc. (A 'Cinderella' story.)
pp. 92–8 Histoire de Con Tam et Con Cam. (A Vietnamese 'Cinderella' story.)
iii. pp. 99–111 Néang Chhouk.
pp. 112–43 Néang Soc Kraaup.
pp. 144–59 Mono-Véan.
4. Contes judiciaires.
i. pp. 161–5 L'étudiant Tissab-Moc.
ii. pp. 166–9 La statue vivifié.
iii. pp. 170–4 Néang Montéa-Vatdey.
iv. p. 175 Tête à tête.
v. pp. 176–8 Le marchand et les trois passagers.
vi. pp. 179–80 Les trois frères.
vii. p. 181 Les trois frères.
viii. pp. 182–4 Les quatre pattes du chat.
ix. pp. 185–8 Les quatre aveugles.
x. pp. 189–91 Le voleur et les quatre femmes.
xi. pp. 192–200 Les quatre hommes vertueux.
5. Jataka du Bouddha.
pp. 201–93 Préa Sang-Sêl-Chey (*Saṅkh Silp Jăy*).
6. Contes malais.
i. pp. 295–300 Le combat du Buffle et du Bufflon.
ii. pp. 301–6 Arrivée des Malais à Kampot.

V 1902 *Le livre de Vésândar le roi charitable (Sâtra Moha Chéadak ou le livre du Grand Jâtaka d'après la leçon cambodgienne).* Paris, Leroux.

V 1903 *Collection de Contes et Chansons populaires XXV. Contes laotiens et contes cambodgiens recueillis, traduits et annotés.* Paris, Leroux.

V S 1906 *Les livres sacrés du Cambodge I.* Paris, Leroux. Contains:

Préas Pathama Sâmphothian (vie du Bouddha). (*Patham Sambodhi*). Introduction pp. 7–12. V pp. 13–114.

Le satra du Tevatat (*Devadatt*). Introduction pp. 121–3. V 125–44.

Maha Chinok (*Mahājanakajātak*). Introduction pp. 145–9. V pp. 151–210.

Nimea-reach-cheadak (*Nimirāj*). Introduction pp. 221–4. V 225–74.

Preas Dime-cheadak (*Temiyajātak*). V 275–340.

V? 1908 *Kâma-Deva. Poésie.* Paris (?), Cordurier et Montégout.

V 1911 *Bouddhisme et Brahmanisme: Trois petits livres. (Le roi Sédathnou et la reine Sépya.)* Paris, Leroux.

V S 1911 'Le théâtre cambodgien.' *Revue d'Ethnographie et de Sociologie.* 1910. Nos. 11–12: 257–82 (17 plates). pp. 264–8, V of Léak-Sènavongs (*Laksanavaṅs*), Part VI, and pp. 270–3, résumé of rest of story.

V 1912*a* *Cambodge. Contes, Légendes et jatakas.* Niort, Clouzot. (Only 50 copies made because some of the 54 tales were pornographic. 1 at Yale University and 1 at Bibliothèque nationale.)

V 1912*b* 'Le roi Sédathnou et la reine Sépya. Bouddhisme et Brahmanisme: Trois petits livres. *BSEI* (1): 35–8.

V S 1914 *Histoire du Cambodge depuis le Ier siècle de notre ère.* Paris, Geuthner. (The author refers to various chronicles, e.g. p. 236 n. 1, but Mak Phœun says he used the chronicle P 58, *Braḥ rāj baṅs sauvaṭār Braḥ mahākrasatr soy-rāj.*)

V 1958 'Un conte khmer. Comment les malais vinrent s'installer à Kampot.' *CA* (2) Feb. 28.

V 1984 (Reprint by Cedoreck of 1912*a*.)

Leroux, Ernest, ed.

T n.d. *Varavaṅs Sūravaṅs.* Paris.

Lesur, Daniel

V 1946 *Chansons cambodgiennes.* Paris, Durand. Contains: p. 2 Le langage des fleurs. p. 4 Sangsar. p. 7 Pirogues. p. 10 L'étang Pesai. p. 12 Le voyage du roi.

Leuba, Jeanne

V 1913 'Pou le niais, Cambodian short story.' *RI* NS 2, 1 (15) 5: 515–.

V 1959 'La réincarnation.' *RC* Nos. 192–3. Dec. 19 and 34. (Also in Anakota 1977. Folktale.)

Levy, Paul

V 1981 'Le Leng Trot ou danses rituelles et rustiques du Nouvel An Khmer.' *Seksa Khmer* 3–4: 59–86. (V of song on p. 73.)

Lewitz, Saveros

S 1972 'Les inscriptions modernes d'Angkor Wat.' *JA* (260) 1–2: 107–29. (Contains some comment on literature.)

T V 1973 '*Kpuon ābāh-bibāh* ou le livre de mariage des Khmers par Ker Nou et Nhieuk Nou traduit et édité . . .' *BEFEO* (60): 243–329. Contains marriage songs, **T**, pp. 299–307, **V**, pp. 293–7 as follows:

Jāv Khān' slā p. 299, L'achat du bol d'arec p. 293.
Jraṅ sraṅāt' p. 299, Le grand calme p. 293.
Ṭoḥ krāl p. 300, Les seins épanouis p. 293.
Kandaen Drāṃṅ p. 300 and pp. 293–4.
Khdo p. 301, p. 294.
Khnaṅ Bhnaṃ p. 301–2, La crête de la montagne p. 294.
Rapaṅ ramās p. 302, La clôture du rhinocéros p. 294.
Dịk jap' pp. 302–3, Le gouffre p. 295.
Krom nāy p. 303, Les terres basses de là-bas p. 295.
Poek vāṃṅnan pp. 303–4, L'ouverture des rideaux p. 295.
Aṅgar or *Nagar rāj* p. 304, La cité royale pp. 295–6.
Stec phdaṃ pp. 304–5, Le roi dort p. 296.
Braḥ Thoṅ p. 305, p. 296.
Jraṅ Sraṅāt' (a 2nd poem with this title) p. 305, Le calme parfait p. 296.
Saṃboṅ p. 306, La belle à l'abondante chevelure pp. 296–7.
Sārikā Kaev p. 306, La merlette mandarine p. 297.
Phāt'Jāy p. 306, Ecartement des rideaux p. 297.
Paṃbe p. 307, Berceuse p. 297.
Ṭamrī yol ṭai p. 307, L'éléphant balance sa trompe p. 297.
Āḷe p. 307, p. 297.
Phāt' Jāy (a 2nd poem with this title) p. 307, Ecartement des rideaux p. 297.

Lī Eṅ Hīek

T 1957 ed. *Rīoeṅ Braḥ Jinavaṅs.* Phnom Penh, Serei Raṭṭh.

Long, *Ḷuṅ*

T 1932 '*Sutadhanajātaka. (Paññāsajātaka)*'. *KS* (4) 7–12: 282–360. (Translation from Pali.)

Long-Chim

T 1954 *Rīoeṅ cau ktāṃṅ pāy niṅ mcās' satrī saen dhipatī.* ('*Cau Ktāṃṅ pāy*' and '*Mcās' Satrī Saendhipatī.*') Phnom Penh.

Long-Seam, *Ḷoṅ-Ŝam*

S 1980 'Povtor v Khmerskom Literaturnom Yazik.' (Reduplicative words in the Khmer literary language.) *Yaziki*: 139–54.

—— and Dementiev, Y. P.

S 1980 'Bibliographie en langue russe sur le Cambodge (1956–1979).

BEFEO (68): 289–311. (Bibliography of works on Cambodian language and literature written in Russian.)

Louis-Em. See Em, Louis.

Louvey

T 1965 *Ayay.* ('Alternating songs') Phnom Penh, Reasmei Kampuchea. (This may be same as *Ayay,* 1965, by Saram Phan (Néang Saram Pak, Néang Lovey, Néang Saram Phan), Reasmei Kampuchea.)

Ly-Nguon, *Lī-Ṅuon*

T 1966 See *Kambujasuriyā* III Texts of folktales and legends 1966 (38) 12 and 1968 (40) 9.

Ly-Théam Teng, *Lī-Dhām Teṅ*

T 1957–8 ed. *Devand.* See Mok, Sandhar.

T [1957] BE 2505 *Prajuṃ atthapad aksarsāstr. Snā ṭai anak nibandh bī satavats dī 16 tal' 20.* Recueil de textes littéraires. Phnom Penh, Seng-Nguon-Huot.

T 1959*a* *Baṅsāvatār khmaer saṅkhep.* ('A short Khmer history.') Phnom Penh, Ching-Nguon-Huot.

S 1959*b* *Siksā aṃbī aksarsāstr khmaer.* Études sur la littérature khmère. Phnom Penh.

T 1960 *Aksarsāstr Khmaer.* ('Khmer Literature') Phnom Penh, Seng-Nguon Huot. (An account of Khmer literature from the inscriptions onwards with lists of works and authors of the various periods and quotations from well-known authors.)

T 1964*a* '*Daṃnīem daṃlāp*' *khmaer. Rapāṃ Kantae-ṙae*'. *KS* (36) 7: 771–7. (Text of song, *Ḷoeṅ bhnaṃ cuḥ bhnaṃ, thma ṭā dhaṃ 2,* p. 775.)

T 1964*b* ed. *Paṇṭāṃ Kram N̈uy.* Phnom Penh, Seng-Nguon Huot.

T 1964*c* '*Rapāṃ rāṃ suor brătr*'. *KS* (36) 9: 989–93. (Texts of 2 songs, *Daṃnuk Sārikā Kaev* (Song of the Myna bird) and *Daṃnuk Uṃ Dūk* (Boat song) p. 992.)

T 1964–8 See *Kambujasuriyā* III Texts of folktales and legends (36) 4, 10 and 12; (37) 5; (40) 4.

T 1966 *Anak Nibandh Khmaer. Bhiramy N̈uy.* ('Khmer Authors. Phirom Ngoy.') Phnom Penh, Séng-Nguon Huot. (Partly translated into French by San Sarin, q.v.)

S 1967 '*Dis ṭau nai silpa: aksarsāstr khmaer (Vicāraṇakathā).*' ('The aims of Khmer art and literature.') *KS* (39) 11: 1145–50.

S 1968 '*Kār srāv jrāv aṃbī lkhon spaek (ṇāṃṅ)*'. ('Research concerning the shadow play.') *KS* (40) 6: 621–41.

S 1969*a* '*Bhār kicc nai anak nibandh knuṅ kār sāṅ jāti*'. ('The duty of authors in improving the nation.') *KS* (41) 2: 136–44.

T 1969*b* '*Daṃnuk purāṇ khmaer*'. *KS* (41) 9: 963–9; 10: 1120–6. Contains **T** of 9 songs, collected from villagers, to be sung by boys and girls:

O mlap' ṭūṅ oey (O, shade of the coconut-tree), 964–6.
Sdoer oey srī sdoer (O, hesitant girl), 966–7.
Sa oey sa s-āt (She is fair and smart), 967.
Ṭamrī dhṅan' bhluk (The elephant has heavy tusks), 968.
Muṃ oey srī muṃ (O, maiden], 968–9.
Caṅvā ṭael kuk (The little fish which lies sleeping), 1120–1.
Phgar lān' īsān (The thunder rumbles to the north-east), 1121–2.
Sra-aem khmau sdoer (The pleasantly dark girl is hesitant), 1122–5.
Srī oey nāṅ srī (O, young lady], 1125–6. (Collected from BEFEO and other publications).

T 1969*c* '*Lpoek Ak*'. *KS* (41) 7: 734–50; 8: 844–60; 9: 970–86; 11: 1249–59. (The last instalment is thought to be *Sāstrā Ak* by *Lok Pamroe Udăy.*)
T 1970*a* '*Lpoek Sīl prāṃ*'. *KS* (42) 1: 67–79.
T 1970*b* ed. '*Lpoek Cacak*' by Mok. *KS* (42) 2: 159–93.
S 1970*c* '*Kār saṅket srāv jrāv caṃboḥ rīoeṅ Varavaṅs-Sūravaṅs*'. (Research into *Varavaṅs Sūravaṅs*.') *KS* (42) 3: 315–22.
T 1970*d* '*Rīoeṅ Varavaṅs Sūravaṅs.*' *KS* (42) 3: 323–50; 4: 426–57; 5: 542–73; 6: 660–91; 7: 774–805; 8: 886–917; 9: 994–1033; 10: 1114–30.
T S 1970*e* '*Anak Srī Siddhi* (1881–1963)'. ('Madame Seth.') *KS* (42) 12: 1350–77.
T 1971 ed. '*Lpoek Juc camlaṅ ceñ bī sāstrā sḷik rịt*'. ('*Lpoek Juc* taken from a palm-leaf manuscript.') *KS* (43) 4: 354–69.
T S 1971 ed. '*Lpoek phgar phtāṃ ktām khyaṅ' (sāstrā purāṇ).* ('*Lpoek phgar phtāṃ ktām khyaṅ* (old manuscript).') *KS* (43) **T** 8: 717–22, **S**: 722–4.
S 1971 '*Srāv jrāv aṃbī lkhon khmaer.*' ('Research on Khmer theatre.') *KS* (43) 9: 793–808.
S 1972 *Recueil des écrivains khmers célèbres.* Phnom Penh, Association des écrivains khmers.

Ly Vou-Ong
S 1967 'Les manuscrits sur feuilles de latanier.' *Annales de l'Université des Beaux-Arts.* (1): 97–108. Phnom Penh, Université des Beaux-Arts. (Description of methods of making, writing, etc.)

Ma Lay Khem
S 1970*a* 'La littérature khmère'/'Khmer Literature'. *CN/NC* (1) 2: 68–70.
S 1970*b* 'La littérature restaurée, d'inspiration religieuse au XVIIIe siècle, par l'apparition d'un conception réaliste de la vie.' *CN/NC* 2: 69.

—— and Ly-Théam Teng
S 1972 'Aperçu sur l'évolution de la littérature khmère.' *CN* (19): 44–9.

Maen-Ton, *Ṁaen-Dan'*

1969 See *Kambujasuriyā* III Texts of folktales and legends. (41) 7.

Mai

T 1901 *Cpāp' Thmī.* Paris, Plon-Nourrit et Cie. Also 1937 *'Cpāp' Thmī'. KS* (10) 4–6: 155–64. (Same text as *Cpāp' Prus.*)

T 1901 *Cpāp' Srī.* Plon-Nourrit et Cie.

T 1911 *Cpāp' Meyyepaṇḍit taeṅ (= Cpāp' Prus).*

T 1911 *Cpạp' Srī Meyyapaṇḍit.*

T 1959 *Cpāp' Prus (ṭoy Paṇḍit Mai).* Phnom Penh, Bouth-Néang.

T 1959 *Cpāp' Srī.* Phnom Penh, Bouth Néang.

T 1964 *Cbap Proch. Cbap Srey.* Phnom Penh, Sérey Râth (*Cpāp' Prus Cpāp' Srī*).

Mak Phœun

V S 1973 *Les Chroniques royales du Cambodge (Partie légendaire).* Traduction française avec comparaison des différentes versions et introduction. Paris. (Thèse de la IVe section de l'École pratique des Hautes Études.)

S 1976 'Présentation des Chroniques royales du Cambodge (Partie légendaire).' *Actes du 29e Congrès international des orientalistes. Section organisée par Pierre-Bernard Lafont. Asie du Sud-Est continental.* II: 102–9.

V S 1980 'L'Introduction de la Chronique royale du Cambodge du Lettré Nong.' *BEFEO* (67): 135–45. (**S** 135–40, **T** (in transliteration) 141–2, **V** 142–5.)

V S 1981 *Collection de textes et documents sur l'Indochine* XIII. *Chroniques royales du Cambodge (de 1594 à 1677).* Traduction française avec comparaison des différentes versions et introduction. Paris, Maisonneuve.

V S 1984 *Collection de textes et documents sur l'Indochine.* XIII. *Les Chroniques royales du Cambodge (des origines légendaires jusqu'à Paramarājā Ier).* Traduction française avec comparaison des différentes versions et introduction. Paris, Maisonneuve.

Malherbes, Paule

V 1958 *Légendes cambodgiennes.* Paris, Sésame.

Malika, Princess, *Braḥ Aṅg Mcās' Ksatrī Mālikā*

S 1938–41 Introductory notes and additional notes on poets or poems in the *Prajuṃ Bāky Kāby* (Collection of poems) by princes, princesses, ladies in waiting, etc. of the 18th and 19th centuries and texts of the poems direct from manuscripts. *KS* (10) 7–8: 101–2 (Foreword); 103–11 and (10) 12: 205–16 (poetry by King Srī Dhammarājā). (11) 1–3: 41–52 Poems by King Srī Dhammarājā with 42 (Note on the circumstances of King Sri Dhammarājā's poem written on the top of a sugar-palm tree), 45–7 (Historical note) and 49–52 (Brief biography). (11) 4: 43–55 *Braḥ Rāj Sambhār*; 5–6:

105–6 (Introduction to poems with texts by various royal persons other than King Sri Dhammarājā), 106–17, 181–96; 7–9: 203–20; 12: 247–59. (12) 1: 35–44; 3: 57–60; 4: 57–63; 5: 85–90; 6: 67–75; 8: 65–71; 9: 51–8; 10: 59–67; 11: 63–7; 12: 55–62. (13) 9: 17–21; 10: 17–20 (repeats (12) 1: 39–40); 11: 20–3 (repeats part of (12) 1: 35–44).

T 1968 *Prajuṃ bāky kāby* (Collection of Poems). Phnom Penh, IB.

Malleret, Louis

V 1941 '*Traditions légendaires des cambodgiens de Cochinchine relevant d'une interprétation ethno-sociologique*'. *IIEH* (4) 1–2: 169–80.

Mann-Eng, *Mān'-Eṅ*

V 1959, 1961 See *Kambujasuriyā* III Texts of folktales and legends. (31) 3 and 7; (33) 4.

Mao (Chuuk Meng), *Mau-Jūk Meṅ*

V 1961 *Contes du Cambodge. Rédigés sous les auspices de la Commission cambodgienne pour l'UNESCO. Document relatif à l'enseignement sur les Cultures Orientales.* Paris, UNESCO. (Stencilled. 9 pp.)

Marounova, I.

V 1972 'Bâton perdu.' *Légendes et récits du Cambodge*. Moscow, Naouka. (Collection of Khmer texts translated into Russian from French and English.)

Martini, François

S n.d. 'La littérature cambodgienne.' *Revue française.* No. 34.

S 1938 'En marge du Rāmāyaṇa cambodgien' *BEFEO* (38) 2: 285–95.

S 1947 '*Bāky banyal' secktī phseṅ gnā knuṅ rīoeṅ Rāmāyaṇa: khmaer.* En marge du Rāmāyaṇa cambodgien' *KS* (20) 321–5. (Note by translator, Ray-Buc, p. 326. Different from the other articles with the same title.)

V 1948 'Les quatre compagnons' *FA* (3) 28: 849–51.

S 1949*a* 'En marge du Rāmāyaṇa cambodgien.' *Actes du XXIe Congrès International des Orientalistes* 225–6. Paris, Imprimerie Nationale. (Summarizes points made in 1938 and 1950.)

V 1949*b* In *FA* (4) 37–8 between pp. 948 and 1031 there are the following:

'Râmakerti (extraits)' pp. 948–52.

'Pour réussir dans la vie. Chbap Ker-Kal (extraits)', pp. 961–2.

'Histoire de Dame Kakèy by Ang-Duong (extraits)', pp. 956–72. (Portrait de Dame Kakèy, pp. 965–6. Dame Kakéy et Garuda s'éprennent l'un de l'autre, pp. 967–8. Les amours de Garuda et de Dame Kakèy, pp. 969–70. Douleurs du roi, pp. 971–2.)

'Légende de la foudre', pp. 995–6.

'Le mariage des quatre chauves', pp. 1020–6.

'Néang Phim', pp. 1027–31. (Version based on 'La femme rusée'.)

T V S 1950 'En marge du Rāmāyaṇa cambodgien'. *JA* (238): 81–90. (Different from the 1938 article with the same title.)

S 1952 'Notes sur l'empreinte du Bouddhisme dans la version cambodgienne du Ramayana'. *JA* (240) 1: 67–70.

V 1955 In *FA* (12) 114–5: 505–11 and 526–7 there are the following:

'Râmakerti (extraits)', pp. 505–10.
'Ker-Kal, petit traité d'Economie domestique', pp. 510–1.
'Légende de la Foudre', pp. 526–7.

S 1961 'Quelques notes sur le Rāmker'. *AA* (24) 3–4: 351–62.

V 1978 *La Gloire de Rām (Rāmakerti).* Paris, Les Belles Lettres. (Translation of the Reamker (Rāmakerti).)

Martini, François and Bernard, Solange

V 1946 *Collection documentaire de Folklore de tous pays. Tome II. Contes populaires inédits du Cambodge.* Preface by J. Przylusky. Paris, Maisonneuve. Contains:

Contes Merveilleux
Les deux frères et le coq chasseur, pp. 17–32.
L'homme au couteau, pp. 33–71.
Le sieur Croûte de Riz, pp. 72–105.
L'homme qui déterrait les crabes, pp. 106–115.
La Bonne Fortune et la Malchance, pp. 116–124.

Contes étiologiques
Les deux amis qui voulaient tarir la mer, pp. 127–33.
Sok le Doux et Sok le Méchant, pp. 134–49.
L'enfant qui tua sa grand' mère, pp. 150–2.

Contes édifiants
L'homme au crottin de cheval, pp. 155–60.
Histoire du paresseux à l'épouse vertueuse, pp. 161–5.

Conte du sorcier, du vieux et de la vieille, pp. 166–8.

Contes judiciaires
Le voleur révélé par un parfum, pp. 171–5.
Histoire d'un vol de bœuf, pp. 176–8.
Histoire d'un contestation d'enfant, pp. 179–80.
Histoire de deux hommes et du parapluie, pp. 181–2.
Histoire des quatre compères qui se partageaient de l'or, pp. 183–4.

Contes plaisants
Histoire des quatre chauves, pp. 186–93.
Histoire du jeune homme à la noix de coco, pp. 194–202.
Histoire du voleur au bon cœur, pp. 203–12.

Contes d'animaux
La légende du Tigre, pp. 215–18.
Histoire du Tigre, du Singe et du Lièvre, pp. 219–27.

Histoire du Lièvre et des deux compagnons, pp. 228–31.
La Tortue et le Singe, pp. 332–4.
Contes divers
Histoire de la vraie mère, du vrai père et de la vraie femme, pp. 237–57.
L'ami et la femme adultère, pp. 258–64.
L'homme au trente sapèques, pp. 265–70.
L'homme qui épousa une fantôme, pp. 271–4.
Appendix: Du mariage cambodgien, pp. 275–89.

V 1949 In *FA* (4) 37–8: between pp. 993 and 1017 there are the following:

'La légende du tigre', pp. 993–4.
'L'homme qui déterrait les crabes, pp. 997–1002.
'Conte du sorcier, du vieux et de la vieille', pp. 1011–12.
'Histoire d'un vol de bœuf', pp. 1014–15.
'Histoire de trois seṭṭhi', pp. 1016–17.

1955 In *FA* (12) 114–15, between pp. 524 and 540 there are the following:

'Légende du Tigre', pp. 524–5.
'Conte du sorcier, du vieux et de la vieille', pp. 536–7.
'Histoire de trois setthi', pp. 539–40.

Martini, Ginette
1991 'Le mariage du Prince Sudhanu'. *Cahiers de l'Asie du Sud-Est*, Nos. 29–30: 159–68.

Marx, J. A.
V 1908 'Les premières larmes du Bouddha (Légende cambodgienne)'. *BSEI* (54) 1: 157–9.

Maspero, Georges
S 1904 *L'empire khmer.* Phnom Penh. Imprimerie du Protectorat.
S 1928–30 'Littérature khmère. '*Un Empire colonial français: l'Indochine.* Paris and Bruxelles, Van Oest: 297–305. 3 vols. (Short **V** of Pra Saṅ (*Săṅkh Silp Jăy*) 3: 305.)

Mathers, E. Powys
V 1929 *Eastern Love. Love Tales of Cambodia and Songs of the Love Nights of Lao.* Vol. X English versions by . . . London, John Rodker. Contains:

How not to treat a son-in-law pp. 1–14.
Sanselkey *(Săṅkh Silp Jăy)* pp. 19–50.
Kung the courageous pp. 54–61.
A woman's artifice pp. 65–76.

Mâm, Bophani
S 1972 'Musique d'accompagnement de "Reamker"'. *Annales de*

l'Université des Beaux Arts (Cambodge) (2): 77–96. 17 pl. (notations).

Mānavī, S.

T 1957 ed. *Īṇāv*. Phnom Penh, Vīriya (Prose account, with verse text given bit by bit).

Méas, *Mās* 1

T 1908 *Rīoeṅ paṇṭāṃ Tā Mās.* Phnom Penh.

Méas, *Mahā Mās, Hmīn Mās, Ukñā Vipul Senā* 2 (Not the same as Meas 1?)

T 1943 '*Paṇṭāṃ bālī*'. *KS* (15) 6: 309–13.

Méas-Ham, *Mās-Hāṃ*

T 1960 See *Kambujasuriyā* III Texts of folkltales and legends (32) 5: 553–8.

Méas-Samioen, *Mās-Samīoen*

T 1952 *Histoire de Mak Payongkéo.* Phnom Penh, Chhung-Nguon Huot. (Reference from Vandy-Kaonn 1981: 81.)

Méas-Yutt, *Mās-Yut*

T 1966 '*Adhippāy bhāsit*' (Explanation of a proverb). *KS* (38) 7: 729–42. (The explanation is given in the form of 2 poems, both explaining the proverb *Ktau ŝī rāk' trajāk' ŝī jrau.*)

Men-Riem

V 1962 *Let's read English.* A collection of Cambodian folktales in simple English. Corrected by M. Gosh, Doch Chhœun.

Menh-Nakri, *Miñ-Ṇagrī*

T 1943 *'Sujātajātak.' KS* (15) 11: 657–62; 12: 709–17.

Menkence, E.

S 1973 'Au sujet de la valeur du poème cambodgien au moyen âge: Prah Raj Sambha (et la Princesse Ang Vodi)'. *La Littérature et le temps',* 207–13. Moscow, Naouka (Russian text) (*re* the drama of the love between Prince-poet and princess and the beauty of the verses).

Mi Chak, *Mī Cak'*

T 1973, 1980 *Rīoeṅ Rāmakerti nai Tā Cak'.* (Mi Chak knew the popular text by heart and recorded it for F. Bizot.) See Bizot 1973, 1980.

Midan, Paul

V 1927 'Le roman cambodgien du lièvre. Légendes recueillies par . . . et illustrées par l'artiste khmer Mao'. *Extrême-Asie/Revue Indochinoise.* (8) 8: 276–92; 9: 315–34; 10: 365–82.

T V 1933 'Histoire du juge lièvre. Recueil de contes cambodgiens traduits et annotés par . . . '. *BSEI* NS (8) 4: i–vi, 1–116. (Introduction, i–vi; translation, 1–39; notes, 41–8; text in orthography, 49–116. Also published as a book by the Société des Études Indochinoises, Phnom Penh, n.d.)

V ? 1933 *Les contes du Lièvre.* Saigon.

Milne, Anthony R.

V 1972 *Mr Basket Knife and other Khmer Folktales.* London, Allen and Unwin. Contains:

pp. 9–11. The story of the greedy family.
pp. 13–15. The origin of the tiger.
pp. 17–21. The story of the jackal and the shrimp.
pp. 23–5. The man who knew how to cure a snake bite.
pp. 27–46. The story of Mr Basket Knife.
pp. 47–9. The trial.
pp. 51–5. The story of Brave Kong.
pp. 57–9. The caterpillar and the crow.
pp. 61–2. Notes.

Mith Yoeng, *Mitt Yoeṅ*, Printing house, Phnom Penh

S T 19— *Maraṇamātā.* School edition. 2 vols. **S**, pp. 1–21.

Mitt Sālā Pāli, Phnom Penh

T 1951 *Cpāp' Braḥ Rāj Sambhār.* (8–9): 331–4. (Same text as *Cpāp' Rājaneti* Cl.)

Moha Meas. See Méas 2.

Mok, Sandhar, *Sandhar M̈uk*

T 1957–8 *Rīoeṅ Devand.* Nhok-Thaem ed. *KS* (29) 2: 144–51; 3: 237–44; 4: 312–23; 6: 546–54; 7: 637–43; 8: 723–32; 9: 815–27; 10: 917–24; 11: 987–1006; 12: 1079–83. (30) 1: 49–56; 2: 117–28; 3: 225–32; 4: 321–36; 5: 429–42; 6: 523–30; 7: 619–27; 8: 705–8; 9: 801–10; 10: 899–908; 11: 979–94.

T 1961 *Duṃ Dāv.* ed. with Preface by Eng Soth, Sam Thang, Hang Thun Hak, and Neang Ho. (Mok's ragged MS was shaped up for printing.)

T 1970 *Lpoek Cacak.* Ly-Théam Teng ed. *KS* (42) 2: 159–43.

Monod, G. H.

V 1922 *Légendes cambodgiennes que m'a contées le Gouverneur Khieu.* Paris, Editions Bossard. Contains:

pp. 9–11. Introduction.
pp. 13–26. Le beau-père qui choisit un gendre.
pp. 27–38. Artifices féminines.
pp. 39–77. Histoire d'Alev.
pp. 79–88. Kung le courageux.
pp. 89–125. Histoire de la perdrix femelle et de la perdrix mâle.
pp. 127–48. La fondation d'Angkor.

V 1932 'Croûte de riz (Légende cambodgienne)' *EA* 61: 396–?

V 1932 'Folklore du Cambodge. Thmenh-Chey: légende cambodgienne'. *EA*, NS (6. 62): 452–7, 467–72.

V 1932 'Prah Botum Sorivong (conte extrait de Kampi Mongkultiphui *(Maṅgaladīpanī)*).' *EA*: 630–4.

V 1933 '*Ākrokkok* [Should be *kuhak*] *sy*.' ('The liar eats.') EA 223–4.

V 1935 *Légendes cambodgiennes.* Illustrations de A. Karpelès. Paris, Librairie du Régionalisme.

T 1935 See *Kambujasuriyā* III Texts of folktales and legends. (7) 1.

V 1943*a* *Contes Khmèrs.* Traduits du cambodgien par ... Feuilles de l'Inde No. 2. Mouans Sartoux, Alpes Maritimes. (From Baruch.)

V 1943*b* *Contes khmèrs traduits du Cambodgien par* ... Feuilles de l'Inde No. 9. Mouans Sartoux, Alpes Maritimes, Chitra C. A. Hogman. Contains:

pp. 14–15. Avant-propos.
pp. 49–97. Thmenh Chey *(Dhmeñ Jăy).*
pp. 98–125. Chau Kdang Bay *(Cau ktāṃṅ pāy).*
pp. 127–39. Neang Lomang Romchék *(Nāṅ lamaṅ raṃcek).*
pp. 141–59. Botum Sorivong *(Padumasūravaṅs).*
pp. 161–99. Neang Mornah Meada *(Nāṅ maraṇamātā).*
pp. 201–46. Satra Kakey *(Satrā Kākī).*
pp. 247–97. Sdech Kmeng *(Stec Kmeṅ).*
pp. 298–302. Glossary.
pp. 302–3. Notes.

V 1985 *Contes Khmers.* Paris, Cedoreck (Reprint of the last item). Contains:

pp. 14–15. Avant-propos de l'éditeur.
pp. 21–48. Sôphea Tonsay. *Le Sôphea Lièvre.*
pp. 51–97. Thmenh Chey. *Celui qui a toujours le dernier mot.*
pp. 101–25. Chau Kdang Bay. *Croûte de riz.*
pp. 129–39. Néang Lomang Romchék. *La fille de l'éléphant blanc.*
pp. 143–59. Prah Botumsorivong. *L'ingrate Princesse.*
pp. 163–99. Néang Mornah Meada. *Protection Maternelle.*
pp. 203–46. Satra Kakey. *La Princesse aux suaves effluves.*
pp. 249–97. Sdéch Kmèng. *Le Roi-Enfant.*
pp. 298–303. Glossaire et Notes.

Moura, Jean

V 1882–3 '"Le poème de Nocor Vat" par Pang, traduit du cambodgien.' *Bulletin de la Société Académique Indo-Chinoise de France.* 2e *s.* II: 197–203. (Translation of *Lpoek Aṅgar Vat.*)

1883 *Le royaume du Cambodge.* 2 vols. Paris, Leroux. Contains:

V Vol. 1, pp. 304–6. La Viméan Chan (*Vimān Cand*).

V pp. 306–8. Extrait du Muchalin (un roman) (*Mucalind*).

V pp. 308–11. Le Tonnerre (poésie).

V pp. 312–15. (Extracts from Mahosot ou Mahos, the *Mahosathajātak.*)

T V Vol. II, pp. 1–185. Chronique royale du Cambodge ou Pongsa Voda pp. 408–10 (**T** in transcription and **V** of 4 short poems). The first lines are: Pi cal bang ban yol (*Bī kāl paṅ pān yal'*), Tang te con cut

(*Tāṃṅ tae kūn giṭ*), Mul srey sap sroc néanéa (*Mūl srī sap (?) sruk nānā*), Phop phnéc bang ban khunh méas mit (*Bhăbv bhnaek paṅ pān ghoeñ mās mitr*).

pp. 413–16. Drama.

V pp. 416–45. Ruong-Eynao. (*Īṇāv*).

pp. 445–58. Réaméa-ke. Episode où Prea-leac est frappé d'un coup de lance. (Part of Reamker concerning Kumbakārṇ's visit to Bibhek, his fight against Sugrīb, the wounding of Laksm(ṇ) and the departure of Hanumān to the Hemavant for medicines.)

V 1959 'Orage'. *CA* (9): 25–6 (Folktale).

N. Onn. See Nouth-Onn.

N. Sukhanari. See Norodom Sukhanari.

Nepote, Jacques, and Khing Hoc Dy

S 1981 'Literature and Society in Modern Cambodia'. Tham Seong Chee ed. *Essays on Literature and Society in Southeast Asia. Political and Sociological Perspectives.* Singapore University: 56–81.

S 1987 'The Chinese Literary influence on Cambodia in the XIXth and XXth centuries'. Cl. Salmon ed. *Literary Migrations: Traditional Chinese Fiction in Asia (17th–20th centuries).* Beijing, International Culture Publishing Corporation: 321–72.

Nevermann, Hans

V 1956 *Die Stadt der tausend Drachen. Götter-und-Dämongeschichten, Sagen und Volkerzählungen aus Kambodscha.*, Eisenach und Kassel, Erich Röth Verlag. Contains:

p. 25. Die Entstehung der Welt.
p. 27. Der Sonnenfresser.
p. 30. Der Mondhase.
p. 31. Buddhas Versuchung.
p. 33. Das Paradies.
p. 39. Noruk, die Hölle.
p. 43. Reams Ruhm.
p. 58. Der Pferde Prinz.
p. 75. Der gebefreudige Prinz.
p. 81. Der Thlok-Baum.
p. 84. Die Gründung von Angkor Thom.
p. 88. Die Stadt der Göttersohnes.
p. 97. Der aussätzige König.
p. 100. Der Geier schützling.
p. 108. Der verdienst volle Preas Krek.
p. 112. Das wunderbare Eisen.
p. 116. Die Tempelteiche.
p. 119. Der goldene Königsschirm.
p. 121. Der Taucher unter der Erde.

p. 125. Die Gründung von Phnom Penh.
p. 127. Die Geschwisterehe.
p. 128. Das vier gesichtige Buddhasbild.
p. 132. Der Smaragbuddha.
p. 137. Das Mädchen im Brunnen.
p. 138. Das Siegel von Sangkeah.
p. 141. Die Schüttelwurzel.
p. 142. Die Reisesserinnen.
p. 143. Die Amazonen.
p. 146. Die Tigeröl.
p. 147. Das Gespenst beim Drachenspiel.
p. 149. Glück lässt sich nicht erzwingen.
p. 154. Die Elefantendiebe.
p. 156. Die Glücksschweine.
p. ?. Der hässliche Prinz.
p. 157. Der Schatz bei Siraphum.
p. 160. Ameise und Grille.
p. 160. Die schwartze Dame.
p. 161. Der einsame Baum.
p. 161. Der Mond.
p. 161. Die Betelkauerin.
p. 162. Auge und Ohr.
p. 162. Sehnsucht.
p. 163. Die Amsel.
p. 163. Liebeskummer.
p. 164. Das Gewitter.
p. 164. Unter den Bäumen.
p. 165. Der Duft.
p. 166. Liebesstreit und -freude.
p. 171–7. Notes.
p. 178. Quellennachweis.

New Cambodia

V 1970 'The tale of the city of Oudong (Province of Kompong Speu).' 1st Year 4: 60–5. (Based on a translation from Khmer to French by René Laporte.)

V 1970 'Legend of the four bald men.' 1st Year, 5: 78–81. (Based on a translation from Khmer to French by René Laporte.)

V 1970 'Story of the Neang Kangrei mountain.' 1st Year, 6: 78–9. (Based on a translation from Khmer to French by René Laporte.)

V 1970 'The two orphans.' Year 1, 8: 52–5. (Based on a translation from Khmer to French by René Laporte.)

V 1971 'The story of Akhvak Akhven (The blind man and the paralytic).' 2nd Year, 9: 44–6. (Based on a translation from Khmer to French by René Laporte.)

V 1971 'The story of Alev.' 2nd Year, 10: 82–8. (Based on a translation from Khmer to French by René Laporte.)

Ngin, or Yos-Ngin, *Yas'-Ṅin*

T 1959 *Sradap Cek.* Phnom Penh, Bouth-Néang. (Parts 1 and 2 for Schools. Parts 3 and 4 to come.)

1967 *Sradap Cek.* Phnom Penh, IB.

—— and Choum-Muong

T 1959 *Rīoeṅ Sradap Cek.* Phnom Penh, Bouth-Néang. (2 vols.)

Ngoy or Ou-Ngoy, *U-N̈uy* (Preah Phirom Pheasa, *Braḥ Bhiram Bhāsā* Ngoy)

T n.d. *Cpāp' dūnmān jan prus srī* ou Préceptes pour l'instruction des hommes et des femmes. Phnom Penh, IB.

T n.d. *Paṇṭāṃ Kram N̈uy.* Phnom Penh, Kim-Séng.

T n.d. *Cpāp' Paṇṭāṃ Kram N̈uy.* Phnom Penh, IB. (4 *Cpāp'* for schools Grade 6, mentioned by Ly-Théam Teng 1966: 6.)

T 1932 '*Cpāp' Lpoek Thmī.*' *KS* (4) 3–6: 149–80.

T 1932 *Cpāp' Lpoek Thmī.* Imprimerie du Gouvernement.

T 1932 *Cpāp' Lpoek Thmī.* Imprimerie Nouvelle.

T 1932 '*Cpāp' Kir Kāl thmī.*' *KS* (4) 3–6: 181–95.

T 1933 '*Secktī raṃlịk ṭaḥ tīoen.* Hommage au Triple Joyau.' *KS* (5) 7–12: 97–118.

T 1937 '*Cpāp' Kūn Cau*'. *KS* (9) 4–6: 111–22.

T 1937 '*Lpoek Cpāp' Săṅgh.* Paroles de Krom Ngoy.' *KS* (9) 7–9: 107–25.

T 1937 '*Cpāp' praṭau jan prus srī*'. *KS* (9) 7–9: 205–20.

T 1940, 1961 *Bāky kāby praṭau jan prus srī.* Phnom Penh, IB. (Another version of *Lpoek Cpāp' Săṅgh.*)

T 1940, 1960 *Cpāp' Lpoek thmī.* Phnom Penh, IB.

T 1951, 1961 *Cpāp' praṭau jan prus srī.* Phnom Penh, IB.

T 1958 *Secktī raṃlịk tās' tīoen.* Phnom Penh, IB.

T 1964 *Cpāp' Lpoek thmī. Cpāp' Kir Kāl thmī.* Phnom Penh, IB.

T 1964 *Paṇṭāṃ Kram N̈uy.* Phnom Penh, Seng-Nguon Huot.

Nguon Kamy

S 1981 'Madame Seth, femme de lettres du début du 20e siècle'. *Vappadharm khmaer*: 133–9. Translation of Ly-Théam Teng 1970.

Nhaem-Khim, *N̈aem-Khịm*

T 1960 and 1961 See *Kambujasuriyā* III Texts of folktales and legends. (32) 11 and 12; (33) 1.

Nhean-Chhin, *Ñāṇ-Jhịn*, ed.

T 1962 '*Sammodamānajātak*'. *KS* (34) 3: 300–5.

Nheuk-Nou, Nhek-Nou, or Nhieuk-Nuv, *N̈ịk-Nū*

T 1944 '*Cpāp' Kram pariyāy.* Chbăp Krămborĭyāy'. *KS* (16) 6: 304–10; 7: 365–72; 8: 430–6; 9: 477–82; 10: 530–47.

T 1964 *Cpāp' Kram Pariyāy.* Phnom Penh, IB.

Nheuk-Nou, Nhek-Nou, or Nhieuk-Nuv, *Ṅ̈ik-Nū* and Nou, *Nū*

T 1965 *Kpuon Ābā-bibāh.* Traité sur le mariage. (Phnom Penh)

Nhok-Thaem, *Ṅ̈uk-Thaem*

S T 1943–4 '*Prajuṃ subhāsit khmaer tām laṃtāp*' *aksar*. Recueil des proverbes k'mèr par ordre alphabétique.' *KS* (15) 12: 666–72 (Introduction 663–6). (16) 1: 22–4; 2: 68–72; 3: 134–7; 6: 311–3; 7: 360–4; 8: 423–9.

S 1948 '*Kathā mukh nai rīoeṅ Bhogakulakumār.*' *KS* (20) 10: 721–7. (Introduction to the story, *Bhogakulakumār*.)

T 1949 *Cpāp' Kram Sāmaṇer. KS* (21) 12: 940–7.

S 1957 '*Amṛtaksatrī Muk.*' (The immortal prince Mok.') *KS* (29) 2: 144–9. (Preface to the work, *Devand*, by Mok.)

S 1959 '*Yopal' niṅ banyal' khlaḥ aṃbī tārāṅ pravattikāl nai aksarsāstr kmaer khlaḥ.* Étude de Monsieur Nhok-Thaem . . . sur la littérature khmère.' *Revue de l'Institut national pédagogique.* 2: 20–9.

T 1960, 1964, 1969 ed. *Mahāvessantarajātak.* Phnom Penh, IB.

T 1962 *Mahāvessantarajātak.* Phnom Penh, *Hāk' Seṅ Grī.*

T 1963 *Paññāsajātak saṅkhep.* Phnom Penh, Faculté des Lettres et des Sciences Humaines. (The 50 *jātak* abbreviated.)

S 1965–8 '*Ekasār sāstrā sḷik ṛit niṅ krāṃṅ ṭael mān nau Vijjāṭhān Buddhasāsanapaṇḍity*'. *KS* (37) 8: 816–31; 9: 953–66; 10: 1051–82; 11: 1151–70; 12: 1276–1323. (38) 2: 188–94; 3: 315–8; 4: 409–12; 5: 524–27; 6: 654–7; 7: 764–7; 8: 858–61; 9: 959–62; 10: 1050–2; 11: 1157–60; 12: 1266–9. (39) 1: 54–7; 2: 174–7; 3: 287–90; 4: 397–400; 5: 505–10; 6: 644–8; 7: 732–44; 8: 825–35; 9: 965–71; 10: 1085–92; 11: 1170–88; 12: 1258–69. (40) 1: 70–88; 2: 232–43; 3: 298–307; 4: 423–32; 5: 544–55. ('MSS of the Buddhist Institute on palm-leaf or in *krāṃṅ* form'. They are briefly described for form and content. Dates and authors are given when possible. The work is incomplete.)

T 1969 '*Jīvapravatti rapas' Lok Ṅ̈uk-Thaem*'. *KS* (41) 2: 162–81 (Autobiography).

T 1977 Extract from *Mahāvessantarajātak*, pp. 281–98. Huffman and Proum 1977: 298–304 (vocabulary 305–8).

T 1982 Preface to Khing Hoc Dy *Rīoeṅ Mahāvessantarajātak* 1982.

Nhoung-Sœung, *Ñūṅ-Sīoeṅ*

T 1946 and 1961 See *Kambujasuriyā.* III Texts of folktales and legends. (19) 3 and (33) 5.

S 1966 '*Pāk' ralaṃ khdec maek truoy*'. *KS* (38) 7: 743. (Poem (2 stanzas) 'explaining' the proverb, *Jhoe buk raluoy, kuṃ ṭāk' kūn aṅguy.* Don't let your child sit on a rotten tree.)

Nicolas, Pierre

V 1947 *108ᵉ Degré Est. Récits d'Extrême-Orient.* Paris, S.E.P.E. (Contains an adaptation of 'Thmenh Chey', *Dhmeñ Jăy.*)

Nong, *Naṅ*

T 1936–8 and 1942–4 *Lokanaya* (Also spelt *Lokaneya, Lokaneyya*). *Bāky Kāby*. *KS* (8) 11: 193–212. (9) 1–3: 133–52; 4–6: 75–106; 7–9: 79–104; 10–12: 179–98. (10) 1–3: 133–47, 193–210; 4–6: 137–44, 241–8; 7–9: 51–61, 138–47 (Contents give pp. wrongly); 10–12: 35–44, 161–72, 249–60. (14) 8: 29–31; 10: 13–15; 11–12: 20–6; 13–14: 24–31; 15–16: 40–8. (15) 1–3: 79–104; 7: 403–11. (16) 1: 46–9; 2: 94–8.

T 1941 '*Cpāp' Subhāsit*. Chbab Subhasit (Poème Khmèr)'. *KS* (13) 1: 12–15; 2: 23–6; 3: 13–17; 4: 23–6; 5: 11–4; 6: 15–18; 7: 13–16; 8: 13–17.

T 1942, 1953 *Cpāp' Subhāsit*. Phnom Penh, BR, IB.

T 1948–50 '*Bhogakulakumār*. Bhog Kul Kumār (en vers)'. *KS* (20) 10: 721–36 (Introduction by Nhok-Thaem 721–7); 11: 817–30; 12: 915–23. (21) 1: 27–36; 2: 132–6; 4: 286–92; 6: 450–5; 7: 525–30; 10: 756–66; 11: 845–54. (22) 2: 124–34; 3: 172–83; 4: 273–82.

T 1958 *Lokanayapakar(ṇ)*. Phnom Penh, IB. 2 vols.

T 1961, 1966 *Bhogakulakumār*. Phnom Penh, IB.

T 1965 *Bhogakulakumār. Histoire de Phauk Kol Komar*. Phnom Penh, Reasmei Kampuchea.

Nop, *Ṇup*

T 1934 See *Kambujasuriyā* III Texts of folktales and legends. (6) 1–3.

T 1939 See *Kambujasuriyā* III Texts of folktales and legends. (11) 4–6 and 7–9.

Norodom Sukhanari, *Narottam Sukhānārī*, Countess Norodom Sukhanari

T 1950 See *Kambujasuriyā* III Texts of folktales and legends. (22) 9 and 10.

Notton, Camille

V 1939 'Légendes sur le Siam et le Cambodge. Illustrations.' *Annales du Siam*. Bangkok, Imprimerie de l'Assomption.

Nou, *Nau* 1

T 1955 *Subhāsit Rājanītisātth*. Phnom Penh.

T 1956 '*Subhāsit rājanīti (bāky kāby)*.' *KS* (28) 2: 147–52; 3: 247–57; 4: 344–8; 5: 447–55.

Nou 2. See Nheuk-Nou.

Nou-Kan, *Nū-Kan*

T 1949, 1950, 1953 *Rīoeṅ Dāv Ek*. Phnom Penh, Kim-Seng.

Nouth-Oun

V 1953*a* 'La légende du Phnom Srey et du Phnom Pros.' *Cambodge: Revue Illustrée*. (1): 29–32.

V 1953*b* 'La jeune fille aux cheveux dénoués: la légende du Phnom-Sampeou ou Légende de Néang Romsay-Sâk.' *Cambodge: Revue Illustrée Khmère*. (2): 45–52.

V 1953c 'Les rivales: une légende khmère inédite.' *Cambodge: Revue Illustrée Khmère*. (3): 44–51.

Nuon-Bouth, *Nuon-Put*, and Choum-Muong, *Juṃ-Muoṅ*

T 1961 *Pramūl Bhāsit, jā ghlāṃṅ saṃrāp' phduk bhāsit.* (Collection of Sayings). Phnom Penh, Bouth-Neang. (Contains proverbs already collected and recorded on palm-leaf manuscripts, proverbs already published and proverbs produced orally.)

Nuon-Neary, *Nuon-Nārī* ed.

T 1960 *Mā Yoeṅ.* Phnom Penh (For schools).

T 1960 *Rīoeṅ Sradap Cek.* Phnom Penh.

Om Ṇāgrī

T 1964 *Atthādhippāy rāmakert(i).* ('Explanation of the *Rāmakert(i)*.') Battambang/Phnom Penh.

Osborne, Milton, and Wyatt, David K.

S 1968 'The abridged Cambodian Chronicle. A Thai version of Cambodian History.' *France-Asie-Asia.* (22) 2 (No. 193): 189–203.

Ou-Chev, *Û-Cev*

T 1951 *Dasajātak.* (The ten *jātak*), ed. from *Samrāy* (Loose translations from Pali).) Phnom Penh, Sumana Suvat(th).

Ou-Ngoy. See Ngoy.

Ou-Srey, *Ū-Srī.* See Srey-Ou.

Ouk, *Ûk* 1

T 1959 *Maraṇamātā*. Editions *Om Ṇāgrī.* Kompung Cham, Khmer samăy.

T 1961 *Rīoeṅ Maraṇamātā.* Histoire de Maranamata. Phnom Penh, IB.

Ouk, *Ûk* 2

T 1929 *Aṃbī ṭaṃṇoer dau kruṅ Pārāṃṅses.* Souvenir d'un voyage en France en l'an 1923. Phnom Penh, Imprimerie du Gouvernement. (Poem.)

Oum-Chhoum, *Uṃ-Jhuṃ*

T 1968 See *Kambujasuriyā* III Texts of folktales and legends. (40) 8.

Oum-Sou, *Ûm-Sū*

T 1930–2 '*Milindapañhā.*' *KS* (3) 1: 35–74; 2: 9–35; 3: 7–32; 4: 31–7; 5: 21–38; 6: 13–32; 7: 1–25; 8: 1–27; 9: 3–25; 10: 3–18; 11: 3–23; 12: 3–36. (4) 1: 3–16; 2: 5–19; 3–6: 3–59; 7–12: 3–112. (Translated from Pali.)

T 1931–2 '*Valâhajâtaka.*' *KS* (4) 3–6: 60–74. (Translated from Pali.)

T 1931–2 '*Ratanapajotajātaka.*' *KS* (4) 7–12: 361–97. (Translated from Pali.)

T 1933 '*Siri Vipulakitti jātaka.*' *KS* (5) 1–6: 94–143. (Translated from Pali.)

T 1942, 1963 *Milindapañhā.* Phnom Penh, IB. 2 vols.

Padānukram Rāmkert(i)

S See Krasem.

Pang-Khat, *Pāṅ Khāt'*

T 196– *Srīhitopades.* Phnom Penh.

T 1971–2 *Srīhitopades.* Phnom Penh, Kim-Séng

T 1981 *Srīhitopades.* Paris, Cedoreck.

Paṇṇāgār Pradīp Khmaer (The Khmer Lantern Bookshop)

S 1960 *Rāmakerti. Pañhā dhaṃ2 knuṅ aksarsāstr khmaer srāv jrāv ṭoy Prajuṃ Sāstrācāry.* ('The Rāmakert(i). Important questions in Khmer literature researched by a group of professors.') Battambang.

Pannetier, A.

T V 1915 'Sentences et proverbes cambodgiennes recueillis par . . .' *BEFEO* (15) 3: 47–71. (250 items in transcription and translation. Brief explanation in some cases.)

V 1949 and 1955 'Proverbes cambodgiennes.' *FA* Nos. 37–8: 975–7 and Nos. 114–15: 515–16. (Translation of just over 30 proverbs.)

Pavie, Auguste

1898 *Mission Pavie. Études I. Recherches sur la littérature du Cambodge, du Laos et du Siam.* Paris, Leroux. Contains:

S pp. v–xlvi Introduction.

V pp. 1–26 Neang Roum-Say-Sock (*Nāṅ Raṃsāy Sak'.* pp. 17–25 entirely illustrations).

V pp. 27–51 **V**, pp. 325–33 Prose **T**. Les douze jeunes filles.

T V pp. 53–154 **V**, pp. 169–324 **T**. Vorvong et Saurivong. (*Varavaṅs Sūravaṅs.* Text difficult to read.)

T V pp. 155–68 **V**, pp. 351–6 prose **T**. Néang-Kakey.

T 1898 (The story of *Varavaṅs* and *Sūravaṅs* in Khmer.) Chartres.

1903 *Contes populaires du Cambodge, du Laos et du Siam. Collection de contes et chansons populaires.* 27. Paris, Leroux. Contains:

S pp. 1–24 Introduction.

V pp. 25–47 Néang Roum-Say-Sock *(Nāṅ Ramsāy Sak').*

V II pp. 48–57 Les Douze Jeunes Filles *(Nāṅ Bīrṭaṇṭap').*

pp. 58–69 Histoire de Rothisen *(Rathasenajātak).*

V III pp. 70–8 Néang Kakey *(Kākī).*

V IV pp. 79–94 Méa Yeung *(Mā Yoeṅ).*

V V pp. 95–209 Vorvong et Saurivong *(Varavaṅs Sūravaṅs).*

1921*a* *Contes du Cambodge: les douze jeunes filles d'Angkor, Rothisen, Neang Roum Say, Neang Kakey, Mea Yeung, Sanselkey, Vorvong et Saurivong.* Paris, Leroux.

S V pp. 32–4 Introduction, 35–6, **V**. Les douze jeunes filles *(Nāṅ Bīrṭaṇṭap').*

S V pp. 57–8 Introduction, 59–65 **V**. Rothisen *(Rathasenajātak).*

S V pp. 66–8 Introduction, 68–81 **V**, Notes, 81–92. Neang Roum Say *(Nāṅ Raṃsāy Sak').*

S V pp. 93–5 Introduction, 97–110 **V**, 111–14 Notes. Neang Kakey *(Kākī).*

V pp. 115–33 Méa Yeung **V** *(Mā Yoeṅ).*

V pp. 135–67 Sanselkey **V** *(Săṅkh Silp Jăy).*

V pp. 169–263 Vorvong et Saurivong **V** *(Varavaṅs Sūravaṅs).*

V 1921*b* *Sangselkey, Conte cambodgien.* Paris, Boissard.

V 1949 'Vorvong et Saurivong (Extrait).' *FA* 37–8: 953–8. (Part of **V** in Mission Pavie.)

V 1969 Série de Culture et Civilisation khmères. No. 1. '*Les douze jeunes filles ou l'histoire de Neang Kangrey.* Extrait de Mission Pavie Tome I.' ed. Léang-Hap An.

V 1988 Reprint of 1921*a*. Paris, Sudestasie.

Peang-Sok, *Bāṅ-Sukh*

T 1944 *Nidān Subhāsit.* ('Narration of a proverb' in Khmer verse.) *KS* (16) 1: 15–21.

Pech-Sal, *Bejr-Sal'*. See also Saris-Yann.

T S 1970 *Aṃbī Laṃṇāṃ Saṅkhep Bhleṅ Khmaer.* ('A short introduction to Khmer music.') Phnom Penh, IB. Contains, on pp. 40–52 **T** of songs, as follows:

1. For girls coming out of 'the shade' (at puberty), p. 40
Pad Sūr Seh.
Chkae pak' kanduy.

2. For weddings, pp. 40–2
Hae kūn prus cūl roṅ (Pad stec ṭoer)
Pad phāt' jāy (kāt' sak')
Pad nagar rāj (kāt' khān' slā)
Phāt' jāy (suṃ kūn srī ceñ phdịm)
Pad kaṅ soy (saen Kruṅ Bālī)
Pad Smoṅ (puk lăkt)

3. For offering food to spirits, pp. 42–3
Pad trabāṃṅ bāy
Pad mlap' ṭūṅ

4. When parents go to work, leaving children in charge, pp. 43–4
Ūn oey geṅ dau
Dūk ṅa paṅ vaeṅ
Sakavā(d) phkā ṭūṅ bhloeṅ
Other songs, pp. 44–52
Pārī caṅ pāc'
Paṅ kralek moel loe
Dūk ṅa lan thmī
Sandhịk phgar grāṃ
Sārikā kaev oey
Phgar lān' cuṅ chnāṃ

Phgar lān' ḷ ṇaen
Sa oey sa hmat'2
Ṭamrī yol smā
Paṅ loeṅ dau sruk loe
Lalak sa oey
Paṅ sraṇoḥ phkā kraṅ
(2 Khmer Loe songs which are translated)
Poe nāṅ puk srūv
Phgar lān' crak bhnaṃ

S 1970 'A folk-show: the Yike.' *NC* 3: 56–7.

S 1984 '*Aṃbī lamnāṃ saṅkhep nai bhleṅ khmaer.*' Paris, Cedoreck. (Reprint.)

Peung-Pam, *Piṅ-Pam*

T 1954–6 ed. '*Rīoeṅ Sau(r) soy (Sisorajātak).* Le Sau-soy ou l'influence saturnienne.' *KS* (26) 5: 351–7; 6: 435–41; 7: 512–17; 8: 606–10; 9: 677–83; 10: 767–73; 12: 908–12. (27) 1: 54–8; 3: 203–11; 4: 269–73; 5: 362–7; 6: 443–9; 7: 506–15; 9: 683–92. (28) 6: 567–77 (not as contents); 7: 684–91; 8: 777–84.

Pheng-Criv, *Pheṅ-Jrīv*

T 1958 See *Kambujasuriyā* III Texts of folktales and legends. (30) 1, 2, and 3.

Pic Bun Nil

S 1971 '*Anak pāṅ niṅ rīoeṅ lpoek aṅgar vatt.*' (Pang et l'histoire du Poème d'Angkor Vat) *Srāv jrāv anak nibandh khmaer*. Phnom Penh, Faculté de Lettres.

Piat, Martine

V 1974 'Chroniques royales khmères.' *BSEI* NS (49) 1: 35–140; 4: 859–94. (Translation into French from the Khmer, *Braḥ Baṅsāvatār Khmaer,* which was itself a translation by In of a Thai composition, Sanā(m)yuddh, by Acary Golab of Bangkok. The unpublished Khmer MS belonged to the Mission des Etrangères, Paris.)

S 1974 'La littérature populaire cambodgienne contemporaine.' P. B. Lafont and D. Lombard eds. *Littérature de l'Asie du Sud-Est.*: 19–27. Paris, Asiathèque. (Colloquium of the XXIXth International Congress of Orientalists.)

S 1975 'Contemporary Cambodian Literature.' *JSS* (63) 2: 251–9.

Pierres D'Angkor, Paris

T 1982 *Rāmakerti (Reamker).* A reprint of the 16 fascicules of the IB edition of the *Reamker* (*Rāmakerti I* and *II*).

T 1985 *Lpoek Aṅgar Vatt.* Preface by Khing Hoc Dy.

Plon-Nourrit et Cie, Paris (publisher)

T 1900 (and corrected 1901) *Cpāp dūnmān khluon.*

T 1900 (" " ") *Cpāp' Kraṃm.*

T 1900 (" " ") *Cpāp' Kram Sakravā.*
T 1900 (" " ") *Daṃbaek dāṃṅ puon.*
T 1900 (" " " 1920) *Kḍān jāp' andāk'.*
T 1900 (" " " 1901) *Rīoeṅ Cau Kaṅkaep.*
T 1900 *Saek Som nīṅ srakā.*
T 1900 (and correct 1901) *Subhāsit.*
T 1901 (" " ") *Cau Ktāṃṅ Pāy.*
T 1901 (" " ") *Cau Kuṃpit (Cau Kaṃpit pandoḥ).*
T 1901 (" " ") *Cpāp Srī* (By Mai).
T 1901 *Cpāp Thmī* (By Mai).
T 1901 (and corrected 1901) *Kel kāl (Cpāp' Kerti Kāl).*
T 1901 (and corrected 1902) *Kruṅ Sabd mīt (Sabbhamitt).*
T 1901 *Kūn cau (Cpāp' Kūn Cau).*
T 1901 *Mā Yoeṅ.*
T 1901 (and corrected 1901) *Pūbit mahārāj (Cpāp Trīneti 1).*
T 1901 *Rājasūbhā.*
T 1901 *Rīoeṅ Kūḷuk Paṇḍit.*
T 1901 *Satrā Rattisaen rī nāṅ bīrṭantap (Rathasenajātak).*
T 1901 *Sek som niṅ srakā (Mahosathajātak 1).*
T 1902 *Bej Mkut' (Bej Mkut).*
T 1902 *Braliṅ mās oey.*
T 1902 (and corrected 1902) *Jai Dāt'.*
T 1902 *Kau Hāy.*
T 1902 *Mā Yeuṅ (Mā Yoeṅ).*
T 1902 *Mtāy bit, ābuk bit, srī bit.*
T 1902 (and corrected 1902) *Nāṅ Kākīy (Kākī).*
T 1902 *Varavaṅs Sūravaṅs.*
T 1903 *Braḥ Cand korup Nāṅ Mujalīn (Mucalind).*
T 1903 *Cau Krabat.*
T 1903 *Nāvaṇ.*
T 1903 *Stec Kmeṅ.*
T 1903 *Suosḍīy (Suostī).*
T 1903 *Trīy netr (Cpāp' Rājaneti).*
T 1905 *Pañasā Sirasā (Puññasār Sirsā).*

Porée, Guy
S 1955 'Personnages comiques des contes populaires.' *FA* Nos. 114–15: 460–66.
V 1949, 1955 'La danse du Léng Trott.' *FA* Nos. 37–8: 842–5 and Nos. 114–15: 371–4. (**V** of song, pp. 845 and 374.)

Porée-Maspero, Eveline
V 1962–9 *Études sur les rites agraires du Cambodge.* Paris, Mouton. 3 vols. (A popular **V** of the story of *Haṅs Yant:*. Vol. 2: 500.)
S 1983 'Le Rāmāyaṇa dans la vie des Cambodgiens.' *Seksa Khmer* 6: 19–24.

Pou, Saveros

T V 1973 *Kpuon Ābāh-bibāh ou Le livre de mariage des Khmers par Ker Nou et Nhieuk Nou. Traduit et édité par . . . BEFEO* (60): 243–328. Contains **T** (pp. 299–307) and **V** (pp. 293–9) of wedding songs. These are:

Jāv khān' slā. L'achat du bol d'arec.
Jraṅ sraṅāt'. Le grand calme.
Ṭoḥ krāl. Les seins épanouis.
Kandaeṅ drāṃṅ.
Khdo.
Khnaṅ bhnaṃ. La crête de la montagne.
Rapaṅ ramās. La clôture du rhinocéros.
Dịk Jap'. Le gouffre.
Krom Nāy. Les terres basses de là-bas.
Poek vāṃṅ nan. L'ouverture des rideaux.
Aṅgar ou *Nagar rāj.* La cité royale.
Stec phdaṃ. Le roi dort.
Braḥ Thoṅ.
Jraṅ sraṅāt'. Le calme parfait.
Saṃboṅ. La belle à l'abondante chevelure.
Sārikā kaev. La merlette mandarine.
Phāt jāy. Ecartement des rideaux.
Paṃbe. Berceuse.
Ṭaṃrī yol ṭai. L'éléphant balance sa trompe.
Ā Ḷe.
Phat jāy. Ecartement des rideaux.

S 1975*a* 'Note sur la date du poème d'Angkor Vat.' *JA* NS 263: 119–24.

S 1975*b* 'Les traits Bouddhiques du Rāmakerti'. *BEFEO* (63): 355–68.

V S 1977*a* 'Deux extraits du Rāmakerti.' *MKS* (6): 217–45. ('L'Odyssée de Rām' and 'Un épisode de la bataille de Laṅkā'. Translated with short introduction and notes.)

S 1977*b* *Études sur le Rāmakerti (XVIe–XVIIe siècles).* Publications de l'École Française d'Extrême-Orient CXI. Paris, EFEO. (Discussion of Middle Khmer literature (*Cpāp'*: 22–31), the Rāmakerti, the characters, a linguistic and a literary study. Includes **V** of part of the *Lpoek Aṅgar Vatt.*)

S V 1977*c* *Rāmakerti (XVIe–XVIIe siècles), traduit et commenté par . . .* Publications de l'École Française d'Extrême-Orient CX. Paris, EFEO. (Translation and commentary.)

T 1979*a* *Rāmakerti (XVIe–XVIIe siècles).* Texte khmer publié par . . . Publications de l'École Française d'Extrême-Orient. CXVII. Paris, EFEO.

S 1979*b* 'Subhāsit and Cpāp' in Khmer Literature.' *Ludwik Sternbach Felicitation Volume.* Lucknow, Akhila Bharatiya Sanskrit Parishad: 331–48.

S 1980 'Some proper names in the Khmer Rāmakerti.' *Southeast Asian Review* (5) 2: 19–29.

S 1981*a* 'Études Rāmakertiennes.' *Seksa Khmer* (3–4): 87–110.

S 1981*b* 'La littérature didactique khmère: les *cpāp'*.' *JA* (269): 454–66.

S 1981*c* 'Rāmakertian Studies.' *Proceedings of the International Ramayana Seminar.* New Delhi, Sahitya Akademi.

S 1982*a* 'Du sanskrit *kīrti* au khmer *kerti*: une tradition littéraire du Cambodge.' *Seksa Khmer* (5): 33–54.

S T V 1982*b* *Rāmakerti II (Deuxième version du Rāmāyaṇa khmer). Texte khmer, traduction et annotations par . . .* Publications de l'École Française d'Extrême-Orient. Paris, EFEO.

(Introduction pp. 1–15, **T** pp. 19–151, **V** 155–278. Short résumé in English, pp. 279–86 + vocabulary, index, and illustrations.)

S 1983*a* 'A propos de *Ramās Bhloeṅ* ou "Rhinocéros du Feu".' *Seksa Khmer* (6): 3–9.

S 1983*b* 'Rāmakerti—the Khmer (or Cambodian) Ramayana.' *Sanskrit and World Culture.* Berlin. Also published in the *Actes de la 1Ve conférence internationale des sanskritistes de Weimar*, Berlin.

S 1983*c* 'Rāmakertian Studies.' *Asian Variations:* 252–62.

S 1986 'Rāmakerti—the Khmer (or Cambodian) Ramayana.' *Sanskrit and World Culture*: 203–11. *Berlin.*

S 1987 'Chroniques et études bibliographiques: études sur le Rāmāyaṇa en Asie (1980–1986).' *JA* (275): 193–201.

S T V 1988 *Guirlande de cpāp'*. 2 vols. Paris, Cedoreck. Contains:

Vol. I. 1. *Cpāp'* Généraux.
pp. 25–7. *Cpāp' Bāky Cās'*.
pp. 29–44. *Cpāp' Mahāpaṭṭhān.*
pp. 45–54. *Cpāp' Hai Mahājan.*
pp. 55–62. *Satrā Ktām.*
pp. 63–9. *Cpāp' Dūnmān khluon.*
pp. 71–82. *Cpāp' Subhāsit.*
pp. 83–95. *Cpāp' Paṇṭāṃ pitā.*
pp. 97–116. *Cpāp' Srī.*
pp. 117–125. *Cpāp' Ariyasatthā.*
2. *Cpāp' Neti.*
pp. 129–36. *Cpāp' Vidhūrapaṇḍit.*
pp. 137–63. *Cpāp' Dhammapāl.*
pp. 165–80. *Satrā Suostī.*
Vol. II. 1. (Transliteration, translation, and notes).
pp. 185–201. *Cpāp' Bāky Cās'*.

pp. 203–48. *Cpāp' Mahāpaṭṭhān.*
pp. 249–79. *Cpāp' Hai Mahājan.*
pp. 281–307. *Satrā Ktām.*
pp. 309–32. *Cpāp' Dūnmān Khluon.*
pp. 333–65. *Cpāp' Subhāsit.*
pp. 365–403. *Cpāp' Paṇṭāṃ Pitā.*
pp. 405–56. *Cpāp' Srī.*
pp. 457–80. *Cpāp' Ariyasatthā 2.*
pp. 483–512. *Cpāp' Vudhūrapaṇḍit.*
pp. 513–89. *Cpāp' Dhammapāl.*
pp. 591–633. *Satrā Suostī.*
Bibliography pp. 635–8.
Photographs pp. 639 ff.

—— and Haksrea, Kuoch, *Kuoc-Hāk' Srā*

S 1981 'Liste d'ouvrages de *Cpāp*'. '*JA* (269): 467–83.

—— and Jenner, Philip N.

T V S 1975 'Les *Cpāp'* ou 'Codes de conduite' khmers: I *Cpāp' Kerti Kāl.*' *BEFEO* (62): 369–94. (Introduction, 369–74; **T** (orthography) 375–8, (transliteration) 379–81; **V** 382–90; Word index, 391–4.)

T V S 1976 'Les *Cpāp'* ou "Codes de conduite" khmers: II *Cpāp' Prus.*' *BEFEO* (63): 313–50. (Introduction, 313–16; **T** (orthography) 317–25, (transliteration) 326–30; **V** 331–43; Word index, 344–50.)

T V S 1977 'Les *Cpāp'* ou "Codes de conduite" khmers: III *Cpāp' Kūn Cau.*' *BEFEO* (64): 165–215. (Introduction, 165–70; **T** (orthography) 171–82, (transliteration) 183–90; **V** 191–206; Grammatical appendix 207–9; Word index, 210–15.)

T V S 1978 'Les *Cpāp'* ou "Codes de conduite" khmers: IV *Cpāp' Rājaneti* ou *Cpāp' Braḥ Rājasambhār.*' *BEFEO* (65): 361–402. (Introduction, 361–8; **T** (orthography) 369–77, (transliteration) 378–83; **V** 383–97; Word index, 398–402.)

T V S 1979 'Les *Cpāp'* ou "Codes de conduites" khmers: V *Cpāp' Kram.*' *BEFEO* (66): 129–60. (Introduction, 129–33; **T** (orthography) 134–41, (transliteration) 142–6; **V** 147–57; Word index, 158–60.)

T V S 1981 'Les *Cpāp'* ou "Codes de conduite" khmers: VI *Cpāp' Trīneti.*' *BEFEO* (70): 135–94. (Introduction, 135–43; **T** (orthography) 144–57, (transliteration) 158–66; **V** 167–87; Word Index, 188–93.)

—— Lan Sunnary, and Haksrea, Kuoch

S 1981 'Inventaires des œuvres sur le Rāmāyaṇa khmer (Rāmakerti).' *Seksa Khmer* (3–40): 111–26.

Poulichet, F.

V 1913 'Douze fables cambodgiennes.' *RI* (69) July: 75–87. Contains:

pp. 75–6. Le roi khmer.
pp. 76–7. Le Hangsa et la tortue.
pp. 77–9. Comment l'éléphant docile devient furieux.

pp. 79–80. Le serpent et la tortue.
pp. 80–1. Le cheval boiteux.
pp. 81–2. Le crocodile et le lièvre.
pp. 82–3. Le gros éléphant et le petit *Thiep.*
pp. 83–4. Le cerf, l'aigle et la tortue.
p. 84. Le singe et le *kleng klong.*
p. 85. Le bonze et le chasseur.
pp. 85–6. L'ours et le figuier sauvage.
p. 87. La vieille femme et le chat.

Pruoch-Phoum, *Bruoc-Bhum*

T 1967 ed. *Lpoek Doc nịṅ Svā. KS* (39) 11: 1189–98.

T 1967 ed. *Lpoek Nāṅ Mān' Pāy Khum. KS* (39) 12: 1270–89.

T 1967 ed. *Braḥ Trai Lakkh(ṇ). KS* (39) 2: 126–33; 3: 239–50.

T 1968 See *Kambujasuriyā* III Texts of folktales and legends. (40) 2, 3, and 4.

T 1969 See *Kambujasuriyā* III Texts of folktales and legends. (41) 3.

Rraghavan, V.

S 1975 *The Rāmāyaṇa in Greater India.* Surat, South Gujerat University.

Rasmei Kampuchea, *Rasmī Kambujā,* publisher, Phnom Penh

T 1963 *Nāṅ Kaṅrī. Ṛddhisaen* (*Rathasenajātak*).

T 1963, 1964 *Dum Dāv.*

T 1965 *Bhogakulakumār.*

Ray-Buc, *Ṙāy-P̂uk*

T S 1949 '*Subhāsit khmaer bhāg dī muoy.* Maximes et pensées. Proverbes et maximes. Tome I.' *KS* (21) 3: 181–5; 4: 271–4; 5: 331–4; 6: 427–31. . . . *bhāg dī bīr.* Tome II. 7: 497–9; 8: 561–3; 9: 672–4; 10: 731–4; 11: 821–4; 12: 891–6 (Khmer text).

S 1956 '*Aksarsāstr khmaer saṅkhep.* Littérature khmère.' *KS* (28) 9: 828–37; 10: 934–43; 11: 1039–49; 12: 1137–44 (Khmer text).

Réalités Cambodgiennes

V 1960 'L'homme aux trente sapèques.' No. 206, 9 Apr.: 18.

V 1960 'Histoire des deux amis qui voulaient tarir la mer.' No. 213, 3 June: 20 and 23.

V 1960 'La Bonne Fortune et la Malchance.' No. 215, 17 June: 15–17.

V 1969 'Histoire de A Pang et de Mlle. Teï.' No. 652: 35.

V 1971 'Les histoires du lièvre juge. Comment le lièvre trompe la vieille marchande de bananas. Le lièvre et le crocodile. No. 733: 27.

V 1971 'Les histoires du lièvre juge (suite). Les évasions du lièvre. No. 734: 25–7.

Rebert (R. Baraba)

V 19— *Relation d'un conteur khmer.* Saigon, A. Portail.

Roeské, J.

S T 1913 'Métrique Khmère. Bat et Kalabat.' *A* (8): 670–87 and 1026–43. pp. 673–82. Description (with examples in orthography, transcription, and translation) of 13 metres. pp. 1027–34. Texts in orthography and transcription of 2 or 3 stanzas of 9 songs. pp. 1034–5. Translations of these stanzas. pp. 1037–40. List of 129 melodies.

S T 1914 'L'enfer cambodgien d'après le Trai Phum (Trī bhūmī). Les trois mondes.' *JA* NS (4): 587–606. pp. 587–602 **T**, 602–6, **S.** (G. Cœdès (1915) demonstrates many mistakes in the translation.)

Ros-Ouch, *Ras'-Ûc*

T 1951 *Cpāp' Bāl-paṇḍit.* Phnom Penh, *Ratanākār.*

S. Mānavi. See *Mānavi, S.*

Saem Sur

T 1965 *Paramādhippāy aksarsilp khmaer.* ('A preliminary exposition of Khmer literature.') Phnom Penh, *Vijjāsākal.*

S 1967 *Artthādhippāy subhāsit srīhitopades. Subhāsit samkhān'2.* ('Explanation of the meaning of the proverbs in Srīhitopades. Important proverbs.') Phnom Penh, Librairie Phnom Penh.

Sak-Khat, *Sak'-Khāt'*

T 1947, 1957 See *Kambujasuriyā.* III Texts of folktales and legends. (20) 9 and (29) 1.

Samāgam Samtec Juon-Nāt, Publisher, Phnom Penh

T 1974 *Duṃ Dāv* by *Śom.*

T 1975 *Baṅsāvatār Ekasār Vatt Sitpūr.* (The chronicle of Vatt Sitpur.') (Phnom Penh).

Samdech Malika. See *Malikā.*

Sam-Soun, *Saṃ-Śun*

T 1947 See *Kambujasuriyā* III Texts of folktales and legends. (20) 1, 2, 3, 4, 6, 10, and 11.

San-Kong, *San-Gaṅ'*

T 1944 ed. *Bāky Subhāsit purāṇ.* ('Old proverbs.') *KS* (16) 10: 505–7.

San Sarin, *San Sarin*

T 1971 'Phirum Ngoy, poète khmer d'après Ly-Theam Teng.' *CN* (16): 25–35. (Translation of part of Ly-Théam Teng 1966.)

S 1975 'Les textes liturgiques fondamentaux du bouddhisme cambodgien actuel.' *Mémoire de l'École Pratique des Hautes Études, IVe Section,* Paris.

Saram Phan, Saram Pak, and Lovey

S T 1965 *Ayay: Chants alternés sous forme de conseils traditionnels.* Phnom Penh, Reasmei Kampuchea.

Saris-Yann, *Sāriḥ-Yān* (also called Pech-Sal)

T 1956 See *Kambujasuriyā* III Texts of folktales and legends. (28) 1.

Sarkar, H. B.

S 19— 'The Ramayana in South-East Asia: A general survey.' *Proceedings of the International Ramayana Seminar.* New Delhi, Sahitya Akademi.

Sarkar, Kalyan Kumar

S 1961 *Contact entre l'Inde ancienne et le Cambodge dans le domaine littéraire et linguistique.* Thèse de doctorat d'Université (inédite). Paris, Faculté des lettres.

S 1963 'Indian literature in ancient Cambodia.' *Proceedings of the 25th session of the Indian History Congress*: 67–9.

S 1968 'Early Indo-Cambodian contacts (literary and linguistic).' *Visva-Bharati Annals, XI,* Santiniketan University, Bengal.

Sdoeng-Chhou, *Stoeṅ-Chū*

T 1969 See *Kambujasuriyā* III Texts of folktales and legends. (41) 2.

Seng-Nguon Huot, *Seṅ-Ṅuon Huot*, printer and editor, Phnom Penh

T 1959, 1962, 1966 *Anak nibandh khmaer. Braḥ Rāj Sambhār.* Léang-Hap An. See under this name for details.

T 1960 *Sabvasiddhi* by Tan.

T 1960 *Kākī* by Ang-Duong.

T 1961 *Jinavaṅs* by Hing.

T 1963 *Cpāp' Ker Kāl.*

T 1963 *Kruṅ Subhamitr.*

T 1963 *Dịk rāṃ phkā rāṃ.*

T 1965 *Cpāp' Prus.*

T 1965 *Mā Yoeṅ*

T 1966 *Duṃ Dāv.* Léang-Hap An ed.

Seth, Sou Seth (or Soeth), *Ŝū-Siddh(i)*

S T 1922 *Paep poek sakrvā(d)* (Phnom Penh).

T 1941 *Bimbābilāp.* Phnom Penh, Kim-Seng.

Sidtha Pinitpouvadal

S 1966 *L'influence khmère dans la littérature siamoise du XIIIe au XVIIIe siècle.* Paris, thèse de Lettres.

Sin-Hean. See Héan-Sin.

Singaravelu, S.

S 1982 'The Rāma story in Kampuchean tradition.' *Seksa Khmer* (5): 17–31.

Sisowath Monireth, Prince. *Ŝīsovatth Muniriddh*

T 1956 *Chants.* Phnom Penh, Maurice Darantière. (7 lithographed items from Elisabeth Gross. In separate boxes.)

Soeth. See Seth.

Sok Bœur, *Sukh-Poer*

T 1952 *Histoire de Chau Kvak Chau Kven.* Phnom Penh, Khemarak. (Same as *Ā Khvāk' Ā Khvin.*)

Som

T 1962, 1966 *Rīoeṅ Duṃ Dāv. Histoire de Tum Teao.* Phnom Penh, IB.

T 1974 *Histoire de Tum Teav.* Phnom Penh, Association Samdach Chuon Nat. (Reference from Vandy-Kaonn 1981: 82.)

T 1977 Extract (*Som* 1966: 52–6) in Huffman and Proum 1977: 189–99 (vocabulary, 200–7).

T 1980 *Duṃ Dāv*. Paris, Cedoreck.

Som-Sukh, a.k.a. *Cān'-Sukh*

T 1950 '*Kār crūt srūv*'. *KS* (22) 2: 135–6. ('Harvesting paddy.' Short folktale on p. 136.)

Song-Siv, *Suṅ-Ŝīv*

T 1953 *Prajuṃ nidān jātak. Prachoum nitean cheatâk.* (Collection of jātak stories retold.) Phnom Penh, Pô Hot.

Soth-Polin, *Suddh P̈ūlīn*

V 1966 *Collection 'Souvenirs du Cambodge'. Contes et récits du Cambodge.* Adaptés par . . . Phnom Penh, Pich-Nil. Contains:

pp. 3–11. Le chasseur des tourterelles.
pp. 12–22. Les caprices de femme.
pp. 23–49. L'Homme au Bantuos.
pp. 50–7. Le serpent Keng Kang.
pp. 58–70. Le malhonnête beau-père.
pp. 71–5. L'anguille longue et la marmite longue.
pp. 76–98. L'incorrigible farceur (Thoun Chey) (*Dhmenh Jǎy*).

Sou-Sokon, *Ŝū-Sugandh,* a.k.a. Nouch, *Ṇuc*

T 1968 See *Kambujasuriyā* III Texts of folktales and legends. (40) 8.

Soung-Phuoy, *Suṅ-Bhuoy*

T 1967 See *Kambujasuriyā* III Texts of folktales and legends. (39) 12.

Spiriagina, N.

S 1973 'La versification classique khmère (traits caractéristiques).' *La littérature et le Temps*: 200–6. Moscow, Naouka (Russian text).

Srey-Ou, *Srī Û*

T 1949 ed. *Paṇṭāṃ mātā*. *KS* (21) 11: 801–5; 12: 897–905.

S 1958 '*Ādhippāy Cpāp' Kerti Kāl*'. ('Explanation of *Cpāp' Kerti Kāl*.') *KS* (30) 8: 726–35; 9: 831–4; 10: 923–32; 11: 1021–6.

—— and Nhoung-Sœung, *Ñūṅ-Sioeṅ*

T 1951 and 1977 '*Ăÿai*'. *Camrīeṅ Jātiniyam. ou Chant patriotique* I: 12–24. Phnom Penh, IB, and '*Aÿai* poem'. Huffman and Proum, 1977: 126–9 (vocabulary, 130–3).

Sugado, Kromokar, *Sugado Kramkār*

T 1934 See *Kambujasuriyā* III Texts of folktales and legends. (6) 4–6. (2 tales.)

Sukhanari, N. See Norodom Sukhanari.

Sunseng, Sunkimmeng

V 1980 'A propos d'une peinture khmère sur le Sāmajātaka, exposée au Musée Guimet de Paris.' *Seksa Khmer* 1–2: 19–43 (pp. 28–36:

Description of the MS, Preas Soeyéam (AC 272) (*Braḥ Sīyām*), and résumé of prologue and story, combined with description of painted illustrations).

Sunthor Chéa

T 1960 *Lpoek Madrī* (poème de Madrī). Phnom Penh, Kim Seng.

Svay Muoy, *Svāy-Muoy*

V 1972 'Histoire de Keo Preah Phleung (d'après les Annales des rois khmers).' *BSEI* (47) 3: 375–94. (Translation of part of Chronicles.)

Tan, *Tan'*

T 1959 *Sabvasiddhi.* Éditions *Om Ñāgrī.* Kompung Cham, Khmer Samay.

T 1962 *Sabvasiddhi.* Phnom Penh, IB.

Tau-Ĥīṅ

S 1955 *Bhāsit samrāy.* Phnom Penh, *Khemarapaṇṇāgār.* (Proverbs explained.)

S 1965 *Bhāsit Saṃrāy.* Phnom Penh, Librairie Phnom Penh.

Taupin, J.

S V 1886*a* 'Études sur la littérature khmère. Néath Outtami. (Poème cambodgien.)' *BSEI* (6) Ier et 2e semestre: 23–47. (Should be Néang not Néath, *Nāṅ Uttamī.* The work is called *Vinā*. pp. 23–4. Short introduction to Khmer literature.)

V 1886*b* 'Une douzaine d'équitables jugements des Bodhisattva traduits des textes kmers recueillis par M. Aymonier.' *BSEI* (7) 2e semestre: 15–31. Contains:

I p. 15. Dispute as to which of 4 men should have a princess as wife.

II p. 16. Gold is left in the care of *Dhmeñ-Jăy*.

III p. 18. Smell of rich man's food reaches poor man living near.

IV p. 20. 4 men, looking for a wife, have to tell a story to the king.

V p. 22. The parasol, cut in two, because 2 people claimed it.

VI p. 23. Admirer came daily to house of married woman. He put a corpse in the house and burned the house down.

VII p. 25. Dispute about ownership of ox. Asked what they gave the ox to eat, they said, 'Grain', 'Haricot leaves'. Ox investigated to determine owner.

VIII p. 26. Dispute between 2 men on a bridge; both carried seeds.

IX p. 27. Owner does not know which of two men stole his ox.

X p. 28. Two women dispute ownership of baby.

XI p. 29. One man's ancestors 'were pelicans', the other's 'were fish'. Dispute when one kills a pelican.

XII p. 30. The caretaker of the king's *Aegle Marmelos* tree catches a suspect thief but the King shows he is innocent.

(These are tales from the *Cpāp' Kịṅ Kantrai.*)

V 1887 'Prophéties khmères. Traduction d'anciens textes cambodgiens.' *BSEI* 2ᵉ semestre: 5–22. (Part from Chronicles. Part is life of Buddha and Buddhist predictions.)

Tā Cak'. See Mi Chak.

Tec-Hong, *Tic-Huṅ,* Publisher, Phnom Penh

T 19— *Saṅkh Silp Jăy.*

T 1957 *Cpāp' Srī Cpāp' Prus.*

T 1958 *Cpāp' dūnmān khluon. Cpāp' dūnmān kūn?*

T 1959 *Haṅs Yant.*

Terral, G.

S 1956 'Samuddaghosa Jâtaka, conte tiré du Paññâsa Jâtaka.' *BEFEO* (48) 1: 249–63. (See 251–2. Translation from the Pali version.)

V 1958 *Choix de Jâtaka.* Paris, Gallimard.

Terral-Martini, Ginette

S 1959 'Les jâtakas et la littérature de l'Indo-Chine Bouddhique'. *FA* 16: 483–92. (Version of *Sudhanajātaka,* 490–2.)

Thang-Vong, *Thaṅ-Vaṅ*

T 1959 ed. *'Surabajātak'*. *KS* (31) 2: 149–68; 3: 264–83; 4: 373–96; 5: 509–20; 6: 623–34; 7: 753–72; 8: 866–70; 9: 985–93; 10: 1099–1106; 11:—; 12:—.

T 1960 See *Kambujasuriyā* III. Texts of folktales and legends. (32) 3 and 8.

Thau Ke, *Thau-Kae*

T 1963 ed. *Dibv Saṅvār.* Phnom Penh, IB.

T 1977 Extracts from *Dibv Saṅvār*, (1): pp. 53–5 and pp. 65–73 in Huffman and Proum: 236–44 (vocabulary, 244–50).

Thay Sok, *Thay-Sukh*

S 1964 *Traité de morale des cambodgiens, du XIVᵉ au XIXᵉ siècle.* Thèse de doctorat d'Université, Paris.

Thierry, Solange

S 1953 'Notes de littérature populaire comparée.' *BSEI* NS (28) 1: 19–24.

T 1955 'L'histoire du serpent Keṅ Kaṅ ou l'Origine des Serpents.' *FA* 114–5: 531–4. (Referred to thus by Thierry 1982 but in fact published in 1949 under Bernard and in 1955 under Bernard-Thierry, q.v.)

S 1959 'La personne sacrée du roi dans la littérature populaire cambodgienne.' *Studies in the history of religion IV.* Leiden, Brill: 219–30.

S 1962 'Manuscrits cambodgiens du Département d'Asie' *Objets et Mondes* II. 1: 13–24.

S 1963 *Les danses sacrées au Cambodge.* Paris. (Reference to literature, pp. 345–70.)

S 1968 'La place des textes de sagesse dans la littérature cambodgienne traditionelle. *Revue de l'École Nationale des Langues Orientales.* 5: 163–84. (Contains résumés of *Cpāp' Kūn Cau,* pp. 176–8, *Cpāp' Srī,* pp. 178–80, *Cpāp' Kerti Kāl,* pp. 180–1 and *Cpāp' Kram,* pp. 182–4.)

S 1969 'Letteratura laotiana, cambodgiana, siamese.' *Storia delle letterature d'Oriente.* Milan, Vallardi: 649–735.

SV 1971–2 'A propos de la littérature populaire du Cambodge: contes inédits.' *L'Ethnographie.* (65): 87–107 and (66): 56–70. Vol. 65 contains:

Introduction, pp. 88–95. Les hommes qui allaient s'instruire, p. 96. Histoire du garçon qui mentait pour manger, pp. 97–100.

Le tigre joué par le crapaud et la tortue, pp. 100–5. Histoire de l'homme qui avait une jolie femme, pp. 105–7.

Vol. 66 contains:

Histoire de l'aigle de Prah Eisur qui voulait manger de l'éléphant blanc, pp. 58–60.

A Khvak A Khvin, pp. 61–9.

Histoire de quatre bonhommes: le chauve, le morveux le chassieux et le boiteux, pp. 69–70.

S 1976 *Étude d'un corpus de contes cambodgiens traditionnels. Analyse thématique et morphologique.* Paris/Lille. Thèse de Doctorat d'État.

S 1977 Le concept d'espace dans les contes cambodgiens. *Cahiers de l'Asie du Sud-Est* (2): 5–14.

S 1978 *Étude d'un corpus de contes cambodgiens traditionnels*. Paris, Champion.

V 1981*a* 'La corneille blanche ou la Mère des cinq Buddha.' *Cahiers de l'Asie du Sud-Est* (9–10): 65–76. (**S** pp. 65–8 and 73–4.)

V 1981*b* 'L'origine du bétel.' *Orients. Pour Georges Condominas.* Paris, Sudestasie/Privat: 247–54.

S 1982*a* 'Brai et Himavant - les thèmes de la forêt dans la tradition khmère.' *ASEMI* (1–4): 121–33.

V 1982*b* 'Une version cambodgienne de l'origine du bétel.' *Orients. Pour Georges Condominas.* Paris, Sudestasie/Privat: 247–54.

S 1985 *Le Cambodge des contes.* Paris, Harmattan.

V 1988 *De la rizière à la forêt: contes khmers. La légende des Mondes.* Paris, Harmattan. Contains:

I *Contes à rire et à sourire.*

pp. 13–17. Le garçon qui mentait pour manger.

pp. 18–23. Les quatre chauves.

pp. 24–6. Le sorcier, le vieux et la vielle.

pp. 27–32. Le jeune homme à la noix de coco.

pp. 33–9. Le voleur au bon cœur.
pp. 40–50. Ceci est l'histoire d'Ā Khvak Ā Khvin ou l'aveugle et l'impotent.
pp. 51–2. Histoire de quatre bonhommes: le chauve, le morveux, le chassieux et le boiteux.
pp. 53–7. L'homme aux trente sapèques.
pp. 58–62. L'ami et la femme adultère

II *Où les animaux mènent le jeu.*
pp. 65–6. Le chien qui voit les fantômes.
pp. 67–8. Le tortue et le singe.
pp. 69–70. Le corbeau qui marie son enfant.
pp. 71–6. Où l'on voit le tigre berné par le crapaud et le tortue.
pp. 77–82. Le tigre, le singe et le lièvre.
pp. 83–4. La civette et la petite poule sauvage.
pp. 85–8. Histoire de l'aigle de Prah Eisaur qui voulait manger de l'éléphant blanc.
pp. 89–108. Les histoires de juge lièvre. Ceci est un conte en prose.
pp. 109–22. Les histoires de juge lièvre. Ceci est conté en vers.

III *Contes à jugements.*
pp. 125–6. Histoire d'un vol de boeuf.
pp. 127–9. Comme un voleur fut révélé par un parfum.
pp. 130–2. Les quatre hommes qui allaient s'instruire.
pp. 133–4. Histoire des deux hommes et du parapluie.
p. 135. Une contestation d'un enfant.

IV *Contes à merveilles.*
pp. 139–45. L'homme qui déterrait les crabes.
pp. 146–51. La Bonne Fortune et la Malchance.
pp. 152–4. Maître Pang et Dame Ti, ou l'homme qui éspouse une fantôme.
pp. 155–7. L'homme paresseux à l'épouse 'marquée des signes'.
pp. 158–61. L'homme au crottin de cheval.
pp. 162–72. Sok le Doux et Sok le Méchant.
pp. 173–7. Les deux amis qui voulaient tarir la mer.
pp. 178–91. La vraie mère, le vrai père, la vraie femme.
pp. 192–213. Le Sieur Croûte de riz.
pp. 214–39. L'homme au couteau de vannier.
Glossary.

Thiounn, Samdach Chauféa

T 1933 *Paep Bāky Sakravā.* (Refrains used at ceremonies.) Phnom Penh, BR.

—— and Cuisinier, Jeanne

S 1956 *Danses Cambodgiennes.* (Phnom Penh), Imprimerie Cambodia. (pp. 91–5. The story of the popular version of *Săṅkh Silp Jăy.*)

Thiounn Veang, *Vāṃṅ Juon*

T n.d. *Braḥ rājabaṅsāvatār kruṅ kambujādhipatī*. La chronique royale du Cambodge. MS G.53/6. Phnom Penh, IB.

Thong-Phan

S 1976 Étude sur Dum-Dāv, roman populaire khmer. Thèse de IIIe Cycle, Paris.

Tieng-Day Chhoun, *Dīeṅ-Tai Jhun*

T 1957 '*Bhāsit khmaer*. Recueil de proverbes khmers.' *KS* (29) 2: 122–8; 3: 221–8. (Proverbs numbered 1–119 and 120–251. Title for *KS* (29) 3 is '*Subhāsit khmaer*. . .'.)

T 1957 and 1958 See *Kambujasuriyā* III Texts of folktales and legends. (29) 12 and (30) 1, 2, 3, and 4.

Tieng-Khen, *Dīeṅ-Khen*

S 1950 '*Pravatti Lok Grū Pān-Teṅ*.' ('Biography of Ban-Teng.') *Mitt Sālā Pālī* (1) 9: 341–6. (Contains extracts from Ban-Teng's works as follows: pp. 344–5, extract from *Bimbābilāp*, pp. 345–6 and 346, 2 extracts from *Chandant* or *Chandantajātak* (*'Kaṃhiṅ Nāṅ Subhitrā'* and *'Brān nịk putr'*).)

Toet, *Dit*

T 1937 and 1942 '*Lpoek Cpāp' Krity Kram*.' *KS* (9) 1–3: 83–95; 4–6: 17–30 and (a separate publication with 86 additional stanzas) (14) 23–4: 27–44.

Tranet, Michel

S T V 1983 'Étude sur la *sāvatār vatt saṃpuk*.' *Seksa Khmer*. (6): 75–108. (**T** 82–7, **V** 87–96. Plates, III–VIII have facsimile of text.)

S T 1987 *Buṅsovaṭār khmaer ('Chronique royale khmère' d'après un manuscrit appartenant à A. Leclère)*. Munich, Khmer Foundation.

Tricon, Albert

S T V 1915 'Les mélodies cambodgiennes.' *BSEI* (67) 1–2: 29–64. (Introduction, pp. 29–37. Notation, text in orthography and translation of 8 songs: pp. 37–44, Om Touk; pp. 45–7, Kanseng krehom; pp. 48–50 Phu Chong le lea; pp. 51–3, Kram Neay; pp. 54–6, Domrey yôlday, pp. 57–8, Srâ-nghe; pp. 59–64, Prom Kut and Sangsar. (*Uṃ dūk, Kansaeṅ kraham, Bhūjaṅ lelā, Krom Nāy, Ṭaṃrī yol ṭai, Sraṅae, Brahmagīt, Saṅsār*).

—— and Bellan, Ch.

S 1921 *Chansons cambodgiennes*. Société des Études Indochinoises. Saigon, Portail.

Introduction by Charles Regismanset, xiii–xvi.

Notation, translation and text in transcription of 57 songs, 17–140.

The songs are:

pp. 17–18. Sangsar (Liaison) (*Saṅsār*).

pp. 19–20. Prôm Kut (*Brahmagīt*).

pp. 21–2. Phu chông li léa (Dragon en marche) (*Bhūjaṅ lelā*).
pp. 23–6. Bom pê (Berceuse) (*Paṃbe*).
pp. 27–8. Si nuôn (*Sī Nuon*).
pp. 29–42. Om Tuk (Pagayer la pirogue) (*Uṃ Dūk*).
pp. 43–4. Komar réo (*Kumār rīev (?)*. The slender (?) boy).
pp. 45–6. Trapéang péai. (L'étang de Péai) (*Drabāṃṅ bāy*).
pp. 47–8. Chol chap (Le passereau chassé) (*Jal' cāp*).
pp. 49–50. Chap kaun khlèng (Prenons les aiglons) (*Cāp' kūn khlaeṅ*).
pp. 51–2. Kombèp (Name of a woman).
pp. 53–4. Phàt cheai (*Phāt' jāy*. Draw the curtains).
pp. 55–6. Srângè (*Sraṅae*. Wild rice).
pp. 57–8. Chau pream (*Cau Brāhm*. The Brahmin).
pp. 59–60. Kânchha vil (Le pavot, chanson d'ivrogne) (*Kañchā vil*. The cannabis causes dizziness).
pp. 61–2. Nuôn Srey. (*Nuon Srī*. Jasmine (*Sida viscosa*)).
pp. 63–4. Préas Bat chum véàng. (Traces de pattes autour du palais) (*Braḥ pād juṃ vāṃṅ*).
pp. 65–6. Komrèng (Name of hill).
pp. 67–8. Dâmbang dèk (Bâton de fer) (*Ṭaṃpaṅ ṭaek*) and Tan toch (Petite et tendre) (*Dan' tūc*).
pp. 69–70. Peak prampel (Les sept paroles) (*Bāky prāmbīr*).
pp. 71–2. Mon.
pp. 73–6. Svai chànti. (Manguier chanti) (*Svāy candī* Cashew nut, *Anacardium occidentale*). Svai knong véat (Manguier dans la pagode) (*Svāy knuṅ vatt*). Svāy muy mek (Une branche de manguier) (*Svāy muoy megh*). Svai muy kuor (Mangues en grappe) (*Svāy muoy kuor*).
pp. 77–8. Angkor réach (*Aṅgar rāj*. The royal city).
pp. 79–80. Chrong Kangar.
pp. 81–2. Sôriya longéach thngay (Soleil du soir) (*Suriyā lṅāc thṅai*).
pp. 83–4. Phot chong chrôi (Extrêmité de la pointe) (*Phut cuṅ jroy*).
p. 85. Poù Pèk.
p. 86. Bok Srou (Chanson pour piler le riz) (*Puk srūv*).
pp. 87–8. Konchanh chêk (Grenouille vert) (*Kañcāñ' cek*).
pp. 89–90. A-Lê (*Ā ḷe*.)
p. 91. Lolok sâr Leo (Tourterelle blanche du Laos) (*Lalak sa lāv*).
p. 92. Pùm nôl (*Baṃnol*).
pp. 93–4. Prâ kom (Invitation des génies).
pp. 95–6. Khlong bândêt (*Khlūṅ panṭaet*).
pp. 97–100. Rômpê (La Mouette) (*Raṃbe*). Krom néai (Au loin) (*Krom nāy* The low land over there). Som nat (Herbes flottantes) (*Saṃnāt'*).
pp. 101–2. Sdêch phtom (Le roi dort) (*Stec phdaṃ*).
pp. 103–4. Sdéch dâr (Voyage du roi) (*Stec ṭoer*).
pp. 105–6. Sômpong (Fille publique) (*Saṃboṅ* Name of Khmer song).

pp. 107–8. Néac péon (For péou? *Anak bau* The youngest?).
pp. 109–10. Sarômê.
pp. 111–12. Phàt chéai (*Phāt' jāy* Draw the curtains).
pp. 113–14. Kâng soi (*Kaṅ Soy* Name of Khmer song).
pp. 115–16. Sô-rèn (*Surendr* Indra).
pp. 117–18. Mon-ro-ngeào (Chant du coq) (*Mān' raṅāv*).
pp. 119–21. Kanlâng thông (Connected with *Braḥ thoṅ*?).
pp. 122–3. Bai khon châng day (*Pāy khun caṅ ṭai.* Name of Khmer wedding melody).
pp. 124–5. Prey è kàt (Forêt de l'est) (*Brai ae koet*).
pp. 126–7. Domrey yôl day (L'éléphant balance sa trompe) (*Ṭaṃrī yol ṭai*).
pp. 128–30. Lolok sar khmer (Tourterelle blanche du Cambodge) (*Lalak sa khmaer*).
pp. 131–2. Khlong.
pp. 133–4. Barang srao pua (Français tirant un cable) (*Pārāṃṅ srāv buor*).
pp. 135–6. Srâca kéo (Le merle) (*Srakā kaev*).
pp. 137–8. Sân thûk phcor kréom (Le tonnerre gronde fortement) (*Sandhịk phgar grāṃ*).
pp. 139–40. Kânsèng krehom (Mouchoir rouge) (*Kansaeṅ kraham*).

Tricon, Albert and Regismanset, C.

T V 1923 *Chansons cambodgiennes. BSEI* (71): 35–58. (Introduction by Tricon, 35–42; Notes, 43–5. Translation of Air d'Angkor, 45, and of Prom Kut, 45–6. 6 songs are given with notation, **T** in transcription and **V** 47–58:

pp. 47–8. Dragon en marche (Phu Chông li léa) (*Bhūjaṅ lilā*).
pp. 49–50. Komrèng (Name of a hill).
pp. 51–2. Chrong Kângkâr (Name of a girl).
pp. 53–4. Grenouille verte (Konchanh chêk) (*Kañcāñ' cek*).
pp. 55–6. L'éléphant balance sa trompe (Domrey yôl day (*Taṃrī yol ṭai*).
pp. 57–8. Le tonnerre gronde (Sân thûk phcor kréom) (*Sandhịk phgar grāṃ*).

Triṅ Ṅār

S 1973–4 *Pravattisāstr khmaer.* ('A Khmer history.') 2 vols. 1973 and 1974.

Trinh Hoanh

S 1967 'Passé et avenir de la littérature khmère.' *RC*: 26–30.

Tvear, *Dvār* (also known as Laporte, René, q.v.)

T 1969 'Histoire des deux hommes qui revendiquaient une ombrelle. Comment fut créé le tigre royal. La femme et le rat blanc.' *RC* (633): 30–1.

T 1970 'Histoire de la création de la limule.' *RC* (718): 24–5.
T 1970 'Une femme cupide.' *RC* (719): 27.
T 1970 'Histoire du singe qui avait volé le diadème royal.' *RC* (722): 25–6.
T 1970 'Le vieux Chan-Romliek.' *RC* (723): 26–7.
T 1970 'Histoire de l'arec et du bétel.' *RC* (725): 26–7.
T 1971 'Légende de la foudre.' *RC* (732): 27.

Université Royale des Beaux Arts
S 1969 'Rāmker (Rāmāyaṇa Khmer). *Kambuja*: Oct. 142–7; Nov. 124–33; Dec. 176–90. Phnom Penh, Imprimerie Sangkum Reastr Niyum. (Same text printed as a book by the Commission du Reamker, 1968.)
S 1974 'Shadow plays in Cambodia'. Osman, M. T. ed. *Traditional drama and music of Southeast Asia,* Kuala Lumpur: 47–50.

Ûk. See Ouk.

Vandy-Kaonn
S 1973 *Vibhāgadān nai kār siksā saṅgam khmaer tām raya: aksarsilp.* (Contribution à l'étude de la société khmère à travers sa littérature.) Phnom Penh.
S 1981 *Réflexion sur la littérature khmère.* Phnom Penh, Institut de Sociologie. Dactylographed. (Contains résumés of Muchalind (*Mucalind*), 26–7; Vimean Chan (*Vimān Cand*) 28; Moranak Meada (*Maraṇamātā*), 35–6; Sabbasiddhi (*Sabvasiddhi*), 38–9; Chau Srâtop Chek (*Sradap Cek*), 41–3; Tong Chin, 45–6; L'histoire de l'aigle de Siva, 47–8; Histoire de Méa Yoeung (*Mā Yoeṅ*), 75–6.
S n.d. Contribution à l'Étude de la Société khmère à travers sa littérature. (Reference from Vandy-Kaonn 1981: 82.)
n.d. Contribution à l'Étude de l'histoire de Thnenh Chey le sage. (*Dhanañjăy*). (Reference from Vandy-Kaonn 1981: 82.)

Vann-Chœung, *Vān'-Jīoeṅ*. See Duong-Ouch and Vann-Chœung.

Vannsak-Keng. See Keng-Vannsak.

Velder, Christian
V 1971 *Liebes-Geschichten aus Kambodscha.* Manesse Bibliothek der Weltliteratur. Zurich, Manesse Verlag.
Contains:

Brautschau und Werbung
1. pp. 9–21. Der Jüngling mit der Kokos schale.
2. pp. 22–5. Der Berg der Frauen und der Hügel der Männer.
3. pp. 26–30. Die redliche Gattin.
4. pp. 31–9. Der magere Turteltaubenjäger.
5. pp. 40–6. Der vergoldete Baum.
6. pp. 47–53. Beil um Beil, Topf um Topf.
7. pp. 54–6. Die Schlangenprinzessin.
8. pp. 57–67. Die vier Kahlköpfe auf Brautschau.

Verführung
9. pp. 71–84. Die vier söhne.
10. pp. 85–95. Die verstossene Königstochter.
11. pp. 96–101. Ein Mann verführt die Frau eines anderen.
12. pp. 102–23. Sprichwörter kosten dreissig Unzen.
13. pp. 124–8. Die Geschichte von Sok und Saü.
14. pp. 129–33. Das Nashorn.
15. pp. 134–8. Die Heuchlerin.
16. pp. 139–45. Die Adler und die Eule.
17. pp. 146–50. Die Geburt des Blitzes.
Vermählung und Ehe
18. pp. 153–64. Das Schwein, das dem Jahr den Namen gab.
19. pp. 165–8. Die Königswahl.
20. pp. 169–82. Der Schutzgeist.
21. pp. 183–94. Das Mädchen und die Katze.
22. pp. 195–203. Die weisse Maus wird Königin.
23. pp. 204–24. Der Blinde und der Lahme.
24. pp. 225–9. Der versunkene Palast.
25. pp. 230–6. Die vier Schwachsinnigen und das Mädchen.
26. pp. 237–41. Der Goldfasan.
27. pp. 242–3. Die Geschichte von der Frau unde dem Rattenkönig.
Schicksal, Liebe und Tod
28. pp. 247–53. Das Aloeholz.
29. pp. 254–8. Die Busse.
30. pp. 259–80. Der Delphin.
31. pp. 281–7. Der Dschunkenberg.
32. pp. 288–92. Die Geschichte von Neang Kongrei.
33. pp. 293–302. Der Herr der Wunderkeule.
34. pp. 303–14. Die malaiische Bananenstaude.
35. pp. 315–22. Prinz Wibol Ker besiegt den grausamen König Hulu.
36. pp. 323–32. Arekanuss und Betelpfeffer.
37. pp. 333–7. Die Gliederkrabbe.
38. pp. 338–48. Der Goldbaum.
Nachwort, Karte von Kambodscha, Register.

Vickery, Michael

S 1977 Cambodia after Angkor, the chronicular evidence for the fourteenth to sixteenth centuries. Thesis. Yale University (University Microfilm, Ann Arbor, Michigan).

S 1982 'Qui était Naṅ/Nong, savant(s) cambodgien(s) des XVIIIe / XIXe siècles?' *ASEMI* (13) 1–4: 81–7.

Vijjādhar, Braḥ Grū

T 1964–7 *Braḥ rājanibandh rāmakert(i) in KS* (36) 3: 307–19; 4: 424–33; 5: 537–47; 6: 651–66; 7: 757–63; 8: 872–79; 9: 976–81; 10:

1067–72; 11: 1169–74; 12: 1242–7. (37) 1: 48–55; 2: 199–206; 3: 303–10; 4: 386–99; 5: 473–88; 6: 603–20; 7: 643–7; 8: 847–58; 9: 939–49; 10: 1042–51; 11: 1171–86; 12: 1258–75. (38) 1 : 52–67; 2: 162–78; 3: 283–98; 4: 381–96; 5: 497–504; 6: 645–51; 7: 743–51; 8: 847–54; 9: 925–32; 10: 1041–9; 11: 1149–56; 12: 1258–65. (39) 1: 46–52; 2: 159–73; 3: 279–86; 4: 387–96; 5: 497–504; 6: 642–43. Compiled by *Vijjādhar*, edited by Dik-Kéam (Incomplete).

T 1964–5 ibid. 6 vols (Incomplete).

Villemereuil, A. B. de

V 1883 *Explorations et missions de Doudart de Lagrée. Extraits de ses manuscrits mis en ordre par*... Paris, Jules Tremblay (pp. 21–57 Chronique royale du Cambodge (Nong's version, as in Garnier 1871–2). pp. 320–33 Histoire d'un centenaire, roi du Cambodge au XVIIe siècle).

Vor Pou, *Var Bau*

S n.d. *Kār siksā aṃbī vijjā taeṅ kāby khmaer.* ('Teaching the art of making Khmer verses.') Roneotyped. Phnom Penh.

Yin, *Yin*

T 1934, 1939, and 1941 See *Kambujasuriyā* III Texts of folktales and legends (6) 1–3; (11) 4–6, 7–9, and 10–12; (13) 1–12.

Yok-Vochir, *Yuk-Vajīr*

T 1959 See *KS* III Texts of folktales and legends. (31) 11 and 12.

Yon (Smean)

S 1965 *Ayay.* ('Alternating songs.') Phnom Penh, Rasmei Kampuchea. (Reference from Vandy-Kaonn, 1981: 82.) (But see Saram Phan, Saram Pak and Lovey 1965.)

You-Oun, *Yūr-Ûn*

T 1947 See *Kambujasuriyā* III Texts of folktales and legends. (19) 12.

T 1960 '*Mahānāradakassapajātak*'. *KS* (32) 7: 734–47.

You-Ponn, *Yūr-Puṇṇ*

T 1944 *Suvaṇṇasāmajātak. KS* (16) 4: 170–4; 6: 322–5; 7: 373–9; 9: 483–90.

Yukanthor, *Yugandhar*, Prince Areno

T? 1923 *La Cantate angkorienne. Bois de Jean Seltz.* Paris, Figuière. 79 pp. (Reference from Baruch.)

Yukanthor, Princess Pingpéang, *Braḥ Aṅg Mcās' Bīṅbāṅ Yugandhar*

V 1947 'Folklore cambodgien: sentences cambodgiennes—Adages et dictons.' *FA* (17): 812–13.

INDEX